Talent Manage ... Hospitality and Tourism

Edite

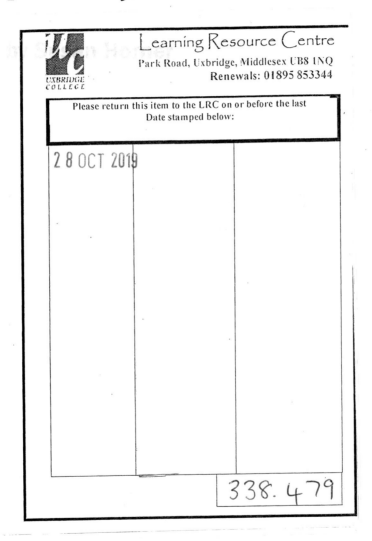

(G) Goodfellow Publishers Ltd

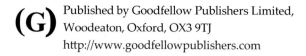 Published by Goodfellow Publishers Limited,
Woodeaton, Oxford, OX3 9TJ
http://www.goodfellowpublishers.com

British Library Cataloguing in Publication Data: a catalogue record for this title is available from the British Library.

Library of Congress Catalog Card Number: on file.

ISBN: 978-1-910158-67-8

 Design and typesetting by P.K. McBride, www.macbride.org.uk

Printed by Marston Book Services, www.marston.co.uk

Cover design by Cylinder

This book is dedicated to my son John, who has become a talent himself in his own specialist field.

Contents

Acknowledgements

I would like to thank the following people for their help in writing this first edition:

- ☐ The students who have asked difficult questions, which have helped to clarify my thinking, and the students from many countries who have provided me with interesting insights into the newly developing topic of talent management.

- ☐ The many colleagues around the world in both the academic and commercial world who have indicated the importance of this topic and encouraged us to write this book.

- ☐ Our colleagues at Goodfellow Publishers who also encouraged us to write the book.

I would also like to thank all of my colleagues from across the world that have been involved with the book and helped me with the considerable amount of research that is necessary as well as the writing of specific sections. Their names and profiles are detailed below.

I would like to thank my parents Norman and Pauline Horner who encouraged me to go to university to study hospitality in the first place, because without this I could not have written this book or achieved so much in my life.

And finally thanks to my partner and fellow writer John who always challenges and inspires me.

Preface

It is now many years since I wrote my first book with John Swarbrooke, and we have recently published the new edition of *Consumer Behaviour in Tourism*. The world of tourism and tourist behaviour has changed dramatically since the late 1990s and it is this that the sector has to address, utilising talented entrepreneurs, business leaders and employees. In that book we explored the ways in which tourism has changed over the last few decades and how terrorism has influenced the way the organisations in the sector have had to react to the rapidly changing market.

In spite of all these threats and problems, tourism has continued to grow. The market has been changing in fascinating ways, from the growth of outbound tourism from China and India to the rapid rise of the Gulf States as major tourist destinations, and the development of the sharing economy with companies such as AirBnB. This has created a demand for talented staff in new operations and in the newly emerging destinations. Over the past few years we have also seen changes in the way tourists access tourism products, with the growth in the use of the Internet by tourists as well as the continued development of budget airlines and cruise ships around the world. These changes have meant that new talents are required by the industry to design and deliver the new products and services that are demanded by tourists.

The issues for the providers in the sector is that they must reflect these new trends, at the same time as beating increasing global competition and reducing operating costs. The talent that they recruit and develop is critical to this process. They must know how to do this more effectively and efficiently so that they can employ the right staff to deliver these new experiences.

Human resource management, as a result, has now morphed into talent management, with many organisations renaming their departments with this new title. But is this just the same thing with a different title, or is it something new? What does this mean and how does it link to the research agendas and educational programmes in the academic world? And what does all of this mean for the individuals who want to have a career in the industry? It is all of these questions and many more that underpinned our desire as authors and researchers to write this new book on the topic of talent management.

I hope this book, which includes chapters from authors across the world on their particular research focus, will help develop understanding and that it will stimulate academics, policy-makers and managers to conduct more research in this field which is still, in my opinion, very underdeveloped.

Happy reading!

Susan Horner

Biographies

Editor

Susan Horner is Associate Professor in Hospitality, Tourism and Events Management at Plymouth University, UK. Susan wrote her first book *Marketing for Hospitality* in 1996 and has gone on to write further books with collaborators including Professor John Swarbrooke and Professor Stephen Ball. Susan's books include key texts such as *Consumer Behaviour in Tourism*, *International Cases in Tourism Management*, *Business Travel and Tourism* and *Leisure Marketing*.
These books are used internationally and have been translated into a variety of languages including Chinese.

Among her other skills Susan has an interest in the learning styles of hospitality students, and relationship marketing and management issues for hospitality. She has also developed an international reputation as a marketing specialist and been responsible for the academic content of hospitality courses at undergraduate and postgraduate level that have been delivered both locally and internationally. During her academic career she has encouraged both undergraduate and postgraduate students to publish their research at various academic conferences.

Authors

Mandy Aggett is a lecturer in Hospitality Management and the Placements and Employability Manager for The School of Tourism and Hospitality at Plymouth University. Her research interests lie in matters relating to employability, business development, service quality and service management. She teaches a number of modules including Facilities and Resource Management, Business Development and Revenue Management, and Managing Service Innovation.

Derek Cameron is a Senior Lecturer in Hospitality Management in the Business School at the University of Huddersfield. He also has responsibility in the role of Designated Academic Liaison Officer for two BA (Hons) degree programmes in Hotel Management and Culinary Arts, which are delivered in India.

In his early career, Derek Cameron worked for the Ford Motor Company in the UK as a training manager for Gardner Merchant, a contract catering company for Trust House Forte. Later he moved to the brewery industry for the public house sector, employed as a catering development consultant. In the 1990s, Derek worked in human resources for Forte (Hotels) Plc. By the mid-1990s he joined the teaching profession and in 1996 moved to Switzerland to teach international hospitality students. His post in Switzerland allowed him to lecture in Greece, Kenya, Australia, and New Zealand. In addition, Derek was a course tutor on the MBA distance-learning programme for the Open University Business School, based in Geneva. His last post before returning to the UK in 2008 was with Ecole Hôtelière, Lausanne, Switzerland.

Derek's compilation of research interests include discourse analysis on commitment with recent studies focused on the behavioural effects of trust on worker occupations, identity within organisational culture, organisational climate and talent management.

Crispin Farbrother has successfully lead the hospitality management academic and professional practice teams at Bournemouth University's Department of Tourism and Hospitality since 2003. Crispin Farbrother is active within CHME and the IoH Southern Branch and is proactive in engaging industry with academia. Crispin holds a number of roles within Bournemouth University and is passionate about enhancing talent through developing engaging and interesting curricula that enhance student learning in developing, technical, interpersonal and professional skills.

Saskia Faulk currently teaches marketing to engineers at the University of Applied Sciences Western Switzerland, building on her experience of hospitality and services management spanning six countries and two continents. She has written and co-authored more than 30 case studies and a book that mainly focuses on two areas: international marketing and public health. At the moment her days are filled with teaching, writing and research as well as working on her doctorate at Plymouth University (UK).

Trishna Gajjar is a PhD Student at the Rosen College of Hospitality Management at the University of Central Florida. She received her Master of Science in Hospitality and Tourism Management in 2014 from UCF Rosen College of Hospitality Management. Her research and teaching interests include strategic management, human resources management, and organizational diversity management.

Philip Gibson is Associate Head of School for the School of Tourism and Hospitality and Director of the University Hotel School at Plymouth University. He is author of *Cruise Operations Management* (first and second editions), which is the core text for students studying Cruise Management, and he has written a number research papers and book chapters on the topic of talent management in both the cruise and hospitality industries.

Philip is a Fellow of the Institute of Hospitality and Fellow and Vice Chair of the Cruise Research Society. He is an advocate of encouraging closer interaction between the worlds of academia and industry. He teaches on a range of modules including talent management and cruise operations management.

Catherine Hine is a Doctoral Teaching Assistant and PhD research student within the School of Tourism and Hospitality at Plymouth University. She gained a Master's Degree in Hospitality Management from the University of Wales, Institute Cardiff in

2011. Prior to embarking on a career in academia Cat spent a number of years working in the hospitality industry for companies including Marriott International, Mitchells and Butlers PLC and Compass Group, predominantly in food and beverage. Her research interest centre around hospitality education and employability within the hospitality industry. She has recently started to publish within these areas.

Anand Iyengar is currently the Dean: Teaching and Learning at the Institute of Hotel Management-Aurangabad (IHM-A). In addition to teaching roles, he has also been in charge of the registry functions at the IHM-A. He has some good publications to his credit with reputed publication houses and indexed journals. He has also presented papers in international conferences and seminars. His current teaching includes Strategic Hospitality Management and Research Methodology modules and research includes Corporate Governance, Family Managed Business and Customer Profitability Analysis

Satish Jayaram has an extensive hospitality experience of two and half decades. He has been the Principal for the Institute of Hotel Management-Aurangabad (IHM-A) since 2006. IHM-A is one of the leading hospitality management school in India and Dr. Satish Jayaram has been responsible for the development and delivery of two prestigious courses under the collaborative provisions of the University of Huddersfield, UK. He has made momentous contribution to the All India Hospitality and Tourism board that charts the path of hospitality education in India and has also presented innovative approaches to develop hospitality talent in prominent forums such as the UK-India Education and Research Initiative popularly referred to as UKIERI. His current teaching involves modules such as Managing Innovation & Change in the Hospitality and Culinary domains while his research interests includes Revenue Management.

Andrew Jenkins is Subject Leader (Principal Lecturer) in Hospitality and Events Management at the University of Huddersfield, UK. He is co-author of the seventh edition of *Introducing Human Resource Management*, published by Pearson. In addition, Andrew has written a chapter on International Assignments with Professor Jawad Syed for the second edition of *Human Resource Management in a Global Context: a critical approach*, published by Palgrave Macmillan. Andrew has written journal articles for *Tourism Management*, the *International Journal of Contemporary Hospitality Management*, *Employee Relations, Equality, Diversity and Inclusion* and the *Journal of Human Resources in Hospitality and Tourism*. Andrew is also a regular reviewer for the *Annals of Tourism Research*, the *International Journal of Contemporary Hospitality Management* and *Employee Relations*.

Andrew's main area of expertise is International Human Resource Management and Strategic Management. He is particularly interested in the working lives of older hotel employees. This was the focus of Andrew's doctoral research at the University of Strathclyde. Andrew is an Academic Member of the Chartered Institute of Personnel and Development, Member of the Chartered Management Institute and Fellow of the Higher Education Academy.

Aliaksei Kichuk is a PhD researcher at Bournemouth University, UK. He is on the final year of his PhD on Exploring Talent Management in the hotel sector: employees' narratives of personal career development. In 2012 he completed his Masters on Talent Management as a source of competitive advantage and business success of an organisation at Bournemouth University.

His research interests centre on Talent Management and personal career development of individual employees in the hotel sector. Having worked in the hospitality industry for more than 15 years, his role has changed over the years from chef to bartender, restaurant supervisor, duty manager, guest services manager and audit manager. Having worked in almost every hotel department, this first-hand experience has equipped him with an understanding of the importance of acknowledging the needs and preferences of individual employees. This, together with a personal high regard for this industry, has inspired him to collect and share the personal stories of employees in the hotel sector.

Deniz Kucukusta is an Assistant Professor at the School of Hotel and Tourism Management at the Hong Kong Polytechnic University. She holds MSc and PhD degrees on Tourism and Hotel Management. Prior to her academic career, Dr Kucukusta spent several years working in the hotel and travel industry. She has industry experience with Hilton Hotels in Turkey and Germany. After her PhD, she worked as a post-doctoral research associate at School of Hospitality and Tourism Management of the Hong Kong Polytechnic University. Her academic research interests are strategic management, human resources management in the hospitality industry, and health and wellness tourism. She published her work in top tier academic journals including *International Journal of Hospitality Management, Tourism Management, Journal of Travel and Tourism Marketing*, and *International Journal of Tourism Research*. She is a Certified Hospitality Educator by AHLA and teaches graduate and undergraduate level courses, namely Lodging Management, Design for Hospitality, Human Resources Management, and Resort and Spa Management.

Adele Ladkin is Professor of Tourism Employment in the Department of Tourism & Hospitality, Faculty of Management, Bournemouth University, UK. She gained her PhD at the University of Surrey in 1995. Her research interests and publications are in the areas of labour mobility and migration, human capital development and employment and employee wellbeing in the tourism and hospitality sectors. She is a co-author of the textbook *Tourism Employment: Analysis and Planning*. She has conducted UK Research Council funded research in the area of tourism work and mobile working and has a research interest in digital interventions in work-life balance. Over the years she has conducted applied research projects for a number of clients including the UNWTO, The Commonwealth Tourism Centre, The European Universities Association and the London Development Agency. Adele is a board member of a number of journals including *Annals of Tourism Research* and the *International Journal of Contemporary Hospitality Management*. She was joint Editor in Chief for the *International Journal of Tourism Research* from 2003-2009. She is an Honorary Professor at the Technological and Higher Education Institute of Hong Kong.

Conrad Lashley is editor of Taylor and Francis' *Hospitality, Leisure and Tourism* series of books. He is Editor Emeritus of the *Hospitality & Society* journal as well as co-editor of *Research in Hospitality Management*. He is author, or editor, of sixteen books including *In Search of Hospitality: theoretical perspectives and debates*, and *Hospitality: a social lens*. He has recently been commissioned by Routledge to edit *Hospitality Studies*, a new volume in their Handbook series. The study of hospitality management and hospitableness has resulted in an array of academic outputs including well over 130 refereed journal papers and conference presentations; as well as twenty books. The dominant theme of much of this enquiry has been to show how the study of hospitality, from wider social science perspectives, can better inform the management of commercial hospitality provision, and the development of future industry managers.

Fevzi Okumus is a Professor in the Hospitality Services Department at the University of Central Florida's Rosen College of Hospitality Management. He was the founding Chair of the Hospitality Services Department from 2007-2013. He received his PhD in Strategic Hotel Management from Oxford Brookes University, UK. His research areas include strategy implementation, strategic human resources management, corporate social responsibility, competitive advantage, knowledge management, crisis management, destination marketing, information technology and developing countries. He has widely published in leading journals. He has h-index of 28 and his publications received over 3137 citations. He is the Editor-in-Chief of the *International Journal of Contemporary Hospitality Management* (IJCHM) and also serves on the editorial boards of 20 international journals. He is a frequent speaker at international conferences.

Ahmet Bulent Ozturk is an Assistant Professor in the Rosen College of Hospitality Management at the University of Central Florida. Dr. Ozturk received his Ph.D. in Hospitality Administration from Oklahoma State University. His research focuses on information technology adoption, e-commerce, mobile commerce and destination marketing.

John Swarbrooke is Head of Plymouth Global at Plymouth University and was formerly Professor of Tourism and Hospitality and Head of Tourism, Hospitality, Events and Food Management at Manchester Metropolitan University. From 2008 to 2011 John was Academic Director of the prestigious Swiss private hotel school, Cesar Ritz Colleges Switzerland. From 1999 to 2014 he was Professor Visitant on the International Hospitality Management programme at IMHI/ESSEC Paris. John has also taught at the Accor Academy in Paris and delivered courses for practitioners at the Ecole Hoteliere de Lausanne. John is the author of nine books and is currently working on a book about the luxury market in tourism and hospitality. In recent years he has delivered invited keynote presentations at tourism and hospitality conferences in places as diverse as Melbourne and Mangalore, Bangkok and Bruges, Mexico and Madeira.

Edwin N. Torres is an Assistant Professor at the University of Central Florida (UCF), Rosen College of Hospitality Management. Prior to joining UCF, he obtained a Ph.D. in Hospitality and Tourism Management from Purdue University. He has several years of experience in the hotel, restaurant, and financial industries. Dr. Torres has built a research agenda on the topics consumer behaviour and organisational behaviour. His work is published in various top-tier academic journals.

Simon Thomas has a wealth of industry experience from his former career as a hotel manager before joining Bournemouth University. Simon's academic areas of interest are in Human Resources, Leadership and Change Management. Simon is also very active in developing industry engagement and student employability through student placement/graduate roles, student consultancy projects, student conferences and alumni. Simon has more recently organised CPD courses for two industry partners.

Andreas Walmsley is Associate Professor in Entrepreneurship at Plymouth University, UK. His research interests revolve around employment in tourism and hospitality, particularly youth employment and the relationship between responsible tourism and employment. He recently (2015) published his first book *Youth Employment in Tourism and Hospitality: A Critical Review* and has published numerous articles relating in particular to student/graduate employment. His other key area of research relates to graduate entrepreneurship and entrepreneurship education where he has also published in a wide range of journals on this topic, most recently a systematic literature review on entrepreneurship education published in the journal *Academy of Management Learning and Education*.

Andreas has worked closely with industry bodies such as ABTA, the Tourism Society Westcountry (for whom he conducted a study on the 'Gove Effect'), the ITT (currently on its Education and Training Committee) and the Association for Tourism in Higher Education where he was on its Executive Committee from 2006-2011. He is currently working on projects relating to attitudes towards careers in tourism and hospitality for the Springboard Charity, and also undertaking research on the impact of the National Living Wage on hotels in the UK.

Wei Wei joined the Rosen College of Hospitality Management at University of Central Florida as an Assistant Professor in August 2014. She received her Ph.D. degree and Master's degree in Hospitality and Tourism Management from Purdue University. At the Rosen College, Dr. Wei has taught a grad-level class – Critical Issues in Hospitality Human Resources, and two undergrad classes – The Hospitality Human Resources Management and The Introduction to the Hospitality Industry. Dr. Wei's research interests include consumer behavior and technological experience. Her academic papers have been published or accepted by highly ranked SSCI journals such as *Tourism Management*, *International Journal of Hospitality Management*, *International Journal of Contemporary Hospitality Management*, and *Journal of Hospitality and Tourism Research*. Dr. Wei is currently a member of Hospitality Human Resources Association (HHRA) of Central Florida.

Craig Wight is a Lecturer in Hospitality and Tourism at Plymouth University. He has a career background in restaurant management and catering, having worked as a chef and front of house manager for Bowland Inns during most of the 1990s and as a head chef in Airlie beach, Australia in the late 1990s. He has led a range of consultancy and research projects including the development of a socio-economic impact study for the 'Freedom' music festival in Hull and a review of tourist information services for Visit Hull and East Yorkshire. He has had academic research published in the fields of visitor attractions, museum interpretation, the role of museums and heritage in nation building and culinary tourism. He has presented at several tourism conferences including the 'Myths of Tourism' conference in Zadar, Croatia in 2012 and the 2nd Advances in Hospitality and Tourism conference in Corfu, Greece in 2011. He also presented research at the first National Association of Interpretation conference in San Juan, Puerto Rico in 2006 (on Lithuanian heritage) and the second in this series in Vancouver, Canada in 2007 (on network marketing in rural tourism). He has a PhD from Plymouth University comprising of a discourse analysis of representations of genocide in museums and sites of memory.

Matthew Yap is Assistant Professor of Hospitality and Gaming Management at University of Macau, China, with more than 15 years of teaching experience in higher education institutions in China, Romania, the Russian Federation and Switzerland. In addition, he has developed and managed postgraduate programmes. His research focuses on human resource management, talent management, organisational behaviour and education management. His publications can be found in International Journal of Hospitality Management, International Journal of Contemporary Hospitality Management, Higher Education and Cities, to name a few. He has also published many cases in edited books and journals to aid students' learning experience.

PART 1

THE **TALENT MANAGEMENT** CONCEPT

1 Talent Management Defined

Susan Horner

Learning objectives

This chapter provides an introduction to the topic of talent management and gives the reader an insight into the underlying philosophy and applications. This chapter should enable you to:

- Gain a preliminary understanding of talent management and the historical development of the concept.

- Get a preliminary understanding of the talent management literature and the sources to enable you to do further reading.

- Understand the research agenda that underpins the topic and be able to source academic reviews of this topic.

- Gain a preliminary understanding of talent management processes in hospitality and tourism organisations and consider the advantages of using the approach.

- Prepare yourself for further reading and debate to help with your development of an understanding of the talent management process.

Introduction

The concept of talent management is not new, and it remains a popular and contemporary concept in hospitality and in wider research fields because of its importance for both individuals and organisations. Talent management is regarded by some commentators as one of the most critical and challenging issues that helps the development of hospitality organisations in the global arena (Cappelli and Keller, 2014). Since the hospitality industry is highly people intensive, the management of talent is a critical factor. Talent in the sector generates high financial performance and also helps to attract new talent to an organisation which adds value to the organisation (Cheese, 2010). It is also argued that it is the talent in organisations that helps them to achieve competitive advantage (Brown *et al.*, 2004). It involves in the simplest form of fitting the right people with knowledge and expertise to the right organisations in order to maintain business success.

There is a wealth of research from the hospitality field on the topic of talent management. This was summarised by Kichuk *et al.*, (2014b) and includes Lashley *et al.* 2007; Baum 2008; Hatum 2010; Steward and Harte 2010, for example, and we will review this in more depth later in the chapter. It is recognised, however, that there are many areas for research and debate that can be pursued. Researchers still debate what actually constitutes talent management. Overall, talent management research to date has focused on the attraction, selection, development and retention of talented individuals, although new research on personal career progression is also starting to develop.

What is talent?

It is important, before we consider the world of work, to think about how we use the word 'talent' in normal language. We can see below the definitions and explanations from the *Oxford English Dictionary* and it can be seen that in normal language we think of talent as being a natural or innate ability. It is also interesting to note that used in an informal way, the term has overt sexual connotations and links to the physical attractiveness of people. This could lead to potential problems when we adapt the term to the organisational context, because individuals may still think of 'talent' as meaning attractive at a subconscious level. Other terms also arose in the twentieth century which referred to talent as people, one example being the term 'talent scout' which refers to a person who hunts for talent, usually in the sporting or entertainment world. Recent programmes such as *Britain's got Talent*, have also encouraged the idea that talent is all about special skills and qualities, such as singing or dancing, and the concept of celebrity judges and TV audiences judging amateurs in this type of talent show have been hugely popular and copied in most developed countries across the world. This has led many people to associate the term talent with either sport or entertainment. In the world of hospitality, which is increasingly about standardisation or scripted service encounters or following procedures, the question is "does it really need creative 'talent'?" It may need it but does it think it needs it. Or are they just using this term because it makes *human resources* sound more 'modern'?

Illustration - the definition of talent

Natural aptitude or skill: He possesses more talent than any other player,
She displayed *a talent for* garden design

People possessing natural aptitude or skill: I signed all the talent in Rome.
Simon is a talent to watch.

British informal - *People regarded as sexually attractive or as prospective sexual partners:*
Most Saturday nights I have this urge to go on the hunt for new talent

Source: Oxford English Dictionary online. Accessed 23/8/16

The term 'talent' started off as a term to describe the characteristics of people, but in more recent times it has been used to refer to people who have special skills and abilities. It is important when we start to apply the term to the business world to understand the background to the term and think about the underlying concepts that underpin the newly developing field of talent management.

Definitions of talent management

The concept of talent management has a variety of meanings both theoretically and in practice. Talent management is a practitioner-generated term, covering a range of long-standing HRM practices that aims to put the right person into the right job, and at the right time (Cappelli and Keller, 2014).

The term has escaped a standard definition, and nearly every academic research article on the topic begins with the debate over the conceptual boundaries of the term (Collings and Mellahi, 2009, Kichuk *et al.*, 2014b). For example:

Lewis and Heckman (2006: 139) note the *"disturbing lack of clarity regarding the definition, scope and overall goals of TM"*.

Collings *et al.* (2009: 1264) argue that *"the concept of TM is lacking in terms of definition and theoretical development and there is a comparative lack of empirical evidence on the topic"*.

Gallardo-Gallardo *et al.* (2013: 291) conclude, *"it appears that TM can mean whatever a business leader or writer wants it to mean, since everyone has his or her own idea of what the construct does and does not encompass"*.

Academics and practitioners agree that talent management constitutes one of the key challenges for organisations worldwide, due to the fact that it can represent a source of sustained competitive advantage in the dynamic and volatile market environment of the 21st century (Collings and Mellahi, 2009; Farndale *et al.*, 2010, Kichuk *et al.*, 2014b). It is not a new area of study, its beginnings largely attributed to McKinsey and Company, who first introduced the term in their report *The War for Talent* (Michaels *et al.*, 2001).

There is a tendency in the talent management literature, however, that the majority of publications do not offer a formal definition of its concepts, due to ambiguity and unclear conceptual boundaries (Lewis and Heckman 2006; Huang and Tansley 2012). However, in order to understand the complexity of the concept of talent management, it is essential to consider some definitions as follows:

According to Hugles and Rog (2008: 746):

"Talent Management is a multi-faceted concept that has been championed by HR practitioners, fuelled by the war for talent and built on the foundations of HRM. It may be viewed as an organisational mind-set or culture which employees are truly valued; a source of competitive advantage; an effectively integrated and enterprise-wide set of sophisticated, technology enabled, evidence-based HRM policies and practices."

Collings and Mellahi (2009) claimed that the TM concept is closely connected to the human capital development, as the latter integrates intangible goods, skills, experience, and is considered to be the greatest investment for all organisations. They argued that organisations should build talent management strategies and invest in talent development, and this should enable them to reach higher goals in the future, and lead the market.

Even though talent management is considered to be a relatively modern and contemporary approach in organisations, some authors (Furusten, 1999) still suggest that in fact it is nothing new, just re-branded human resource management practices. Chuai *et al.*, (2008: 901) claimed that talent management is not a new concept, on the contrary, it is "old wine in new bottles". Finding the right people and fitting them into the right organisations are really just human resource strategies. What is clear is that management development and talent management are inextricably linked.

The history of talent management

The first mention of talent management in the management arena was by the McKinsey group of consultants who proposed that there was a 'war for talent' and suggested that organisations must recognise the importance of talent management if they were to achieve organisational excellence. It could be suggested that what they were talking about was recruiting and retaining staff rather than talent management. This was later written about in a book – *The War for Talent* – which was published on the basis of the earlier research (Michaels *et al.*, 2001). There has been a rapid expansion in the talent management debate over the last decade but commentators have suggested that there is confusion and ambiguity surrounding the topic, largely because most of the literature is consultancy or practitioner based (Lewis and Heckmann, 2006, Iles *et al.*, 2010). According to Chambers *et al.* (1998), for McKinsey and Company, TM refers to the process of developing new employees through the framework of interviews, hiring, orientation, and helpful integration into an organisation's culture. The most important corporate resource, which leads organisations to competitive advantage, are well-educated, smart, business people, with talents that are technologically advanced, savvy and mobile. McKinsey and Company claimed that there was only way to win the war for talent: *"organisations must elevate TM to a burning corporate priority"* (Chambers et. al., 1998: 1, Kichuk *et al.*, 2014b). True talent is always passionate and difficult to manage yet hospitality looks for people who are easy to control. That is perhaps why it does not attract so many 'talented' people.

At that time, the concept started to emerge and develop, shaping new approaches to human resource management. Talent management refers to the process of developing new employees through the framework of interviews, hiring, orientation, and helpful integration into an organisation's culture. Certainly, since this time the topic has been written about endlessly and organisations are adopting talent management as a new approach, replacing their human resource departments to reflect the new trend. This move has prompted academics to carry out more research to discover whether talent management is just human resource management in a different guise or whether there are fundamentally different perspectives that have been adopted.

Gallardo-Gallardo *et al.*, (2013) suggested that there has been ongoing confusion about the meaning of 'talent' in the work place and that a suitable framework should be adopted to encapsulate the underlying concepts that are involved. This includes grouping theories into two broad areas. The first of these is the theoretical approach to talent as 'object'. This is where talent is considered as a natural ability: talent as master; talent as commitment and talent as some people. The second approach is to conceptualise talent as 'subject', i.e., people possessing special skills or abilities. They summarise these two approaches in a framework for the conceptualisation of talent which is shown in Figure 1.1.

OBJECT approach	SUBJECT approach
Talent as natural ability	**Exclusive approach**
Talent as mastery	Talent as high performers
Talent as commitment	Talent as high potential
Talent as fit	Or
Innate abilities, acquired skills, knowledge,	**Inclusive approach**
competencies and attitudes	For all employees

Figure 1.1: Framework for the conceptualization of talent within the world of work.
Source: Adapted from Gallardo-Gallardo *et al.*, p297 (2013)

They suggest that the approach taken in the adoption of talent management will depend on the mission of the organisation and its culture, but that the key decisions for organisations will be whether they want to focus their management effort on talent identification (buying talent) or talent development (building talent) (Gallardo-Gallardo, 2013). We will return to this topic later in the book when we consider inclusive and exclusive practices in talent management.

Both academics and practitioners argue that talent management is one of the most pressing issues now as they face the dynamic and intensely competitive market of the 21st century. Despite this, organizations have often struggled to develop and implement effective and efficient talent management programmes. Particular issues that underpin the problems with talent management strategies seem to be a general shortage of talent, fierce global competition for the 'best talent', and the need for talent in rapidly emerging markets such as India and China. Other researchers have argued that it is important to develop underlying philosophies on talent management, test them out in a thorough research programme, and implement them in a well thought out management process (Meyers *et al.*, 2013). It is however, necessary to distinguish here between senior management and operative levels. The main challenge appears to be in recruiting and retaining operatives but the competitive global market relates to senior managers.

The literature underpinning the topic

A recent review of the talent management literature tried to bring together the key themes in the 7,000 articles that had been written about talent management up to the date of the analysis. Some of the themes that were identified from the literature are as follows:

- ☐ Talent management is a phenomenon rather that a theoretical construct and there is no 'one right way' of approaching or studying it.
- ☐ Talent can mean different things to different people, and it can be suggested that the research is being conducted by people who do not have the theoretical underpinning to make their studies anything other than superficial and simplistic.
- ☐ One of the main discussions that appears is the inclusive versus exclusive approaches to talent management. Talent management often tends to be an exclusive field.
- ☐ A valuable approach for talent management research is social exchange theory, where the employee-employer relationship is investigated.
- ☐ Some of the research has focused on the ethical dimension of talent management in relation to corporate social responsibility, business ethics, organizational justice, and employee well-being, burn out and stress.
- ☐ The researchers suggest a critical approach to talent management as a topic of study, because many existing claims in the literature do not originate from empirical research.

The paper ends by suggesting that there are many unanswered questions because of a lack of empirical research and the newness of the topic. This includes controversy as to whether researchers should settle on one underlying theme, questioning whether organizations should have humanistic goals and responsibilities, and carrying out empirical research on previously assumed truths (Dries, 2013).

Other researchers have suggested that there are important contexts that can be a focus of talent management research. These are summarised in Figure 1.2, and it can be seen that it is appropriate if empirical research is planned that decisions are made as to the underlying concepts and the context of the research. All of the contexts are interesting, but the consideration of the individual and their personal career development is one that warrants particular attention (Kichuk et al., 2014b).

Key levels	Specific themes
Individual level	Individual or personal agency, strategy, and experience, such as work-life balance, impacting upon talent development.
Organizational level	Firm-wide policies and practices – both conscious and unconscious – and HRM strategies that shape TM.
Institutional context	Legislative, political, and legal frameworks at regional, national, and international levels that institutionalize TM in employment, education, and other fields both formally and informally.
National/international/ sectoral context	TM analysed with respect to its context; recognition of how TM practices can transcend (or not) national borders among different industries, networks, and organizations.

Figure 1.2: Key levels and contexts that define TM research.

Source: Ariss *et al.*, p177 (2013).

Individuals and talent management

The traditional views of career, which used a primary linear upward sequence of jobs within a single organisation, have changed in recent decades (Baruch and Peiperl, 2000). This has happened due to broad environmental changes, such as globalisation, increased diversity of a workforce, and the increased prevalence of knowledge-based talented workers in organisations (Cappelli and Keller, 2014). There is also the creation of new types of jobs and disappearance of others due to technology. The new career patterns of modern reality are often boundary-less (Briscoe and Hall, 2006, de Vos and Soens, 2008) Employees are often less committed to the organisations they work for, as shown by the fact that they are more independent, and are more likely to leave, if their personal needs are not being fulfilled by the employer. Work-life balance and stress have become major issues for employees, especially those from the younger generation who are less loyal to organisations than their predecessors.

According to Baruch and Peiperl (2000) talent management practices are outdated and out of touch with the current-day needs of the individual (Kichuk et al, 2014b). Ever since Michaels *et al.*, (2001) introduced the term 'war for talent', there has been a massive increase in the popularity of talent management as a concept, both among the academics and the practitioners (Silzer and Dowell 2010, Kichuk *et al.*, 2014b). Recent careers literature states that the more talented employees in the hospitality organisations are acting like 'free agents' (Tulgan 2001). At the heart of the talent management concept, there is the notion that different career management strategies should be adopted for employees from different talent categories in the organisation (Lepak and Snell 1999). The use of technology allows this type of personalisation, and this is a theme that we will return to later in the book.

Management development and talent management

A review of articles of research carried out in the hospitality industry has shown that management development processes have an impact on both management development and talent management in the sector (Watson, 2008).

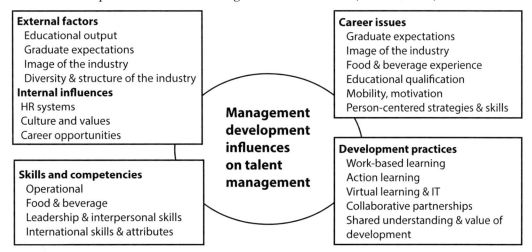

Figure 1.3: Management development issues influencing talent management in hospitality
Source: Watson, 2008, p775.

It can be seen that there are both external and internal influences which have an effect on individuals and their development. It is interesting to note that both culture and values and the career opportunities that are on offer to the individual, as well as the human resource systems, all have an influence on talent management. The skills and competencies of an individual are critical in combination with their educational background. It is also important for the organisation to think about the numerous career issues, including graduate expectations. Finally, the development practices that are adopted by the organisation are also critical to the talent management process.

Talent management in hospitality and tourism

The hospitality and tourism industry is described as a synthesis of aspects that are concerned with producing and supplying certain physical products: food and drink, and accommodation (Lashley *et al.*, 2007). The ideas underpinning hospitality will be explored in more depth later on in the book. Hospitality is a labour-intensive industry, requiring employees with different skills and levels (Baum, 2008). Research has been conducted on talent management in the hospitality and tourism sector by a number of influential authors. Barron (2008), Baum (2008), D'Annunzio-Green (2008), Deery (2008), Hugles and Rog (2008), Maxwell and MacLean (2008), Scott and Revis (2008), Watson (2008), Davidson *et al.* (2011), and Bharwani and Butt (2012) are examples of these and are included in the references at the back of this chapter.

It can be seen from a review of these articles that the research agenda in hospitality up to this time has been focussed on a number of fronts, but has particularly concentrated on the issues surrounding the attraction and retention of employees, which the industry sees as a particular issue in terms of financial success and competitiveness.

The advantages of talent management

The talent management process is said to produce a number of real advantages for organizations that are facing an increasingly competitive situation in the marketplace. These advantages can be summarised as follows:

☐ The hospitality or tourism organisation must identify the sort of talents that are required for the business. These are changing and developing and the talent management process helps them to identify them more accurately.

☐ One of the biggest challenges facing the hospitality and tourism sector is how to attract the best talent in a competitive market. The use of talent management practices allows the company to achieve this more effectively.

☐ Once the organisation has attracted the best people to work for them, they then need to develop the raw talent into individuals and teams who can help the company become more successful. It is argued that talent management helps in this process.

☐ Hospitality and tourism has particular challenges with seasonality and turnover of staff and the talent management process helps the organisation to cope with these challenges.

☐ It is clear that management development practices are needed to engage employees in hospitality and tourism companies, and talent management helps with this process.

☐ The organisations in the sector should try to attract the brightest and best graduates to join the work force, and well thought out talent management processes help with this.

☐ Hospitality and tourism organisations have both a diverse labour force and customer base, and the talent management process helps with the management of both groups.

☐ Talent management is more sophisticated that human resource management. Its focus on individual career development and inclusive approach allows the organisation to move to a stronger competitive position.

☐ Hospitality and tourism is all about a complex balance between technical, personal and creative skills, and talent management helps in the development of these amongst the employees.

We can finish this introductory chapter by considering a short illustration of what a large hotel company actually does currently to attract new talent. The Hilton

Elevator programme, outlined in the illustration below, shows how the company is trying to attract newly qualified graduates who have a good educational level and language abilities. In return the company offers good career prospects and a well thought out management development programme. You will find it interesting to look at the programme in more detail on the internet and consider how it fits in with the concepts and ideas that we have considered earlier in the chapter.

Illustration: Hilton Elevator Programme

Hilton elevator programme duration: 18 months The Hilton Worldwide Europe Elevator Programme is regarded as one of the best graduate hotel training courses in the industry. It aims to fast-track you to become the General Manager of your own hotel within five-to-eight years. For us, that's a significant investment in nurturing your talent. This highly structured programme will expose you to different areas of our business and offer new cultural experiences. Over two nine-month placements within Europe, you'll take on real business projects with bottom-line impacts. We'll equip you with the skills to conduct feasibility studies, document your findings, and present your project to the hotel management team. Keen to hear your creative ideas, we welcome new approaches, so you'll have the support of your senior managers to share your opinions too. Join us an 'Elevator' and you can expect to become part of a team that values relationship building and career progression. You'll have genuine networking opportunities with leaders during meetings and cocktail receptions, and also receive support from assigned buddies, mentors, and even General Managers. It is a fantastic experience for anyone who is ready to work hard and enjoy the adventure. To find out more and apply, visit: http:jobs.hiltonworldwide.com/universities/europe

'When I graduated from the University of Applied Sciences Bad Honnef earlier in 2014, there were two things that I was really looking for in companies to help me build my career. The first was the opportunity to learn about all of the departments in a hotel. While I was at university, I completed an apprenticeship in hospitality but I didn't get to discover the full range of hotel departments, so I was curious to know more. The second was genuine support for my ambition to work all over the world. It's important for me to know that my seniors know about my career goals. That's why it feels like the Elevator Programme was tailored exactly to my needs. At Hilton, I get to work in different cities across Europe, and I also have a support network of General Managers and Managers, a mentor and a talent management team that help me to develop toward my final goal – becoming a General Manager.' Antonia Ahlers, Elevator programme 2014.

Entry requirements

- A strong and serious interest in becoming a General Manager with Hilton Worldwide
- A 2.1 Bachelor's Degree
- To speak English plus preferably one other European

Source: Hilton Elevator brochure http://jobs.hiltonworldwide.com/files/universities/europe/Hilton_Brochure_EU_digital.pdf

Conclusions

This chapter has introduced the concept of talent management and provided a brief overview of the research agenda that underpins the topic. It has also tried to give an idea of the origins of the subject, and the key commentators in the area. It has also considered why the talent management process has become important and the advantages that the process offers for organizations in the sector.

The references and further reading at the end of the chapter allows you to read more widely on the topic and develop your understanding of the topic. You may also have started to think about the sort of research that you are interested in doing in the area, or the chapter may just have helped you with an assignment. The chapter has exposed you to some of the complexities of the topic of talent management, including the underlying philosophies and the practical applications in the real business world.

The following activities allow you to carry out your own research and think in more depth about the issues that individuals and organisations face when they consider the complex issue of talent management in the increasingly competitive business world.

Activities

1   Design an interview that you could use to discover the personal career aspirations of a junior manager from a hospitality or tourism company. Try to link each of the questions to a theory from the literature. Test out the interview on a chosen manager and analyse your findings with reference to the literature.

2   Consider the model presented in this chapter in Figure 1.1. Critically analyse the model and discuss in detail what it tells you about the talent management process.

3   Choose an organisation from the hospitality or tourism sector and critically analyse what they say about their talent management process on their web pages, in relation to the theory in this chapter.

4   Provide a short 2000 word summary of the key areas of literature that underpins the topic of talent management and highlight the key authors in each of the areas that you identify.

The content of the book to follow

This chapter has provided the underpinning to read the rest of the book and it is worth discussing the content to come, so that you can read broadly or focus on the area in which you have a particular interest. The first section of the book is arranged in three chapters and gives you the ideas about the talent management process in general and the role of higher education in the development of talent for the hospitality and tourism sectors. The two remaining chapters are as follows:

Chapter 2: Talent management in the hospitality and tourism curriculum, John Swarbrooke

Chapter 3: Talent management in the hospitality and tourism context, Philip Gibson

At the end of Part 1 you should have developed a preliminary understanding of the ways in which talent is developed in the hospitality and tourism industry, and differing views on this. The final chapter in this part of the book considers the special nature of hospitality and tourism, and how the talent management process can be applied in this setting.

Part 2 of the book considers the role of the individual in the talent management process. This is an area that has been neglected in the literature to date, with much more emphasis being placed on the organisational agenda for the talent management process. The second part is composed of seven chapters as follows:

Chapter 4: Personal career development - the concept of 'Hospitableness', Conrad Lashley

Chapter 5: Individual career progression in hospitality and tourism settings, Adele Ladkin

Chapter 6: Human resource strategy and talent management, Andrew Jenkins.

Chapter 7: The cultural and occupational roles attributed to 'trust' in talent management, Derek Cameron

Chapter 8: Talent management and youth employment, Andreas Walmsley

Chapter 9: The role of the professional body in the development of talent, Crispin Farbrother

Chapter 10: The role of situated learning in shaping talent, Craig Wight

These chapters aim to give you a more detailed insight into issues that are related to individual career progression, including what it takes to deliver the concept of 'hospitableness', how individuals develop a career in the sector, the role of the organisation in this, and the very interesting topics of 'trust' in the talent management process and the critical development of young talent. At the end of this part of the book, you will have considered a number of critical topics in depth, and may be interested in further developing an interest in one or more to underpin your academic development or help you in the workplace.

Part 3 of the book considers the role of the organisation in the talent management process and has five chapters as follows:

Chapter 11: The inclusive or exclusive concept in practical talent management, Susan Horner

Chapter 12: The role of diversity in talent management, Matthew Yap

Chapter 13: The role of internships and placements in the talent management process, Mandy Aggett

Chapter 14: Local, national or international strategies for talent management, Deniz Kucukusta

Chapter 15: Technology and talent management, Fevzi Okumus, Edwin Torres and Ahmet Ozturk

This part of the book starts by focusing on whether organisations should try to include all their human resources in the talent management process, or develop an elite band that are given resources and are seen as being the future senior management talent pool. Diversity and cultural differences and the need for specially developed approaches to talent management are also considered, and well as the role of technology in the talent management process.

The final part concludes the book and considers the future of the talent management process in one chapter:

Chapter 16: The future of talent management – meanings for hospitality organisations and educational delivery, Susan Horner

The cases at the end of the book illustrate the practical implementation of the talent management process in both small to medium enterprises (SMEs), and in large organisations in the sector.

References

Arris, A.A., Cascio, W.F. and Paauwe, J. (2013). Talent management: Current theories and future research directions. *Journal of World Business,* **49** (2014), 173-179.

Barron, P., (2008). Education and talent management: implications for hospitality industry. *International Journal of Contemporary Hospitality Management,* **20**(7), 730-742.

Baruch, Y. and Peiperl, M. (2000). Career management practices: an empirical survey and implications. *Human Resource Management,* **39** (4), 347-366.

Baum, T., (2008). Implications of hospitality and tourism labour markets for talent management strategies. *International Journal of Contemporary Hospitality Management,* **20**(7), 721-729.

Bharwani, S. and Butt, N. (2012). Challenges for the global hospitality industry: an HR perspective. *Worldwide Tourism Hospitality Themes,* **4**(2), 150-162.

Briscoe, J. and Hall, D., (2006). The interplay of boundaryless and protean careers: Combinations and implications. *Journal of Vocational Behaviour,* **69**, 4–18.

Brown, P., Hesketh, A. and Williams, S. (2004).*The Mismanagement of Talent. Employability and jobs in the knowledge economy*. Oxford: Oxford University Press.

Cappelli, P. and Keller, J. (2014). Talent management: conceptual approaches and practical challenges. *Annual Review of Organisational Psychology. Organisational Behaviour,* **1**(2), 305-331.

Chambers, E., Foulon, M., Handfield-Jones, H., Hankin, S. and Michaels, E. III, (1998). The war for talent. *McKinsey Quarterly,* **3**, 1-8.

Cheese, P. (2010). Talent management for a new era: what we have learned from the recession and what we need to focus on next. *Human Resource Management International Digest,* **18** (3), 3-5.

Chuai, X., Preece, D. and Lles: (2008). Is talent management just "old wine in new bottles"? The case of multinational companies in Beijing, *Management Research News*, **31**(12), 901–911.

Collings, D. and Mellahi, K. (2009). Strategic talent management: A review and research agenda. *Human Resource Management Review*, **19**(4), 304–313.

Collings, D., Scullion H. and Dowling P. (2009). Global staffing: a review and thematic research agenda. *International Journal of Human Resource Management*. **20**(6), 1253–1272.

D'Annunzio-Green, N. (2008). Managing the talent management pipeline: Towards a greater understanding of senior managers' perspectives in the hospitality and tourism sector. *International Journal of Contemporary Hospitality Management*. **20** (7), 807 – 819.

Davidson, M., McPhail, R. and Barry, S. (2011). Hospitality HRM: past, present and future. *International Journal of Contemporary Hospitality Management*, **23** (4), 498–516.

Deery, M. (2008). Talent management, work – life balance and retention strategies. *International Journal of Contemporary Hospitality Management*, **20** (7), 23-28.

De Vos, A. and Soens, N. (2008). Protean attitude and career success: The mediating role of self-management. *Journal of Vocational Behaviour*, **73** (2008) 449–456.

Dries, N. (2013). The psychology of talent management: A review and research agenda. *Human Resource Management Review*, **23** 272–285.

Farndale, E., Scullion, H. and Sparrow: (2010). The role of corporate HR function in global talent management. *Journal of World Business*, **45**, 161–168.

Furusten, S. (1999). *Popular Management Books: How They are Made and What They Mean for Organisations*. Routledge: London.

Gallardo-Gallardo, E., Dries, N. and Gonzalez-Cruz, T. (2013). What is the meaning of talent in the world of work? *Human Resource Management Review*, **23**, 290-300.

Hatum, A. (2010). *Next Generation Talent Management. Talent Management to survive turmoil*. Basingstoke: Palgrave Macmillan.

Huang J. and Tansley, C. (2012). Sneaking through the minefield of talent management: the notion of rhetorical obfuscation. *The International Journal of Human Resource Management*, **23**(17), 3673-3691.

Hugles, J. C. and Rog, E. (2008). Talent Management: A strategy for improving employee recruitment, retention and engagement within hospitality organisations. *International Journal of Contemporary Hospitality Management*, **20**(7), 743-757.

Iles, P. , Preece, D. and Chuai, X. (2010). Talent management as a management fashion in HRD: towards a research agenda. *Human Resource Development International*, **13**(2), 125-145.

Kichuk, A., Horner, S. and Ladkin, A. (2014b). Understanding Talent Management in Hospitality: Developing the conceptual framework. 32nd EuroCHRIE Conference, Dubai 6-9 October. Dubai: the Emirates Academy of Hospitality Management

Lashley, C., Lynch: and Morrison, A. (2007). *Hospitality: a social lens*. Elsevier: Oxford

Lepak, D. and Snell, S. (1999). The human resource architecture: Toward a theory of human capital allocation and development. *Academy of Management Review*, **24**(1), 31–48.

Lewis, R. and Heckman, R. (2006). Talent management: A critical review. *Human Resource Management Review*, **16**, 139–154.

Maxwell, G. and MacLean, S. (2008). Talent management in hospitality and tourism in Scotland: Operational implications and strategic actions. *International Journal of Contemporary Hospitality Management*, **20** (7), 820–830.

Meyers, M.C., van Woerkom, M. and Dries, N. (2013). Talent –Innate or acquired? Theoretical considerations and their implications for talent management. *Human Resource Management Review*, **23**(4), 305-321.

Michaels, E., Handfield-Jones, H. and Axelrod, B., (2001). *The War for Talent*. Harvard Business School Press: Boston.

Scott, B. and Revis, S. (2008). Talent management in hospitality: graduate career success and strategies. *International Journal of Contemporary Hospitality Management*. **20** (7), 781 – 791.

Silzer, R. and Dowell, B. (2010). Strategy-driven talent management: A leadership imperative. Jossey-Bass: San Francisco.

Steward, J. and Harte, V. (2010). The implications of talent management for diversity training: an exploratory study. *Journal of European Industrial Training*, **34**(6) 506-518.

Tulgan, B. (2001). Winning the talent wars. *Employment Relations Today*, **23**(1–2), 37–51.

Watson, S., (2008). Where are we now? A review of management development issues in the hospitality and tourism sector. Implications for talent management. *International Journal of Contemporary Hospitality Management*, **20**(7), 758-780.

2 Talent Management in the Hospitality and Tourism Context

Philip Gibson

Learning objectives

- Introduce the reader to the special nature of hospitality and tourism and the implications for the talent management process.

- Provide an analysis of contemporary hospitality business realities to explain the nuances of managing a workforce while operating a hospitality business.

- Discuss employment factors in order to make sense of theories concerning personnel and talent attributes.

- To identify a range of talent management issues that are relevant for managers in the industry

Introduction

Hospitality and tourism businesses operate in ever changing socio-cultural and socio-political environments. The constancy of change establishes the conditions for entrepreneurial innovation (Olsen, 1999), which can lead to evolutionary business opportunities for this sector, but this never-ending cycle of business generation and regeneration creates the often volatile reality for managing the human resource (Solnet, Kralj, and Baum, 2015). The people who are employed in hospitality and tourism make critical differences in the levels of success that are achieved by their employers thus underlining why talent management requires careful attention (Zhang, Kandampully, and Choi, 2014). Without talent, hospitality and tourism have no dynamism (Law, Bai, Crick, and Spencer, 2011). Globally, talented people are at the heart of successful hospitality and tourism organisations and businesses (Hsu, 2015; Mathew, 2015; Nzonzo and Chipfuva, 2013).

This chapter considers the special nature of hospitality and tourism and reflects on the unique or important features of the sector and the implications for the talent management process. An analysis of contemporary hospitality business realities is provided in the first section in order to help to explain the nuances of managing a workforce while operating a hospitality business. Thereafter, a discussion of employment factors is considered in order to make sense of theories concerning personnel and talent attributes. This is developed further in the penultimate section which identifies talent issues as identified from within a research project and provides an interpretation of how businesses respond to challenges identified from within hospitality and tourism contexts. In the conclusion, a range of key issues is identified that are relevant for managers in the industry.

The special nature of hospitality and tourism

How are hospitality and tourism different to other industries? It is possible to argue that all businesses are alike and that they depend on their success by deriving a profit from the sale of goods and services (Drucker, 1995). Yet this rather simplistic and mechanistic response ignores fundamental qualities that exist which differentiate one business type from another. For example, according to Stutts (2013), hospitality is both large scale and diverse but ultimately unique in the centrality of human interaction and service. In addition, Guerrier (2013) identifies that hospitality and tourism businesses are frequently subject to fluctuations in demand, because of business patterns or seasonality, and they thrive when they are flexible. She also draws attention to the 'paradox' (p88) of those hospitality businesses that utilise the lowest paid labour to undertake the most important customer contact roles. Furthermore, Nickson (2013) highlights the reality for some businesses that have the largest numbers of staff, often described as having 'low skills', employed at the lowest pay levels and the smallest number of 'high skilled' employees at the highest pay levels, but with no real mid-level employees. From a people and employment perspective hospitality and tourism appear to possess particularly challenging characteristics.

Clearly the diversity of hospitality and tourism can undermine attempts for a tidy interpretation. Hospitality and tourism enterprises often attract those with an ambition to start their own business. Start-up costs can be proportionately less than for other business types thus ensuring that hospitality and tourism as sectors are predominantly constituted by small-scale independent operators. Small to medium sized businesses including: ambitious family concerns; entrepreneurial innovators; and regional operators, focus on a broad market base in urban and rural areas. Large organisations flourish in the lucrative mass markets of international cities refining their brands so they become targeted and process driven.

Hospitality and tourism employers have certain unique as well as certain shared features. Invariably, hospitality and tourism jobs are co-related because of the close connections between the business of tourism and the management of hospitality; so tourism careers are frequently seen by many as overlapping with hospitality careers. Hotels and restaurants are, after all, located at the heart of tourism activities. Yet the nature of tourism is that its scope goes beyond that which is typically hospitality in focus. Tourism includes occupations connected with: planning and development (both public and private sector related); travel providers; travel agencies; tourist attractions, tourism related accommodation and hospitality services, as well as numerous closely related activities (Page and Connell, 2006).

While many casual observers would consider hotels to be synonymous with hospitality, the sector is as much about restaurants and catering than it is about any other type of activity. Yet the sector is goes beyond restaurants and hotels. Hospitality includes: any form of subsidised catering and facility management (e.g. education, health care, military and workplace); travel related catering and facility management (e.g. cruise, ferry, airport, trains motorway); leisure venues (casinos, retail, sports stadia, theme parks, night clubs, theatres and cinemas) and stand-alone hospitality businesses (restaurants, hotels [including variants such as aparthotels, 'botels' etc.], bars, resorts, time share and holiday centres). The relationship between hospitality and tourism is close but not complete and, as a result, there are opportunities within each sector for individuals to craft careers that can see them claiming membership of one or both sectors depending on the focus of their employment (see Figure 2.1).

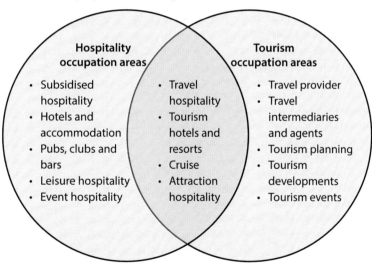

Figure 2.1: The relationship between hospitality and tourism occupations (Career Scope, 2016; Hospitality Guild, 2016; Institute of Hospitality, 2016 and Prospects, 2016).

In the UK, the government classifies employment into categories that are known as the Standard Occupational Classification (SOC). In April to June 2015, according to national data relating to the SOC, the number of individuals employed as managers and/or proprietors in various categories of hospitality and leisure services were as follows:

	Total (000's)	Employees (000's)			Self employed (000's)		
		Full time	Part time	Both	Full time	Part time	Both
Hotel and accommodation managers and proprietors	52	21	*	23	12	15	27
Restaurant and catering establishment managers and proprietors	129	77	6	82	38	8	46
Publicans and managers of licensed premises	49	29	*	31	16	*	18
Leisure and sports managers	62	45	7	52	7	*	10
Travel agency managers and proprietors	8	5	*	6	*	*	*
Managers and proprietors in hospitality and leisure services	**302**	**177**	**18**	**195**	**76**	**28**	**104**

(* = sample size too small for estimate)

Table 2.1: Numbers of m anagers and proprietors in hospitality and leisure services in employment in the UK, April-June 2015. Adapted from information obtained from the Office for National Statistics (ONS, 2015).

The data identify that there were a total of 302,000 managers and proprietors in hospitality and leisure services. According to this government analysis there were 3,182,000 managers for all occupational areas, thus suggesting managers and proprietors in hospitality and leisure services represent 9.49% of the total.

Employment area	Total employees
Food preparation and hospitality trades	495,000
Housekeeping and related services	103,000
Cleaning & housekeeping managers/supervisors	69,000
Kitchen and catering assistants	454,000
Waiters and waitresses	287,000
Bar staff	204,000
Leisure and theme park attendants	30,000
Leisure and travel related services	173,000
Transport related (includes 122,000 coach drivers and 213,000 taxi drivers)	412,000
Total	**2,227,000**

Table 2.2: Numbers employed in hospitality, tourism and leisure services in the UK, April -June 2015. Adapted from information from ONS (2015). Note this figure does not include support services employees.

The same source identified that there were 2,227,000 employees in hospitality and tourism related occupations, which equates to 7.2% of all employees. The government figures state that there were 30,950,000 people in employment at this time (ONS, 2015). The figures are broadly in accord with international estimates, with the International Labour Organisation (ILO, 2011) claiming that tourism accounts for 9% of the world's GDP and 8% of its employment. On the basis of these data, it seems that the scale of hospitality and tourism is significant both nationally and internationally in contributing towards generating opportunities for employment.

Hospitality and tourism can be viewed and interpreted through a number of lenses. For example, a sociological description of hospitality could focus in on the criticality, centrality and interactivity of the host-guest relationship. A psychological view could reflect on the host satisfying a guest's need for safety and comfort. An operational lens could highlight the component parts of the industry such as facilities, food, drink and entertainment. A business economics perspective could refer to the cash-rich trading environment, where different elements of the hospitality business contribute to revenue generation or a sales mix. Each element within this sales mix would have varying levels of profitability because of the types of costs (e.g. consumables, labour, direct costs, indirect costs, fixed costs and variable costs). Equally in tourism, the subject could be deconstructed using a broad range of conceptual approaches. These could include: geo-tourism; sustainable tourism; tourism and society; tourism and culture; and tourism and business. While this list is in no way complete, it does give a sense of comparison between those who have a tendency to consider hospitality pragmatically as a business subject and those who see tourism as a rich and diverse research field. That said, each lens helps to construct a more intricate picture of contemporary hospitality and tourism with direct implications for employability and talent management.

Increasingly hospitality and tourism exist in a brand defined world, with the largest multinational brands such as TUI, Hilton Hotels and Carnival Corporation meeting the diverse needs of specific markets for specific products. These large corporations make use of the trust that has been created for the parent brand (Bhat and Reddy, 2001), e.g. with TUI operating extension brands such as: Thomson Holidays, Hapag-Lloyd Cruises and Thomson Airways; with Hilton developing extension brands such as: Garden Inn, Hampton Inn and All Suites (made up of Embassy Suites, Homewood Suites and Home2 Suites); and with Carnival Corporation operating extension cruise brands such as: Holland America Line, P&O Cruises and Princess Cruises. In some cases brand extensions arise from a merger or acquisition and at other times it is a specific act of brand development and engineering in response to an identified market opportunity. The challenge for these groups, in terms of their staff, is to develop and maintain a unique brand identity and encourage brand specific staff loyalty, while simultaneously harnessing the corporate power of the parent brand to derive strategic advantages in terms of cost saving and efficiency of process management.

A considerable quantity of work has been undertaken to identify issues concerning culture in the workplace. For example, Pizam *et al.* (1997) emphasised the conflicting nature of types of culture that exist, with the result that a chef employed by a large hotel company could at varying times describe her organisational culture, her occupational culture, her industry culture, her national culture, her ethnic culture and even a supranational culture. This aspect of employment is important in understanding employee identity or motivation, but also in ensuring that brand identity is appropriate and achievable. An organisational culture can therefore be a vital element in the corporate toolkit to ensure a platform is established that helps to define the way the workplace functions (Schein, 1985, Handy,

1996, Robbins 2001). For multinational brands there are additional complexities to be considered concerning multicultural dimensions to do with both employees and customers, and in promulgating the host-guest relationship.

When you take into account the plethora of contextual and circumstantial factors described so far, all of which relate to the occupational opportunities that exist in hospitality and tourism, it becomes clear that there are important issues and distinctive factors that confirm the special nature of hospitality and tourism. There are, for example, issues at hand that identify:

☐ A compelling need to ensure staffing levels meet guest expectations in customer settings that rely predominantly on people skills,

☐ A complexity of business types and services that fall under the umbrella terms 'hospitality' or 'tourism', from business start-ups through to global multi-brand corporations,

☐ The scale of hospitality and tourism which correlates with the demand for employment and the diversity that relates to the employment opportunities.

Personnel and talent attributes

Hospitality and tourism guest experiences are frequently described as being like a mix or cocktail, derived from the various tangible (product related) and non-tangible (service related) elements that exist at the time of engagement. These guest interactions are examples of what Pine and Gilmore (1999) refer to as the 'experience economy', which describes an evolved state of consumerism where guests place value on the form of involvement that is derived from the hospitality or tourism activity. Bharwani and Jauhari (2013) believe employees play vital roles to become 'enablers' of positive guest experiences, and that the desired characteristics of effective employees are, as a result, more complex than some industry commentators would suggest.

There have been a number of studies undertaken to extrapolate key issues concerning service related roles, which try to make sense of the nuanced realities that seem to exist for hospitality and tourism guest-facing personnel. For example, Ladhari (2009) and Guerrier and Adib (2003) examined the notion of emotional labour, a theory made popular by Arlie Hochschild (1983), where the employee presents what could be described as an artificial construct and accepts that in undertaking their role they bring to bear human emotional characteristics. In this sense the authors identify that, for example, the smile is a tradable commodity and the theory draws attention to challenges such as: maintaining consistency in customer service; avoiding burnout when dealing with high pressure customer related situations; and developing some kind of balance in job satisfaction.

From this focus on emotional labour, it is but a short mental hop to then consider the part performativity has for this type of employee. When employees aim to develop and enhance experiences for guests, they are in effect becoming supporting actors or even directive participants in a custom built service oriented world. The world may exist only for the time the sales activity plays out, but during that time the employee is both an interlocutor or guide for easing the guests' transitions through the process, and an agent to provide stimulus to make the experience even better (Van Dijk, Smith, and Cooper, 2011). Hospitality and tourism have long been connected with theatre (Hemmington, 2007), as the guest experience is manufactured and, in some service settings, even scripted, but for the entire event, be it a service encounter or a tourist activity, there exists an importance in the way the experience is planned, cast, staged and performed in order to create a desirable level of authenticity (Taylor, 2001).

For the tourism and hospitality employee, such levels of engagement can present contradictions. Guests can be demanding and the guest encounters can be physically and emotionally draining, yet guest interaction can also be rewarding and the positive guest encounter can be highly motivating (Arnett, Laverie, and McLane, 2002). Bharwani and Jauhari (2013) believe, in addition to technical proficiency, it is essential that tourism and hospitality employees are capable of possessing high levels of competence in terms of understanding and responding to guest needs, co-operating and operating effectively in teams to provide enhanced service and demonstrating 'cultural empathy' (p. 836). This capability is therefore an important element in considering talent for hospitality and tourism.

The implications of ensuring high-level guest to host interactions, infer that there would appear to be potential problems in identifying the best employees to undertake such guest relations. Crawford (2013) believes that it is vital to screen applicants carefully to find those who possess attributes including: heightened and empathetic communication skills; capability to respond to guest needs without direction; genuinely caring to guests; ability to create an appropriately comfortable atmosphere through their engagement with guests; and the ability to go beyond the basics in dealing with guests. In addition, Lee and Ok (2012) focus on the need to ensure recruitment considers emotional intelligence or *"the ability of an individual to recognize his/her own feelings and those of others and to motivate and manage his/her own emotions well in relationship with others"* (p. 1101) so that employees are better able to cope with the emotional challenges of the job. In addition, Bolton (2004) draws attention to the dichotomy that exists in many businesses who recruit low pay employees but then expect highly skilled emotional labour performances from those recruits.

In the food service part of the industry, operators frequently struggle to find ways of sourcing qualified and competent chefs or similar food production employees (Rodgers, 2009). The scarcity of skilled production staff has become endemic and is an item of regular interest for a media reflecting on the implications for city centre restaurants (Guardian Newspaper, 2015; Independent Newspapers, 2015). In the UK this scarcity has evolved in Darwinesque style as a result of initiatives such as: de-skilling in the kitchen and the introduction of centralised production kitchens in order to reduce staffing costs; the erosion of government and business support for culinary skills development in Colleges of Further Education (CFE); and the inexorable focus by central government on London as a magnet for business and high paid jobs, together with the demand for high calibre chefs to service city dwellers' gastronomic ambitions. The implications for talent management are that too few trainee chefs emerge from CFEs, because opportunities tend to be concentrated in relatively centralised locations. In addition CFEs lose funding because of recruitment and can't maintain expensive resources to support provision and recruitment in those centralised locations affected by expensive housing. An outcome of these circumstances can lead to high-end food service businesses blaming CFEs for not meeting their needs. For example, chef and businessman Mark Hix says:

> The chef shortage is an on-going crisis and that's why I opened the Hix Academy in Weymouth last year. Catering colleges are not what they once were. They don't teach students to innovate or work under pressure, and we can't just sit back and wait for staff to come to us. We have to go out to find and train them. (Independent Newspapers, 2015).

Ultimately, hospitality and tourism employers are faced with a quandary in recruiting talented staff, who must have and use superior social skills. This difficulty also exists for businesses seeking staff with particular attributes, who are hard to find because of the way that businesses have evolved. The industry is faced with complex, ever-changing recruitment and talent management challenges that are affected by technological developments, economic circumstances, trading patterns and social trends. These various issues are developed further in the next section and are considered so as to highlight implications for talent management processes.

Talent management: Challenges and implications

The challenges facing employers to manage their talented staff so as to maintain competitive advantage are significant. In the final section of this chapter a number of issues are identified and reflected upon in respect of typical talent management processes. The evidence relating to the issues is drawn from a research project undertaken between 2011 and 2013, in which a number of high profile employers and industry professionals were interviewed about their approach to talent management (Gibson and Hine, 2013).

A synopsis of comments received from the aforementioned employers and industry professionals about their considered responses to the challenges that relate to the nuanced realities of managing talent in hospitality is provided in a series of tables in this section. The responses are framed in an analysis that identifies specific approaches within talent management namely: sourcing, recruiting, developing, retaining, deploying and engaging (Hughes and Rog, 2008). While details relating to each of these approaches can be found elsewhere in this book, a definition of engagement is provided later in this section to assist the reader.

The employers and professionals who participated in the study were promised confidentiality but are described by type in the following rubric (Table 2.3):

Description of interviewees
Large national limited service hotel brand
Iconic luxury city centre hotel - part of a multinational hotel group
Independent city centre hotel - part of a small international group
4 star branded city centre hotel – part of a multinational hotel group
City centre branded boutique hotel - part of a multinational hotel group
Luxury cruise brand - part of a multinational cruise corporation
International cruise brand - part of a multinational cruise corporation
International cruise brand - part of a multinational cruise corporation
Organisation focused on hospitality careers

Table 2.3: Employers and professionals interviewed

Table 2.4 shows a summary of challenges that relate to two talent management approaches: sourcing and recruiting. Industry professionals were invited to identify challenges and to comment on their method of dealing with the challenge.

Talent management practice	Challenges	Commentary
Sourcing	How can the business respond to the problems associated with identifying and targeting potential recruits? How can the business address skills shortages?	Networks with employee support groups, CFEs and universities and the way relations with networks are cultivated and maintained are vital. Employer branding (the way the employer communicates the brand to employees) plays a significant part in attracting new talent. Importance of the website in attracting interest. Some hospitality and cruise brands target 'trusted' universities and colleges. Awards matter so the employer is identified as a purveyor of good employment practice. Talent recruitment can be multi-level but work experience helps to facilitate the process.
Recruiting	How can the business attract employees in a competitive employment market?	Criticality of the website as the interface for recruitment. Importance of social media for recruitment communications. The need to identify behaviour traits in relation to 'fitting in' to ensure the recruitment process is efficient. Common sense attributes are seen to be important.

Table 2.4: Challenges and employer responses in respect of sourcing and recruiting

Employers spoke of the need to be proactive in tackling talent management issues head on. Those who spent time and money on developing their brand image for employees appeared to at an advantage. Employer branding seemed to have the potential to develop positive perceptions about the employer, providing it was seen by potential employees as reliable and valid. Organisations that work on behalf of employers to develop employee awareness about working in hospitality were highlighted as being excellent network partners and a closely nurtured relationship with this type of organisation was said to be strategically valuable.

Employers were also aware that they needed to be in tune with contemporary practices in terms of social media and internet communications. The internet presents a challenge in that it is constantly changing and driven by popular reaction to emerging trends. The interviewees noted that employees and guests viewed this set of circumstances as being normal and believed that businesses who failed to keep up to date with IT practices were out of touch. Table 2.5 shows employer responses relating to the challenges of developing, retaining and deploying employees.

Talent management practice	Challenges	Commentary
Developing	How can the business make sure investment in training and development is effective?	Many employers encourage training and development with a particular focus on leadership and responsibility. Performance management and/or appraisal made use of address this aspect. Career mapping is important to show routes for progression and linked development needs. It is important to train and develop employees even if they leave. Placement programmes for students need to be handled with care.
Retaining	How can the business ensure the best employees are retained and staff turnover is minimised?	Review employee performance regularly and personalise development linked to the job. Evolve systems to identify and nurture key talent. Importance of harnessing the brand in retention strategies.
Deploying	How can the business maximise potential of employees to benefit the business?	Promotion should be based on performance, levels of training and aptitude for the promoted post. Importance of communicating options for career paths. Establish strategies for cross brand deployment to open up alternative routes. Ensure plans in place to cover succession planning.

Table 2.5: Challenges and employer responses in respect of developing, retaining and deploying

Training and development were said to be critical for establishing motivated and effective employees. Most employers recognise that the way businesses manage their training and development is directly linked to matters such as their reputation as employers, the effectiveness of their employees and the long term profitability of the business. Some also noted that if a trained employee left and spoke well of their former employer, that was invaluable for employer branding.

The quandary of minimising staff turnover is a constant challenge. Those businesses that had managed to reduce staff turnover had sophisticated systems in place to monitor performance and linked to that an inter-related approach to develop talent, identify key talent and show clear opportunities for progression.

Table 2.6 provides a reflection of interviewee responses to challenges concerning staff engagement. For the purposes of this chapter it is useful to consider a definition of engagement. Gibbons (2006: 5) states that:

> employee engagement is a heightened emotional and intellectual connection that an employee has for his/her job, organization, manager, or co-workers, that in turn influences him/her to apply additional discretionary effort to his/her work.

This implies that engagement is a vital component for business success.

Challenges	Commentary
How can the business ensure employees are motivated and engaged?	Actively seek feedback to measure engagement and monitor engagement continuously.
	Disengagement should be seen as a problem and addressed immediately.
	Management relations with employees are a major issue and may require development and investment.
	Business units may have different engagement environments depending on the variables .
	Employees should have an active part in deciding on their own welfare.
	Employee services are very important to promote engagement (e.g. staff dining).
	Investigate ways of making connections with employees for developing social engagement associated to the workplace.

Table 2.6: Challenges and employer responses in respect of engaging

Much of what was said by employers in relation to the talent management challenges of sourcing, recruiting, developing, retaining and deploying was connected with engaging. The most effective strategy for talent management could be undermined at local level if engagement was mishandled or ignored. In many ways employers regarded the issue of engagement as a kind of 'holy grail', or a measure of the wellbeing at the heart of a business. Two aspects seemed to emerge as pertinent: understanding the form and level of engagement; and devising a continuously evolving plan for encouraging and developing positive engagement. From the research data collected, it was apparent that employers were active in addressing staff engagement and the evidence suggests that various approaches were taken in the way this was done. Some employers created and nurtured staff social committees, and then supported plans that were subsequently developed in an effort to generate a social culture. Other employers sought to develop and manage engagement at various levels in the business hierarchy. Those businesses that appeared to be most successful in creating the best conditions for engagement treated the topic strategically. In those particular businesses there was a philosophy that staff were central to the success of business, and a commitment to establishing openness, honesty and equality in all dealings with employees.

Conclusion

This chapter has presented a discussion concerning the structure, scale and complexity of hospitality and tourism businesses. It is a business setting that relies on its employees' talent for its success, yet is imbued with characteristics that complicate the process of managing that talent. Contemporary hospitality and tourism businesses require a particular type of guest focused talent: one which is emotionally mature and empathetic but also capable of anticipating guest needs and highly responsive to changing requirements. Yet, for most hospitality and tourism businesses it has become an industry norm that the employee with these set of skills may not be well rewarded compared to other industries. The implications of this reality has created problems in recruiting employees, led to skills shortages in some geographical locations and also influenced staff turnover.

In the final section, the findings of a research project that examined employer and professional perceptions of challenges for talent management approaches were discussed. The resultant reflection on practice presented a portrait of the complex machinations that have been devised by businesses who are proactive in managing their talent effectively. These businesses approach the task of engaging with their employees as a serious task. They recognise the need to invest in long term strategies that are focused on developing their labour base, creating a sound reputation as employers and seeking to be regarded as the employer of choice.

Learning activities

1   What are the industry-related challenges that exist for Hospltality and tourism that impact on talent acquisition?

2   Describe the types of skills that are required in hospitality and tourism.

3   What are the reasons for possible skill shortages in hospitality and tourism and what can be done about this?

4   What is staff engagement?

5   Why is staff engagement of critical importance for hospitality and tourism employers?

References

Arnett, D. B., Laverie, D. A. and McLane, C. (2002). Using job satisfaction and pride as internal-marketing tools. *The Cornell Hotel and Restaurant Administration Quarterly,* **43**(2), 87-96.

Bharwani, S. and Jauhari, V. (2013). An exploratory study of competencies required to co-create memorable customer experiences in the hospitality industry. *International Journal of Contemporary Hospitality Management,* **25**(6), 823-843.

Bhat, S. and Reddy, S. K. (2001). The impact of parent brand attribute associations and affect on brand extension evaluation. *Journal of Business Research,* **53**(3), 111-122.

Bolton, S. (2004). Conceptual confusions: emotion work as skilled work, in C. Warhurst, I. Grugulis and E. Keep (Eds.), *The Skills That Matter,* (pp. 19-37). Basingstone: Palgrave Macmillan.

Career Scope. (2016). About the industry. Retrieved 25 April 2016 from http://careerscope. uk.net/industry

Crawford, A. (2013). Hospitality operators' understanding of service: a qualitative approach. *International Journal of Contemporary Hospitality Management,* **25**(1), 65-81.

Drucker: F. (1995). *People and Performance: The best of Peter Drucker on management.* New York: Routledge.

Gibbons, J. (2006), *Employee Engagement: A review of current research and Its implications,* the Conference Board, New York, NY: 1-21.

Gibson,P. and Hine, C. (2013). *Hospitality's got talent: investigating best practice.* Paper presented at the EuroCHRIE 2013 Conference, Freiburg, Germany.

Guardian Newspaper. (2015). Too few chefs: how a staffing crisis could change what we eat. Retrieved 7th January, 2016, from http://www.theguardian.com/lifeandstyle/2015/ sep/18/chef-shortage-could-change-way-we-eat-restaurants

Guerrier, Y. (2013). Human resource management in hospitality. In R. C. Wood (Ed.), *Key Concepts in Hospitality Management.* London: Sage.

Guerrier, Y. and Adib, A. (2003). Work at Leisure and Leisure at Work: A Study of the Emotional Labour of Tour Reps. *Human Relations,* **56**(11), 1399-1417.

Handy, C. B. (1996). *Gods of Management: The changing work of organizations*: Oxford University Press, USA.

Hemmington, N. (2007). From service to experience: Understanding and defining the hospitality business. *The Service Industries Journal,* **27**(6), 747-755.

Hochschild, A. R. (1983). *The Managed Heart.* (Vol. 31). Berkeley: University of California Press.

Hospitality Guild. (2016). Hospitality careers map. Retrieved 25 April 2016 from http:// www.hospitalityguild.co.uk/A-Career-in-Hospitality/Career-Map

Hsu, Y.-L. (2015). The review of human resource strategies applying in hospitality industry in South California. *International Business Research,* **8**(3), p133.

Hughes, J.C. and Rog, E. (2008). Talent management: A strategy for improving employee recruitment, retention and engagement within hospitality organizations. *International Journal of Contemporary Hospitality Management*, **20**(7), 743-757.

Institute of Hospitality. (2016). Careers guidance. Retrieved 25 April 2016 from https://www.instituteofhospitality.org/Careers/careers_guidance

International Labour Organisation. (2011). Hotels, catering & tourism - Sustainable tourism. Retrieved 08/12/15, 2015, from http://www.ilo.org/global/industries-and-sectors/hotels-catering-tourism/WCMS_162197/lang--en/index.htm

Independent Newspapers. (2015). Restaurants are booming in Britain, but the chronic shortage of chefs and other staff is threatening the industry. Retrieved 7th January, 2016, from http://www.independent.co.uk/news/uk/home-news/restaurants-are-booming-in-britain-but-the-chronic-shortage-of-chefs-and-other-staff-is-threatening-10457551.html

Ladhari, R. (2009). Service quality, emotional satisfaction, and behavioural intentions: A study in the hotel industry. *Managing Service Quality*, *19*(3), 308-331.

Law, R., Bai, B., Crick, A. P. and Spencer, A. (2011). Hospitality quality: new directions and new challenges. *International Journal of Contemporary Hospitality Management*, **23**(4), 463-478.

Lee, J. J. and Ok, C. (2012). Reducing burnout and enhancing job satisfaction: Critical role of hotel employees' emotional intelligence and emotional labor. *International Journal of Hospitality Management*, **31**(4), 1101-1112.

Mathew, A. (2015). Talent Management Practices in Select Organizations in India. *Global Business Review*, **16**(1), 137-150.

Nickson, D. (2013). *Human Resource Management for Hospitality, Tourism and Events.* Abingdon: Routledge.

Nzonzo, J. C. and Chipfuva, T. (2013). Managing talent in the tourism and hospitality sector: A conceptual view point. *International Journal of Academic Research in Accounting, Finance and Management Sciences*, **3**(2), 92-97.

Olsen, M. D. (1999). Macroforces driving change into the new millennium—major challenges for the hospitality professional. *International Journal of Hospitality Management*, **18**(4), 371-385.

ONS (2015). Occupational statistics. Retrieved 7 November 2015, 2015, from http://www.ons.gov.uk/ons/publications/re-reference-tables.html?edition=tcm%3A77-381603#tab-Employment-tables

Page, S. and Connell, J. (2006). *Tourism: A modern synthesis.* London: Cengage Learning EMEA.

Pine, B. J. and Gilmore, J. H. (1999). *The Experience Economy: Work is theatre and every business a stage.* Harvard Business School Press, Boston.

Pizam, A., Pine, R., Mok, C. and Shin, J. (1997). Nationality vs industry cultures: which has a greater effect on managerial behavior? *International Journal of Hospitality Management*, **16**(2), 127-145.

Prospects. (2016). Travel and Tourism. Retrieved 25 April 2016 from https://www. prospects.ac.uk/careers-advice/what-can-i-do-with-my-degree/travel-and-tourism

Robbins, S.P. (2001), *Organizational Behavior*, Prentice-Hall, Upper Saddle River, NJ.

Rodgers, S. (2009). The state of technological sophistication and the need for new specialised tertiary degrees in food services. *International Journal of Hospitality Management*, **28**(1), 71-77.

Schein, E. H. (1985). Defining organizational culture. *Classics of Organization Theory*, **3**, 490-502.

Solnet, D., Kralj, A. and Baum, T. (2015). 360 degrees of pressure the changing role of the HR professional in the hospitality industry. *Journal of Hospitality & Tourism Research*, **39**(2), 271-292.

Stutts, A. T. (2013). Hospitality as an Occupation. In K. S. Chon, C. W. Barrows & R. H. Bosselman (Eds.), *Hospitality Management Education* (pp. 21-32). New York: Routledge.

Taylor, J. P. (2001). Authenticity and sincerity in tourism. *Annals of Tourism Research*, **28**(1), 7-26.

Van Dijk,P. A., Smith, L. D. and Cooper, B. K. (2011). Are you for real? An evaluation of the relationship between emotional labour and visitor outcomes. *Tourism Management*, **32**(1), 39-45.

Zhang, T. C., Kandampully, J. and Choi, H. Y. (2014). The role of employee wellness programme in the hospitality industry: a review of concepts, research, and practice. *Research in Hospitality Management*, **4**(1/2).

3 Talent Management in the Hospitality and Tourism Curriculum

John Swarbrooke

Learning objectives

At the end of this chapter the reader should be able to recognise the current issues in tourism and hospitality education and the likely future challenges in relation to talent management. They will have read a number of proposed solutions which they will then be able to critically evaluate. Finally, they should have deepened their understanding of what talent management means in tourism and hospitality.

Student learning activities

Students should, in groups, discuss the programme of study they are undertaking and evaluate its relevance to talent management. They should then present their findings face-to-face to a tutor and an industry representative and take feedback from both. In light of this feedback they should then finalise their conclusions and present them through the medium of a written report.

Assessment: Essay question

Critically evaluate the statement that 'talent management in tourism and hospitality relies heavily on the tourism and hospitality curriculum in higher education institutions'.

Introduction

This is a fascinating topic to be discussing during a period of great, and perhaps even unprecedented, uncertainty and change in politics, business and society. It is against this volatile background that this chapter is set.

The author will argue that the traditional approaches to tourism and hospitality education are failing to meet the needs of the two industries in terms of talent management. Indeed in some cases they are in danger of becoming irrelevant to the nurturing of future talent in tourism and hospitality due to their focus on research and bureaucratic quality systems

At the same time it will be suggested that the two industries are struggling to attract and retain the best talent due to outdated and sometimes downright unethical approaches to managing people. We are seeing improvements here but they are not fast enough to be effective in a rapidly changing labour market.

We therefore appear to be heading towards some kind of 'perfect storm' in which, if we are not careful, tourism and hospitality sectors will become the preserve of those with few other career options, not a desired destination for the brightest and most talented in our countries. However, the author does not wish to simply present a critique of current practice. Instead the intention is to highlight the challenges and suggest ways in which they might be tackled in future.

While the author is UK based and most familiar with the UK situation, the chapter will endeavour to present a global view of the subject and it will be up to the reader to judge how successful he has been in this, based on how what is said relates to where they are reading this book.

The author wishes not to offer a traditional chapter with references but instead to present a personal view as a basis for discussion and debate. However, suggestions for further reading will be found at the end of the chapter.

Finally, it is important to stress that the major focus in this chapter will be on higher education and particularly universities, and is not meant in any way to devalue what is done in other types of institution.

A brief history of the subject areas

By general consensus, formal hospitality education is said to have originated in Switzerland in 1893 with the creation of the *Ecole Hôtelière de Laussanne* or EHL. This was created to help meet the demand for skilled labour for the growing tourism industry in Switzerland, which catered for rich and demanding clients. Switzerland later went on to develop a very strong hospitality education 'brand' with the opening of further hotel schools, particularly in the 1980s. In the Netherlands the *Hotel School the Hague* commenced operations in 1929. Across the Atlantic, the *Culinary Institute of America* opened its doors in 1946 while in the UK the first university in the country to launch a hospitality programme accepted its first students on to a Hotel and Catering Administration undergraduate programme in 1966.

Tourism, by contrast, was a somewhat later development and often started out as an elective subject on hospitality programmes. However, it became widely accepted in universities quite quickly, so that the University of Surrey, a pioneer in the field, awarded its first PhD in tourism in 1972 and launched its first postgraduate programme in tourism in 1981, two years before it launched the equivalent programme in hospitality.

The historical evolution of the two areas perhaps provides hints as to how they have developed in different ways since their early days. Hospitality education has its roots in the 19th century and has a longer heritage than tourism, which may partly account for its more traditional and conservative nature. It also grew out of industry needs rather than academic interest unlike tourism, which probably explains why it has developed differently to tourism in the ways we will discuss in the next section.

As a further comment in this section, it is perhaps worth noting that when EHL opened its doors there were no aeroplanes or motels, when the Culinary Institute of America launched there were no fusion cuisine restaurants or Mc Donalds and when the University of Surrey started its first postgraduate tourism programme there were no budget airlines or mobile devices! In other words, most of the leading players were created before the developments that have revolutionised tourism and hospitality were even in existence!

Finally, we also need to note that, until recently, tourism and hospitality education was dominated by institutions in Europe and the USA. Yet it is in other parts of the world, notably Asia and the Gulf States, that we have seen the most growth and innovation in the tourism and hospitality sectors.

Key differences between tourism and hospitality education

The author has always been intrigued by the fact that hospitality and tourism education are often so different, when the subjects are so closely related. What follows is a highly generalised view that is not true for everywhere, but is a fair summary of the global situation as a whole.

Hospitality education is not accepted as a university level subject in many countries and is seen as a subject to be taught at vocational rather than academic institutions. It is rooted in business as a subject and is concerned mainly with operational management and customer service. Industry links would have been strong on such programmes traditionally but research would have been a very low level priority. Hospitality academics have largely refrained from criticising the hospitality industry in terms of salary levels, for example. A major concern of educators concerned about the employability of graduates has been the social skills and appearance of students, as employers have stressed the importance of these in recruitment decisions.

One result of the lack of conventional university level hospitality education in many countries has been the rise of alternative providers, often private sector organisations, who have sought to offer degree programmes in cooperation with universities in other countries. At the same time some hospitality corporations have developed their own higher education level programmes through partnerships with universities

Tourism education by contrast is accepted as a university level subject much more widely, although not universally. As a result one does not see equivalents of the Swiss hotel schools in the tourism field. It is rooted in the social sciences and is generally concerned with policy and the role of the public sector. Research has usually been quite high on the list of priorities but industry links, particularly with the private sector, have often been limited. Tourism academics have often been critical of the actions of the tourism industry. Tourism educators have generally been more concerned with the intellect of their students and have been largely unconcerned about their social skills or appearance.

This is not to say that all hospitality and tourism academics have taken these approaches. Conrad Lashley has long campaigned for hospitality education to take a broader, more philosophical view of hospitality and its role in society, while Harold Goodwin has had great success in building links between academia and the tourism industry in the field of sustainability. However the existence of these two rather lone voices perhaps proves the point being made by the author.

In terms of talent management therefore, we might make the following observations. Hospitality educators may have focused too much on the practical side of employment roles and have encouraged compliance without too much questioning of how employers operate. Tourism educators have encouraged questioning and critical analysis but perhaps have rather neglected to give sufficient attention to developing the business management skills and experience of their students

What 'talent' does hospitality and tourism need?

This is an obvious question but it is more complex than one might expect. Traditionally the word 'talent' was not used and the focus was on individuals with a set of technical competences, together with a general 'service mentality'. It was expected that over a period of years those who did particularly well in their areas of technical expertise or departments would rise to management positions. The difficulties of the transition from technical specialist to departmental manager were often underestimated, which partly accounts for the poor reputation of our industries in terms of management quality, and particularly the ability to motivate and manage people. The traditional manager was often someone who had to focus on regulation and discipline to ensure a diverse workforce worked as a team and did not indulge in bad behaviour. The emphasis was on consistency at routine tasks and following set procedures.

There is no doubt that there is still a place for elements of this traditional management practice. However, for these industries to be successful in a modern economy and attract the best talent there is a need to take a rather different approach as many leading organisations have realised.

First, if managers are there to manage and plan strategy, do they all need to start at the bottom in the industry and work their way up? Maybe some should be brought in from other sectors to bring new thinking into the industry.

Second, we need managers who are creative and innovative, rather than just those who are good at following systems. We also need disruptive thinkers who will challenge the status quo and question how things are done. This needs to be seen as a strength rather than a problem. They need to be problem solvers and people who can take responsibility and flourish on empowerment. In terms of personality, they need to have great social skills and be flexible and adaptable as the workplace is changing every day. Most importantly perhaps they need to be people who have the ability to lead and motivate a team. All of this is not to ignore the importance of technical competence in tourism and hospitality. Waiting staff need to be able to serve food and beverage, and travel agents to process bookings, but managers need to be able to manage.

When discussing this question we also need to discuss the impact of recent changes in our industry which are having an impact on the type of talent we need. The rise of online travel agents and the growth of the online travel media have created new job opportunities for younger people with ICT skills. In this world, long years of experience are more of a handicap than a benefit as the experience is unlikely to have included ICT expertise, and long years means more mature age, and more mature age generally means a reduced ability to learn new skills such as ICT.

It is therefore no surprise that some of the most dynamic players in the market, such as AirBnB and TripAdvisor, recruit young people in direct competition with more traditional tourism and hospitality organisations.

Higher education curricula, talent and tourism and hospitality

Before moving on to spend most of the chapter looking at the future challenges we will be facing and how we might respond to them the author would like to make a few observations about the current curricula whilst recognising the difficulty of generalising about such a diverse subject.

First, many curricula are simply failing to keep pace with changes in the 'real world' not least because they are underpinned by academic literature that may well be based on research which was several years old when published. It also happens because university quality systems can mean it can take up to one year or more to change the content of the curriculum. If he was being petty, the author might also point to the many 'Contemporary Issues' modules on programmes as further confirmation that even universities recognise that most of the curriculum is outdated!

Second, too little attempt has been made to differentiate institutions through their curricula. Instead we have had benchmarks and talk of core curriculum based on the idea that a tourism or hospitality student needs a certain body of knowledge to be credible. Yet not only are these industries changing rapidly, but they are incredibly diverse. So instead of general programmes in hospitality and tourism we may need to develop programmes tailored to the needs of specific sectors, so that programme A focuses on airline management, B on tour operations,

3

C on luxury hotel management, D on bar management and E on fast food and casual dining. This approach would have its challenges too; not least would be ensuring that young people chose the right programme for them and that numbers were viable. However, this approach would gain more buy-in from industry that would see a product that was much more aligned to their particular sector.

Third, few university programmes pay enough attention to the development of personal skills and attributes, particularly as they are difficult to assess and give credits for, and universities tend to be concerned with credits and assessment.

Fourth, when we ask students to do a major piece of individual investigation it is in the form of a traditional dissertation or thesis. Whilst there are a number of approaches that can be taken, most institutions tend to use the very traditional aims and objectives, literature review, methodology, results, discussion, conclusions model. This positively discourages creative thinking, which is what our industries need, and also discourages students from taking risks, because if you do a subject with little existing literature you will risk getting lower marks. Furthermore, we insist in dissertations being submitted in a language and style that students will probably never use again. The author wholly accepts the validity of this traditional approach for science subjects, but rejects its value in the development of talent in hospitality and tourism. There are more appropriate ways of developing critical thinking skills amongst future tourism and hospitality professionals.

Finally, not enough curricula are as yet embracing the new approaches to business that we are seeing, whether it be social enterprises, pop-up restaurants and hotels, or crowd funding. This gap will reduce the relevance of curricula unless it is addressed.

On the more positive side we are seeing the emergence of a small number of initiatives in terms of developing the hospitality and tourism curriculum to ensure that it will meet the future needs of industry. Of these perhaps the most exciting is Hotel Icon, developed by Hong Kong Polytechnic University, which is already well known. However, sadly there are few such examples of true innovation.

Future challenges

If hospitality and tourism education wants to play a role in future talent management it first of all has to survive! As universities in many countries seek to focus more on research and less on vocational education, many hospitality programmes are under threat or are being subsumed in to business schools. Tourism faces fewer such threats but is no longer the cash cow, beloved of university finance managers, that it was a few years ago.

And this trend in hospitality and tourism education, whereby the subjects are in apparent stagnation or even decline, does not seem to be drawing howls of protest from industry.

There seems a general view in industry that hospitality and tourism educators are not producing the right graduates to meet the needs of the sector. This came out clearly at a recent conference in Finland that the author attended, so it is not just a UK issue. In fairness it has to be said that educators would deny this and place the blame on industry, perhaps for not knowing what it needs. However, the fact is that industry is in the driving seat, deciding who it will and will not employ.

Industry seems to be saying increasingly that specialist technical skills are less important than the attributes of the person in terms of problem-solving skills, flexibility, social skills, adaptability and so on. These can be found in students on many other programmes, and training can resolve any skills gaps. To cut costs, many institutions are reducing the practical element of programmes so that if gaining practical experience ever was a competitive advantage for hospitality programmes, it probably is not any longer. In any event, we also need to recognise that industry is changing so quickly that any technical knowledge or skill a student acquires in their final year will be out of date in a few years or even months.

Perhaps we should abandon hospitality and tourism programmes and just focus on producing smart, highly motivated graduates in management or geography or languages and so on, whom industry can develop through training once appointed!

However, the author believes that, partly because of the vested interest and inertia built in to higher education worldwide, this is unlikely to happen in the short term so we will proceed to discuss possible courses of action if these programmes are to continue. If universities are going to play a vital role in talent management in hospitality and tourism they made need to change their approach dramatically. Instead of recruiting people in their late teens who study for three or four years to gain a degree, they may need a much more flexible offer.

As sectors where staff often have relatively low levels of academic qualifications we need to fully embrace the idea of lifelong learning and get away from the idea that your formal education ends when you graduate from a university degree programme. Higher education institutions need, first, to be working in schools with industry representatives to start identifying young people who have an aptitude for, and an interest in, these two industries. They should then be encouraged and supported to undertake programmes at universities.

The programmes themselves may need to look very different to how most of them look today.

First, they do not need to be three or four years long with the long summer breaks, which are more beneficial for staff than students. The Swiss hotel school which I had the pleasure of teaching at for three years, taught 44 weeks a year so students completed a full undergraduate programme in three years, including two six-month duration paid internships. That put great pressure on staff certainly but the intensity was actually good experience for the students in terms of the pressures of working in a dynamic industry. Staff do not have to work 44 weeks, they could have contracts for 22 or 33 weeks, for example, if they wanted time to do research or consultancy work.

Second, instead of, or in addition to, internships we could integrate assessed work-based learning into the curriculum with the involvement of industry partners. Indeed in the UK, degree level 'apprenticeships' are being introduced in industries, including hospitality, whereby students study for a degree and work in industry at the same time so that they can relate theory to practice throughout their studies.

Third, to help the employability of students, and indeed to develop them as people, universities need to go well beyond academic content in programmes. There is a need to focus on the development of the individual, including everything from confidence building to presentation skills, cultural awareness to social skills, professional behaviour to having a sense of responsibility towards others. We also need experienced credible mentors working with students. This is very resource–intensive activity that most universities seem unwilling or unable to support. But it works, as the best Swiss hotel schools, for all their faults, clearly demonstrate.

The curriculum also needs updating with more focus being placed on issues such as ICT and digital technologies, ethics and corporate social responsibility, creativity, design, innovation and disruptive thinking. We should be establishing innovation labs where students – and industry – can use simulation technologies and computer aided design to experiment with designs for new hotel or airports, as well as testing out alternative approaches to service delivery.

Furthermore, as these are service industries, perhaps programmes need to devote more attention to the issue of service and what it means in the modern era, when customers are taking more and more ownership of the service process, undertaking functions previously delivered by staff from airline check-in to being their own travel agent through their mobile devices.

Finally in terms of the university curriculum, the author would like to suggest that gaming has a role to play in tourism and hospitality talent development. There are games around airline and hotel management available that were designed to entertain rather than educate. However, in the hands of a skilled tutor they can both improve students' understanding in their early studies, as well as motivating them to wish to learn more. We can also develop our own educational games and simulations where students have to react to unforeseen changes in circumstances, which is obviously what they will experience in industry

Perhaps we can also sometimes learn at the premises of our industry partners, instead of always basing learning on a higher education campus. By learning in an hotel or restaurant or airport environment students will begin to gain an awareness of the actual context in which they will work. In turn this should help them relate theory to practice in their studies.

However, the changes in the programmes need to start before the student even enrols. Students who are going to be successful in these industries need more than just good high school grades. It is about attitude and motivation and ambition, and this means we need a more thorough selection process that helps students decide if this career path is right for them.

Returning to the subject of lifelong learning, we need to make sure that universities are offering programmes that help people to continue to develop throughout their careers, as the industry changes. This means programmes being available part time and at times that work for employers and employees. This may require evenings and weekends but is more likely to mean delivering in blocks when industry is in its off-peak season.

Given the time pressures on hospitality and tourism, employees we may also have to rethink the idea that delivery takes place at particular times and in specific locations where the student has to attend. Online learning is probably the most effective tool for delivering this lifelong learning, given that people can access it at any time in any location. However it needs to be backed up by personal interaction from tutors and in-workplace mentors. Universities also need to cease to be obsessed about everything having to be assessed and carry credits. Education does not always have to be based on counting and measuring; it is about meeting the needs of individuals and society.

If we look at the demographic trends in some countries we also need to recognise that a growing number of staff may come from the older age groups, which will make the term 'lifelong learning' particularly appropriate. The whole debate about lifelong learning brings into question the traditional distinction between education and training, with higher education only wishing to be involved in the former. If all higher education is seen as ending when people finish their Bachelor's or Master's or PhD we are saying that most people will have finished their education by the time they are in their mid-twenties. Given the trend in life expectancy and a rapidly changing world, are we saying that people will neither need nor want any further education for the last fifty or sixty years of their life?

At the same time as more and more tasks in the workplace are de-skilled or standardised, there will be an increasing focus in staff development and continuing professional development for improving job quality and satisfaction to aid retention. The rapidly changing environment in which we will be working in tourism and hospitality in the future will also create a need for managers who are creative innovators, quick thinkers and disruptive thinkers. This is an education rather than a training challenge, as it involves the encouragement of critical thinking skills.

Social inclusion

In terms of future challenges, I would now like to move on to look at two issues relating to what might be termed 'social inclusion' in relation to talent management in hospitality and tourism.

In many countries the labour force in hospitality and tourism includes, indeed sometimes relies upon, people from ethnic minorities or recent immigrants. We are living in an era in which tolerance towards both communities sadly often appears to be in short supply. These people often face discrimination in the market place and are often relegated to the lowest skilled jobs, regardless of their previous experience and qualifications. This means that industry is potentially ignoring a source of talent here that it could develop if it were so inclined. Undoubtedly this would require effort but it would be worthwhile. A major priority should be helping recent immigrants in particular to learn the language of the country, not least because this will help them deliver a better service for customers. However, the action would need to also attend to cultural issues and prejudice that may be holding back the progress of recent immigrants and those from ethnic communities. Higher education institutions, the author would argue, have not only a role but a duty to be involved as part of their social inclusion policies.

The second group I would like to focus upon are those from disadvantaged backgrounds, whether that be based upon poverty, childhood abuse or criminal activities. Hospitality and tourism can really be a way out of despair for such people. Hotels and restaurants in particular can provide a support structure somewhat akin to a family, and the work discipline can help people to build new lives. However, to engage with these individuals, industry organisations will need to reach out into communities and put systems in place to ensure they are not discriminated against in terms of both recruitment and promotion.

Again I would stress that working with these groups is not just about altruism for industry, it is enlightened self-interest, particularly at a time when many employers complain about the difficulty of attracting and retaining good staff.

While a great deal has been done in industry to address the gender imbalance in relation to management positions in hospitality and tourism, the fact remains that it is still a reality. However while pressure is mounting quite rightly on companies to do more, the author, an elderly well-travelled academic, knows of no higher education institution that has an overt, clear programme in place to encourage and support female hospitality and tourism students to aspire to reach the very highest management positions.

The geography of consumption

One of the most striking developments in recent years in tourism and hospitality has been a dramatic change in the geography of consumption. Whilst most international tourists are still residents of Europe and North America, there has been a massive growth in inbound and domestic tourism in other parts of the world, most notably Asia and the Gulf States. This has led to a substantial increase in the need for properly educated and trained personnel.

However, many of these countries which are relatively new to hospitality and tourism have struggled to keep up with the growth in demand for suitably skilled labour. This has had two main results. First, they have tended to import senior management from abroad, so that many managers are foreign. If this continues it will be a vicious circle, where local people have to emigrate to progress because opportunities are not available in their own country. Second, in many countries foreign universities have set up transnational education programmes that have certainly helped developed local human resource development, but have not always been contextualised to the local environment. It must be remembered that they are ultimately controlled by foreign universities with their own agendas, largely based around income generation. In addition we have seen some very good development aid programmes around capacity building in these countries, but many are not sustainable and robust enough to survive once the funding ends. There is thus a need for industry players and governments in these countries to invest more in tourism and hospitality education to meet their own needs.

Universities around the world have sought increasingly to attract international students, largely one would have to say for financial reasons. This has brought really talented young people to countries such as the USA, UK and Australia. The tourism and hospitality sectors in these countries have benefitted greatly from the arrival of this talent. However their home country has lost out from this 'brain drain' to foreign countries.

Notwithstanding the issue of income for the universities therefore, the author would argue that 'responsible higher education' should focus on transnational education initiatives designed to help students gain a high quality education within their own country. Then, the government and industry in these countries need to put in place structures to create good career opportunities for indigenous talent. Major international hotel companies could support them by putting in place training and mentoring programmes for local people so that there will be much less use of expatriate managers 'parachuted' in to manage units.

On a different note, in terms of talent management, we also need to recognise that not all talent management is about the people who will be employed. We also need to be concerned with the development of entrepreneurial talent and the development of those who wish to set up their own enterprises.

Hospitality and tourism can have relatively low barriers to entry, so a student can, in many countries, develop an enterprise with very little money. This could be anything from setting up a travel website funded by advertising, to becoming a party organiser at night clubs, to renting a room through AirBnB, to running a pop-up restaurant in their home! Mobile devices and the Internet have created more opportunities for smart, dynamic young people to develop their own enterprises than has ever been the case before. Our curricula must provide the opportunity for these young people to get started even while they are students. More universities need to provide 'incubator' space for fledgling student enterprises and allow young entrepreneurs to relate formal assessment to their enterprise.

At the same time tourism and hospitality has traditionally attracted career changers who wish to change career in everything from their 20s to their 60s. Their aspirations usually revolve around setting up their own enterprises, with bank managers wanting to become bakers and administrators dreaming of running a bed and breakfast establishment. Our higher education offer needs to be able to support these people to achieve their dreams, as many of the best customer experiences in our sectors are delivered by such highly motivated entrepreneurs.

Higher education staff

Before concluding this section on future challenges for higher education and moving on to look at the role of industry we will look at two crucial issues relating to higher education staff in tourism and hospitality education.

The first issue is staff development, where it is clear that, through no fault of their own, tourism and hospitality academics are currently not in a position to lead the change that is needed in tourism and hospitality education. Many have no experience of working in the sector and an increasing number may go straight from high school through to PhD with no experience at all that is not higher education. These staff need the opportunity to develop their industry knowledge and keep their knowledge up to date through constant interaction with industry, including regular short term secondments to work in industry.

The author realises that he is about to alienate many of his friends in tourism and hospitality academia, but he wants to talk, at this stage, about what he might term 'research distraction'. The contribution which we are able to make to talent development, as well as to our sectors, is being reduced because of the focus placed by universities on research. This forces academics to focus more and more energy on their own research, which can only mean less time to spend teaching, mentoring and supporting their students. However, it is not research per se which is the problem, but rather the obsession with publication in journals. It feels as if part of our motivation is our need to prove we are as good as the older established disciplines, when in fact we have nothing to prove. What we do as educators and academics is of great value to society and helps students transform their lives and realise their dreams. Yet the fear is that this contribution will be eroded if we continue to focus our energy largely on getting published in the 'top' refereed journals, which brings few if any benefits for either the students or the industry.

Research and scholarship is important to underpin any higher education delivery, but it should be relevant to the needs of society, the sector and our students. If we were to rethink research in this way it would allow us to make a much more effective contribution towards talent management in tourism and hospitality. Students should work on joint research projects with industry along with their tutors. This would improve the subject knowledge of students more than reading many journal papers, given the data in many of the latter are already several years old when published. In doing so both tutors and students would gain access to up to date data, that no student or academic would normally ever get close to seeing. Academics when doing their own personal research would focus on topics that have more direct industry applications. When publishing, we would not only send work to journals but would also, as a matter of course, produce short versions that highlighted the implications for industry and make these readily available to industry and government decision-makers

At the same time we need to be prepared to do research that, while highly relevant to industry, is critical of its current practice, but which goes on to suggest practical ways forward. This is very relevant to talent management where we need to work with the more enlightened industry players on issues such as discrimination in the workplace, gender imbalance in management positions, the role of tourism in poverty reduction and corporate social responsibility.

Academics with no industry experience might be surprised to learn that most of the most intellectually challenging and fascinating conversations the author has had in recent years have been with senior managers and entrepreneurs in tourism and hospitality, rather than with academic colleagues. These people would make excellent partners in university research projects.

Of course not all industry people are interested in research but there are enough who are, for academics to work with. But we have to be able to tell them something they do not know. Too often we tell them what is already obvious to them or what appears to them, based on years of experience, to be not true in their particular context.

Finally, in terms of talent management, there are great research opportunities for looking at what talent means in hospitality management, staff motivation, and responsible human resource management. Industry will be very interested in the results of this research even if they may not always like the results.

Industry, talent management, and higher education

Having discussed the challenges facing higher education in relation to talent management in tourism and hospitality it is now time to turn our attention to the role of industry. The industry clearly has a vested interest in managing talent as its future success depends on how it attracts, retains and nurtures talent.

However, in terms of attracting talent, the sectors still face challenges from the idea that these are not 'real jobs', but rather jobs on the margin for those with few other options. This is an ignorant opinion but it is a perception that in many countries leads talented people to eschew these sectors in favour of those with a better image.

Talent may also look elsewhere for employment due to the reputation of the sectors for long hours and low wages, so that staff rely on gratuities for their livelihood. At the risk of upsetting colleagues in the industry the author believes that a successful modern industry should not make its employees into virtual beggars, relying on charitable handouts from customers to allow them to earn a decent living. This is demeaning for staff and unethical behaviour on the part of companies no matter how much it is part of the tradition of the sectors. In a modern economy customers should pay a fair price that allows all employees a decent salary, and guests should not be asked to, in effect, pay extra for a service they are supposed to receive anyway. This kind of old fashioned thinking may well be one of the reasons why many talented young people, even those who chose to go to hotel school, choose to seek employment outside hospitality.

There are still challenges in how tourism and hospitality, and particularly hospitality, are managed that make it more difficult to attract talent. First, is the idea that managers must work in hospitality from the beginning, so very few have any other background. This can lead to a lack of new thinking that is a disincentive for talent to join the industry. Second, in many places the industry is very hierarchical so that new talent has little autonomy and is expected to simply follow orders, almost like the military.

Retaining and nurturing talent is a challenge in both sectors, but let us start with tourism. As a highly seasonal industry, tourism is often unable to retain talent simply because many jobs are seasonal and the industry is often unable to offer the all-year-round permanent jobs that people need to settle down or start a family. This is one of the reasons why we should pay more attention to seasonality in the debate over sustainable tourism

In the case of hospitality, this can also be an issue but other major issues resolve around training and discrimination. Many hospitality organisations remain wary of training, as they fear trained staff will simply leave for a 'better job'. This is a depressingly negative attitude. Second, there still seem to be problems in terms of workplace discrimination, particularly in terms of promotion, for women and people from ethnic minorities. It is not that they cannot find employment in the sector; indeed most hospitality organisations rely very heavily on both groups. It is just that their chances of reaching higher level jobs are poorer. Thus, the industry is in danger of wasting a talent pool that is available.

The author could go on but believes that his point has now been sufficiently made. If you listen carefully, you may be able to hear the screams of industry representatives accusing the author of ignoring all the good practice that is occurring in both tourism and hospitality. This is certainly true and there is some exemplary work going on, but there is not enough of it! The same industry figures also say the image of hospitality in particular outlined above is out of date and no longer true. They claim the situation is a perception not a reality. Any academic who is supervising students on hospitality internships can quickly dispel this argument, as can any researcher who investigates industry practice.

However, on the other hand the best employers in tourism and hospitality offer talented individuals the chance to develop well paid, highly satisfying careers with plenty of opportunities to travel and take on new challenges.

If higher education is going to help tourism and hospitality, it will have to make the first move. Industry will only very rarely approach universities for all kinds of reasons. They may think they have nothing to offer, or they may find what we publish to be esoteric and not easily accessible, or they may feel academics are too 'clever' for them to work with.

We have a lot to offer industry, but only if we are prepared to see things from their perspective. We need to understand that their world is one of action not reflection, of short timescales not years, and one of straightforward communication not obtuse academic language.

The experience of the author is that if we reach out a hand, many in industry, but certainly not all, will grab it gratefully. So what can all this mean for talent management in tourism and hospitality?

First, we need to move beyond the traditional ideas of industry cooperation that many higher education institutions operate. This usually involves getting a few supportive industry people, often alumni, to sit on validation panels or advise on curriculum development. We will also invite guest speakers to bring their industry experience into the classroom. All of this is good, but it is not enough given the challenges we have discussed so far in this chapter. Instead, let us look what a week in a university could look like for tourism or hospitality students.

On Monday morning, new first year students attend a job workshop where local employers offer part-time job opportunities for students who want them. Those who take these jobs will be able to reflect on this experience as part of one of their coursework assignments, because that is built into their assignment marking criteria. In some institutions, this part time work will be counted towards any internship requirements the programme may have.

The employers will then be staying for a networking lunch and will be using this opportunity to identify students they think could join them after graduation even though this is several years in the future.

That afternoon, second year students are working on a live consultancy project for a tour operator based in another country. And they are working on the project with students from an institution in that other country via Skype.

In the evening an alumnus comes to tell her story of her career to date to show the students what can be achieved by a motivated graduate from their programme.

Next morning the Revenue and Yield Management class is held not in the university but in a local hotel, in one of their conference rooms. After the theory class the hotel's own Revenue and Yield Manager comes to tell the group all about their job and the revenue and yield management issues in their particular hotel.

In the afternoon, the CEO of an airline catering company comes in to the university to act as judge for a student project around developing new healthy menus for long-haul flyers. Afterwards the CEO interviews final year students for a job vacancy within their organisation.

In the evening there is a joint presentation by an academic and an industry person about a local visitor attraction. The academic has just finished a four week secondment working with the management team and the industry person has spent one day a week over the past three months at the university doing research on the future of the visitor attraction market.

Wednesday is the Student Conference where students present the results of pieces of research they have done in cooperation with industry organisations who provided both the problem to be solved and access to relevant data. Presentations must be no longer than five minutes with a one page executive summary, and they must provide potential solutions to problems. The event is a competition and the ten winners will be given the opportunity to shadow one of the industry partners for a day to see what their job is all about. It is likely that some of these 'shadows' will be offered jobs on graduation, if they impress the employers.

On Thursday there is an Employability Fair which goes on into the evening. In the morning second year students have mock interviews with employers based on a mock application they made for a range of real jobs. The interviews will be very realistic and students will get feedback on both their interview and their application. In the afternoon employers will interview final year students for real jobs including interviews via Skype or video conference with international employers. The day ends with an evening 'masterclass' on how to network.

Friday morning is the Entrepreneurship Workshop, where tourism entrepreneurs come in to mentor students who have ideas for new businesses they want to set up immediately or when they graduate.

On Friday afternoon the development team from a major hotel chain comes to the university to visit the Hospitality Innovation Laboratory. There, in the presence of final year students, they explore with academics what their future hotel rooms could look like, both in terms of mock ups and virtual reality representations.

The week ends on Friday evening with a 'Young Talent' awards evening, part sponsored by industry partners. Amongst other awards, six second year students will be given an industry sponsored scholarship covering their final year fees together with a job offer on graduation.

Clearly all of this is easier said than done, but all of it is possible if the will is there on the part of both academia and industry.

The relationships that could lead to this kind of week of activities need to start somewhere and as we noted earlier it is probably the academics who will need to take the first step. We need to demonstrate that we have knowledge that is valuable to industry and that we can work with them to develop the talent that they need to run their businesses.

However, the arrangement needs to be one which demands responsible behaviour from employers. They must contribute time, money or expertise to support the higher education institution and the education of the students if they expect to benefit from this talent pool. We also need to ensure that academia only works with ethical employers and should be prepared to terminate any partnership where an employer behaves unethically.

This has been written largely from the point of view of an academic working in a so-called developed country in northern Europe and it should be read with that fact in mind. He acknowledges that the situation highlighted above in terms of the industry is not the same throughout the world. In many developing counties tourism and hospitality are seen as modern, clean sectors offering good jobs with excellent prospects. There it is often a more attractive career option, but even so these countries face other challenges in relation to talent management. These include the drain of their best talent to more developed countries in search of higher salaries although the money sent home by these migrant workers certainly benefits their home countries. In terms of the Gulf States, the use of imported labour and the role of recruitment agents also distorts the labour market.

Conclusions

Rather than attempt to summarise what has been said the author would like to end with some broader observations as stimuli to encourage the reader to think further about the issues discussed above.

In the first instance we need to be dedicated to, and focused upon, our role as hospitality and tourism educators. We need to be proud that we are involved in vocational education, rather than having a 'chip on our shoulder' that we are not treated as 'proper academics', whatever that means in the modern world. Our main task is to motivate and support our students to develop to their full potential and help them achieve their ambitions within tourism and hospitality. Our first duty is to our students, but we also have a responsibility to industry and consumers to ensure that those who graduate from our programmes can meet the demands placed upon them as employees, managers and service deliverers.

In terms of our research, the need is for humility. Our research does not find a cure for terrible diseases nor do we find answers to the question of 'why are we here?' Nor do we develop intellectually stunning theories. We are not disciplines and we should cease to be concerned about this. Instead we need to recognise that the value of our research is in terms of its application for the improvement of industry practice, the enrichment of the consumer experience, shaping of public policy, *and* the education of the future talent in hospitality and tourism. Our research can change the world in a way which much so-called academic research will never be able to do. This is something to be proud of, rather than being seen as less important than publishing in journals. Perhaps most important, all research needs to directly benefit our students rather than being irrelevant to their studies. This is a challenge given the culture and performance metrics of universities but it is a battle we must be prepared to fight.

At the same time we need to bring industry and academia together as true partners with a mutually beneficial interest in talent development. Academia needs to be seen as part of the industry, not a separate entity and like all good friends it should criticise industry when it feels it is not behaving as it should. However, the partnership needs a third partner and that partner is the talent, all those people who could enrich hospitality and tourism and in doing so create good working lives for themselves.

The fear is that if we do not take this opportunity, tourism and hospitality education will become irrelevant and disappear, and the industry and the consumer experience in tourism and hospitality will be the poorer as talent goes into other sectors of the economy

Further reading

As the reader will have noticed this has been a personal opinion piece with no academic references. However, there are many excellent works on this subject, some of which are listed below for those who, I hope, wish to read further.

Airey, D. and Tribe, J. (2005). *An International Handbook of Tourism Education*. Elsevier. Oxford.

Alexander, M. (2007) Reflecting on changes in operational training in UK hospitality management programmes. *International Journal of Contemporary Hospitality Management.* **19**(3), 211-220

Amoah,V. and Baum,T. (1997). Tourism education : Policy versus practice. *International Journal of Contemporary Hospitality Management.* **9** (1), 5-12

Barron,P. (2008). Education and talent management: implications for the hospitality industry, *International Journal of Contemporary Hospitality Management.* **20** (7), 730-742

Belhassed, Y. and Caton, K. (2011). On the need for critical pedagogy in tourism education. *Tourism Management.* **32** (6), 1389-1396

Cantoni, L. (2009). E-learning in tourism and hospitality. *Journal of Hospitality, Leisure, Sport and Tourism Education.* **8** (2), 148-156

Chang, T-Y. and Hsu, J-M . (2010). Development framework for tourism and hospitality in higher vocational education in Taiwan. *Journal of Hospitality, Leisure, Sports and Tourism Education.* **9**(1), 101-109

Cho, W. and Schmelzer, C.D. (2000). Just-in-time education: Tools for hospitality managers of the future? *International Journal of Contemporary Hospitality Management.* **12**(1), 31-37

Chon, K.S., Barrows, C.W. and Bosselman, R.H. (2013). *Hospitality Management Education*. Routledge: New York.

Dopson, L. and Nelson, A.A. (2003). Future of hotel education: Required program content areas for graduates of U.S. hospitality programs beyond the year – Part two. *Journal of Hospitality and Tourism Education.* **15** (3), 11-17.

Fidgeon,P. (2010). Tourism education and curriculum design: a time for consolidation and review? *Tourism Management.* 31 (6), 699-723

Harkison, T., Poulston, J. and Kim, J-HG. (2011). Hospitality graduates and managers: the big divide. *International journal of Contemporary Hospitality Management*, **23**(3), 377-392.

Harper, S., Brown, C. and Irvine, W. (2005). Qualifications; a fast track to hotel general manager? *International Journal of Contemporary Hospitality Management*, **17**(1), 51-64

Haywood, K.M. (1989). A radical proposal for hospitality and tourism education. *International Journal of Hospitality Management.* **8** (4),259-264.

Jafar, J. and Brent Ritchie, J.R. (1981). Towards a framework for tourism education: Problems and prospects. *Annals of Tourism Research.* **viii** (1), 13-34.

Jayawardena, C. (2001). Challenges in international hospitality management education. *International Journal of Contemporary Hospitality Management.* **13** (6), 310-315.

Jayawardena, C. (2001). Creating hospitality management educational programmes in developing countries. *International Journal of Contemporary Hospitality Management .* **13**(5), 259-266.

Jenkins, A.K. (2001) Making a career of it? Hospitality students future perspectives: an Anglo-Dutch study. *International Journal of Contemporary Hospitality Management.* **13**(1),13-20.

King, B., McKercher ,B. and Waryszak, R. (2003). A comparative study of hospitality and tourism graduates in Australia and Hong Kong. *International Journal of Tourism Research.* **5**, 409-420.

Lashley, C. (1999). On making silk purses : developing reflective practitioners in hospitality management education. *International Journal of Contemporary Hospitality Management.* **11** (4), 180-185

Lashley, C. and Alexander, M. (2007). Reflecting on changes in operational training in UK hospitality management degree programmes. *International Journal of Contemporary Hospitality Management.* **19** (3),211-220

Li, L. and Li, J. (2013). Hospitality education in China: a student career-oriented perspective. *Journal of Hospitality, Leisure, Sports and Tourism Education.* **12**(1), 109-117

Littlejohn, D. and Watson, S. (2004) Developing graduate managers for hospitality and tourism. *International Journal of Contemporary Hospitality Management.* **16** (7), 408-414.

Mayaka, M. and Akama, J. S. (2007) Systems approach to tourism training and education: The Kenyan case study. *Tourism Management.* **28** (1), 298-306.

Morgan, M. (2004) From production line to drama school:higher education for the future of tourism. *International Journal of Contemporary Hospitality Management.* **16** (2), 91-99

Morrison, A. and O'Mahony, G.B. (2003) The liberation of hospitality management education. *International Journal of Contemporary Hospitality Management* **15** (1), 38-44.

O'Leary, S. and Deegan, J. (2005) Career progression of Irish tourism and hospitality management graduates. *International Journal of Contemporary Hospitality Management.* **17**(5), 421-432

Pearce,P. L. (2005) Australian tourism education. *Journal of Teaching in Travel and Tourism.* **5** (3), 251-267.

Rimmington, M. (1999) Vocational education: Challenges for hospitality management in the new millennium. *International Journal of Contemporary Hospitality Management* **11**(4),186-192.

Zagonari, F. (2009) Balancing tourism education and training. *International Journal of Hospitality Management.* **28** (1) 2-9.

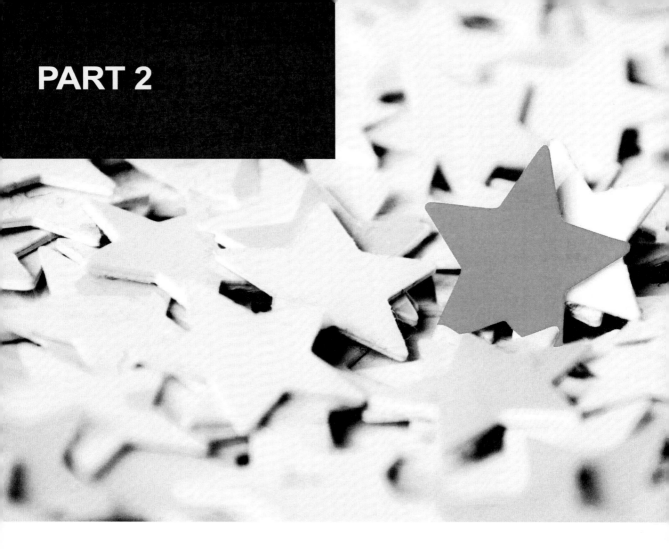

PART 2

PERSONAL CAREER DEVELOPMENT

4 The Concept of 'Hospitableness'

Conrad Lashley

Learning objectives

At the end of this chapter you should be able to:

■ Understand the morality of hospitality and obligations on hosts and guests.

■ Recognise an array of motives for offering hospitality to guests.

■ Identify the qualities of hospitableness.

■ Appreciate the value of guest/host relationship in building commercial competitive advantage.

■ Evaluate different approaches to talent management suited to hosting commercial guests.

Introduction

Increased demand for eating, drinking and staying away from home over the last half century has resulted in a growth in the numbers of cafes, snack bars, restaurants, bars and hotels and other businesses organisations to meet these demands. Recognising that there are many similarities and overlaps in the service provided by these organisations, the word *'hospitality'* emerged as a collective noun to describe this whole sector.

As a consequence of the emergence of the word, many academics undertaking research and consultancy in the field began to question the nature of hospitality and hospitableness. This led to the study of hospitality from an array of social science perspectives and the publication of numerous books including *In Search of Hospitality: Theoretical perspectives and debates* (Lashley and Morrison, 2000) and *Hospitality a Social Lens* (Lashley, Lynch and Morrison, 2007). Some academics from social science disciplines concurrently began to explore hospitality as a human experience. The collaboration between these two groups of academics has resulted in, amongst other publications, the journal *Hospitality & Society,* and the upcoming *Hospitality Studies* (Lashley, 2017) in the Routledge Handbook series.

The study of hospitality engages the notion of *hospitableness*, that is the qualities demonstrated by hosts to their guests. The requirement for hosts to offer shelter to guests is a common feature of all religions and can be seen as a fundamental strand of human morality. In practice, the motives for hospitality to others can vary and this chapter highlights a range of reasons for offering hospitality, with altruistic hospitality being the most consistent with hospitableness.

Attempts to develop an instrument to measure the hospitableness, although at an early stage, do suggest that some individuals are more prone to be hospitable to guests, than others. This chapter features one instrument that was developed based upon thirteen questions, using a seven point Likert scale. The chapter provided insights into the instrument and its potential benefit in both academic study and in commercial organisations. The relationship between host and guest can, when genuinely offered, be the source of competitive advantage because it cannot be easily replicated.

4

Hospitality morality

The obligation to be hospitable to strangers has been a constant feature of human social existence through time and across the world. All societies have something to say about strangers; mostly there is a moral obligation to welcome those from outside, and to *'turn the stranger into a friend'* (Selwyn, 2000). That said, fear of the stranger could be a powerful strand in any society, particularly when times are challenging. Some find it easier to blame the outsider rather than look to the selfish and greedy ruling elite that causes most of the problem. Oxfam, for example, estimate that in 2016 the world's one per cent own 50 per cent of the world's wealth. In Britain, the Office of National Statistics report that the top one per cent own more than 55 per cent of the poorest citizens. At the same time, as consequence of neo-liberalism, many middle and low-income families have seen wage rates fail to keep in line with costs of living, leading to a decline in living standards (Lashley 2017a). These inequalities, particularly for those on the lowest incomes, can cause anxieties and anger that fuels a fear of strangers and anti-hospitableness.

Most religions have either consciously, or unconsciously, recognised these potential tendencies and make it a moral obligation of the faithful to be hospitable to strangers. Without wishing to deny the multi-faith nature of most Western societies, the dominant religions of the faithful are Abrahamic in origin; both Christianity and Islam are founded on the Judaic scripts of the 'Old Testament'.

The Old Testament advocates the customary sharing of meals and as a way of distributing excess to the poor and the needy. The practice of hospitality in settings where it was unlikely that the guest could repay the host was fundamental. Indeed, many of the biblical stories advocate generosity by hosts in contexts where they could not expect repayment (Casselberry, 2009). For example, Abraham generously received three strangers who turned out to be angels (Genesis: 18). At another point, Lot was spared the destruction of Sodom and Gomorrah because he had offered hospitality and protection to two visitors who were later identified as angels (Genesis: 1). Through the stories of the Israelites, it is argued that through their experiences of movement and being strangers in foreign lands, they developed an intensive awareness of the need for hospitality and the need to offer food, drink and accommodation to strangers and those in need.

Several of the teachings of the New Testament also highlight hospitable treatment of Christ and the disciples. However, the requirement to be hospitable to strangers goes beyond the immediate treatment of Jesus and the disciples. It is claimed that the faithful demonstrate their faith when they honour the poor and the needy. Luke (14:13) advocates giving to the poor, the needy, lame and the blind as way of demonstrating faithful behaviour. In the gospel of Matthew the behaviour of those who will be most favourably blessed refer to their host behaviour, 'For I was hungry and you gave me something to eat, I was thirsty and you gave me something to drink, I was a stranger and you invited me in, I needed clothes and you clothed me, I was sick and you looked after me' (Matthew 25:34-36). Luke says, 'When you give a banquet, invite the poor, the crippled, the lame, the blind, and you will be blessed' (Luke 14:13). Furthermore the faithful are instructed to 'love your neighbour as yourself' (Matthew 22:39). At these and other points the scriptures clearly show that offering hospitality to strangers is a basic requirement of the Christian faithful. 'Come, everyone who thirsts, come to the waters; and he who has no money, come, buy and eat! Come, buy wine and milk without money and without price' (Isaiah. 55:1).

Those writing from an Islamic perspective (Meehan, 2013), for example, claim that only the Muslim faithful understand the need to be hospitable. It is claimed that non-believers will only offer hospitality with an expectation of worldly gain (repayment or reciprocity). The true believer offers hospitality to strangers to honour god (Jafar, 2014). Mohammed is quoted as saying, 'Let the believer in Allah and the day of judgment honour his guest' (Meehan, 2013). It is required that all must be welcomed and treated with respect, whether they are family or non-family members, believers or non-believers. Stories are recounted concerning the behaviour of Mohammed as being hospitable to strangers, and never dining alone. One parable has Mohammed feeding three strangers who are angels in disguise, and reveal themselves after they have been shown generous hospitality by their host. Another popular story has hosts feeding guest with the hosts' own food because they have little to share (Schulman and Barkouki-Winter, 2000). These acts of generosity to either share, or to give all they have to the stranger, is claimed to be an exclusive perspective of the faithful, but in reality can be seen to be a feature of all these religions. Indeed, the story of guests turning out to be god, gods, or angels is a common theme to be found in all these religious parables. Either acts of extreme generosity to the stranger results in excessive reward, or in other cases the failure to be hospitable results in the hosts' goods being taken away.

Whilst the Muslim faith emerges at some time in the seventh century AD, and Christian teaching two thousand years ago, the writing of the Jews surface around seven hundred years before that. In all three cases, these monotheistic religions advocate hospitable behaviour that builds on religious traditions that go back even further. Hindu ideas and teachings, for example, are said to have originated some 4,000 years BCE (ISKCON, 2004). Offering hospitality to strangers is a fundamental feature of Hindu beliefs and culture. In particular the unexpected guest was to be particularly honoured. The unpredicted guest was called *atithi* that translates literally as 'without a set time' (Khan, 2009). A popular proverb says, '*The uninvited guest should be treated as good as a god*' (Melwani, 2009). Tradition teaches that even the poorest should offer at lease three things, sweet words, a sitting place and refreshments (at least water). '*Even an enemy must be offered appropriate hospitality if he comes to your home. A tree does not deny its shade, even to the one has come to cut it down*' (Mahabharata, 12.372).

Hospitality motives

Combing the work of Heal (1984), Nouwen (1998), Telfer (2000) and O'Gorman (2007a; 2007b) it is possible to detect a number of motives for hosts offering hospitality to guests. Figure 4.1 provides a graphical representation of this array of motives. These can be mapped along a continuum showing the more calculative reasons for providing hospitality through to the most generous. In other words, where hospitality is offered with the hope of gain, to situations whereby hospitality is offered merely for the joy and pleasure of hosting.

Ulterior motives hospitality | Containing hospitality | Commercial hospitality | Reciprocal hospitality | Redistributive hospitality | Altruistic hospitality

Figure 4.1: *A continuum of hospitality*

Telfer (2000) identified the offering of food, drink and accommodation for some thought of subsequent gain as *ulterior motives hospitality*. It is assumed that the guest is able to benefit the host and hospitality is offered as a means of gaining that benefit. Here the business lunch or dinner for the boss, or the client, can be examples of hospitality being offered with the intention of creating a favourable impression with the hope that this will ultimately benefit the host. Writing in the early 1500s Nicholo Machiavelli says: '*Keep your friends close, but your enemies closer.*' In this sense, *containing hospitality* is motivated by a fear of the stranger, but which advocates close monitoring by including the stranger in the household. Wagner's opera *Die Walkure*, involves Hunding offering Seigmund hospitality even though he knows Seigmund to be an enemy. This provides an insight into both the obligation to offer hospitality to all, irrespective of who they are, but also suggests the motive is to monitor and contain the enemy (Wagner, 1870).

On one level, '*Treat the customers as though they were guests in your own home*' is attempting to tap into restaurant workers' hosting experience in domestic settings (Ashness and Lashley, 1995). Ideally, service workers will engage on an emotional level as hosts serving their customers as personal guests. Yet the provision of *commercial hospitality* involves a financial transaction whereby hospitality is offered to guests at a price, and is withdrawn if the payment cannot be made. Hence commercial hospitality can be said to represent a contradiction, and cannot deliver true hospitableness (Warde and Martens, 2000; Ritzer, 2004; 2007). Telfer (2000) however, reminds us that this is a somewhat simplistic view because it may be that hospitable people are drawn to work in bars, hotels and restaurants, and offer hospitableness beyond and in spite of, the commercial transaction and materialistic instructions from owners. In addition, it may be that hospitable people are drawn to set up hospitality businesses in guesthouses, pubs and restaurants, because it allows them to be both entrepreneurial and hospitable at the same time.

A number of writers suggest that hospitality involves reciprocity, whereby it is offered on the understanding that it will be reciprocated at some later date (O'Gorman, 2007a,b). Hospitality practiced by elite families in Augustinian Rome was founded on the principle of reciprocity as an early form of tourism. Affluent Romans developed networks of relationships with other families with whom they stayed as guests, then acted as hosts when their former hosts travelled. Cole's (2007) work with the Ngadha tribe in Indonesia provides some fascinating insights into hospitality and tourism in a remote community today. The tribe practice reciprocal hospitality through tribe members hosting pig-roasting events for other members. This *reciprocal hospitality* involves hospitality being offered within a context whereby hosts become guests and guests become hosts at different times. Yet another form of hospitality takes place when *redistributive hospitality* is offered in settings where food and drink are provided with no immediate expectation of return, repayment or reciprocity. The study of the potlatch practiced by North American Indians is a clear example, of this redistributive effect, though there is overlap with other forms (Zitkala-Sa, 1921). Clearly the inclusion of the poor and needy in hospitality settings offered in the early middle ages, noted by Heal (1990), also had a redistributive effect. Finally *altruistic hospitality* involves the offer of hospitableness as an act of generosity and benevolence, and a willingness to give pleasure to others. It is this that is the key focus here because it provides an ideal, or pure, form of hospitality, largely devoid of personal gain for the host, apart from the emotional satisfaction arising from the practice of hospitableness (Telfer, 2000; Derrida, 2002).

The study of hospitality engages with research and academic enquiry informed by social science, and encourages the development of critical thinking. These aid and inform research, academic thought and the development of reflective practice within those being developed as managers destined for careers in hospitality organisations. Hospitality represents a robust field of study in it own right, but it also encourages critical thinking and a concern for host guest relations that influence the practice and development of those entering managerial roles in the sector. Flowing from this is the study of the motives being engaged by those offering hospitality. These motives can be perceived in a ranking system that ranges from hospitality offered for ulterior motives through to hospitality offered for the joy of giving.

Identifying hospitableness

The preceding has established definitions of hospitality and hospitableness, extending across religions and through time, that stress altruistic hospitality as being concerned with generosity and the pleasure of providing food and/or drink and/or accommodation to others without any consideration of personal gain in return. The philosopher Telfer (2000) reminds us that the qualities of hospitableness include the following points.

- ☐ The desire to please others, stemming from general friendliness and benevolence or from affection for particular people; concern or compassion.
- ☐ The desire to meet another's need.
- ☐ A desire to entertain one's friends or to help those in trouble.
- ☐ A desire to have company or to make friends.
- ☐ The desire for the pleasures of entertaining what we may call the wish to entertain as a pastime.

Whilst this provides a definition of the qualities of hospitableness, there has been no attempt, until now, to identify individuals who express these qualities. The following describes the development of a bank of questions that are consistent with identifying individuals who appear to demonstrate strong support for hospitableness.

Reporting on the instrument developed by Matthew Blain (Blain and Lashley, 2015) the following gives an overview of the process and the various iterations it went through, following a process suggested by Churchill (1979). This was tested for validity against a framework outlined by Cook and Beckman (2006) and the instrument demonstrated high levels of internal reliability. The following briefly shares the experience of developing an instrument that identifies genuine, or altruistic, hospitality (hospitableness). The instrument was developed and field-tested in a relatively limited setting and needs wider use and exposure. It is hoped that one of the outcomes of this publication will be greater interest in critical application of the questionnaire.

Blain's research commenced with an initial study of the experiences of hosting, when he set up an event whereby different couples acted as hosts for an evening dinner, and then as guests, when other couples acted as hosts. Following from this he conducted interviews with the parties. Importantly, the hosts all reported that a driving ambition of their hosting of the event was to give their guests pleasure, with one host summing up the views of most hosts when he said he felt happy by *'seeing the smiles on guest's faces, and knowing that they are enjoying themselves'* (Blain and Lashley, 2015: 6). From this qualitative study, the research went on to engage in the development of survey instrument in the form of a questionnaire. The instrument development stage went through several iterations but eventually arrived at the thirteen questions, reflecting three themes, that are listed below in Table 4.1.

Table 4.1: The question bank identifying genuine hospitality (hospitableness)

Desire to put guests before yourself	I put guests' enjoyment before my own
	I do whatever is necessary to ensure that guests have a great time
	I always try to live up to my idea of what makes a good host
	The comfort of guests is most important to me
Desire to make guests happy	I get a natural high when I make my guests feel special
	I enjoy taking responsibility for the wellbeing of guests
	It means the world to me when guests show their approval of my hospitality
	It's important to do the things that people expect of a good host
	I seek out opportunities to help others
Desire to make guests feel special	When hosting I try to feel at one with the guests
	I try to get on the same wavelength as my guests
	Guests should feel that the evening revolves around them
	I find it motivating to take accountability for other people's welfare

Source: Bain and Lashley, 2014

This instrument was initially developed in the context of a pub company and has, at the time of writing, not been subject to extensive testing to establish validity and reliability. That said, there are a couple of studies underway that aim to explore these issues. The current version of the instrument has been tested with employees at two Movenpick hotels, one in Amsterdam and one in Dubai. It is perhaps that start of an instrument development cycle, but one that promises an opportunity to identify individuals who have positive attitudes towards the act of hosting, that has important potential for the commercial sector.

Commercial hospitality

One of the key issues relating to hospitality provision in the commercial sector relates to the authenticity of the hospitality provided. Are commercial hospitality products and services merely another service? Can commercial hospitality ever be genuinely hospitable? Are models of cultural and private hospitality of any value? Slattery (2002) argues that restaurant, bar and hotel services are essentially economic and involve a management activity. The study of hospitality from wider social science perspectives has, therefore, limited utility. In this view the guest-host transaction is essential a monetary transaction.

Ritzer (2007) supports this view by suggesting that there are powerful drivers in commercial hospitality organizations that will lead hospitality provision to become 'inhospitable'. Ritzer's comments on McDonaldization says that corporate drivers to increases efficiency, calculability, predictability and control, lead ultimately to the creation of systems that act as a barrier to the frontline delivery of hospitableness. These McDonaldizing processes inhibit performances that are hospitable, and at the same time they generate customer feelings of being under-valued as individuals. Standardizing and systemizing processes, therefore, are a fundamental aspect of the approach to managing hospitality services in bars, restaurants and hotels, and in effect remove the 'hospitality' from the transaction. In Telfer's (2000) terms, the commercial transaction provides an ulterior motive for offering hospitality and therefore prevents 'genuine' hospitality. Warde and Martens found that interviewees regarded eating out in restaurants as less than authentic. In contrast to the somewhat pessimistic views by Warde and Martens (2000) and Ritzer (2007), Telfer (2000) does suggest that it is not inevitable that commercial hospitality will invariably be less authentic than hospitality in the home. She suggests that it is possible that those who have an interest in, and who value, hospitality will be drawn to work in the commercial hospitality sector. They may run their own hospitality businesses, or choose to work in roles that enable them to be hospitable.

Work by Lashley, Morrison and Randle, (2003) on 'memorable meals' suggests that the emotional dimensions of the meal were much more significant than the quality of the food in creating memorable meals. The research asked respondents to provide a written account of their most memorable meal. The texts were sub-jected to semiotic analysis and a multi-dimensional image of the meal emerged – nature of the occasion of the meal; fellow diners who made up the company with whom they dined; characteristics that contributed to the atmosphere; food eaten; overall setting; and the service provided. The occasion was typically some significant event in which the social dynamic of the meal reinforced the emotional significance of the event. Hospitality settings create an added significance. The occasion of the meal, or holiday, is often a celebration of bonding and together-ness with family and friends. The company of others comes across strongly in these accounts, and although one report involved the company of just one other person, most involved groups of people, and none involved an individual diner alone. The atmosphere created by the setting, other people and their treatment by hosts provide emotional dimensions to meal occasions that are vital to creating memorable occasions. Interestingly, few of the respondents mentioned the food consumed or quality of dishes as part of their descriptions. The dominant impres-sion is that these emotional dimensions of hospitality are what make these meal occasions special, and it will be these emotional dimensions of their visit that will make for memorable hospitality and tourism events. Interestingly, when asked to recount their most memorable meal experiences, about half the respondents quoted occasions that were in domestic settings, whilst the other half of occasions were in commercial restaurants, pubs or bars.

The problem is that many hospitality and tourism operators give priority to tangible aspects of the customer offer, such as the quality of the food, facilities and comfort of the room, the range and quality of the drinks on offer, etc., but they fail to see that it is the quality of the employee performance which creates the guest emotional experience that impacts upon long-term customer satisfaction and loyalty. Herzberg's (1966) concept of motivation theory provides a useful metaphor: the physical aspects of the resort, the décor, physical facilities, the meals and drinks supplied are potentially '*dissatisfiers.*' If standards do not meet expectations, customers will be dissatisfied. However, exceeding their expectations in these tangible aspects will not produce satisfaction (Balmer and Baum, 1993). Customer satisfaction will be created by the quality of the emotions generated from their experiences; staff performance, the qualities of hospitableness, fellow diners and the performance of line management are the keys to producing customer satisfaction, through their emotional experiences as guests. Long-term customer loyalty, and repeat custom to the venue are dependent on the emotions generated by these elements. Highly satisfied hospitality and tourism visitors are more likely to return, or to recommend the establishment to family and friends.

This chapter suggests that the study of hospitality from wider social science perspectives enables an understanding of guest and host transactions that can inform much management practice and prerogatives. Traditional understandings of hospitality require hosts to be primarily concerned with ensuring the well-being and emotional needs of their guests. Using some of these traditional models of hospitality offers the opportunity to convert strangers into friends. In a commercial context, this could be translated to converting customers into friends (Lashley and Morrison, 2000), thereby providing the basis for competitive advantage and building a loyal customer base. At root, operators can be trained to recognize and engage with the provision of hospitality experiences that rely heavily the emotional dimensions of these experiences. Figure 4.2 is an attempt to show how these various factors interact to create guest experiences

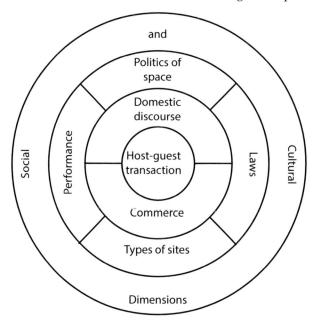

Figure 4.2: A contextual understanding of commercial hospitality

Acceptance of the central importance of the guest experience has some major implications for the management of hospitality and tourism service providers (Lashley, Lynch, and Morrison, 2007). Policies that train, support and empower frontline staff become essential, and have to be seen as core to the management task. Training frontline staff in how to build friendly relations with the stranger/guest is not just a nice idea, or an expensive luxury to be jettisoned when times get tough. Similarly, the management of staff retention is core to being able to build the relationship. It is impossible to train frontline staff appropriately if there is a constant churn of new employees through the organization. It is also difficult to build these relationships if customers rarely see the same service face twice.

Figure 4.2 provides a visual representation of the potential commercial advantage to be gained from focusing on the guest host transaction. The human chemistry created between the individual host and the individual guest cannot be replicated because it is unique to the individuals concerned. The customer feels special and values the relationship with the host. This enhances the desire to always (or frequently) use the same establishment. Customer churn will be reduced because of the increase in customer loyalty. Customer churn is not formally measured by most hospitality business organisations, but it exists and costs the organisations, even if most are not able to show how much it costs.

Accepting that the interactions between host and guest take place in a social cultural context that shapes the expectations of the two actors, research in the immediate relationship between guest and host has to be sensitive to these wider issues. In particular, the role and extent of commercial hospitality are likely to shape the extent to which individuals suspend disbelief about hospitableness. Do customers have lower expectations about their treatment as guests in a commercial setting? Do those with genuine hospitableness qualities display these even in the commercial setting?

Managing hospitality talent

The impact of the relationship between individual hosts and their guests has the potential to create unique selling points that can be the source of competitive advantage. Employees are therefore not just providing physical labour serving food and drinks, and receiving guests; they delivering the customer experience and are the assets upon which customer satisfaction is built. They are not merely a cost that has to be increased or reduced in line with levels of demand. They are potentially able to build relationships with customers that embed customer loyalty and competitive advantage.

In these circumstances the recruitment and retention of staff is a crucial strand in the style and management of hospitality employee talent. Figure 4.3 identifies the three dominant styles in managing employees.

		DIRECTIVE		CONSULTATIVE		PARTICIPATIVE		NONE
		Tell	Tell and sell	Tell and test	Seek	Joint problem solving	Delegate	Abdicate
Manager involvement		makes decisions and instructs	makes decisions and instructs with reasons	makes decisions but reviews after seeking views	defines problem and seeks employees view before deciding	defines problem and makes decision jointly with employees	defines scope of decision making authority –monitors decisions	provides limited direction or support to employees
Staff involvement		acts on instructions	acts on instructions and explanation given	gives views on bosses proposed decision	discusses alternatives and makes suggestions	joins in the decision making process	makes decisions within boundaries set by boss	employees decide for themselves and react to events

Figure 4.3: Mapping leadership styles. Source: Lashley 2000

Three different approaches to controlling employees can be matched against different management and team leadership styles, classically know as:

Directive	Also known as command and control. Managers tell, or tell and sell, make decisions and instruct staff - though they may give reasons (the sell). Staff receive and act upon instruction.
Consultative	Managers tell and test, or seek employee's views about problems or decisions to be made. Staff comment or make suggestions before the manager decides.
Participative	Managers jointly solve problems and make decisions with staff, or delegate decision-making authority to employees. Employees are either involved with managers in making decisions or make the decisions themselves, within set limits.

Directive management

The directive style of management is widely practiced across the hospitality industry, though in some cases this descends into management abdication, where managers who are untrained and the resulting management style is idiosyncratic. Top down decision-making involves managers making all strategic and tactical decisions, and employees act upon the instructions. The most directive form involves mangers instructing employees, and the workforce act out the instructions. A slightly softer approach aims to win commitment to the instructions by sharing the reasons why the actions are needed. Talent management in a directive manner allows little employee influence on working practices or decisions, but managers aim to win commitment by an array of employment practices. Managers who want employees to be committed have to recognise that employees have some expectations about good employment practice. Loyalty is a two way street, employers who demand loyal employees have to meet some of the these basic expectations.

Employees are often bullied and paid low wages, with minimal training and base level development. Given the low level of trade union membership in the commercial sector, employee resistance to the directive style typically takes individualised forms. High levels of staff turnover, high levels of absenteeism and poor levels of staff satisfaction are all symptoms of the negative effects of directive management amongst employees in bars, restaurants and hotels.

There may be some circumstances where the directive management style is appropriate, particularly where the tangible and intangible offer to customers is dependent on uniformity and standardised practice. Customers are buying in to brands that are reassuringly consistent. Customers know what they are going to get, how much it will cost and how long it will take. Brands such as McDonald's in the fast food sector are prime examples of this. In these circumstances there is one best way of doing things, because it delivers the uniformity that customers are buying into. Staff are instructed and managed according to the one best way. There are limited opportunities for employees to adapt the service experiences, because that would undermine uniformity.

Where directive management is undertaken as a personal preference of the manager, without any basis in the service principle, it is likely to lead some of the negative impacts discussed earlier. It is unlikely that it will be consistent with managing employees who are shown to have levels of hospitableness as the key source of customer satisfaction, and of generating competitive advantage. Performance is often highly prescribed and dialogue scripted and hospitable employees are not able to respond flexibly to customers, or demonstrate their qualities of hospitableness.

Consultative management

The consultative style of management aims to inform decision-making by gaining information from employees. Given the immediate relationship between frontline employees and customers, the workforce are often best placed to report upon the impact of managerial decisions, service successes and failures, and customer feedback. Managers continue to make decisions, but they are informed by input from staff. Consultative styles can take two distinct forms. It might simply be mangers telling employees what they intend to do, but gaining advice from employees about their plans. More intense approaches actively seek employee ideas and suggestions

Employee suggestion schemes are one example of a mechanism for seeking input from the workforce. These schemes take a number of formats, from simple feedback forms and a suggestion box available in the staff canteen, to a more structured questionnaire given to all staff on a regular basis. In some cases the suggestions from staff are anonymous, in others they are incentivised so that employees receive a bonus if the suggestion is adopted and results in business benefits.

Over recent years there has been increasing use of quality circles, quality improvement groups or focus groups as a means of increasing employee involvement and gaining improvements in service quality. At an operational level, quality circles involve groups of employees who meet regularly to discuss common operational issues. Usually, these meetings involve volunteers, are weekly and last about one hour. In the majority of cases the quality circle's activities are co-ordinated by a trained facilitator. Typically, the facilitator is a management appointment, either a supervisor or manager. In some cases the facilitator is a manager from another department. Unlike suggestions schemes that potentially involve all employees, quality circles are usually made up of representatives from the workforce.

Team briefings are another technique for both informing the workforce and getting feedback from them. The whole team on a shift meet, typically before the shift, to discussing upcoming bookings and business activities. The benefit is that the workforce is fully briefed about the upcoming shift and can make suggestions about how events can be handled. This form of consultation involves all staff and all participate, and overcomes some of the shortcomings of both suggestion schemes and quality circles. The key weakness is that these sessions are usually organised by management and are less likely to generate critical comments.

These various consultative devices are helpful in gaining employee insights, and do have a positive impact on employee morale, because employees are likely to feel valued as their views are being sought. The problem from a hospitableness point of view is that managers are still in control and are able to approve or disapprove suggestions made. They do not allow employees to be empowered enough to display their hospitableness and do whatever it takes to generate customer satisfaction. Truly hospitable employees must be empowered to make the decisions that make customers feel like welcome guests in their own right.

Participative management

This involves employees making decisions that might be made by managers alone in more traditional cultures. In most hospitality settings in the UK, these decisions are at an operational level. However there are some arrangements where employees participate in strategic decisions. German two tier boards and works councils are examples from the European Union. Interestingly, this is the most powerful economy in Europe – a point missed by some of the conservative observers, practitioners and commentators in the UK. Amongst this set of observers, the notion of employee participation is deemed to be deeply threatening.

The joint problem solving style involves owners/managers making decisions with the workforce. The German two tier boards are an example where employee representatives sit as directors on the supervisory boards. The business decisions covering investment, policy, strategic planning etc., are made by directors reflecting both owners and workers.

At a more operational level, work teams can be allocated responsibilities for issues like complaint handling and dealing with unusual requests from guests. Though frontline employees are empowered to deal with these issues, managers may have inputs in reviewing decisions made and performance experiences.

If employees are meant to be truly hospitable, they need to be empowered to do whatever it takes to make customers to feel welcome. Customers need to feel valued as guests and this means that employees need to be given the authority to do whatever is necessary to make that happen. Extending responsible autonomy allows frontline workers to make the service decisions that are needed to ensure customer satisfactions. Whilst the principle of extended responsible autonomy is appropriate it needs to be managed. Variations in the way different employees respond to similar situations may result in customer confusion and dissatisfaction.

Job enrichment suggests that employees can be trained and empowered to respond to customers in a way that is appropriate to the development of hospitableness as a competitive strategy. Job enrichment starts with the recognition the frontline employees are the immediate interface between the hospitality organisation and its customers. This goes beyond the happy worker syndrome famously promoted by Marriott hotels (Lashley, 2000). Clearly there are emotional dimensions to the service interaction, but this needs to be focused on the guests as valued individuals in their own right, and employees must be supported in their experiences of emotional labour, where they are expected to display one emotion whilst feeling another. The recruitment of workers who appear to display genuine hospitableness would minimise the emotional labour element, because they are displaying a service emotion that is consistent with their desire to be hospitable.

The treatment of employees as valued assets and human beings is the cornerstone of tapping into these qualities: paying decent wages pitched at the independently verified, living wage, not just the legal minimum wage; providing job role training that equips staff with the tools they need to do the job. This may involve training programmes, but can also include case-sharing amongst employees. Positive reactions to customer needs will be based on a toolkit of options. Overly formulaic responses will not build customer satisfaction or customer loyalty.

The step-by-step guide

1 Define the qualities of hospitableness and their relationship with the job role. Front of house and back of house need to understand this but in different ways, and it will impact differently on their performance with guests.

2 Carefully focused recruitment and selection may commence with in-house recruitment from existing staff – people from other units, or on part-time or fractional contracts. Also using existing staff contacts to suggest potential recruits from family and friends. People who are 'known' are less likely to leave, and there is a more detailed knowledge of the individual.

3   This might include hospitableness tests, or case study settings and exploring responses to own experiences as well as setting in the up-coming operation. Multi-stage selection including potential work colleagues as well as managers. Role play might be used to gain insights into the individual and how he/she deals with workplace experiences.

4   Induction training to include both a pre-service stage to establish role expectations, duties and responsibilities, and in-service training working with experienced employees. In the latter stage, build upon the individual's skill profile and their future development needs. Build a personal development plan agreed with the individual reflecting ambitions and family circumstances.

5   Appraisal procedure to be two-way, so as to both help the individual access feedback but also make suggestions and discuss future employment needs.

6   Reward package that is fair and based upon the living wage, with bonus options in line with organisational targets. This might link to sales performance, cost reduction, quality improvement, complain handling and actions in response to customers' requests and complaints.

7   A transparent and fair promotion process so that all employees at each stage understand what is needed to progress through the hierarchy. Provide case studies of more senior staff that have moved through the organisation.

8   An open and clearly managed equal opportunities strategy informed by research into barriers to development and actions to address these.

9   An annual report on employment practice covering, staff development, staff feedback, equal opportunities practices and profile.

10 All set within a participative culture in which people are empowered to provide the customer with hospitableness experiences.

Conclusion

This chapter has argued that operations providing food, drink and accommodation as commercial service can build competitive advantage through the study of hospitality and hospitableness. For the strategy to be effective, guests need to feel valued and welcome on their own terms and not just as customers who will make a contribution to sales and profits. The quality of the welcome delivered by hosts who are permanent and not ever-changing is key to the chemistry of the host guest relationship.

Clearly a culture of hospitableness is necessary, and this needs to go beyond the mechanistic notion that guest is always right! Hospitableness has to be based upon an emotional bond between the guest and the host(s). This has implications for the recruitment and development of talent able to deliver hospitableness, who are supported by employment practices that see employees as the key asset upon which to build success.

Activities

1   Design a recruitment and selection process that would identify a candidate's approach to guests and their understanding of the qualities of hospitableness.

2   In small groups discuss your individual experiences of being both a guest and a host in domestic settings.

3   Identify examples from your own experiences of being well and badly treated as a guest. Links this back to issues raised in the chapter.

4   Prepare a 2000 word discussion of the value of hospitableness as the source of competitive advantage in commercial service organisations.

References

Ashness, D. and Lashley, C. (1995). Empowering service workers at Harvester Restaurants. *Personnel Review* **24** (8), 501-519

Balmer, S. and Baum, T. (1993). Applying Herzberg's hygiene factors to the changing accommodation environment. *International Journal of Contemporary Hospitality Management,* **5** (2), 203-214

Blain, M. and Lashley, C. (2015). Hospitality and hospitableness. *Research in Hospitality Management.* **5**(1)1-9

Casselberry, R. (2009). Giving in the Old Testament, *The Bible on Money,* internet.

Cole, S. (2007). Hospitality and tourism in Ngadha: an ethnographic exploration, in Lashley, C., Lynch: and Morrison, *Hospitality: a social lens,* Oxford: Elsevier.

Cook, D. and Beckman, T. (2006). Current concepts in validity and reliability for psychometric instruments: theory and application. *The American Journal of Medicine,* **119,** 166-166.

Churchill J. R. G. (1979). A paradigm for developing better measures of marketing constructs. *Journal of Marketing Research,* **16**(1), 64-73.

Derrida, J. (2002). *Acts of Religion,* London, Routledge.

Heal, F. (1984). The idea of hospitality in early modern England, *Past and Present,* **102** (1), 66-93.

Heal, F. (1990). *Hospitality in Early Modern England,* Clarendon Press: Oxford.

Herzberg, F. (1966). *Work and the Nature of Man,* Staple Press: New York.

ISKCON (2004). *The Heart of Hinduism,* International Society for Krishna Consciousness, http://iskconeducationalservices.org/HoH/index.htm.

Khan, N. (2009). Definitions of hospitality in religions & regions, www.slideshare.net/ nayeemk/definitions-of-hospitality-in-religions-regions-presentation.

Lashley, C. and Morrison, A. (2000). *In Search of Hospitality: Theoretical perspectives and debates*, Butterworth-Heinemann: Oxford.

Lashley, C., Lynch,P. and Morrison, A. (2007). *Hospitality: A Social Lens,* Amsterdam: Elsevier.

Lashley, C., Morrison, A.J. and Randall, S. (2003). My most memorable meal ever: hospitality as an emotional experience. In Sloan, D., (ed) *Culinary Taste: Consumer Behaviour in the Restaurant Industry. Hospitality, Leisure and Tourism.* Butterworth – Heinemann.

Lashley, C. (2017). *Routledge Handbook of Hospitality Studies*, Routledge: Oxford.

Lashley, C. (2017a). Liberating wage slaves, in Lashley, C. (Ed.) *Routledge Handbook of Hospitality Studies*, Routledge: Oxford.

Meehan, M.W. (2013). *Islam, Modernity, and the Liminal Space Between*, Newcastle upon Tyne: Cambridge Scholars Publishing

Melwani, L., (2009). Hindu Hospitality: The Gods Amongst Us, *Hinduism Today.*

Nouwen, H. (1998). *Reaching Out: A Special Edition of the Spiritual Classic including Beyond the Mirror*, London: Fount (an Imprint of Harper Collins).

O'Gorman, K. D. (2007a). The hospitality phenomenon: philosophical enlightenment? *International Journal of Culture, Tourism and Hospitality Research,* **1,** 189 – 202.

O'Gorman, K. D. (2007b). Dimensions of hospitality: exploring ancient and classical origins. In Lashley, C., Morrison, A. and Lynch: (Eds.) *Hospitality: A Social Lens.* Amsterdam: Elsevier.

Ritzer, G. (2004). *The McDonaldization of Society: Revised New Century Edition,* London, Sage.

Ritzer, G. (2007). Inhospitable hospitality? In Lashley, C., Morrison, A. and Lynch: (Eds.) *Hospitality: A Social Lens.* Amsterdam: Elsevier.

Schulman, M. and Barkouki-Winter, A. (2000). The extra mile: The ancient virtue of hospitality imposes duties on hosts and guests, *Issues in Ethics,* **11** (1), 12-15.

Selwyn, T., (2000). An anthropology of hospitality, in Lashley, C. and Morrison, A., *In Search of Hospitality, Theoretical perspectives and debates*, Butterworth Heinemann: Oxford.

Slattery, P. (2002). On being a pompous pratt, *Journal of Hospitality, Leisure Sport and Tourism,* **1** (1).

Telfer, E. (2000). The philosophy of hospitableness. in Lashley, C., Morrison, A. (Eds.) *In Search of Hospitality: Theoretical perspectives and debates.* Oxford, Butterworth-Heinemann.

Wagner, R. (1870). *Die Walkurie,* Libretto

Warde, A. and Martens, L. (2000). *Eating out: Social Differentiation, Consumption, and Pleasure*, Cambridge: Cambridge University Press.

Zitkala-Sa. (1921). *American Indian Stories*, Washington: Hayworth Publishing House.

 5 Career Progression in Hospitality and Tourism Settings

Adele Ladkin and Aliaksei Kichuk

Learning objectives

After reading this chapter you will be able to:

- Understand the characteristics of tourism and hospitality employment

- Define careers and career development

- Explore the way individuals build careers in tourism and hospitality

- Explain the relationship between career development and talent management

Introduction

This chapter considers the career journey that individuals make in hospitality and tourism settings, and the role of talent management in the career development process. Career development is facilitated both by organisations in terms of their current and future human resource needs, and by individuals who make choices concerning their career needs and aspirations. Career development plans and prospects take place in numerous industry sectors, each with their own labour market characteristics and norms for career development opportunities.

In this chapter, the nature of tourism and hospitality employment is outlined as a starting point to set the context of careers in the tourism and hospitality sectors. This is followed by an exploration of the aspects that are relevant to the topic: careers, career development and career progression. The career journey then becomes the focus of discussion, outlining what constitutes a career journey before examining them in the tourism and hospitality contexts. The remaining part of the chapter turns its attention to talent management in the career context. The relationship between talent management and careers is outlined. A summary is then offered.

Tourism and hospitality employment

The ever-growing tourism sector provides opportunities for employment creation. Estimates by the World Travel and Tourism Council anticipate that over the next ten years there will be 347 million tourism jobs worldwide (World Travel & Tourism Council, 2014). Tourist activities create direct, indirect and induced employment opportunities. As discussed elsewhere by Ladkin and Szivas (2015), direct employment refers to employment in tourist sectors such as hotels, tour operators, transport, travel agencies etc. Indirect employment refers to jobs created by people working in activities that are partially dependent on tourism, for example, financial services, construction, car hire, etc. Induced employment is the additional employment resulting from the effects of the tourism multiplier as residents spend money on activities earned from tourism (Fletcher *et al.*, 2013). What this provides is a wealth of employment opportunities in numerous sectors, some more directly related to tourism and hospitality settings than others.

In terms of employment issues and labour markets, information is more readily available concerning the hospitality sector, partially due to jobs in this sector being more evident and less hidden than those in tourism. In the UK, for the tourism and hospitality sectors, figures from People 1st for 2013 indicate that:

☐ The sector accounts for just over 2 million jobs

☐ Restaurants employ the largest workforce in the sector

☐ 35% of businesses expect the workforce to increase

☐ By 2020, the sectors' workforce will have grown by 6%

☐ An additional 660,200 people will need to be recruited by 2020

☐ Nearly half of the workforce is part-time

☐ The sector has a young workforce, two in five workers are aged under 30

☐ 57% of the sector are female

☐ 32% of employers have female senior managers

☐ 22% of the workforce are migrant workers

(People 1st, 2013, p11)

Despite the diversity in the tourism and hospitality sectors, it is possible to identify certain characteristics of employment in the sectors. These broad characteristics have been identified and discussed elsewhere (Duncan *et al.*, 2013; Janta *et al.*, 2011), however a selection of these are presented here as they require consideration due to their relevance to how people develop their careers in the sectors. The characteristics that have an influence on career development include:

☐ Tourism and hospitality occupations vary widely in terms of skill requirements, ranging from unskilled to highly skilled and professional occupations. This presents a range of opportunities for different skill levels, and provides a means for up-skilling throughout a career journey.

☐ Many of the occupations have low barriers to entry (Liu and Wall, 2005; Vaugeois and Rollins, 2007). For example, if they are unskilled or semi skilled, they are open to a wide range of people and may be seen as a 'first job' to gain experience. This can be drawback, creating the perception of low skilled, low paid menial transient jobs (WTTC, 2014). However, it could also be viewed as a positive aspect as it means that many jobs are open to everyone. Unskilled or low skilled jobs provide the entry points for work into the sectors.

☐ The contractual arrangements are varied, for example they may be part-time or full-time, permanent, temporary or seasonal. This again can be viewed both as positive or negative. Positive in that the flexibility of contracts suits different individual needs, but negative as the security of full-time permanent work is not always available.

☐ Some of the occupations have clear career progression, others do not. The lack of clear career pathways is one of the main reasons leading to a poor image of the sectors and the negative impact of this on recruitment (WTTC, 2014).

☐ Turnover rates can be high (Yang, 2010). One feature of the sector that is felt in most countries and appears to be universal is higher turnover rates compared to occupations in other sectors.

☐ The sector is one that employs economic migrants due to the ease of obtaining employment in the sectors. (Matthews and Ruhs, 2007; Janta *et al.*, 2011). A low skill specificity, few educational requirements and short term contracts make many of the jobs available to a wide range of individuals. High turnover also ensures a constant supply of available employment opportunities for migrant workers seeking their first job in a new country.

☐ Associated poor labour conditions conform to stereotypes and are well documented, consisting of issues such as low pay, shift work, long hours, and poor career advancement opportunities (Baum, 2007; McIntosh and Harris, 2012).

☐ Cultural and social issues in some countries make travel and tourism less attractive than other sectors. For women, this may place a 'glass ceiling' on their participation rates (WTTC, 2014).

Careers, career development and progression

A career

A career is the *"evolving sequence of a person's work experiences over time"* Arthur, Hall and Lawrence (1989: 8). The traditional understanding of a career is seen in terms of professional employment with progression and advancement in the organisational position (Gunz and Heslin, 2005). However, traditional concepts

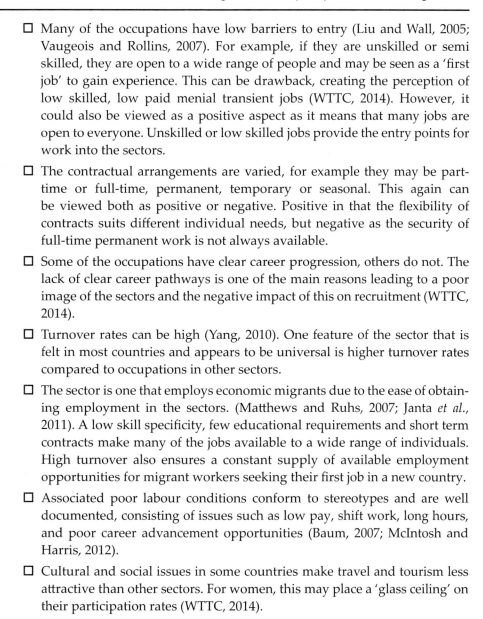

of a career based on organizational structures and hierarchies are in decline (Eaton and Bailyn, 2000; Sullivan, 1999) and are being replaced by careers with less developed structures. The modern career is multi-dimensional, developing beyond the constraints of a single organization or occupational setting (Arthur, 1994; Collin and Young, 2000). It is associated with increased mobility and is increasingly 'boundaryless' (Arthur, Inkson and Pringle, 1999, p 11) reflecting contemporary work practices.

However defined, careers are the outcome of structural opportunities available to an individual, for example the size of the industry, organizational structure, and knowledge requirement, human ability and ambition. The structural opportunities in an industry provide the framework for any occupation, and individual ability and ambition determine how people make choices within the structural opportunities (Ladkin and Weber, 2009). From an individual's perspective, how people's experiences and occupations change across a life course is essentially what defines a career.

Within the broad field of career theory, career development and progression form an integral aspect.

Career development

Career development is closely aligned with career planning. It is an essential component of human resources management (Nebel, Braunlich and Zhang, 1994). In the organisational context, career development is concerned with:

- ☐ How individuals manage their careers within/between organisational structures;
- ☐ How organisations structure the careers of their members.

From a personal perspective, career development is concerned not only with how individuals manage their careers, but also how individuals view and direct their own careers in terms of their goals, values, beliefs aspirations etc.

Essentially, labour market and structural opportunities are presented by the industry context but it is a range of personal choices, opportunities and constraints that make one person's career different from others.

As careers are part structure, part individual choice, we can argue that the responsibility for career development rests neither solely with the individual nor the organisation, but is shared by both (Pazy, 1988, Orpen, 1994). It is the outcome for the individual from both organizational and personal career planning (Simonsen, 1986). It is widely accepted that joint responsibility is the best way to achieve successful career development (Kong *et al.*, 2010; Lewis and Arnold 2012). Both organisational needs and personal career goals can be considered together and be mutually beneficial. This practice is in line with contemporary ways of working, as individuals are now less likely to spend all of their working lives with a single organisation.

Career progression

Career progression is a term that is often used in discussions of career development. It can be taken loosely to mean the process of making progress towards better jobs, implying an upward trajectory. As individuals gain more experience, they take on more challenging roles and responsibilities, usually rewarded with higher levels of pay. Implicit in progress through a career is the assumption of ever improving occupations and status. One factor that significantly affects career progression is that some careers have clear progression routes, and these are largely professional careers, for example, as in the case of a medical practitioner or an airline pilot. Other careers follow a much less well defined route, developing in a more ad hoc way with greater fluidity and variability. This is certainly the case for many tourism and hospitality careers, and will be returned to later in the chapter.

The career journey

In recognition of the many structural and individual factors that impact upon a person's career, one way in which an individual's career development can be explored is through the career journey. As implied by 'journey' we are concerned with how a career develops going from one job to another over time.

There is little doubt that the career journey looks quite different now to the past (Arthus, Inkson and Pringle, 1999). As discussed earlier, traditional career development largely took place within one organisation, and was characterised by a series of structured job changes with an upward trajectory. They were based on hierarchical, highly rigid structures (Baruch, 2004). Hall (2004) discusses the shift towards a *protean* career, characterised by proactive career management by the individual and involving multiple job and organisational changes. Related to this is the concept of the *boundaryless* career, advocated by Arthur (1994). In this type of structure, a career is not limited to one organisation but involves many different organisations and occupations. The implication is that careers cross multiple boundaries, the corporate boundaries of hierarchy and status, occupational, trade and job boundaries of specialist skills and function, and alongside this the social boundaries of separating work from home are no longer applicable (Arthur, Inkson and Pringle, 1999: 11).

Career journeys therefore can no longer be seen as following a one directional route, but take on different forms according to the changing structures of labour markets and individual choice and opportunity. This type of career journey is possible where there are opportunities in both the internal and external labour markets, as individuals make the most of opportunities offered by their existing employer or in moving to a new one. This type of mobility will have an impact on turnover if there are more job moves in the external rather than the internal labour market. This notion of a more fluid career structure is useful to set the context of career journeys in the tourism and hospitality settings, where these characteristics are evident.

Career journeys in tourism and hospitality settings

Tourism and hospitality employment involves a multitude of different activities, types of establishments, working arrangements and employment contracts. The diversity of the industries provides a wide range of job opportunities, which are difficult to categorise. One consequence of this is that the choice of career path opportunities is bewildering.

There are many different ways in which the tourism and hospitality industries are classified, providing an indication of the vast array of job opportunities. For example, the Office of National Statistics (2016) identifies that following industry groups for employment purposes:

- ☐ Accommodation for visitors
- ☐ Food and beverage activities
- ☐ Passenger transport, vehicle hire, travel agencies etc.
- ☐ Cultural, sports, recreational and conferences etc.

People 1st (2013) has these hospitality employment categories:

- ☐ Events
- ☐ Food and service management
- ☐ Gambling
- ☐ Hospitality services
- ☐ Hotels
- ☐ Pubs, bars and nightclubs
- ☐ Restaurants
- ☐ Self catering accommodation, holiday parks, and hostels
- ☐ Tourist services and
- ☐ Visitor attractions

The type of organisation for employment opportunities is vast, including for example airlines, cruise ship operators, rail companies, coach companies, tour operators, travel agents, theme parks, cafes, museums, resorts, hotels, restaurants etc. Added to this myriad of employment sectors are the various job functions, including for example sales and marketing, food and beverage, accounting, finance and purchasing, human resources management, information technology and systems, education, customer services and generic leadership and management.

Given the importance of human resources to the tourism and hospitality industries, surprisingly little is known about how people develop careers in these sectors. There are some exceptions, one being the case of hotel managers in which there is a wealth of research (Guerrier 1987, Baum 1988, Riley and Turam 1989,

Ladkin and Riley, 1994, 1995, 1996, Ladkin, 1999; 2002). One of the reasons for this body of research is that the hotel sector presents one of the more structured employment sectors in terms of a developmental hierarchy. Medium to large hotel companies offer a range of different functions for employment (for example front office, food and beverage, human resources management, finance and accounting, sales and marketing, housekeeping etc.) and recognised job levels (for example, operative, supervisor, department section head, department head, assistant manager, deputy general manager, general manager). The occupation of hotel general manager is widely seen in the industry as a target job, and one that attracts commitment to the career, therefore undertaking career tracking surveys is possible for this occupation. The nature of the hotel industry suggests that career patterns of hotel managers are likely to involve mobility (Ladkin and Riley, 1996). This mobility is both between and within organisations, but showed little movement outside of the hotel sector. In a related sector, this has been supported by McCabe and Savery (2007) who through an exploration of the careers of professional conference organisers, employees in hotels and convention, identified a new career pattern, which they named '*butterflying*'. This term refers to having more than one career route through different sectors, where respondents flutter between sectors according to the opportunities of employment and career growth. In essence, individuals make the most of job opportunities as they arise to facilitate their career development. There is no one specified career journey, but rather the journey is opportunistic, and in some ways reflects an extension of the boundaryless career McCabe and Savery, 2007). However, traditional careers that follow an upward trajectory were also evident (Kong *et al.*, 2011; Wang, 2013).

Specifically in terms of career development, previous studies in the context of hospitality (Ladkin, 1999; 2002) and the events industry (McCabe, 2008) have explored a range of career choice and development issues. These confirm that the tourism and hospitality sectors have few structured career opportunities. Often occupations are seen as transitory, with many people working in the sector for short periods of time and with notions that it will only be temporary (Ladkin, 2013). Those who intend to remain in the sector, may become frustrated by the lack of career opportunities and therefore do not remain.

Careers and their relationship with talent management

Despite the wealth of research from the hospitality field on the topic of talent management (Lashley *et al.*, 2007; Barron, 2008; Baum 2008; Hatum 2010; Steward and Harte, 2010; Collings and Mellahi, 2009; Kalaisevan and Naachimuthu, 2011) very little is known about the relationship between talent management and careers. In tourism, there is a dearth of talent management discussion, beyond the recognition that the loss of talented individuals is a significant problem for the industry (Ladkin, 2013). In hospitality, talent management is largely confined to discussions around talent management practices and activities (Kichuk, Ladkin, and Horner, 2014). Broadly, discussion focuses on attraction, selection, development and retention of talented individuals (Watson, 2008).

This is not surprising, as the existence of talent is important for the sustainability of organisations. Optimising talent is instrumental in determining whether the organisation is successful or not. The importance of talent in a people based industry is paramount (Sonia and Neetu, 2012; Watson, 2008) and without a doubt, hospitality organisations have to retain the best and brightest talents in order to succeed (Tuglan, 2001). Hotels continue to operate in an environment that is often unpredictable and characterised by rapid seasonal change (Poescu and Avram-Ratiu, 2012). Specific industry challenges include labour shortages both in terms of quality and quantity (Sonia and Neetu, 2012), a lack of skilled candidates for leadership positions (Pricewaterhouse Coopers, 2012) and the negative employer image that can lead to difficulties of attraction to the industry (Hughes and Rog, 2008). The reliance on temporary and or migrant workers can also be problematic in terms of labour turnover (Janta and Ladkin, 2009). Essentially, developing and managing talent in hotels is bound within the nature of the hospitality industry. High mobility, short term contracts, the employment of a large percentage of low or semi skilled workers, and problems of recruitment and retention all have an impact (Kichuk, Ladkin and Horner, 2014).

Aligning career progression to the talent management is now seen as a priority (Sparrow *et al.*, 2011). Career management practices could be designed to assist the career development of employees as well as considering organisational needs (Kong *et al.*, 2010). Essentially, this widens the traditional requirement of talent management for the benefit of the organisation, to consider how talent management will also benefit individuals and enable them to better plan and manage their careers. While talent management is widely used by organisations' human resource departments to enable organisational goals for recruitment, retention and development of vital employees (Stahl *et al.*, 2007), it is important to remember that individuals join organisations to develop and fulfil their own careers (Panda and Sahoo, 2015). In recognition of the duality of needs from both the organisation and the individuals, the narrow scope of talent management as purely organisational human resource practices is contested. Thunnissen *et al.* (2013a, 2013b) advocate for talent management to also consider the aspirations, needs and preferences of individual employees and their career development.

Organisational human resource current and future needs and the experiences and aspirations for the personal career development of employees is the basis of the relationship between talent management and careers.

Attracting and retaining talent through career development

The tourism and hospitality sectors are facing a problem in terms of attracting and retaining talent (WTTC, 2014). Talented employees are recognised as vital for ensuring the success of organisations (Kusluvan *et al.*, 2010) with organisations paying particular attention to how they might attract, retain and develop the careers of talented individuals (Cappelli and Keller, 2014). Attracting the right employees can lead to better customer service, and cost efficiency where turnover is reduced (Bharwani and Butt, 2012).

People 1st (2015) have outlined the concerns of the growing skills gap and high turnover rates in the tourism and hospitality sectors. The number of employers in this sector with vacancies has increased from 16% in 2011 to 18% in 2013, with those vacancies that are considered 'hard to fill' rising by 12% in the same timeframe (UKCES, 2013). Recruitment appears to be getting more problematic, with reasons given for this including the low number of applicants with required skills, attitude and motivation; a lack of work experience; not enough interest in the sector; and an unwillingness to undertake jobs that have shift work and/or unsociable hours (UKCES, 2013). High turnover rates are continually driven by the sector's overreliance on young workers, migrant workers, flexible contracts and low pay (People 1st , 2015).

In response to this on-going problem, there are a number of responses by employers to both attract and retain talent. This include flexibility in working arrangements, work design practices to make work more challenging and varied, and employee engagement. However, given the characteristics of the sector and the nature of many jobs, this is problematic.

The implementation of career development practices is also seen as a way forward. For example, strategies that motivate employees by job design and reward (Clayton, 2006) and those that develop marketable skills and feelings of value to the organisation (CIPD 2014). Specific career development strategies to attract and retain talent from an organisation perspective include:

☐ In-house training programmes

☐ Coaching and mentoring opportunities

☐ Job rotation

☐ Work-shadowing.

However, often the high labour turnover rates act as a barrier for organisations to invest in staff, only to lose them later on.

The Manpower Group talent shortage survey (2014) identified that human resources management should focus on three areas: people practices, talent sources, and work models. Examples of each include clear development opportunities during recruitment, providing training for existing staff, recruiting from outside the region and patterning with educational institutions to align skill requirements and to take the best from education, and redesigning work procedures offering more flexible working arrangements.

Recent research by Ladkin and Buhalis (2016) has advocated the use of online and social media recruitment as one of the ways to facilitate recruitment. A web presence can formulate an identity for organisations through brand awareness and reputation, as a means to attract talented employees.

The skills shortage and problems of recruiting and retaining talent individuals for the tourism and hospitality sectors look unlikely to be solved in the near future. However, due to the positive benefits that talented individuals bring to the workplace, any mechanism to foster the process has to be considered. An improvement in defining career development routes and training opportunities represents one positive strategy to attract and retain employees.

Summary

This chapter has sought to explore the career journeys that individuals make in tourism and hospitality settings. The value of career progression and development for individuals has been highlighted, along with the role that talent management might play in these processes. Due to the structure of the tourism and hospitality sectors, there is no one set career development route, which is one of the reasons for the difficulty in attracting and retaining individuals. There is considerable choice in terms of employment opportunities in the sectors, a shortage of applicants for many jobs, along with predicted growth in the sectors. These factors combined present the opportunity for employment and positive job prospects. Recruiting and encouraging people to develop careers in the sector is crucial. Incorporating talent development practices as part of career development programmes may be one of the ways forward.

Learning activities

The following activities can be undertaken in the form of small group discussion to facilitate an understanding of jobs and career development in the tourism and hospitality sectors.

1　Have you ever worked in any of the tourism and hospitality sectors? Think about the job you did, and reflect on a) the skills you needed to be able to perform your work, and b) what the opportunities were for further training and career development.

2　Many of the jobs in the tourism and hospitality sectors are customer facing. What do you consider to be important skills for being able to undertake customer-facing roles and deliver excellent customer service?

3　Reflect on the characteristics of the tourism and hospitality labour force. For employers, what are the challenges in providing career pathways for people who wish to develop a career in these fields?

4　Consider how a career is defined and reflect on how career development and career paths have changed over time.

5　Identify different talent management practices that could be used to assist career development in the tourism and hospitality sectors. Consider how talent management practices might be utilised by a) employers and b) individuals.

Assessment suggestions

6 Design a questionnaire that would help organisations understand the career development needs of the different employees in their organisations.

7 Write a report that identifies different talent management strategies, and how they might be used to benefit both the organisational and the individual.

8 Write an essay on the following. "Identify and discuss the characteristics of tourism and hospitality sector employment and the challenges they present for attracting and retaining talent."

References

Arthur, M. B., (1994). The boundaryless career: A new perspective for organizational inquiry. *Journal of Organizational Behaviour,* **15**, 295–306.

Arthur, M. B., Hall, D.T. and Lawrence, B.S. (1989). *Handbook of Career Theory.* Cambridge University Press. Cambridge.

Arthur, M.B., Inkson, K. and Pringle, J.K. (1999). *The New Careers. Individual action and economic change.* Sage, London.

Barron,P. (2008). Education and talent management: Implications for the hospitality industry. *International Journal of Contemporary Hospitality Management,* **20**(7): 730-742.

Baruch, Y. (2004). Transforming careers from linear to multidirectional career paths. Organizational and individual perspectives. *Career Development International,* **9**(1),58-73.

Baum, T. (1988) Ireland: Toward a new definition of hotel management. *Cornell Hospitality Quarterly,* **29**(2): 35-40.

Baum. T. (2007). Human resources in tourism: Still waiting for change. *Tourism Management* **28**(6), 1383-1399.

Baum,T. (2008). Implications of hospitality and tourism labour markets for talent management strategies. *International Journal of Contemporary Hospitality Management,* **20**(7), 721-729.

Bharwani, S. and Butt, N. (2012). Challenges for the global hospitality industry: an HR perspective. *Worldwide Tourism and Hospitality Themes,* **4**(2), 23-37.

Cappelli,P. and Keller, J.R. (2014). Talent management: Conceptual approaches and practical challenges. *Annual Review of Organizational Psychology and Organizational Behaviour,* **1**,305-331.

CIPD (2014). *Learning and Development. Annual Survey Report 2014.* Chartered Institute of Personnel and Development. London.

Collin, A. and R.A. Young, R.A. (2000). The future of careers. In *The Future Career,* Cambridge: Cambridge University Press.

Collings, D.G. and Mellahi, K. (2010). The barriers of effective global talent management: The example of corporate elites in MNEs. *Journal of World Business,* **45**,143-149

Clayton, G. (2006). Key skills in retention and motivation: the war for talent still rages and retention is high ground. *Industrial and Commercial Trading*, **38**(1), 37-45.

Duncan, T., Scott, D G. and Baum, T. (2013). The mobilities of hospitality work: An exploration of issues and debates. *Annals of Tourism Research*, **41**(1), 1-19.

Eaton, S.C. and Bailyn, L. (2000). Career as life path: tracing work and life strategies of biotech professionals. In *Career Frontiers: New Concepts Of Working Lives*, edited by T. Morris. (pp.177-198). Oxford: Oxford University Press.

Fletcher, J., Fyall, A., Gilbert, D. and Wanhill, S. (2013). *Tourism Principles & Practice*, 5th Ed. Pearson Education Limited, Harlow.

Guerrier, Y. (1987). Hotel managers' careers and their impact on hotels in Britain. *International Journal of Hospitality Management*, **6**(3), 121–130.

Gunz, H.P. and Heslin, P. A. (2005). Reconceptualising career success. *Journal of Organizational Behaviour*. **26**, 105-111.

Hall, T. (2004). The protean career: A quarter-century journey. *Journal of Vocational Behavior*. **65**(1), 1-13.

Hatum, A. (2010). *Next Generation Talent Management. Talent Management to survive turmoil*. Basingstoke: Palgrave Macmillan.

Hughes, J. C. and Rog, E. (2008). Talent Management: A strategy for improving employee recruitment, retention and engagement within hospitality organisations. *International Journal of Contemporary Hospitality Management*, **20**(7), 743-757.

Janta, H. and Ladkin, A. (2009). Polish migrant labour in the hospitality workforce: Implications for recruitment and retention. *Tourism, Culture and Communication*. **9**(1/2), 5-15.

Janta, H., Ladkin, A., Brown, L. and Lugosi, P. (2011). Employment experiences of Polish migrant workers in the UK hospitality industry. *Tourism Management*, **32**(5), 1006-1019.

Kalaiselvan, K. and Naachimuthu, K.P. (2011). A synergic model to training and development. *The Indian Journal of Industrial Relations*, **47**(2), 366-379.

Kichuk, A., Ladkin, A. and Horner, S. (2014). *Understanding talent management in hospitality: A career perspective?* CHME Annual Research Conference, University of Derby, May.

Kong, C., Cheung, C. and Zhang, H.Q. (2010). Career management systems: what are China's state-owned hotel practising? *International Journal of Contemporary Hospitality Management*, **22**(4), 467-482.

Kong, H., Cheung, C. and Song, H. (2011). Hotel career management in China: Developing a measurement scale. *International Journal of Hospitality Management*, **30**, 112-118.

Kusluvan, S., Kusluvan, Z., Ilhan, I. and Buyruk, L. (2010). The human dimension: A review of human resources management issues in the tourism and hospitality industry. *Cornell Hospitality Quarterly*. **51**(2), 171-214.

Ladkin, A. (1999). Hotel general managers: A review of prominent research themes. *International Journal of Tourism Research*, **1**(3), 167–193.

Ladkin, A. (2002). Career analysis: a case study of hotel general managers in Australia. *Tourism Management* **23**(4), *379-388.*

Ladkin, A. (2013). Tourism human resources. In C. Costa, E. Panyik and D. Buhalis (Eds). *Trends in European Tourism Planning and Organisation.* Channel View Publications. Bristol.

Ladkin, A. and Buhalis, D. (2016). Online and social media recruitment: hospitality employer and prospective employee considerations. *International Journal of contemporary Hospitality Management,* **28**(2), 327-345.

Ladkin, A. and Riley, M. (1994). A research update, *Tourism Management,* **15**(3), 221-222.

Ladkin, A. and Riley, M. (1995). Hotel management careers: Research update 2. *Tourism Management.* **16**(6), 475-476

Ladkin, A. and Riley, M. (1996). Mobility and structure in the career paths of UK hotel general managers: A labour market hybrid of the bureaucratic model? *Tourism Management,* **17**(6), 443–452.

Ladkin, A. and Szivas, E. (2015). Green jobs and employment in tourism. In M.V. Reddy, and K. Wilkes (Eds). *Tourism in the Green Economy.* Routledge, Taylor and Francis Group, Oxon. 115-127.

Ladkin, A. and Weber, K. (2009). Career analysis of convention professionals in Asia: The case of Hong Kong. In T. Baum, M. Deery, C. Hanlon, L. Lockstone and K. Smith (Eds). *People and Work in Events and Conventions: A research perspective.* CABI: London. 39- 50.

Lashley, C., Lynch,P. and Morrison, A., (2007). *Hospitality: A social lens.* Elsevier: Oxford.

Lewis, S. and Arnold, J. (2012). Organisational career management in the UK retail buying and merchandising community. *International Journal of Retail and Distribution Management,* **40**(6), 451-470.

Liu, A. and Wall, G. (2005). Human resources development in China. *Annals of Tourism Research* **32**(3), 689-710.

Matthews, G. and Ruhs, M. (2007) *Are you being served? An exploration of the demand for migrant labour in the UK's hospitality sector.* Working Paper No. 51. University of Oxford, Oxford.

McCabe, V. and Savery, L. (2007). 'Butterflying' a new career pattern for Australia? Empirical evidence. *Journal of Management and Development,* **26**(2),103-116.

McCabe, V. (2008). Strategies for career planning and development in convention and exhibition industry in Australia. *International Journal of Hospitality Management,* **27**(2), 222-231.

McIntosh, A and Harris, C. (2012). Critical hospitality and work: (In)hospitable employment in the hospitality industry. *Hospitality and Society* **2**(2), 129-135.

Manpower Group (2014). Manpower Group 2014 Talent shortage Survey Results: Available at www.manpoergroup.co.uk/media/137404/2014_talent_shortage_wp_us2.pdf

Nebel, E. C., Braunlich, C.G. and Zhang, Y. (1994). Career paths in American luxury hotels: Hotel food and beverage directors. *International Journal of Contemporary Hospitality Management,* **6**(6), 3-9.

5

ONS (2016). Characteristics of tourism industries, 2014. Office for National Statistics. 3rd February. Available at www.ons.gov.uk Accessed 3rd April 2016.

Orpen, C. (1994). The effects of organizational and individual career management on career success. *International Journal of Manpower,* **15**(1), 27-37.

Panda, S. and Sahoo, C.K. (2015). Strategic talent development interventions: an analysis. *Industrial and Commercial Training,* **47**(1), 15-22.

Pazy, A. (1988). Joint responsibility. The relationship between organizational and individual career management and the effectiveness of careers. *Group and Organizational Studies,* **13**(3), 311-331.

People 1st (2013). *State of the National Report 2013.* Available at http://www.people1st.co.uk/research/state-of-the-nation-2013 (Accessed 14th April 2016).

People 1st (2015). *The skills and productivity question: Hospitality and tourism sector.* http://www.people1st.co.uk/getattachment/Research-policy/Research-reports/The-Skills-and-Productivity-Problem/Report-The-Skills-and-productivity-problem-Oct-15.pdf.aspx

Poescu, C. and Avram-Ratui. (2012). New trends in resource management in the hospitality industry. International Conference of Scientific paper AFASES, 2-6.

Pricewaterhouse Coopers (2012). *Delivering results through talent - the hr challenge in a volatile world.* 15th Annual Global CEO Survey. Available at: www.pwc.com/talent management

Riley, M. and Turam, K. (1989). The career paths of UK hotel managers: A developmental approach. *Signet Quarterly,* **1**(1), 1–13.

Thunnissen, M., Boselie,P. and Fruytier, (2013a). Talent management and the relevance of context: Towards a pluralistic approach. *Human Resources Management Review,* **23**(4), 326-336.

Thunnissen, M., Boselie,P. and Fruytier, (2013b). A review of talent management: infancy or adolescence? *International Journal of Human Resource Management* **24**(9), 1744-1761.

Simonsen,P. (1986). Concepts of career development. *Training and Development Journal,* 40(1): 70-74.

Sonia, B. and Neetu, B., (2012). Challenges for the global hospitality industry: An HR perspective. *Worldwide Hospitality and Tourism Themes,* **4**(2), 150-162.

Sparrow,P., Hird, M. and Balain, S. (2011). Talent Management: Time to question the Tablets of Stone? White paper 11/01, October, Lancaster University Management School.

Stahl, G.K., Bjorkman, I., Farndale, E., Morris, S.S, Paauwe, J., Syiles,P., Trevor, J. and Wright,P. M. (2007). Global Talent Management: How leading multinationals build and sustain their talent pipeline, INSEAD Faculty and Research Working Papers.

Steward, J. and Harte, V. (2010). The implications of talent management for diversity training: an exploratory study. *Journal of European Industrial Training,* **34**(6), 506-518.

Sullivan, S.E. (1999). The changing nature of careers: A review and research agenda. *Journal of Management,* **25**(3), 457-484.

Tuglan, B., (2001). Winning the talent wars. *Employment Relations Today*, **23**(1/2), 37-51.

UKCES (2013) *UK Commission Employer skills Survey 2013: UK results Evidence Report 81.* London: UK Commission for Employment and Skills www.ukces.org.uk/publications

Vaugeois, N. and Rollins, R.(2007). Mobility into tourism: Refuge employer, *Annals of Tourism Research*, **34**(3), 630-648.

Wang, Y.F. (2013). Constructing a career competency model of hospitality industry employees for career success. *International Journal of Hospitality Management*, **25**(7), 994-1016.

Watson, S. (2008). Where are we now? A review of management development issues in the hospitality and tourism sector, *International Journal of Contemporary Hospitality Management*, **20** (7), 75.

World Travel and Tourism Council (2014). *Global Talent Trends and Issues for the Travel & Tourism Sector.* London. Oxford Economics, London.

Yang, J.T. (2010). Antecedents and consequences of job satisfaction in the hotel industry. *International Journal of Contemporary Hospitality Management* **29**(4), 609-619.

5

6 Human Resource Strategy and Talent Management

Andrew Jenkins

Learning objectives

After reading this chapter you will be able to:

- Explain how strategy develops in organisations

- Explain how an organisation's strategic orientation affects how it manages people

- Discuss the key characteristics of strategic human resource management

- Discuss the principal features of a strategic approach to talent management in organisations

- Identify future factors likely to influence an organisation's strategic approach to talent management in organisations

Introduction

This chapter will start with a discussion of strategy and strategic management in order to provide the reader with a good overview of how strategy develops in organisations and how strategy may affect the organisation's approach to managing human resources. Thereafter, the concept of strategic human resource management and strategic talent management is examined and the chapter concludes with a discussion of future issues concerning strategic talent management.

Strategic management

Strategy concerns the long-term direction of an organisation (Johnson *et al.*, 2014). There are many definitions of strategy and strategic management. David (2011: 37) defines strategic management as '*the art and science of formulating, implementing, and evaluating cross-functional decisions that enable an organisation to achieve its objectives'*. According to Wheelen and Hunger (2010), strategic management relates to managerial decisions and actions that affect the long-term performance of an organisation. Wheelen and Hunger (2010) further state that strategic management includes scanning the environment, formulating and implementing strategy, and the evaluation and control of strategy. However De Wit and Meyer (2014) state that a clear definition of strategic management is illusive, given differing opinions about what strategic management is and the key issues associated with it.

Essentially, there are two different approaches to explain how strategy develops in organisations: the *intended* (also called *prescriptive* or *deliberate*) and the *emergent* approach (Barney and Hesterly, 2010; Lynch, 2012; Johnson *et al.*, 2014). The intended approach is where strategic development is linear, rational and where the main elements of strategy are determined in advance. The emergent approach is where strategy emerges over time and, as a result, cannot be usefully summarized in a plan (Lynch, 2012). Johnson *et al.* (2014) comment that deliberate strategy involves intentionally formulating or planning strategy and this could take many forms including strategy intentionally being made by the strategic leader; strategy being made by the process of strategic planning involving many managers; and strategy imposed on the organisation. It is not necessarily the case that one approach is better than another, but there are situations where one approach is better suited to the prevailing conditions. Thus Lynch (2012) asserts that the prescriptive approach works perfectly well where growth is continuous, linear and predictable, but is much less suited to conditions where there is rapid change taking place.

In the intended approach to strategic management, strategy is defined as a plan of action for the future. There are typically three common questions that can assist an organisation to determine its strategy: Where are we now? Where do we want to be? How do we get there? A strategic plan will provide data and argument to support the organisation's strategy (Johnson *et al.*, 2014). Typically, strategic plans have a long-term focus with business plans usually being developed around a three to five-year time-frame, although, because of increased uncertainty in the environment, the time-horizon is become shorter (Tyson, 2012). The aim of designing and following a strategic plan is to create competitive advantage for the organisation. Competitive advantage relates to a firm's ability to create more economic value than its competitors (Barney and Hesterly, 2012). In attempting to create greater economic value, a firm must be able to supply products and services that more closely match the needs and wants of its customers and be able to actually develop and supply these products and services (De Wit and Meyer, 2014).

Strategy can be formulated and implemented at different levels, and there are recognised generic forms that organisations or sub-divisions of organisations might adopt. The levels at which strategy are formulated and implemented are most frequently identified as corporate, business and operational or functional (see, for example, Boxall and Purcell, 2008; and Johnson *et al.*, 2014). Wheelen and Hunger (2010) recognize three types of strategy: corporate, business and functional. Corporate strategy is about the organisation's overall strategic direction relates to growth and how it manages its various businesses, products and services; business strategy focuses on improving the firm's competitive position in relation to its products and services, usually at the business-unit or product level; and functional strategy relates to the approach taken by a functional area, such as marketing, human resource management or research and development, to achieve corporate and business unit objectives by maximizing the productivity of the given resource (Wheelen and Hunger, 2010).

As previously stated, corporate strategy is concerned with the overall direction that an organisation follows. For large corporations, such as multinational organisations, this is a question of which sectors of business they choose to be engaged in, and these organisations would then develop separate business level strategies for their strategic business units, each focusing on a discreet range of products or services. Corporate-level issues concern the geographical coverage of the organisation, the products and services offered, the methods used to develop the business and how resources are allocated within the organisation whilst typical business-level issues concern innovation, scale and response to competitors (Johnson *et al.*, 2014).

Operational strategies concern the delivery of corporate and business strategies in relation to resources, processes and people (Johnson *et al.*, 2014). The functions an organisation has will depend on the type of business, its structure and its size. Functional areas include human resources, operations, marketing and sales, logistics, procurement, research and development, human resources and finance. Each of these functional areas needs to follow strategic plans that are consistent with the corporate and business plans adopted by the respective organisation. The strategic plans followed by the functional departments must be integrated to ensure success as they are interdependent and cannot be formulated without reference to each other.

Strategy involves gathering and processing data in order to make long-term decisions. There is a need to focus on relevant information to the firm, but it is also important to be as comprehensive as possible in order that potentially important information is not overlooked. Since planning is concerned with forecasting future actions, there is always the potential for developments that are not foreseen. This means that planning is an on-going process, and that a five year strategic plan cannot be followed slavishly until the end of the five year period but will probably need to be adjusted to take into account unforeseen developments.

Identifying pertinent issues, and collecting relevant information concerning them, is referred to as *environmental scanning*, defined by Wheelen and Hunger (2010: 64) as '*the monitoring, evaluating, and disseminating of information from the external and internal environments to key people within the corporation*'. The acronym PEST, or its alternative forms of PESTEL or PESTLE, are commonly used as an aide memoire of the issues that organisations need to take into consideration when formulating their strategies. The initials in PEST stand for Political, Economic, Social and Technological issues whilst the E and L in variations of the acronym stand for Environmental and Legal issues (Thompson, Scott and Martin, 2014).

There are various strategic options that an organisation may wish to follow. These include growth, stability and retrenchment (Millmore *et al.*, 2007). There are different ways of pursuing each of these strategies. Growth, for example, can be achieved through the development of new products and services, by increasing the market share for existing products and services in domestic or international markets, through mergers and acquisitions or by means of growing the business using franchising or management contracts. The strategic directions of growth, stability and retrenchment are normally associated with the life cycle stages of products and markets. The idea behind the Boston Consulting Group (BCG) Matrix is that large corporations would aim to have a balanced portfolio of businesses which have products that are stable and products that are growing (Lynch, 2012).

The work of Michael Porter (1980, 1985 and 1988) is frequently cited in discussions of business strategy. Porter's generic strategies, as cited in Johnson *et al.* (2014), are cost leadership, differentiation, cost focus and differentiation focus. Cost leadership focuses on obtaining advantage by reducing costs so that they are below those of the firm's competitors (Barney and Hesterly, 2012). A differentiation strategy is the ability of the firm to supply products and services that offer superior value to the consumer in terms of build quality, special features or quality of after-sale service (Wheelen and Hunger, 2010). A focus strategy targets an activity or segment, tailoring products and services to the needs of the segment (Johnson *et al.*, 2014). There are two variants of focused strategies: cost focus and differentiation focus. Porter (1980) states that the generic strategies offer alternative and viable approaches to a firm's competitive forces. However, a firm that is 'stuck in the middle' is in a very weak strategic position.

One or a combination of the generic strategies can be adopted in order to achieve the organisation's chosen corporate strategy. A strategy based on cost will involve an organisation attempting to improve efficiency by reducing staffing, production and other costs. A strategy based on differentiation means emphasising the uniqueness of the firm's products or services, for example by being known for the aesthetic design of its products. A focused strategy entails concentrating on a particular segment rather than the whole industry or sector. As a strategic direction, innovation can also provide a major focus. In this respect, Guest, Storey and Tate (1997) make the point that all business strategies need some element of innovation.

A major strand of strategic management literature relates to the Resource-Based View (RBV) of the firm. RBV views organisational resources as unique bundles that can give an organisation advantage over its competitors (Saunders, Millmore and Lewis, 2007). Firm resources, according to Barney (2002: 155) consist of '*all assets, capabilities, competencies, organisational processes, firm attributes, information, knowledge and so forth that are controlled by the firm and that enable the firm to conceive of and implement strategies designed to improve its efficiency and effectiveness.'*

According to Fleisher and Bensoussan (2003), RBV theory recognises four categories of resources which, potentially, can give a firm competitive advantage: tangible assets; intangible assets; organisational capabilities and core competencies. De Wit and Meyer (2014) state that the strategist needs to compare the firm's resources to other companies to establish their relative strength to determine if the firm's resources are unique, superior or inferior to other firms' resources. This is a difficult analysis to perform as it requires in-depth knowledge of other firm's resources. Knowing other firms' intangible resources is particularly problematic

RBV states that an organisation's internal resources, such as its people, can form the basis of sustainable competitive advantage if the resources are scarce, valuable, inimitable and non-substitutable (Paauwe and Boon, 2009). It could be stated that HRM provides resources that are scarce, valuable, imitable, and non-substitutable by providing people who are productive, engaged, relatively scarce and difficult to copy (Marler and Fisher, 2013). Moreover, Barney (2002) states that human capital is an important resource for any organisation and includes te experience, training, judgement, relationships, insight and intelligence of managers and employees.

RBV theory has been criticised by a number of authors. Kaufman (2015) claim that RBV is often presented in an incomplete form and key aspects are superficially represented. Therefore, writers and researchers need to be more critical of the theory before making potentially harmful recommendations to managers. Spender, Kraaijenbrink and Groen (2010) state that there are eight key criticisms of RBV: it has no managerial implications; it implies infinite regress; its applicability is too limited; sustained competitive advantage is not achieved; it is not a firm-based theory: VRIN/VRIO[1] is not necessary or sufficient for sustainable competitive advantage to be achieved; a resource's value is too indeterminate to be useful theoretically and the definition of a resource is not workable. Spender, Kraaijenbrink and Groen (2010: 349) conclude that *'the RBV's core message can withstand criticism from five of these* (criticisms: see above) *provided the RBV's variables, boundaries, and applicability are adequately justified'*.

In relation to the hospitality industry, Enz (2010) claims that businesses are pursuing a more strategic approach to management. However, it has to be remembered that the hospitality industry, and the tourism industry as well, are very diverse in nature. There are major differences between firms in terms of primary activity, profit motive, size and geographical coverage (Okumus, Altinay and Chathoth, 2010). Invariably, some hospitality and tourism businesses will be adopting a strategic approach to management whereas other will be reacting to events. Similarly, there will be diversity in terms of the generic strategy followed.

---

1 Two approaches to viewing the resources: by characteristics – valuable, rare, inimitable, non-substitutable; by questions of value, rarity, imitability, organisation's ability to exploit.

Some businesses will focus on quality and innovation, resulting in a differentiation strategy, whereas other firms will focus on cost.

Having explained how strategy develops in organisations, the next section will examine the concept of strategic human resource management (SHRM).

Strategic human resource management (SHRM)

Armstrong (2011: 48) defines strategic human resource management as '*an approach to managing people that deals with how the organisation's goals will be achieved through its human resources by means of integrated HR strategies, policies and practices*'. Armstrong (2011) further comments that SHRM is based on five propositions: a firm's human resources play a strategic role in the firm's success; HR strategies should be integrated with the firm's overall business strategies; human capital represents an important source of competitive advantage; business strategy is implemented by people; and a systematic approach is needed to develop and implement HR strategies.

According to Foot, Hook and Jenkins (2016), the human resource strategy arises from the firm adopting a strategic approach to managing people, where the human resource strategy is aligned with the firm's overall business strategy. It is reflected in a set of human resource policies specifically designed to achieve the firm's strategic goals. This implies that an appropriate human resource strategy, linked to the corporate strategy, provides the 'best fit' between the firm's overall business strategy and the human resource strategy. This is discussed in detail by Marchington and Wilkinson (2005: 106–113). Ideally, human resource issues should support the organisational strategy and affect what it includes (CIPD, 2015a). Indeed, the costs associated with pursuing a human resource strategy, and the probability of the strategy succeeding, should have been a key consideration in the decision to pursue the particular business strategy in the first place.

The philosophy of senior management regarding the treatment of people in the organisation will affect the choice of human resource strategy to be followed. This, in turn, will result in a set of human resource policies and practices that help the organisation achieve its strategic objectives. The human resource function helps the firm achieve its strategic goals by developing and implementing human resource policies and practices that engage employees, encouraging them to channel their efforts towards the achievement of corporate objectives (CIPD, 2005). These policies and practices normally address the different aspects of human resource management, such as recruitment and selection, learning, training and talent management, diversity management, rewards and employment relations. Rather than being able to identify an organisation's human resource strategy, it is more common to be able to identify an organisation's recruitment and selection strategy or its diversity or reward strategy, either explicitly stated as a strategy or reflected in the organisation's human resource policies and practices (Foot, Hook and Jenkins, 2016).

6

Strategic human resource management (SHRM) is undoubtedly a complex subject. Theoretical interpretations of SHRM are constantly evolving and any definition of SHRM and the relationship to strategy and planning are not absolute but are subject to interpretation, based on an author's understanding of the phenomena (CIPD, 2015b). The CIPD (2005) has produced a toolkit for creating HR strategy, consisting of a nine-step development process. The steps are:

1 Decide who is to be involved and their role
2 Define what the business strategy is
3 Analyse the context
4 Identify the needs of the business
5 Identify the key HR issues
6 Develop the strategic framework
7 Define the specific HR strategies
8 Assess HR capability and resources required
9 Prepare action plans

As there are so many important aspects of HR strategy, it is essential that these aspects are coherent and support each other as well as being aligned with the organisation's overall business or corporate strategy. Other key aspects of successful strategic HRM are effective change management and effective communication (CIPD, 2005). In order for an organisation to achieve its strategic goals, its employees need to understand what is required of them and how their efforts contribute to the success of the organisation. Operating in a strategic manner also means having to deal with change, since strategy involves planning for the future and adjusting to an uncertain business environment (Foot, Hook and Jenkins, 2016). The CIPD (2005: 3) has produced a number of questions to consider before formulating, developing and implementing HR strategy. These questions help the HR practitioner focus on the more general aspects of project and change management, as well as developing the HR strategies per se. Questions include: Are the resources available to develop and implement the strategy? How are staff generally likely to react to the strategy? Is this the first time the strategy is formulated or is this an updating of an existing strategy? Will line managers support strategy initiatives and do they have the skills to implement them?

The discussion of SHRM thus far has emphasized the role of the HR practitioner as a business partner. However, in many organisations, HR responsibilities have been delegated to line managers. Front-line managers, defined as line managers with no managerial staff reporting to them, play a crucial role in ensuring that HR strategies are carried out effectively (Hutchinson and Purcell, 2003), The CIPD Factsheet (2015d) on the role of line managers in HR, states that line managers should have the necessary skills to perform HR activities and should reflect on their behaviour and how this affects employees' motivation and performance. These managers need to be selected in a thoughtful manner and need to be supported by strong organisational values to clearly show what behaviour is acceptable and what behaviour is unacceptable.

Because of the important role that line mangers play in relation to an organisation's HR strategy, HR practitioners involved in strategic aspects of HR need to solicit and incorporate the view of line managers into the HR strategy planning process to ensure that line managers are actively engaged with the HR strategy (Foot, Hook and Jenkins, 2016). However, the achievement of mutual understanding between HR strategists and line managers can be problematic (Smethurst, 2005). This understanding can be improved by more effective communication, involvement, participation and more effective change management.

Whatever strategy a firm chooses to follow, there is likely to be considerable change which will affect the firm, the industry in which the firm operates and the society in which the firm is located and interacts. Work and employment are constantly changing and evolving, and new work methods require new sets of employee skills (Foot, Hook and Jenkins, 2016). This highlights the need for effective human resource planning which takes a longer-term view and helps an organisation prepare for its future requirements, facilitating achievement of its strategic objectives and helping it achieve sustainable competitive advantage. The information acquired through undertaking human resource planning, incorporating aspects of environmental scanning (discussed earlier in this chapter), will provide an organisation with a basis for the formulation and development of its human resource strategies.

In his book on *Human Resource Management and Performance*, Paauwe (2004) suggests a model of HRM, the contextually based human resource theory (inspired by Resource Based Theory), that goes beyond focusing purely on the relationship between HRM, strategy and performance to a model in which ethical HRM is an enabling factor. In Paauwe's model, the development of HRM is affected on the one hand by product market combinations and appropriate technology (competitive mechanisms) and, on the other hand, by the socio-political, cultural and legal contexts (institutional mechanisms). In addition to these two factors, HRM policies and practices are influenced by the historical and grown configurations of the organisation (configuration mechanisms). The competitive configuration and institutional mechanisms influence the 'dominant coalition' (the role of different stakeholders – or actors – and the influence they have on strategic choices). The dominant coalition shapes HRM policies and practices so that they fit with the firm's strategy, organisation, environment and are coherent, helping the firm achieve competitive advantage. Chosen HR strategies are aimed at resources that are valuable, inimitable, rare and non-substitutable (see the discussion on RBV earlier on in this chapter). This, in turn, generates HR outcomes and contributes to the firm achieving higher levels of performance.

Like many HR writers, Beardwell and Claydon (2007) discuss two schools in relation to SHRM: the 'best fit' (or contingency) school and the 'best practice' school. In relation to the first, the relationship between strategic management and HRM is explored to establish the extent to which there is vertical integration between an organisation's business strategy and its HR policies and practices. In relation to the second, there is a notion that there are best HR practices that, if enacted, will result in improved organisational performance. Boxall and Purcell (2000) state that 'best fit' models of SHRM argue that HR strategy is more effective when it is designed to fit critical contingencies in the firm's context, whereas 'best practice' models of SHRM consider that organisational performance can be enhanced by adopting certain HR practices. Recognising the key discussion between 'best fit' and 'best practice', Boxall and Purcell (2000) call for more debate around the type of market regulation and social capital needed to offer more rewarding and secure work to a larger number of people in society.

Millmore (2007) has identified three models of strategic HRM: universal, closed matching and open matching models. Universal models of SHRM claim that there is one best way of achieving HR effectives and represent a 'best practice' approach to HR. However, Millmore (2007) criticises this approach because of lack of agreement of what constitutes the key HR practices that enhance organisational performance; the lack of focus on the context in which SHRM operates; and the lack of focus on the employee. Closed matching models focus on the clear and beneficially supportive relationship between business strategy and HR strategy, giving rise to specific HR initiatives. The main problems associated with this school of thought, according to Millmore (2007), are the difficulties of clearly defining business and HR strategy; lack of focus on the employee; and the problem of implementation due to the changing nature of the environment. Finally, open matching models, like closed matching models, recognise the clear and supportive relationship between organisational strategy and HR strategy but do not prescribe HR strategy initiatives. Once again, there are limitations of this school of thought: there is ambiguity and it is difficult to operationalise the model (Millmore, 2007).

In spite of the growing focus on strategic HRM by writers and organisations, the concept of SHRM, at least to some extent, remains vague and unclear (Darwish, 2013). Moreover, Paauwe et al. (2012) criticise writings and research on SHRM (and the role of 'fit') in that it does not sufficiently focus on the role of the line manager; there is insufficient focus on the role of the employee; and there has been insufficient attention paid to how intended, actual and perceived HR practices are aligned. Pilbeam and Corbridge (2010) also comment that it is difficult to establish clear links between corporate strategy and HR strategy, and between HR strategy and business performance.

With reference to the hospitality and tourism industry, Kusluvan et al. (2010) comment that, given the differences amongst tourism and hospitality organisations, it is not possible to prescribe a single approach to HRM practices. Many businesses have not yet implemented a strategic approach to HRM. The industry, it seems, is still grappling with SHRM (Davidson et al., 2011). However, a survey of hotel managers in Barbados by Alleyne et al. (2008) revealed widespread implementation of a strategic approach to HRM, supporting the findings of similar research undertaken by Baptiste and Bailey (2003) in Trinidad and Tobago and by Hoque (2000) in the UK.

Having discussed strategic management and strategic human resource management, the next section will discuss the concept of strategic talent management.

Strategic talent management (STM)

Given the increased competition for skilled employees in different sectors of the economy, many organisations have developed and implemented a strategic approach to talent management, or have developed and implemented talent management processes (Ready and Conger, 2007; Wooldridge, 2006; Vaiman and Collings, 2013). Managing talent is a strategic priority in today's complex and dynamic global business environment (Newhall, 2012), and business leaders expect that the intense competition for talent will have a major impact on their businesses (Thunnissen, Fruytier and Boselie, 2013). The need to acquire and/or retain talented employees is not just important when an economy is growing, and jobs are being created. It is also important during an economic downturn, as the organisation needs to ensure that it has the appropriate human resources when the economy recovers and when business opportunities arise (Murphy, 2009).

Essentially, there are two approaches to talent management: the *individualistic* (or star) approach and the *strategic* approach (Jones *et al.*, 2012). In relation to the individualistic approach, talent is viewed as a form of human capital and the organisation's performance is a result of attracting and retaining talented people. However, this approach has been criticized because it can reduce rather than enhance organisations, teams and individuals (Beechler and Woodward, 2009). Furthermore, upon leaving and joining a different organisation, a talented individual's performance may deteriorate (Groysberg, Nada and Nohria, 2004). Whilst there are many interpretations of what strategic talent management is, having a strategic orientation to talent management entails focusing on systems-level issues (Jones *et al.*, 2012). These issues relate to teams, networks, relational and social processes (McDonnell *et al.*, 2010). Jones *et al.* (2012) have stated that, with a maturing of research and writings on talent management, there have been calls to move from an individualistic to a strategic approach.

A qualitative study of talent management practices in Australia by Jones *et al.* (2012) revealed a lack of explicit links between talent and strategy, with organisations following an individualistic (or star) approach rather than a strategic approach. Based on interviews with 22 senior managers, the study found that there was diversity in terms of how human resource managers in firms defined talent and approached talent management, with some firms following a re-labelled human resource management approach, whilst others used a more strategic approach. The authors found evidence of an emphasis on identifying key positions that help an organisation achieve competitive advantage and, in some organisations, differentiated human resource 'architecture' related to a more strategic perspective.

6

Collings and Mellahi (2009: 304) define strategic talent management (STM) as '*activities and processes that involve the systematic identification of key positions which differentially contribute to the organisation's sustainable competitive advantage, the development of a talent pool of high potential and high performing incumbents to fill these roles, and the development of a differentiated human resource architecture to facilitate filling these positions with competent incumbents and to ensure their continued commitment to the organisation*'. In addition to defining STM, Collings and Mellahi (2009) have developed a theoretical model of STM. In relation to this model, the authors state that the first stage is to identify pivotal talent positions. These represent strategically important posts. The talent pool fills the pivotal positions, either from the internal or external labour market. Differentiated human resource architecture involves deploying human resource practices relevant to the organisation's context. The outcome of STM is to have a positive impact on employees and the organisation, but this is mediated by three key variables (work motivation, organisational commitment and extra-role behaviour). Thus, if undertaken successfully, STM will enhance the organisation's performance.

An organisation's human talent can help it achieve its strategic objectives (Lengnick-Hall *et al.*, 2009).

According to Ashton and Morton (2005), good talent management is strategically important and can help differentiate an organisation. Furthermore, it can be seen as a strategic and holistic approach to human resource management and business planning, or a new way of achieving organisational effectiveness (Ashton and Morton, 2005). However, it is widely acknowledged that the process through which human resource strategy leads to increased performance is not as straightforward as the talent management literature suggests (Thunnissen, 2016).

In her (2016) paper on 'Understanding how employees respond to talent identification over time', Karin King advocates a theoretical model concerning the talent deal and talent journey, illustrating how employees experience STM. King (2016) conceptualises the talented-employee perception of exchange as the 'talent deal' and their experience of STM over time as the 'talent journey'. The model proposed by King (2016: 95) theorises that '*the psychological contract of talented employees is modified by talent identification and strategic talent management is experienced through a series of significant career events*'.

Dries (2013) comments that, while most talent management authors assume that talent management is part of an organisation's general human resource management strategy, some authors (e.g. Chuai *et al.*, 2008) claim that talent management is a 'mind-set', a characteristic of an organisation similar to organisational culture. Al Ariss, Cascio and Paauwe (2014) state that, in order to address the challenges and opportunities presented, the broader national and institutional contexts should be considered in relation to talent management, rather than focusing solely on organisational performance. It is important that talent management practices have a strategic focus, supporting the capabilities of the firm. Furthermore, in addition to building new capabilities, talent management practices must consolidate and support gains the company has already made (Joyce and Slocum, 2012).

In developing a talent management strategy, Armstrong (2011) states that an organisation will need to address the following:

☐ Who the programme includes

☐ What is meant by 'talent'

☐ What the future talent requirements of the organisation are

☐ How to develop the organisation as an 'employer of choice'

☐ How to apply appropriate recruitment and selection methods

☐ How to identify talented people and their development needs

☐ How to design jobs that are interesting and challenging

☐ How to provide talented employees with opportunities for career development

☐ How to create rewarding jobs and ensure an appropriate work-life balance

☐ How to develop a positive psychological contract

☐ How to reward achievement, excellence and enterprise

☐ How to introduce succession planning for management.

Armstrong (2011) further states that developing and implementing a talent management strategy requires good leadership and support from senior management, including HR managers.

According to the Chartered Institute of Personnel and Development (2015c), the key issues when developing a talent management strategy are to closely align the talent management strategy with the corporate strategy; to decide whether an 'inclusive', 'exclusive' or hybrid approach to talent is adopted; to decide who is involved (employees and managers); and to consider the four areas of the 'talent management loop' (attracting talent, developing talent, managing talent and tracking and evaluating talent).

According to Baum (2008), given that most hospitality and tourism organisations operate in a weak and complex labour market, there is a need for firms to adopt creative approaches to talent identification and acknowledgement; to have an inclusive approach towards talent; to invest in training and development for all staff; and to improve working conditions. Implementing an effective talent management strategy for hospitality and tourism businesses is crucial given its benefits. These include improved employee retention, enhanced employee engagement and better financial performance (Hughes and Rog, 2008).

Having discussed strategic talent management, the next section will provide a conclusion to the chapter and discuss future perspectives.

Conclusion and future perspectives

This chapter opend with a discussion of strategy and strategic management. This was necessary as strategic human resource management and strategic talent management are based on principles of strategic management. Essentially, companies achieve competitive advantage by following a strategy based on differentiation of their products and services, or focusing on low cost. Whichever strategy is followed, a firm must use its resources effectively to help it achieve competitive advantage. These will only help the company gain advantage if they are valuable, inimitable and non-substitutable (Paauwe and Boon, 2009). Increasingly, firms have the same technology, similar products and services and physical assets. What differentiates one firm from another are its human resources. To fully capitalise on its human capital, a firm will need to nurture its talent. A strategic approach to talent management will help an organisation take a pro-active approach, identifying what human resources it needs in the future to be competitive.

Al Ariss, Cascio and Paauwe (2014) state that the landscape for talent management will change drastically in the next 5 to 10 years and foresee these trends:

- ☐ Talent which is globally abundant but locally scarce
- ☐ Depending on the demographic context, ageing of the population
- ☐ More differences, as well as similarities, across different generations at work
- ☐ Different attitudes to work as more people work remotely and virtually
- ☐ New ways of working and new relationships between those supplying talent and those using talent

TM and STM will certainly continue to evolve and develop. The future is uncertain, but the search for talent will continue to grow in importance. To achieve sustainable competitive advantage, hospitality and tourism organisations will need more effective talent management, not just operationally but also strategically.

Learning activities

1   For a firm of your choice, evaluate the generic strategy followed (cost leadership, differentiation, cost focus and differentiation focus) and assess how this strategy might affect the firm's approach to HRM, in general, and talent management, more specifically.

2   In relation to the hospitalityindustry, examine whether 'best-fit' or 'best-practice' models of strategic HRM are more effective. How might a hospitality organisation develop a strategic approach to manage its talent?

3   Assess the advantages and disadvantages of using an 'inclusive', 'exclusive' or 'hybrid' approach to managing talent in a hospitality business.

4   Evaluate how hospitality firms might approach strategic talent management in ten years' time.

References

Al Ariss, A., Cascio, W. F. and Paauwe, J. (2014). Talent management: Current theories and future research directions, *Journal of World Business*, **49**(2), 173-179.

Alleyne,P. A., Greenidge, D., Corbin, A., Alleyne,P. G. and Devonish, D. (2008). The practice of HRM and SHRM in the Barbados hotel sector. *Journal of Human Resources in Hospitality & Tourism*, **7**(2), 219-240.

Armstrong, M. (2011). *Armstrong's Handbook of Strategic Human Resource Management*, 5th Edition, London: Kogan Page Ltd.

Ashton, C. and Morton, L. (2005). Managing talent for competitive advantage: Taking a systemic approach to talent management. *Strategic HR Review*, **4**(5), 28-31.

Baptiste, R., Bailey, V. (2003). The status of strategic human resource management in Trinidad and Tobago. *Journal of Eastern Caribbean Studies*, **28** (1), 1–16.

Barney, J. B. (2002). *Gaining and Sustaining Competitive Advantage*, 2nd Edition, Upper Saddle River: Prentice Hall.

Barney, J. and Hesterly, W. (2010). *Strategic Management and Competitive Advantage: Concepts and Cases*, 3rd Edition, Pearson: Upper Saddle River.

Barney, J. and Hesterly, W. (2012). *Strategic Management and Competitive Advantage: Concepts*, 4th Edition, Upper Saddle River: Pearson.

Baum, T. (2008). Implications of hospitality and tourism labour markets for talent management strategies. *International Journal of Contemporary Hospitality Management*, **20**(7), 720-729.

Beardwell, J. and Claydon, T. (2007). *Human Resource Management: A contemporary approach*, 5th Edition, Harlow: Pearson Education.

Beechler, S. and Woodward, I. C. (2009). The global 'war for talent'. *Journal of International Management*, **15**(3), 273-285.

Boxall, P. and Purcell, J. (2000). Strategic human resource management: Where have we come from and where should we be going?. *International Journal of Management Reviews*, **2**(2), 183-203.

Boxall, P. and J. Purcell (2008.) *Strategy and Human Resource Management*, 2nd Edition, Basigstoke: Palgrave Macmillan.

Chartered Institute of Personnel and Development (2005). HR Strategy: Creating the Framework for Successful People Management, CIPD. Available at www.cipd.co.uk. Accessed 05.01.15.

Chartered Institute of Personnel and Development (2015a). HR Business Partnering', CIPD. Available at www.cipd.co.uk. Accessed 09.04.16.

Chartered Institute of Personnel and Development (2015b). Strategic human resource management, CIPD. Available at www.cipd.co.uk. Accessed 09.04.16.

Chartered Institute of Personnel and Development (2015c). Talent management: an overview, CIPD. Available at www.cipd.co.uk. Accessed 07.04.16.

Chartered Institute of Personnel and Development (2015d). The role of line managers in HR, CIPD. Available at www.cipd.co.uk. Accessed 09.04.16.

Chuai, X., Preece, D. and Iles, P. (2008). Is talent management just 'old wine in new bottles'?: The case of multinational companies in Beijing. *Management Research News,* **31**(12), 901-911.

Collings, D. G. and Mellahi, K. (2009) Strategic talent management: A review and research agenda, *Human Resource Management Review,* **19**(4),304-313.

Darwish, T. K. (2013) *Strategic HRM and Performance: Theory and practice.* 1st Edition, Newcastle upon Tyne: Cambridge Scholars Publishing.

David, F. (2011) *Strategic Management: Concepts and Cases (Global Edition),* 13th Edition, Upper Saddle River: Pearson.

Davidson, M., McPhail, R. and Barry, S. (2011) Hospitality HRM: Past, present and the future, *International Journal of Contemporary Hospitality Management,* **23**(4) 498-516.

De Wit, B. and Meyer, R. (2014) *Strategy: An International Perspective,* 5th Edition, Andover: Cengage Learning.

Dries, N. (2013). The psychology of talent management: A review and research agenda., *Human Resource Management Review,* **23**(4), 272-285.

Enz, C.A. (2010), *Hospitality Strategic Management Concepts and Cases,* 2nd Edition, Hoboken: John Wiley & Sons Inc.

Fleisher, C. S. and Bensoussan, B. E. (2003) *Strategic and Competitive Analysis: Methods and techniques for analyzing business competition,* 1st Edition, Upper Saddle River: Pearson.

Foot, M., Hook, C. and Jenkins, A. (2016) *Introducing Human Resource Management,* 7th Edition, Harlow: Pearson.

Groysberg, B., Nanda, A .and Nohria, N. (2004). The risky business of hiring stars. *Harvard Business Review,* **82**(5), 92–101.

Guest, D., Storey, J. and W. Tate (1997). *Innovation: Opportunity through People.* Consultative Document. Institute of Personnel and Development, June.

Hughes, J. C. and Rog, E. (2008). Talent management: A strategy for improving employee recruitment, retention and engagement within hospitality organisations. *International Journal of Contemporary Hospitality Management,* **20**(7), 743-757.

Hutchinson, S. and Purcell, J. (2003). *Bringing Policies to Life: the Vital Role of Front Line Managers in People Management,* London: CIPD.

Johnson, G., Whittington, R., Angwin, D., Regner: and Scholes, R. (2014) *Exploring strategy,*10th Edition, Harlow: Pearson Education Limited.

Jones, J. T., Whitaker, M., Seet,P. and Parkin, J. (2012). Talent management in practice in Australia: Individualistic or strategic? an exploratory study. *Asia Pacific Journal of Human Resources,* **50**(4), 399-420.

Joyce, W. F. and Slocum, J. W. (2012). Top management talent, strategic capabilities, and firm performance. *organisational Dynamics,* **41**(3),. 183-193.

Kaufman, B. E. (2015). The RBV theory foundation of strategic HRM: Critical flaws, problems for research and practice, and an alternative economics paradigm. *Human Resource Management Journal*, **25**(4), 516-540.

King, K. A. (2016). The talent deal and journey: Understanding how employees respond to talent identification over time. *Employee Relations*, **38**(1), 94-111.

Kusluvan, S., Kusluvan, Z., Ilhan, I. and Buyruk, L. (2010). The human dimension: A review of human resources management issues in the tourism and hospitality industry, *Cornell Hospitality Quarterly*, **51**(2), 171-214.

Lengnick-Hall, M. L., Lengnick-Hall, C. A., Andrade, L. S. and Drake, B. (2009). Strategic human resource management: The evolution of the field. *Human Resource Management Review*, **19**(2),64-85.

Lynch, R. (2012). *Strategic Management*, 6ᵀᴴ Edition, Harlow: Pearson Education Limited.

Marchington, M. and A. Wilkinson (2005). *Human Resource Management at Work: People Management and Development*, 3rd Edition, London: CIPD.

Marler, J. H. and Fisher, S. L. (2013). An evidence-based review of e-HRM and strategic human resource management. *Human Resource Management Review*, **23**(1), 18-36.

McDonnell, A., Lamare, R., Gunnigle, P. and Lavelle, J. (2010) Developing tomorrow's leaders – Evidence of global talent management in multinational enterprises, *Journal of World Business*, **45**(2), 150-160.

Millmore, M.P., Lewis, M. Saunders, A. Thornhill and T. Morrow (2007) *Strategic Human Resource Management: Contemporary Issues*, 1ˢᵗ Edition, Harlow: Financial Times Prentice Hall.

Millmore, M. (2007) *Strategic Human Resource Management: Contemporary issues*, 1ˢᵗ Edition, Harlow: Pearson Education.

Murphy, N. (2009).Talent management's role in a time of recession. *IRS Employment Review 927*. Available at www.xperthr.co.uk. Accessed 05.01.15.

Newhall, S. (2012). A global approach to talent management. *Human Resource Management International Digest*, **20**(6), 31-34.

Okumus, F., Altinay, L. and Chathoth: (2010). *Strategic Management for Hospitality and Tourism*, 1ˢᵗ Edition, Oxford: Butterworth Heinemann.

Paauwe, J. (2004). *HRM and performance: Achieving long-term viability*, 1ˢᵗ Edition, Oxford: Oxford University Press.

Paauwe and Boon (2009). Strategic HRM: A critical review, in Collings, D. G., and Wood, G. (Eds.) (2009). *Human Resource Management: A critical approach*, Abingdon: Routledge Ltd.: 38-54.

Paauwe, J., Boon, C., Boselie: and den Hartog, D. (2012). Reconceptualizing fit in strategic human resource management: Lost in translation?' In Guest, D. E., Paauwe, J., and Wright, P. (Eds.) *HRM and Performance: Achievements and challenges*, Hoboken: Wiley: 61-78.

Pilbeam, S. and Corbridge, M. (2010). *People Resourcing and Talent Planning: HRM in practice*, 4th Edition, Harlow: Pearson Education.

6

Porter, M. E. (1980). *Competitive strategy: Techniques for analyzing industries and competitors,* 1st Edition, New York: The Free Press.

Ready, D.A. and J.A. Conger (2007) Make your company a talent factory, *Harvard Business Review,* June, 68–77.

Saunders, M., Millmore, M. and Lewis: (2007) *Strategic Human Resource Management,* 1st Edition, Harlow: Financial Times/ Prentice Hall.

Smethurst, S. (2005). HR roles: the long and winding road. *People Management,* 28 July, 25–29.

Spender, J., Kraaijenbrink, J. and Groen, A. J. (2010). The resource-based view: A review and assessment of its critiques, *Journal of Management,* **36**(1), 349-372.

Thompson, J., Scott, J. and Martin, F. (2014). *Strategic Management: Awareness and change,* 7th Edition, Andover: Cengage Learning.

Thunnissen, M. (2016). Talent management: For what, how and how well? an empirical exploration of talent management in practice. *Employee Relations,* **38**(1), 57-72.

Thunnissen, M., Fruytier, B. G. M. and Boselie,P. (2013). Talent management and the relevance of context: Towards a pluralistic approach, *Human Resource Management Review,* **23**(4), 326-336.

Tyson, S. (2012). *Essentials of Human Resource Management,* 5th Edition, Oxford: Butterworth Heinemann.

Vaiman, V., and Collings, D. G. (2013). Talent management: Advancing the field. *The International Journal of Human Resource Management,* **24**(9), 1737-1743.

Wheelen, T. and Hunger, J. (2010). *Concepts in Strategic Management and Business Policy: Achieving Sustainability,* 13th Edition, Upper Saddle River: Pearson.

Wooldridge, A. (2006). A survey of talent. *The Economist,* 7 October: 3–20.

7 The Cultural and Occupational Roles Attributed to 'Trust' in Talent Management

Derek Cameron

Learning objectives

This chapter provides:

- An explanation of talent and trust expressed through cultural complexity using in-group organisational and out-group occupational processes

- An application of talent recognition through the concept of cultural mutual-equivalence based on trusting beliefs as to what is valuable for the organisation and occupation

- An assessment of motivational considerations in the workplace and the assertion that talent potential should be a developmental process, inclusive to all

- An analysis of trust and talent through the influence of corporate values and human resource policies

- An examination of talent and connotations of trust to problematic scenarios based on operational *push-pull* realities given to an organisational climate subjected to the management and development of change.

After reading this chapter you will be able to:

- Reflect on the importance of trust and trusting beliefs to applications of talent management

- Understand the relationship of in-group, out-group processes through the concept of cultural mutual-equivalence

- Discuss cultural complexity within organisations in the deployment of talent management

- Observe problematic dilemmas of talent and trust brought about by the management change from the perspective of HR management and the labour market.

Introduction

This chapter considers the significance of 'trust' in talent management and assesses its critical nature through cultural and occupational roles, by observing group dynamics within the social framework of mutual-equivalence. Positive forms of trusting beliefs can create an organisational climate that conveys a sense of confidence. This in turn, could inspire generative learning and an innate driving force for talent to manifest itself throughout an organisation's workforce. Notwithstanding, realities of work-life balance and the management of change could, for example in recessionary times, impede notions of mistrust, replacing confidence with some degree of suspicion. By implication this could cause reduced productivity and talent potential. Managing social diversity or unpredictability to on-going organisational dilemmas can be assisted when observed within a cultural setting of in-group (e.g. organisation), out-group (e.g. occupations) processes. Using an applied concept known as mutual-equivalence (Wallace, [1961], ed.1964), an analytical insight could assess positive or negative *push-pull* environmental and operational behaviours such as, for example, a 'recession push' vs. 'prosperity pull' (e.g. Brünjes and Diez, 2013). Such social perceptions (and others) could affect opportunities for talent acquisition or create or inhibit inspired aspirations amongst employees, for which trust would be an important variable to consider.

Trust and talent: in-group, out-group cultural complexity

The question of talent relative to work-performance can be seen as an occupational affiliation with that of corporate culture. From a socio-cultural perspective, organisations are functional entities whose role is to serve society. Applied to the hotel industry, organisations can provide talent opportunities for occupational out-groups; for example, an aspiring chef can play out a quasi-professional role as an occupational member within an in-group (e.g. an organisational culture and its corporate identity). This relationship can be of a reciprocal nature (Cameron *et al.*,1999; Cameron, 2001). An organisational climate could alternatively be adversarial to less positive forms of trusting beliefs where, for example, there could be a sense '...*that management is not making wise or even prudent decisions*' (Shaw 1997: 45). Where there is such an effect on trust, this will invariably affect talent and its potential for organisational development. An example of mistrust (e.g. the lack of confidence) among occupational group members can create a work climate of suspicion in an organisation. Moreover, discourses attributed to distrust (e.g. to have no confidence) can intensify organisational low-trust perceptions to suspicions of disbelief and cynicism (Warnock-Smith *et al.*, 2016).

In contrast, fundamental to corporate policies and practices, there should therefore notably be an avoidance of motivational loss. This could be achieved by addressing issues of commitment and trust to what is mutually 'valuable'

(Becker, 1960) to both the in-group and out-group(s). Talent attributed to shared trusting beliefs among occupational members and a corporate organisation provides an interesting premise when observed through the conceptual framework of cultural 'mutual-equivalence' (Wallace, [1961] ed.1964). A key component of this theory resides in the principle *'that societies are held together by an organisation of diversity'* (Wallace 1985: 24). As an applied concept, mutual-equivalence confers self-percept to an individual's social-concept that is, for example, through a series of in-group/out-group(s) consensuses that are attributed to cultural norms, practices and values. These are based on standardised cognition but not necessarily cognitive sharing (Wallace [1961] ed.1964: 40) where performance outcomes are culturally beneficial for the occupation (e.g. from the perspective of self–achievement, personal development) and for the organisation (e.g. corporate identity and good reputation). In short, organisations can be talent management gateways for an individual to be inspired through a cultural representation of occupational outgroup identity. Moreover, the management of group dynamics can assist in maintaining adaptive strategies-in-use and competence-base functions that effectively engage in human capital and knowledge. Related to the principle of a learning organisation, knowledge learned can and should culturally transcend, disperse and defuse as an accumulation of internalised tacit knowledge. Subsequently, the tacit process (in the form of knowledge) would need to externalise and transform to a mind-set of business strategy.

In short, organisations are systemised processes resembling outcomes of tacit and explicit knowledge, transformed to represent products and services (e.g. Saint-Onge (1996), Leroy and Ramanantsoa (1997), Haldin-Herrgard 2000, Becker 2001). In essence, the process of what has been learned, albeit developmental or otherwise, should be a reciprocal process. For example, strategically a learning organisation is capable of synergising knowledge processes with those of opportunities for innovation. Likewise for occupational groups, a learning organisation allows for career progression such as for example, developmental opportunities for aspiring chefs (Cameron, 2001), or waiters and pursers on board cruise-ships (Dennett *et al.*, 2014). To elaborate briefly, Senge (1990) sees a 'learning organisation' as operationally representing:

> '...shift in the mind-set of employees to readily foster generative learning and ultimately, a personal mastery of their job...employees, often inspired by leaders, work in multi-functional teams and are invariably encouraged to see the company, its environment and its systems as a whole rather than in parts'

> (cited in: Cameron, *et al.*, 1999: 227).

Put simply, a high performing learning organisation infers constant renewal as it evolves and innovates and therefore, can be the bedrock for talent management within in-group and out-group processes.

Trusting beliefs, behaviours and talent

Shaw (1997), cited in Caproni ed. (2012: 84), perceptively observed: *'the importance of trust becomes clear when we try to imagine a world without it'*. Trusting beliefs and behaviours more often rely on the confidence of others. To reiterate, this can be conveyed by social categorisation to forms of group dynamics. In the employment world, this is invariably expressed by the culture and identity of occupational and organisational work systems and subsequently transmitted to an affiliation of norms, practices, policies and procedures. The trustor, in this case the employee, and the trustee in a typical organisation is likely to be the basis for psychological *'propensity'* given to *'perceived risk'* as an association that develops with components of *'ability, benevolence and integrity'* and; where a *'relationship is likely to alter the relative importance of the factors of trustworthiness'* (Mayer *et al.* (1995: 715-722). In other words, the notion of trustworthiness would need to be manifested in commitment such as an *'identification [of] pride in the organisation [and] the internalisation of the organisation's goals and values'* (Cook and Wall 1980: 40). The aforementioned, when observed, could infer an alignment with the cognitive sharing that would involve the inclusion of occupational values. Notably, the representation in some literature tries to draw the concepts of trust and talent more closely together to characteristics such as *'loyalty and integrity'* with themes relative to *'congruence between individual and organisational values and the role of organisational culture in retaining and attracting talented people'* (Martins and von der Ohe, 2002: 56). Other perspectives link trust to issues of corporate social responsibility as a management tool for *'...combining talents to better processes...'* (Rok and Mulej, 2014: 358). Moreover, in a recent survey *'high-trust companies are far more likely than low-trust companies to have highly engaged and involved workforces and better employee retention ...[when]... leaders prioritize policies to talent acquisition and retention...'* (Atkins 2014/2015: 15). A consensus suggests that the underlining concept of trust and talent needs to be synergised. This can be enacted upon by a work-engagement and involvement being relative to confidence. Here, self-esteem, and esteem from others where work-outcomes are to be competence-based, would be important criteria to consider if talent management is to thrive.

In a review given to hospitality and tourism issues, Kusluvan *et al.* (2010) observed skills (amongst others) to be more effectively employed when organisations demonstrate transparent-functionalist attributes based on: a *'high-trust culture'* (p.185) where for example; *'...jobs with employees characteristics, needs, and talents...'* (p.197) have been effectively realised within human resource policies and procedures. Further research suggests high trust organisations are better able to deploy and develop talent to *'capabilities levering the power of collaborative action'* that effectively aligns employee engagement with strategies of high performance (Dunki, 2009: 63). On a similar sentiment, recent research purports a need for employee engagement to *'actively'* transcend to *'involvement'*, thereby allowing *'opportunities for employees to give their input and/or participate in the decisions that affect them'* (Atkins 2014/2015: 19). It is worth noting that a collaborative approach has the potential to interact with reciprocal processes based on occupational and organisational value systems which moreover, provide the presumption for Wallace's [1961], (ed.1964) conception of 'mutual-equivalence'. For example, Atkins (2014/15: 13), give emphasis on 'why we trust' to 'any one of three primary reasons which attributes to a trusting belief mind-set – namely:

1   consistency, predictability and quality of people's work and actions;

2   confidence that they are focused on achieving shared goals;

3   expectations associated with a person's role in the organization.'

Talent, trust and cultural mutual-equivalence

Concepts of talent can be observed through the centuries. Themes afforded to the contemporary refer to examples of 'talent as an object' (e.g. performance related to organisational benchmarks such as: ability, knowledge, competence, capability, etc.) and 'talent as a subject' (e.g. aspiring, achieving individuals, etc.), which when unrecognised or mismanaged can operationally collide (see Gallardo-Gallardo *et al.*, 2013: 293 and Iles, 2013). Organisational policy shifts in times of economic downturn can be detrimental to successful talent management programmes. The need for personal growth expressed through cultural-occupational identity (e.g. talent as a subject) could become compromised if corporate survival reverts to short-term policy tactics. For example, not too distant from recent economic times, the *Economist* (Kellaway 2009: 140) in the advent of the much published credit crunch, predicted corporate boardrooms in 2009 will be *'less of vision and much more of value'*. To elaborate, Kellaway (2009: 140) speculated that *'..."talent" will be a word we wave goodbye to … In 2009 the word "staff" will make a comeback, as will "headcount"'*. For talent to flourish, organisations would need to internalise the instrumental worth of 'talent as an object' whereby competence owned by the organisation needs to align more closely with 'talent as a subject', i.e., to competencies owned by individuals and expressed through their occupations. Moreover, reciprocal in-group, out-group homogeneity (e.g. Brewer, 1993) can operationally facilitate the interplay with cultural mutual-equivalence. This can be achieved when corporations proactively support quasi-professional needs expressed through occupational identity. To capture talent, organisational processes would therefore need to be synonymous with inclusive and developable talent management philosophies (e.g. Meyers and van Woerkom, 2014) and arguably, be less exclusive of others.

Meyers and van Woerkom (2014:192) speak of talent resembling *'salient tension concerns'* referred to as either 'exclusiveness' or 'inclusiveness' in disposition. Within this setting, exclusiveness can refer to organisational needs and therefore becomes a metaphor for ownership (i.e. talent as an object). In contrast, inclusiveness takes the assumption that talent is the ownership of the individual and their affiliation to their quasi-profession and occupation. However, where a reciprocal relationship is fragile, for example through weak human resource – personnel functions, then there is likely to be competing tensions between occupational and organisational cultural values. Hofstede (1994) observed that when it comes to cultural values people are likely to be more strongly attached to their occupation than to any one organisation. Research suggests accumulated *side bets* proposed by Becker (1960), such as for example, an occupational calculus for career progression, are important for chefs working in 4-5 star hotels (Cameron 2004). Moreover, chefs tended to be more behaviourally committed to the organisation where they worked, reserving stronger cultural values by way of attitudinal commitment to occupational membership (Cameron 2004).

The intensity of what is intrinsically 'valuable' (Becker, 1960) to the cultural values of an occupation can hold strong motivational prospects attributed to valence. For example, Lewin speaks of the importance of valence and comments *'anyone who wishes to influence likes and dislikes has to be aware of the change in valence'* (Lewin [1951], (ed.1963: 79) cited in Cameron *et al.*, 1999: 231). Similarly, the term 'equivalence' proposed by Wallace [1961], (ed.1964) is closely related to valence within expectancy theory. Put simply, mutual-equivalence seeks to relate cultural ideational symbolic interpretation to material relationships. Wallace [1961], (ed. 1964: 32) equates symbol '...*as a reasonable interpretation of the logical relationship of material implication'*. In Figure 7.1, this is referred to as representing *'primary and secondary equivalence structure'* (Wallace [1961], ed.1964: 31).

Mutual-equivalence

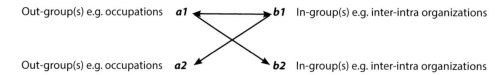

Figure 7.1: Cameron (2004) based on Wallace's [1961] (ed. 1964) Model for mutual-equivalence adapted to incorporate in-groups, out-groups.

Symbolic forms will invariably interact and identify with synchronic components of the socio-cultural system, such as the need for innovation within forms of group dynamics. Hence, both primary and secondary equivalence structures form the basis of a mutual-equivalence. By way of conceptual transfer, this can be achieved by identifying *'sets of valuables with which side bets can be made'* (Becker 1960: 39). If we were to use as an example that of the quasi-professional chef, it is likely that they would see their craft in terms of an art and science. Contextually, this is likely to be exceeded by passion based on the work-related skills, in which they would need to excel. In contrast, for a hotel corporation, what is valuable (Becker, 1960) would contextually be the corporate identity, its reputation and competitive advantage. Based on this premise, a hotel corporation would be party to and dependant on high-performing talented out-groups, such as in this example, the occupation of chefs. When applied to Figure 7.1, *a1* and *a2* could be related to the occupation of chefs, and *b1* and *b2* to the hotel/organisation where they work.

Here, Wallace [1961], (ed. 1964: 32) comments '...*we may interpret acts a1 and b1 as instrumental acts*' (primary equivalence structure) e.g. goal-setting an expectancy set by occupational and organisational values and *a2* and *b2* as '*consummatory acts*' (secondary equivalence structure), e.g. a pathway towards consuming. Equated to 'talent as an object' (*b2*) there would be a need to demonstrate instrumental worth with out-group occupational values (*b1*) should in-group organisational goal-setting and performance satisfy an alignment to talent, i.e. both as an object and subject. From a motivational perspective, trusting beliefs would need to embrace features of talent through a psychological state, attributed to personal self-esteem and organisational esteem from others. Here, the capacity and opportunity to perform, when applied to Figure 7.1, should be 'inclusive' (rather than exclusive), 'stable' and 'developmental' (Meyers and van Woerkom, 2014) with in-group organisational facilitations (i.e. talent as an object) that are attributed to out-group occupations (i.e. talent as a subject).

A study of tourist hotels in Taiwan identified a lack of trust as an issue that invariably stifled opportunities for management and supervisors to effectively utilise or develop talented staff (Yang *et al.*, (2012). Similarly a study in Turkey noted perceptions of talent management and organisational trust to be higher in 5-star hotels compared to those in 4-star hotels (Altınöz *et al.*, 2013). An emerging theme indicates a need for transparency that includes a 'culture of trust' with 'differentiated' potential among workers in talent management (Kovack, online 2015). Interestingly, the term 'differentiated' infers a need for the realisation for self-esteem and esteem from others. This should be where individuals as employees consume mutual-equivalence as an instrumental process.

Talent and the socio-cultural context

The argument here is for talent philosophies for business organisations to be all-inclusive to out-groups. In short, organisational culture needs to be viewed beyond a unitary cultural mind-set by avoiding the exclusion (partially or otherwise) of sub-cultures in decision-making processes. For example, the social concept for career development to given out-groups should be reciprocally embraced by the in-group to avoid unitary cultural traits. In a similar vein, Transley *et al.*, (2013: 228) state that '...*there should be more of a focus on talent and their work, with particular regard to both the employment and work relationship*'. Notably, Herzberg (1974), in a presentation given to business executives, expressed the motivational aspirations of employees, in which Herzberg gave representational voice on behalf of workers by stating: '*treat me the way I am, not the way you need me to be*'. This observation suggests management should not wittingly or unwittingly stifle a passion or aptitude for excelling talent but rather, in the language of Herzberg (1974), '*give people the opportunity to use their ability*' for which '*all jobs should be a learning experience - a growth experience, inherent in the job*'. To some degree, the sentiment of Herzberg still rings true today, for it is interesting to observe Fernández-Aráoz's

(2014) viewpoint in talent spotting for the 21st century in which the author discusses the need for *'the right kind of motivation'* (p.51), *'the ability to adapt'* (p.49) to *'grow into increasingly complex roles and environments'* (p.49) grouped to *'share organisation's core values'* (p.53). Organisational cultural values would therefore need to transcend to a workable vision and to a reality that embraces an ideation of cultural sharing, based on mutuality with occupational out-groups. Arguably this represents a process that cannot be assumed but one that needs to be worked upon through systemised processes of mutual-equivalence. This would require shared core values of a reciprocal and seamless nature replicating in-group, out-group homogeneity.

Talent and trust aligned to corporate values and vision

In more recent times companies have placed greater emphasis on the importance of *corporate values* for which the *corporate vision* is used as a communication and motivational tool for ensuring positive forms of emotional engagement to workforce practices. Moreover, a firm's *corporate vision* for most organisations embeds policies of corporate strategy for which *the vision* is required to be enduring and equally adaptable to embrace 'disruptive technologies' (e.g. Wessel and Christensen, 2012). For talent and trust to excel, a firm's *corporate values* transcended to the *corporate vision* would therefore need to necessitate a diffusion of mutually-shared occupational values. To reiterate, this infers moving away from a unitary cultural concept to a diversified mutual-cultural concept in which *corporate values* share ethical and moral standing embedded by processes of corporate citizenship, corporate governance and corporate social responsibility. As a series of processes, they bring together a social community context expressed by *corporate identity* where trust and talent are better empowered to flourish and synergise through workforce practices.

Trust and talent: human resource policies and the labour market

Retaining trust and talent in a climate of economic austerity creates operational and strategic challenges for most corporate organisations. In particular, this can become problematic for firms who tend to practise weak HR–personnel functions alongside a weak internal labour market, where often there exist reoccurring skill shortages. This invariably leads a firm to rely on the external labour market thereby placing greater cost on training budgets. By way of comparison, a strong internal labour market infers entry is restricted by employers to people who have the appropriate professional skills, competence-based knowledge and the potential for talent acquisition. This creates a primary labour force that is specific to an industry, for example, the hotel industry (Simms *et al.*, 1988). Markedly, in times of austerity, a situation sometimes transpires where in the case of a strong internal labour market, the supply of labour exceeds demand for certain occupational skills. As a consequence, firms can be tempted to engage in weak HR–personnel functions. This can create a lack of opportunity for personal development (temporary or otherwise) for existing employees leading to a negative 'sunk cost' (McGee and Ford, 1987). When workers are faced with a lack of alternatives then this could create a sense of job insecurity and a socio-climate that leads towards low-trust in the organisation they work for. In the context of mutual-equivalence this may create a work-environment of mistrust through a lack of confidence, where the inspiration to excel one's talent could be unwittingly compromised. In a similar vein, Cappelli (2015: 59) commented in observations made in the United States, that *'with the effects of the Great Recession of 2008 still lingering, most people with jobs aren't jumping ship yet, so executives feel no urgent need for HR programs. HR must make a case for them'*.

Whether organisations operate within the characteristics of a strong or weak labour market, day-to-day HR–personnel functions have an important socio-cultural functional role that is ultimately determined by the core values of an organisation. Notably in past recessions, a sentiment '*...not to cut back on training...*' was held by Horst Schulze, the founding President and Chief Operating Officer of The Ritz-Carlton Hotel Company and recipient of the 1992 and 1999 prestigious Malcolm Baldrige National Quality Award. Notwithstanding, organisations in times of recession, will in all probability most likely apply stringent financial controls to employment policies. By implication this will put pressure on traditional work practices, a notable characteristic commonly documented in previous recessions (e.g., Arron, 1992; Cameron 2001, 2009). Should there be a low priority for talent within a corporate vision, then this will invariably affect trusting beliefs among employees. Related to a need for adaptive strategies-in-use Cappelli (2015: 61) comments *'one of traditional HR's biggest difficulties has been supporting business strategy, because it's such a moving target these days'* noting that *'companies seldom have long-term plans with straightforward talent requirements'*. To summarise, policies rest on assumption about how companies engage with the necessities of numerical, financial and functional flexibility and their use of the internal and external labour market (Atkinson 1984). Nonetheless, a key function for embracing talent would be to go beyond the basis of the labour market with a proactive view of 'retooling HR' and with a commitment *'to take time to manage talent that is not part of the elite group'* (Boudreau 2013: 288) but arguably, inclusive to all workers.

Unfortunately, breakdowns in trust commonly occur in times of recession where capital presides over labour in a 'functional-structural' form (e.g. Radcliff-Brown (1952), Allaire and Firsirotu (1984)), which is positivistic in nature for objective radical pursuits and processes based on efficiency drives. Notably, literature on trust, mistrust and distrust provides some essential features on the 'psychological state' of workers in their contractual relationship with their employer. In the case of Fraher and Gabriel's (2014) study on US airline pilots in the decade after 9/11, the frequent lay-offs that occurred led to high levels of distrust among those pilots who were affected. In a similar vein, levels of trust, when compromised, can have a varied impact on an employee's psychological state and resultant behaviour across a range of on-going organisational dilemmas. For example, in an earlier case related to corporate downsizing. Fraher (2013) observed discourses of mistrust among airline pilots causing amongst other things, some adverse effects on organisational commitment.

As a cultural and identity construct, the behaviour of some occupations can at times overtly portray discourses that resemble an 'affinity' characterised by ethnocentrism (Cameron *et al.*, 1999: 227). Notably, a play on corporate ethnocentrism can also be used to assist the promotion of a product or brand. For example, the iconic and talented Rupert D'Oyly Carte [1876-1948] commented in 1930, '*The Savoy is always up-to-date and, if possible, a little ahead*' (Cameron, 2009: 4; Savoy, 2009). This quotation was used in 2009 as part of a marketing strategy by Fairmont Hotels and Resorts to keep The Savoy (London) visible prior to launching the hotel's reopening after major restoration, which took place from 15th December, 2007 until 10th October, 2010 (Savoy, 2016). This example amplifies the value of talent noted by a documented speech given by Rupert D'Oyly Carte from the *past* and used as a marketing tool for the *present*. On arguably a not dissimilar sentiment, corporate policies in the *present-future* need to be more assertive on the call for *strong* as opposed to *weak* HR–personnel functions in the promotion of inclusive talent management philosophies. This was noted in Dennett *et al.* (2014: 492), which goes some way to embracing the conceptual modelling proposed by Etzioni (2011: 1111) for which, '*there should evolve through emotional engagement, an embracement of cultural mutual-equivalence that is fundamentally shaped by organisational and occupational "normative and effective choices"'*.

Organisational realities: organisational push-pull in a climate of managing change

Linked to push-pull theory, cultural mutual-equivalence can be a useful concept in understanding the occupational potential of trust in talent management. Case study research by Maqsood, Walker and Finegen (2007: 98) in the context of facilitating knowledge, identified the importance of the group-concept. As an applied concept, the authors view 'knowledge processes' (p.98) as an important operational activity to outcomes which facilitate '*integrating shared understanding and mutual adjustment*' in the management of organisational change. Moreover, they refer to '*culture providing a means to interpret and share insights [to] internal knowledge building [with conceptual] push and pull*' (p. 98). Perceptions of trust and opportunities for talent recognition can become powerful behavioural tools when applied to an operational context and attached to an industry's socio-cultural and strategic environment (such as, for example, the hospitality industry). To reiterate, the socio-cultural system, by corporate representation, exists to serve society for which it is required to have a functional fit (e.g. Burrell and Morgan 1979). This will inevitably place on-going *push-pull* challenges for management in the planning and development of change. For example, related to a given context, levels of job security (McAulaya, Zeitz and Blau (2006: 571), given to 'push and pull theory' can suggest that '*job insecurity does not automatically* push *the employee toward professional commitment, but rather that such commitment stems from the* pull *of perceived occupational professionalization*'. To summarise, Table 7.1 highlights scenario settings of *push-pull* based on positive and negative environmental and operational dilemmas such as intervening case variables brought about by capital over labour.

Cultural mutual-equivalence, potentials of trust and talent management

- ☐ **Positive scenario:** PUSH (talent potential inclusive to all workers) PULL (opportunities for personal growth and career development for all workers).

  Talent potential supported by strong HR–personnel functions designed to facilitate inclusive opportunities for personal growth and career development for all workers: trusting beliefs are likely to be causal to the work environment, giving workers a sense of confidence in trusting beliefs where for example, all jobs are a learning experience in an organisational climate, which permits talent to excel.

  Resulting factor: inclusive forms of cultural mutual-equivalence by processes of in-group, out-group homogeneity.

- ☐ **Negative scenario**: PUSH (talent exclusive to few workers) PULL (opportunity for personal development of only the few).

  Talent potential using strong HR–personnel functions designed to facilitate exclusive opportunities for personal growth and career development for only a minority of workers: trusting beliefs are likely to be causal to a work environment that initiates a lack of confidence for the majority of workers due to lack of opportunity for personal growth and career development (e.g. negative *push-pull* initiated by the organisation for the majority of workers). This is likely to create an organisational climate of mistrust or even distrust for workers who have been excluded. Moreover, this could be further compounded should there exist negative 'sunk cost' due to a lack of alternatives for occupational members to find employment elsewhere.

  Resulting factor: restricted forms of cultural mutual-equivalence by processes of in-group, out-group heterogeneity.

- ☐ **Scenario for labour, capital and economic constraints:** PUSH (e.g. labour over capital) PULL (e.g. economic constraints). Scenarios given to strong or weak personnel functions and the interplay between a strong and/or weak internal labour market and the external labour market.

Resulting factors: policies curtailed by moral and ethical principles ascribed to:

- strategies,
- longevity and sustainability,
- innovation,
- the management of disruption,
- maintaining competitive advantage,
- leadership expressed within the cultural values and vision and adaptive decision making processes of the corporation.

Table 7.1: Push-Pull in given scenarios.

Conclusion

Positive forms of trusting beliefs aligned to the potential for talent can be effectively attributed to mutual-equivalence based on socio- and ideational cultural value systems given to organisational in-group, and occupational out-group processes. A behavioural element for avoiding motivation-loss is recognising talent with an opportunity for occupational members to use their ability. This goes to suggest (amongst others) that there needs to exist a *primary equivalence structure* which facilitates instrumental acts such as cultural values that transcends *valence* to a *secondary equivalence structure*, i.e. the pathway to consuming and realising expectancies. This could represent a realisation for on-going organisational development aligned to synergies of occupational personal development. Trust can be compromised when the potential of talent is restricted to a mutual-equivalence that only represents a minority of stakeholders. In any sense, this is likely to slow down an organisation's ability to adapt to foreseen or unforeseen disruption should strategic direction require it. Looking from an optimist viewpoint, an occupational relationship with an organisation is likely to be distinctive to behavioural commitment and in some cases to attitudinal commitment. The probability will rest on the fulfilment of cultural variables that accommodate a work-culture to, esteemed opportunities, ability and ultimately achievement; an entrustment arguably attributed to talent recognition.

Learning activities

1   Identify occupational groups working in the hotel or tourist industry and assess the challenges for management to ensure mutual opportunities for talent recognition.

2   Discuss how a lack of trusting beliefs might affect a perception that an organisation is not committed to recognising talent amongst its employees.

3   Assess the influence of corporate values on policies of trust and talent.

4   Assess the importance of valence, and the potential benefit when applied to mutual-equivalence, to outcomes of trust and talent.

5   How could weak personnel functions inhibit developmental talent acquisition for a hospitality or tourist corporation?

6   Discuss the implications and challenges of *push* and *pull* in assuring talent and potential talent is not lost or minimised for an organisation.

7

References

Allaire, Y. and Firsirotu, M.E. (1984). Theories of organizational culture. *Organization Studies*, **5**(3): 193-226.

Altınöz, M., Çakıroğlu, D., and Çöp, S. (2013). Effects of talent management on organizational trust: a field study. *Procedia-Social and Behavioral Sciences*, **99**, 843-851.

American Society for Quality (ASQ) (1999) Ritz-Carlton Again: Hotel Wins Second Baldrige Quality Award, Retrieved from http: //asq.org/teamwork/1999/12/news-for-a-change-v53-i12-feature-article-ritz-carlton-again-hotel-wins-second-baldrige-award.html. Accessed on: 20th April, 2016.

Arron, C. (1992). Gourmet chefs are trimming the fat for leaner times, *The Daily Telegraph*, 13th October: 4.

Atkins, A. (2014/15). Building workplace trust: trends and high performance, Report prepared for Interaction Associates, Inc. Boston. USA.

Atkinson, J. (1984) Manpower strategies for flexible organisations, *Personnel Management*, August: 28-31.

Becker, H.S. (1960). Notes on Commitment, *American Journal of Sociology*, **66**(1), 32-40.

Becker, M.C., (2001). Managing dispersed knowledge: organizational problems, managerial strategies, and their effectiveness. *Journal of management studies*, **38**(7), 1037-1051.

Boudreau, J.W. (2013). Appreciating and 'retooling' diversity in talent management conceptual models: A commentary on "The psychology of talent management: A review and research agenda", *Human Resource Management Review*, **23**(4), 286-289.

Brewer, M. B. (1993). Social identity, distinctiveness, and in-group homogeneity, *Social Cognition*, **11**(1), 150-164.

Brünjes, J. and Diez, J.R. (2013). 'Recession push' and 'prosperity pull' entrepreneurship in a rural developing context, *Entrepreneurship and Regional Development*, **25**(3-4), 251–271.

Burrell, G. and Morgan, G. (1979). *Sociological Paradigms and Organisational Analysis*, England: Area Publishing.

Cameron, D. (2001). Chefs and occupational culture in a hotel chain: a grid-group analysis. *Tourism and Hospitality Research*, **3**(2), 103-114.

Cameron, D.S. (2004). Organizational and Occupational Commitment: Exploring Chefs from a Cultural Perspective, PhD. Thesis, University of Surrey.

Cameron, D. (2009). Unravelling the complexity of organizational and occupational culture through an exploration of eight cultural schools: a case study of chefs working in luxury hotels and restaurants, in: *18th CHME Annual Hospitality Research Conference*, 13th -15th May, University of Brighton.

Cameron, D., Gore, J., Desombre. T. and Riley, M. (1999). An examination of the reciprocal affects of occupation culture and organisation culture: the case of chefs in hotels, International *Journal of Hospitality Management*, **18**, 225-234.

Cappelli, P. (2015). Why we love to hate HR...and what HR can do. *Harvard Business Review*, **93**(7/8), 54-61.

Caproni, J. (2012). *Management Skills for Everyday Life: The Practical Coach*, ed. 3, New Jersey: Pearson.

Cook, J. and Wall, T. (1980). New work attitude measures of trust, organizational commitment and personal need non-fulfilment, *Journal of Occupational Psychology*, **53**(1), 39-52.

Dennett, A., Cameron. D., Bamford. C and Jenkins. A. (2014). An investigation into hospitality cruise ship work through the exploration of metaphors. *Employee Relations*, **36**(5), 480-495.

Dunki, L. (2009). Building trust in business: best practices in trust, leadership and collaboration, Report prepared for Interaction Associates, Inc. Boston. USA.

Etzioni, A. (2011). Behavioral economics: toward a new paradigm, *American Behavioral Scientist*, **55**(8), 1099-1119.

Fernández-Aráoz, C. (2014). The big idea: 21st century talent spotting (Digest summary). *Harvard Business Review*, **92**(6): 2-11.

Fraher, A.L. (2013). Airline downsizing and its impact on team performance, *Team Performance Management*, **19**(1/2), 109-126.

Fraher, A.L. and Gabriel, Y. (2014). Dreaming of flying when grounded: occupational identity and occupational fantasies of furloughed airline pilots. *Journal of Management Studies*, **51**(6), 926-951.

Gallardo-Gallardo E., Dries. N. and Gonzalez-Cruz T.F. (2013). What is the meaning of Talent in the world of work? *Human Resource Management Review*, **23**(4), 290-300.

Haldin-Herrgard, T. (2000). Difficulties in diffusion of tacit knowledge in organizations. *Journal of Intellectual capital*, **1**(4), 357-365.

Herzberg, H. (1974). *Management classics: jumping for jelly beans*, From BBC Training Videos, [video: VHS], London: British Broadcasting Corporation.

Hofstede, G. (1994). *Cultures and Organizations: Software of the mind*, London: Harper Collins.

Iles: (2013). Commentary on "The meaning of 'talent' in the world of work", *Human Resource Management Review*. **23**(24), 301-304.

Kellaway, L. (2009). The Year of the CFO in: The World in 2009. *The Economist*, December: 140.

Kovack, K. (2015). Along the spectrum of transparency, what is the optimal level in sharing performance management assessments with employees? *Cornell University ILR School*, ILR Digital Collection, Available from http: //digitalcommons.ilr.cornell.edu, Accessed on: February 8th, 2016.

Kusluvan, S., Kusluvan. Z., Iham, L. and Buyruk, L. (2010). The human dimension: A review of human resources management issues in the tourism and hospitality industry, *Cornell Hospitality Quarterly*. **51**(I), 171-214.

Leroy, F. and Ramanantsoa, B. (1997). The cognitive and behavioural dimensions of organizational learning in a merger: An empirical study. *Journal of Management Studies*, 34(6), 871-894.

Lewin, K. ([1951], ed. 1963). *Field Theory in Social Science-Selected Theoretical Papers*, London: Social Science Paperbacks in association with Tavistock Publications.

Martins, N. and Von Der Ohe, H. (2002). Trust as a factor in determining how to attract, motivate and retain talent, SA *Journal of Industrial Psychology*. **28**(4), 49-57.

Maqsood, T., Walker, D.H.T. and Finega. A.D. (2007). Facilitating knowledge pull to deliver innovation through knowledge Management: a case study. *Engineering, Construction and Architectural Management*. **14**(1), 94-109.

Mayer, R. C., Davis, J. H. and Schoorman, F. D. (1995). An integrative model of organizational trust. *Academy of Management Review*, **20**(3), 709-734.

McAulaya, B. J., Zeitz, G. and Blau, G. (2006). Testing a "Push–Pull" theory of work commitment among organizational professionals, *The Social Science Journal*. 43, 71–596.

McGee, G. W. and Ford, R. C. (1987). Two (or more?) Dimensions of organizational commitment re-examination of affective and continuance commitment. *Journal of Applied Psychology*, **77**(4), 638-642.

Meyers, M. C. and van Woerkom, M. (2014). The influence of underlying philosophies on talent management: theory, implications for practice, and research. *Journal of World Business*, **49**(2), 192-203.

Radcliffe-Brown. A.R. (1952). *Structure and Function in a Primitive Society*. Oxford: Oxford University Press.

Rok, M. and Mulej, M. (2014). CSR-based model for HRM in tourism and hospitality, *Kybernetes*, **43**(3/4), 346-362.

Saint-Onge, H. (1996). Tacit knowledge the key to the strategic alignment of intellectual capital. *Planning Review*, **24**(2), 10-16.

Savoy (2009). Leading the Past. London: Pentagram. Available https://vimeo.com/18047582

Savoy (2016). Savoy Hotel History. Retrieved from: http://www.fairmont.com/savoy-london/hotelhistory. Accessed on September 25th , 2016.

Senge, M. (1990). *The Fifth Discipline: The art and practice of the learning organization*, Broadway Business.

Shaw, R. (1997). *Trust in the Balance*. San Francisco. CA: Jossey- Bass.

Simms, J., Hales, C. and Riley. M. (1988). Examination of the concept of the internal labour markets in UK hotels, *Tourism Management*, **19**(1), 3-12.

Transley, C., Kirk. S. and Tietze, S. (2013). The currency of talent management - A reply to "talent management and the relevance of context: towards a pluralistic approach", *Human resource Management Review*, **23**(4), 337-340.

Wallace, A.F.C. ([1961], ed. 1964). *Culture and Personality*, New York: Random House.

Wallace, A.F.C. (1985). The week's citation classic, *Institute for Scientific Information*. 21, May 27th.

Warnock-Smith. D. and Cameron. D. and O'Connell J. F. (2016). Organizational trust: an application to the airline sector. (work-in-progress).

Wessel, M. and Christensen, C. M. (2012). Surviving disruption, *Harvard Business Review*, **90**(12), 56-64.

Yang, J.T., Wan, C.S. and Fu, Y.J. (2012). Qualitative examination of employee turnover and retention strategies in international tourist hotels in Taiwan, *International Journal of Hospitality Management*, **31**(3), 837-848.

8 Talent Management and Youth Employment

Andreas Walmsley

Learning objectives

After reading this chapter you should:

- Be able to explain the potential of youth to the success of the hospitality organisation within the context of the resource-based view of the firm

- Be able to apply the concept of aesthetic labour to youth employment in hospitality

- Be familiar with the concept of generation theory and how managers may use it to manage young talent within their organisations

Introduction

This chapter focuses on young people as a source of talent and thereby a source of competitive advantage for the hospitality organisation. It is structured in three main sections. The first section provides a theoretical foundation for understanding talented individuals as a source of competitive advantage in alignment with the resource-based view of the firm. The following section explores characteristics of youth, or young people, that make them particularly suited to some forms of hospitality work, and thereby a talent to be recruited and managed. The final section seeks to better understand the work values, broadly defined, of today's youth, which may arguably assist in their recruitment and retention, as well as their management. It should be noted from the outset that this line of investigation, i.e. a focus on youth attributes and their relationship to the hospitality firm, is fairly novel and as such the discussion is necessarily theoretical in the main for want of empirical evidence. Nonetheless, in an increasingly competitive world, being able to recruit and manage talented young people may very usefully feature as part of a competitive strategy of the hospitality firm.

Human resources as a source of competitive advantage

Today, much literature extols the value of people to organisational success to the extent that it might appear churlish to suggest otherwise. This view is not natural or inevitable, however, as a historical review illustrates. Frederick Taylor's notion of scientific management, which emerged at the close of the 19th century, has clear leanings towards traditional economics' view of labour as a factor of production, and therefore to be regarded as a cost. Taylor's preoccupation with finding the most efficient way of organising labour was thereby particularly suited to standardised business processes. Ethical considerations aside, treating employees like cogs in a well-oiled machine was possible where there existed an abundant supply of labour, where costs associated with high rates of labour turnover were mitigated by low wages in the knowledge that replacing workers was unproblematic. Work effort was maintained by close monitoring and efficiency wages (MacDuffie, 1995: 201).This admittedly reductionist view of labour persisted, and some might argue still persists in some quarters today, although a change in attitudes is often promoted by drawing attention to a shift in terminology, i.e. from the use of the term Personnel Management to Human Resources (or Human Resource Management) (Ulrich and Dulebohn, 2015). HRM has been interpreted as elevating the position of employees in other words, indeed regarding HRM functions (e.g. recruitment, selection, human resource development, performance and reward management etc.) as fundamental to a firm's success. The debates around the need for the term 'strategic human resource management', given that HRM is arguably strategic in nature, are indicative of this shift also (see for example Price, 2007) and a recent preoccupation with talent management is equally indicative of this shift.

It is not just the academic literature that is preoccupied with human resources and their management. The practitioner literature in hospitality unfailingly promotes people as the source of business success and as such it is 'their people' who should be nurtured and cared for. The following claims serve to provide a flavour of these espoused beliefs. The International Hotel Group (IHG, 2015) states that:

> We're a company which passionately believes that it's our people who have brought us to where we are today and our people that will help us grow.

Marriott International (2015) explains that its core values and culture are underpinned by the notion to 'Take care of your employees and they'll take care of the guests', which is in fact their founding philosophy. At Marriott, caring for people and the community is part of who we are.

Hilton Hotels (2015) claims:

> Great guest experiences begin with Team Members who feel appreciated, valued and respected.

The elevation of the status of employees, in theory at least, in recognition of their role in determining organisational success, was further driven by a shift in perspective in the strategic management literature. Despite the long-held understanding in strategic management of the importance of the resource position (strengths and weaknesses) of the firm (e.g. Andrews, 1971), which itself extends back to Penrose's (1959) seminal work that regards the firm as a broader collection of resources, it was not until the 1980s and early 90s that the resource-based view of the firm began to attract notable scholarly interest (see for example Barney, 1991; Wernerfelt, 1984). Wernerfelt (1984: 172) suggests that *'by a resource is meant anything which could be thought of as a strength or weakness of a given firm. More formally, a firm's resources at a given time could be defined as those (tangible and intangible) assets which are tied semi-permanently to the firm.'* Within this statement lies one of the premises of talent management: to provide a sustained competitive advantage the resource needs to conform to certain characteristics, notably it must be tied to the firm. Wernerfelt (1984) alludes to a resource position barrier; within the context of this chapter and book we might refer to a talent position barrier.

Barney (1991) similarly picks up on Wernerfelt's position establishing that a focus on sustained competitive advantage must result in firm resource immobility as well as heterogeneity. The point around heterogeneity is in reality about scarcity, if all firms had access to the same resource, i.e. it wasn't rare, then no competitive advantage could be achieved. Barney (1991) concludes therefore that for a resource to provide sustained competitive advantage it must be valuable (to the organisation), rare, inimitable and non-substitutable (i.e. another bundle of firm resources cannot be exploited to achieve the same strategic results).

Although talent management is still a relatively recent concept in the spheres of the broader business management literature, the potential of human resources and their management to provide a sustained competitive advantage for the firm is not as new and draws heavily on ideas such as those initially expressed by Wernerfelt (1984) and Barney (1991). Indeed there is a clear link between (strategic) HRM and the resource based view of the firm. However, Wright *et al.*'s article reviews competing approaches as to whether the management of human resources can in fact provide a sustained competitive advantage. On the one hand Wright *et al.* (1994), who distinguish between a firm's human resources (i.e. its human capital pool) and HR practices (i.e. the tools used to manage that pool), argue that HR practices cannot offer a source of sustainable competitive advantage since individual HR practices can be copied by competitors. Lado and Wilson (1994) counter this by suggesting it is the overall HR system which is inimitable.

Part of the appeal of a focus on HR systems in achieving sustained competitive advantage is precisely the difficulty in establishing in detail what the system consists of and how it works, thus making it problematic, if not impossible, to imitate. As Spender and Grant (1996: 8), with reference to the resource-based view, have identified *'the variables which are most theoretically interesting are those which are least identifiable and measurable'*. This is just one of the paradoxes of the resource-based view and has led to some criticism of the 'theory' because not being able to measure the resource means empirical verification of its impact on firm performance is hampered (Lado *et al.* 2006). To put it bluntly, we can say all we like about the virtues of HRM but we have limited actual evidence of its success, certainly if we discard anecdotal evidence. This is not to say that HRM does not have an impact, just that it has been difficult to verify its impact empirically, which is in large part down to measurement of what precisely is the cause (i.e. the HRM systems) and how to disentangle this from other factors that impact on firm performance (such as general economic climate, industry forces, a firm's resource endowments and so forth).

The difficulty in establishing causality has not prevented researchers from tackling the issue. Numerous studies exist both within and outside of the hospitality context that explore the HRM – business performance relationship. Examples within hospitality include Cho *et al.* (2006) who for 219 publicly traded hotel and restaurant companies in the U.S. only found a positive relationship between certain HRM practices (not overall systems) and non-managerial labour turnover rates, but were unable to establish statistically significant associations for managerial turnover rates, productivity and return on assets. A more recent study based in Croatia is that conducted by Ruzic (2015), who from the outset clarifies that the search for HRM's impact on firm performance has moved from *whether* to *how*. It is more about understanding the conditions where impact can occur rather than trying to establish a universally applicable 'law' determining the HRM-firm performance relationship. Nonetheless, Ruzic's (2015: 64) findings while multi-faceted point to a clear overall relationship between HRM and firm performance: '*The key conclusion is that, in a hotel environment, HRM directly contributes to the HRM result performance, both at individual and organisational levels, as well as to hotel company financial performance.*' Notwithstanding the theoretical strength of claims seeking to justify HRM's impact on performance (be that measured at the level of the individual, the department, or the firm) there is still much scope for research in this area.

In sum, talent management may be regarded as typifying the resource-based view of the firm, in that as a resource it can provide a competitive edge to it. Moreover, because the management of talent goes beyond the existence of a resource but exemplifies a core competence in the way HR systems and procedures are organised to manage talent, it may in fact provide a sustainable competitive advantage, or at least make it more difficult for competitors to imitate.

The discussion now turns to how young people can provide a ready source of talent for the hospitality organisation.

The promise of youth within hospitality

Having laid the foundations in terms of seeing people and their management as a source of competitive advantage we now focus our attention on youth within hospitality organisations, and specifically how youth attributes can offer the hospitality organisation a competitive edge. The discussion focuses on the delivery of service excellence via youth's ability to provide aesthetic labour, youth's ability to endure the physically demanding nature of much hospitality employment, and more general characteristics such as enthusiasm and drive. The section concludes with a critical view at hospitality organisations' ability to harness youth talent.

Controversially, we first draw attention to a query about the usefulness of special training programmes for young staff. Results from a study conducted by Cairncross and Buultjens (2007) suggest that some managers felt a training programme for young people was ill-conceived because many are impatient and without enthusiasm to learn. This claim is provided simply to act as a counter-point, to highlight the frequently diverging views on youth and their employment. Thus, this chapter lays the foundation for the promotion of youth talent but acknowledges that opinions on this matter will differ, and indeed, empirically age has received scant attention as an explanatory variable in studies of human resources in hospitality.

Our first port of call in the quest to understand the potential of young talent is the notion of service excellence. Parasuraman *et al.*'s (1985) seminal work on the SERVQUAL model recognises the need for staff to be courteous and understanding of customer needs in delivering service excellence. The notion of understanding customer needs requires emotional intelligence, in other words empathy and social deftness (Goleman, 1996). Furthermore, to be courteous despite varying and often difficult customer and superordinate demands epitomises emotional labour, i.e. the ability to manage one's own emotions which thereby become commodified (Bolton and Boyd, 2003; Hochschild, 1983).

In addition to the provision of emotional labour and the display of emotional intelligence, many of today's leading hospitality organisations rely on the related concept of *aesthetic labour* to provide a competitive edge. Aesthetic labour has been defined as '*the employment of workers with desired corporeal dispositions*' (Warhurst and Nickson, 2007: 107). The recognition that employers in the service industries frequently seek more than skills and attitudes is long held. As long ago as 1956 the existence of a market for personalities was noted, whereby the employer buys the employee's personality (Mills, 1956). Aesthetic labour is about more than personality however, as the embodiment of brand image, the corporeal disposition, combines personality with the visual and aural, and with aesthetics therefore.

This is where being young can provide an advantage for the prospective employee, because they are better at representing the brand image of many types of hospitality organisation (although certainly not all). This 'image-driveness' is so important for select hospitality organisations that Witz *et al.* (2003) write of the existence of a 'style labour market', something which has only received limited academic interest however. Aesthetic labour understood as the (literal) embodiment of an organisation's desired image by the employee, works in favour of youth if the organisation is trying to exude a youthful image, or indeed other attributes associated with youth.

Many hospitality organisations are staffed by young people. Admittedly, the high levels of youth employment in tourism and hospitality are in part due to the attractiveness of the sector or to labour market circumstances (see for example Walmsley, 2015). From Warhurst *et al.*'s (2000) study of the 'New Glasgow' it became evident however that 'style market companies' were directly developing aesthetic labour. Moreover, recruitment and selection practices demonstrated aesthetics as an important feature in terms such as 'smart young person', 'smart appearance', 'well-spoken and of smart appearance' and 'very well presented' (Warhurst *et al.*, 2000: 11).

Although all societies across all ages have been concerned with appearance, according to Fox (1997), technological developments and the rise of mass media in particular have led to an obsession with it. This fixation with appearance finds repercussions in a 'race to be forever young' (Archer, 2013), or as Robert Harrison, author of the book *Juvenescence* explains, for the first time in human history, '*The young have become a model of emulation for the older population, rather than the other way around*' (cited in Stanford Report, 2014). Evidently, employees who are young have by definition an advantage over older employees when it comes to embodying youthful ideals. The rise of aesthetic labour, while not exclusively the domain of organisations trying to promote a youthful image, frequently emphasises youth and associated attributes.

A further attribute, albeit not immediately related to aesthetics, where young people may have an advantage over older employees is physical endurance. Much work in tourism and hospitality is undoubtedly physically demanding. A Eurofound report into working conditions in 15 EU countries in hospitality and catering (Eurofound, 2004: 25-26) suggests, for example, that physical endurance is frequently required in relation to:

- ☐ Noise (in kitchens, bars, discotheques and nightclubs)
- ☐ Low lighting conditions (associated risks include falling, burning and eye strain)
- ☐ Temperature and breathing problems
- ☐ Physically demanding work (long periods of standing, sometimes carrying loads, repetitive movements, having to wear high-heeled shoes)

As a consequence of these features the Eurofound (2004: 25) report argues that '*employees need to be of a good physical condition*'. There is no arguing that non-youth cannot undertake physically demanding tasks. It is similarly difficult to argue against the notion that physical endurance declines with age.

A further advantage in hiring young people in hospitality is their generally higher degree of flexibility with regard to working hours. Indeed, marginal employment in the sector, notably that of women, migrants and youth, is very common in hospitality because of the requirements of working non-standard working hours (see for example the International Labour Office's work in this area). The period of youth is often associated with freedom, the lack of commitments, family and financial. The hospitality sector draws, in some locations heavily, on student labour precisely because students are more able to 'fit in' with irregular working patterns (Rowson and Lashley, 2005).

Sometimes it is difficult to disentangle stereotypical views of youth from actual youth characteristics. Thus, youth are described as 'bringing ideas to the workplace', are 'eager and willing to learn' or are 'not afraid of technology or change' according to a Canadian government-sponsored website in Newfoundland that is trying to promote the advantages of hiring youth to employers. These descriptors probably resonate with many people and yet there exist plenty of youth who would not fit these ideals. Nonetheless, even where youth enthusiasm, zeal, willingness to learn and technological prowess amongst other positive attributes exist, there is no guarantee that the hospitality firm will utilise them. Froy (2013) explains that employers are not always best placed to use, or even understand, the skills that their new hires have.

Froy's (2013) point is possibly less true of large graduate recruiters, but then the hospitality sector is not made up solely of this type of firm – far from it. The structure of the tourism and hospitality sector is one dominated by small and medium-sized enterprises (Thomas, 2000). Although levels of education are rising globally, many of the owner/managers of hospitality firms, especially SMEs, are not degree-educated and tertiary education in hospitality is still a relatively recent phenomenon. Without empowering the employee, without listening to their suggestions, giving them a voice, the organisation will not benefit from the education and training these individuals have received, education the organisation could now be benefitting from. Some hospitality organisations are characterised by low demand for higher level skills, which in turn results in the employment of individuals with low skills levels. This is the so-called low skills equilibrium scenario (Finegold and Soskice, 1988). This is not to say the organisation would not benefit from employing people with higher skills levels, but without the vision and willingness on the part of owner/managers to draw on these skills, to develop and retain them, the skills will not benefit the organisation.

What do young people want?

We now turn to the final part of the chapter: the issue of how to attract and also, but to a lesser degree, manage and retain talent. In fact, these latter two points are only addressed indirectly as entire chapters could be written here. The fact remains though that if we want to attract, manage and retain young talent an understanding of young people's work orientations are critical. So, for example, Farndale, *et al.* (2014) suggest that approaches to talent management should be more closely aligned with an individual's goals and expectations. This general insight is not new, but Farndale *et al.*'s (2014) point stresses that for some organisations focussing on what may initially be regarded as their own needs may in fact run contrary to them. The premise is that a business that lacks the desire to address, or indeed is unaware of its employees' needs is likely to face difficulty attracting and retaining talent. This then leads to the question as to what young people's attitudes towards work are? What values do they hold or needs do they have that might assist in attracting and retaining them?

Clearly, it would be too simplistic to suggest all young people share the same values, attitudes and more specifically work orientations. However, as will be discussed, some characteristics may be generalizable and businesses that are keen to attract and retain talent would be well advised to understand something of this generation of young people's attitudes towards work and career. The chapter also provides some defence of educational institutions against calls that they should better prepare individuals for work, which is often the cry emitted by industry. Likewise, it provides some solace to industry too in explaining apparently disappointing early work experiences in hospitality on the basis of inevitable symptoms associated with organisational entry. That both educational institutions and employers can do more to ease the transition into hospitality employment is nonetheless a given and this too shall be briefly discussed.

At the outset we need to be mindful to not confuse differences in work values and attitudes as a result of ageing, from changes in work values as a result of generational differences (Leuty and Hansen, 2014). Age effects are a result of the maturation process as opposed to generation effects which are the result of shared political, cultural and generally historical experiences (Mannheim, 1952). Staying with generation theory as much has been written about the differing values between generations, there is no universal agreement as to where the boundaries of one generation end and where those of the next begin. Certainly, to pin this down to a particular year ignores Mannheim's (1952) explanation of a generation as being determined by socio-political events and climate that shape an individual's economic and political orientation. Furthermore, generation theory is predicated on the assumption that an individual's most enduring beliefs are shaped during youth (Mannheim, 1952). If this were not the case then youth, middle-aged and elderly would all be shaped in equal measure by prevailing socio-political events rendering generation meaningless as an explanatory variable for beliefs and attitudes.

Just what the most momentous events were in a given epoch is easier to establish with the benefit of hindsight (Roberts, 2012) and so there is general agreement that the baby boomers (sometimes referred to as Generation X), are the generation born in the aftermath of World War II. Despite others pronouncing the arrival of other generations since (notably Generations Y and Z, but also the Internet Generation, Millennials, the Ecstasy Generation and the Lost Generation) Roberts (2012) makes the case that only now are we witnessing the possible emergence of a new generation, at least in North America and Western Europe. The reason for this, so Roberts (2012), is that until fairly recently each cohort born in the second half of the Twentieth Century had expected a standard of living higher than that of their parents. Although the reasons for this are manifold, the main one, and arguably the one most difficult to argue against, is the abnormally high economic growth rates witnessed immediately after the Second World War (often referred to as the glorious years) which made possible the rapid and consistent rise in living standards. Current youth and those in their late twenties and early thirties may be among the first generation however to experience a reversal of fortunes.

An advocate of a recent change in young people's attitudes towards work is Noreena Hertz who describes twenty and thirty year-olds as the 'Yes We Can' generation, the generation who believed the world was their oyster. By contrast, she argues that teenagers today feel more uncertain about the future (echoing Roberts' (2012) work, albeit drawing the boundaries around generations slightly differently). Data from her sample of 1,000 girls aged between 13 and 20 in the US and the UK suggested 86% worried about getting a job. Hertz's work proposes that today's youth have woken up to a new uncertain future and are therefore more career-driven, understanding that they cannot simply expect to have success handed to them on a plate. This might not however mean that they are willing to accept poor working conditions and discriminatory employment practices. Hertz explains that today's youth are more socially and environmentally conscious and value their uniqueness; they are less willing to conform.

A lot of advice exists on how to attract and manage Generation Y. Kerslake (2005), for example, echoes some of what Hertz describes as current youth's attitudes towards work, drawing the conclusion that today's youth value their individuality and independence more than previous generations. As a consequence of having witnessed the era of corporate downsizing and delayering, Generation Y is more transactional in its approach to work. Generation Y are willing to work hard but need recognition. Reflecting developments in career theory, specifically the notions of protean (Hall, 1996) and boundaryless (Arthur and Rousseau, 1996) careers, Generation Y individuals no longer assume or indeed expect long-term employment with one organisation.

Despite the existence of numerous studies documenting hospitality (and tourism) students' perceptions of careers in the sector (e.g. Airey and Frontistis, 1997; Getz, 1994; Kusluvan and Kusluvan, 2000; Nachmias and Walmsley, 2015; Roney and Oztin, 2007; Walmsley, 2012; Wan *et al.*, 2014) by contrast, there exist few studies that seek to understand hospitality students' career values, broadly defined. One of the difficulties in studies of career values in tourism and hospitality, and one that this chapter has thus far equally ignored, is what the precise focus of the investigation should be. For the sake of expediency this chapter proposes the notion of career values, but a number of related concepts feature in studies that seek to make sense of the relationship between the individual and employment. This includes work values, work attitudes, career orientation and vocational interests. These are all concepts that have received much attention in the generic literature but little discussion within the context of tourism and hospitality.

Kim *et al.* (2010) sampled undergraduate students majoring in hospitality and/ or tourism management in seven universities located across the U.S. (total sample

= 442). This study included an investigation of the importance of 'career choice factors' which resulted in the identification of eight such factors:

- ☐ People relationships
- ☐ Service to society
- ☐ Job security
- ☐ Public status
- ☐ Advancement chances
- ☐ Job autonomy
- ☐ Leadership development
- ☐ Location

Of these, extrinsic factors (e.g. advancement changes and job security) seemed to be more influential than internal factors (e.g. public status, service to society). Although subgroup differences had almost no effect on the results of the rankings, differences in career choice factors were evident based on gender (job autonomy and leadership development were more important for males, service to society was more important for females). The authors explain the importance of extrinsic factors on the basis of the tough economic climate.

Richardson and Butler (2012), whose study involved a sample of 229 tourism/hospitality students at a Malaysian university, make reference to other studies that have looked at tourism/hospitality students' career values (preferences). Thus, in Damonte and Vaden's (1987) study an importance ranking of factors is as follows: (1) interesting work; (2) advancement potential; (3) secure future; (4) good salary; (5) opportunity for service to society and (6) social prestige. For Blumenfeld *et al.* (1987) the five most important factors when deciding whether to accept a job were (1) type of work; (2) advancement opportunities and (3) company reputation; (4) salary; (5) job security. Richardson and Butler's (2012) own study comprised an importance rating of twenty factors. The most important factor was 'A job that I will find enjoyable' which 81.6% of respondents found important. The next three most important factors were 'A pleasant working environment' (71.3%), 'Good promotion prospects' (67.2%) and 'High earnings over the length of career' (65.8%).

Based on these studies alone it is difficult to draw any firm conclusions as to whether a change in career values has occurred over the years in the hospitality/tourism student and recent graduate population. The above-mentioned studies are geographically dispersed which adds another layer of complexity. Perhaps the one thing that continues to dominate in this type of student career preference survey is the importance of earnings and opportunities for career progression. While we would agree therefore with Richardson and Butler's (2012:267) statement: '*If employers can understand better the psyche of the Generation Y worker, it will allow them to provide greater opportunities for them based on their ideals and expectations*', there is to date simply not enough data from youth employed in tourism and hospitality to be able to provide much generic advice. For now it appears that those responsible for recruitment will have to rely on non-sector-specific sources in an attempt to capture the attitudes of young people's towards work and careers.

More worryingly, irrespective of young people's career values, the uptake of hospitality employment during or soon after students' studies appears to detract from it. This is the message numerous studies convey (e.g.Barron and Maxwell, 1993; Chuang *et al.*, 2007; Jenkins, 2001; Kusluvan and Kusluvan, 2000). While possibly down to poor working conditions, low wages or limited career progression opportunities, this conclusion is nonetheless not inevitable. To a degree it could indicate a discrepancy between perceptions, untested, of working life more generally and the actual experience of working life. Louis' (1980) seminal work on the encounter with new organisational settings provides a useful framework upon which to understand organisational newcomers' experience. The wording of the title of the paper 'surprise and sense-making' provides an indication of the content: it is quite common for organisational newcomers to face surprises; in Louis' (1980: 228) words: '...*unmet expectations, broadly defined, may be an inevitable accompaniment to the experience of entering an unfamiliar organizational setting*'.

With regard to labour turnover, Louis (1980 distinguishes between unrealistic expectations and unmet expectations. Although two sides of one coin, i.e. where expectations are unrealistic they are by definition not going to be met, this approach provides the basis for an explanation of labour turnover that emphasises the nature of the expectations as much as the nature of the organisational setting. In crude terms, unmet expectations are the result of personal and organisational factors, and consequently disappointment upon organisational entry may have as much to do with the false image of work inculcated by society and by educational institutions, as it does by the employing organisation itself. In defence of the role of education in not being able to provide a realistic understanding of work experience, Louis' (1980) framework points to a source of surprise that results from difficulties in forecasting internal reactions to new experiences. She refers to the difference in the cognitive 'knowing about' as opposed to the experiential being 'acquainted with'. In practice, while educational institutions may advise students of working conditions in the sector, until the individual actually experiences work, they will not know for sure how they will react to it. It is this that Collins (2002) refers to as the 'sting of battle' in describing the placement experience, similar to the placement's description as a shop window of the industry (Sherrel, 1987).

Although part of the responsibility of providing students with an understanding of the realities of the workplace rests on the shoulders of the educational institutions, employers too share this responsibility. Overly positive images of work are frequently portrayed by employers. One needs only look at a selection of recruitment videos and company promotional material to realise that some hospitality businesses create a false image of organisational life in their quest to recruit suitable individuals. Although Wanous (1992) has undertaken much work in the area of realistic job previews (RJPs) and provides a review of literature going back to Weitz (1956, cited in Wanous, 1992) that alerts practitioners to the usefulness of employee expectations being as realistic as possible, empirically the effectiveness of RJPs is equivocal. This could however be down to methodological weaknesses in trying to assess their impact as Breaugh (2008) has argued, and in theory at least the case for RJPs is strong. Thus, even though RJPs may detract talented recruits and so may be frowned upon by some employers (see for example Baur *et al.*, 2014 for an historical overview of RJPs), an exaggeratedly positive outlook on employment will not wash with youth today, if they are indeed more transactional in approach to work as argued above (Kerslake, 2005). Returning to the issue of poor early work experiences in hospitality and the notion that these may in part be a consequence of inflated expectations of work more generally, instead of RJPs Buckley *et al.* (1998) introduce expectation lowering procedures which are less related to a specific job. The message however remains the same, if the recruiting organisation promises more than it delivers, today's young recruits are unlikely to simply shrug these false promises off.

Conclusion

Despite the recognition that the tourism and hospitality sectors rely heavily on youth employment (Walmsley, 2015), youth as an analytical category has remained largely absent from studies of hospitality work. This chapter has provided a theoretical discussion of the relationship between youth and talent management that may serve as a basis for future work in this under-researched and therefore poorly understood area. Initially it was outlined how talent management was itself couched in the broader resource-based view of organisations and their strategic management. Upon this backdrop the chapter sought to outline reasons why youth, or young people, can present a valuable resource for hospitality organisations. Here the notions of aesthetic labour, the associated style labour market from which many hospitality organisations recruit, as well as the more mundane but nonetheless important aspect of physical endurance related to youth were discussed. Youth attributes such as dynamism, drive and enthusiasm were mentioned, although here there is very limited empirical work upon which to draw and some would argue that these attributes are not over-represented in youth. More work is clearly called for in this area. It was also recognised that a young person's talent would not automatically be utilised by the hospitality organisation, particularly for SMEs which are more likely to adopt informal approaches to managing their human resources.

The discussion concluded with a review of the literature outlining hospitality students' work orientations. The reasoning here is that if an organisation wants to recruit and retain talented individuals, it needs to understand how these individuals relate to work, what meaning work holds for them and what they might therefore expect from a job and a career (Farndale *et al.* 2014). Data here, while more abundant than perhaps data on the potential contribution youth can make to organisational success, are still equivocal and unsurprisingly so given temporal and geographical differences. Perhaps what is surprising is that work orientations have not in fact changed that much in the last 20-30 years, although again the paucity of data does not permit a robust comparison. Youth's more transactional approach to work has been offered by some commentators and if indeed this is true, i.e. that youth today are more transactional, care is needed not to overpromise and then under-deliver. Realistic job previews may be more relevant than ever in this scenario, as may expectation lowering procedures (Buckley *et al.* 1998). Attracting talent is but a first step in the 'war for talent' (Rynes, 1991) after all.

Learning activities

1   Drawing on your work experience, identify a process or competence that you feel provided the organisation with a source of competitive advantage. How easy or difficult would it be for a competitor to imitate this?

2   With reference to Froy (2013), who argues that employers are not always best placed to use, or even understand, the skills that their new hires have, consider what an employer could do to promote the use of all employees' talent.

3   Consider your own work values: how transactional are you compared to your colleagues/ peers? Do you believe youth are more transactional today than in the past? What consequences might your answer have for talent management policies and practices?

4   Thinking about your own organisation (or ones you have previously worked for), to what extent do you feel the organisation provided a realistic image when recruiting talent? What might an expectation lowering procedure (Buckley *et al.*, 1998) actually look like?

8

References

Airey, D. and Frontistis, A. (1997). Attitudes to careers in tourism: an Anglo Greek comparison. *Tourism Management*, **18**(3), 149-158.

Andrews, K. (1971). *The Concept of Corporate Strategy*. Homewood: Dow Jones-Irwin.

Archer, D. (2013). Forever young: America's obsession with never growing old. *Psychology Today*. Retrieved from Psychology Today website: https://www.psychologytoday.com/blog/reading-between-the-headlines/201310/forever-young-americas-obsession-never-growing-old.

Arthur, M. and Rousseau, D. M. (1996). *The Boundaryless Career: A New Employment Principle for a New Organizational Era*. Oxford: Oxford University Press.

Barney, J. (1991). Firm resources and sustained competitive advantage. *Journal of Management*, **17**(1), 99-120.

Barron,P. and Maxwell, G. (1993). Hospitality management students' image of the hospitality industry. *International Journal of Contemporary Hospitality Management*, **5**(5), 5-8.

Baur, J., Buckley, R., Bagdasarov, Z. and Dharmasiri, A. (2014). A historical approach to realistic job previews. An exploration into their origins, evolution, and recommendations for the future. *Journal of Management History,* **20**(2), 200-223.

Bolton, S. and Boyd, C. (2003). Trolley dolly or skilled emotion manager? Moving on from Hochschild's managed heart. *Work, Employment and Society,* **17**(2), 289-308.

Breaugh, A. J. (2008). Employee recruitment: Current knowledge and important areas for future research. *Human Resource Management Journal,* **18**(3), 103-118.

Buckley, R., Fedor, D., Veres, J., Wiese, D. and Carraher, S. (1998). Investigating newcomer expectations and job-related outcomes. *Journal of Applied Psychology,* **83**(3), 452-461.

Cairncross, G. and Buultjens, J. (2007). Generation Y and work in the tourism and hospitality industry: problem? what problem? *Centre for Enterprise Development and Research Occasional Paper, No.9.*

Cho, S., Woods, R., Jang, S. C. and Erdem, M. (2006). Measuring the impact of human resource management practices on hospitality firms' performance. *Hospitality Management,* **25**(2), 262-277.

Chuang, N.-K., Goh, B., Stout, B. and Dellmann-Jenkins, M. (2007). Hospitality undergraduate students' career choices and factors influencing commitment to the profession. *Journal of Hospitality & .Tourism Education,* **19**(4), 28-37.

Collins, A. B. (2002). Gateway to the real world, industrial training: dilemmas and problems. *Tourism Management,* **23**(1), 93-96.

Damonte, T. and Vaden, A. G. (1987). Career decicisons in hospitality management. *Hospitality Education and Research Journal,* **11**(2), 51-63.

Eurofound. (2004). *EU hotel and restaurant sector: work and employment conditions.* Retrieved from http://www.eurofound.europa.eu/sites/default/files/ef_files/pubdocs/2003/98/en/1/ef0398en.pdf

Farndale, E., Pai, A., Sparrow, P. and Scullion, H. (2014). Balancing individual and organizational goals in global talent management: A mutual-benefits perspective. *Journal of World Business,* **49**(2), 204-214.

Finegold, D. and Soskice, D. (1988). The failure of training in Britain: Analysis and prescription. *Oxford Review of Economic Policy,* **4**(3), 21-53.

Fox, K. (1997). Mirror, Mirror. A summary of findings on research image. . *Vox Rationis.* Retrieved from Social Issues Research Centre website: http://www.sirc.org/publik/mirror.html.

Froy, F. (2013). Global policy developments towards industrial policy and skills: skills for competitiveness and growth. *Oxford Review of Economic Policy,* **29**(2), 344-360.

Getz, D. (1994). Students' work experiences, perceptions and attitudes towards careers in hospitality and tourism: a longitudinal case study in Spey Valley, Scotland. *International Journal of Hospitality Management,* **13**(1), 25-37.

Goleman, D. (1996). *Emotional Intelligence. Why it can matter more than IQ.* London: Bloomsbury Publishing.

Hall, D. T. (1996). Protean careers of the 21st century. *Academy of Management Executive,* **10**(4), 8-16.

Hilton Hotels (2015) *Hilton Worldwide. It's Your World.* http://jobs.hiltonworldwide.com/en/why-choose-us. Accessed 07.11.15

Hochschild, A. (1983). *The Managed Heart: Commercialization of Human Feeling.* Berkeley, CA: University of California Press.

Intercontinental Hotels Group (2015) *Who is IHG?* http://careers.ihg.com/about-ihg. Accessed: 15.11.15

Jenkins, A. K. (2001). Making a career of it? Hospitality students' future perspectives: an Anglo-Dutch study. *International Journal of Contemporary Hospitality Management,* **13**(1), 13-20.

Kerslake, P. (2005). Words from the Ys. Leading the demanding dot-coms. *New Zealand Management,* **52**(4), 44-48.

Kim, B., McCleary, K. and Kaufman, T. (2010). The new generation in the industry: hospitality/tourism students' career preferences, sources of influence and career choice factors. *Journal of Hospitality and Tourism Education,* **22**(3), 5-11.

Kusluvan, S. and Kusluvan, Z. (2000). Perceptions and attitudes of undergraduate tourism students towards working in the tourism industry in Turkey. *Tourism Management,* **21**(3), 251-269.

Lado, A., Boyd, N., Wright, P. and Kroll, M. (2006). Paradox and theorizing within the resource-based view. *Academy of Management Review,* **31**(1), 115-131.

Lado, A. and Wilson, M. C. (1994). Human resource systems and sustained competitive advantage: A competency-based perspective. *Academy of Management Review,* **19**(4), 699-727.

Leuty, M. and Hansen, J.-I. (2014). Teasing apart the relations between age, birth cohort, and vocational interests. *Journal of Counseling Psychology,* **61**(2), 289-298.

Louis, M. R. (1980). Surprise and sense making: What newcomers experience in entering unfamiliar organizational settings. *Administrative Science Quarterly,* **25**(2), 226-252.

MacDuffie, J. (1995). Human resource bundles and manufacturing performance: Organizational logic and flexible production systems in the world auto industry. *Industrial and Labour Relations Review,* **48**(2), 197-221.

Mannheim, K. (1952). *The Problem of Generations. Essays on the sociology of knowledge.* London: Routledge.

Marriott International (2015) *Learn About Marriott.* http://www.marriott.co.uk/careers/working-for-marriott.mi accessed: 07.11.15

Mills, C. W. (1956). *White Collar.* New York: Oxford University Press.

Nachmias, S. and Walmsley, A. (2015). Making career decisions in a changing graduate labour market: A hospitality perspective. *Journal of Hospitality, Leisure, Sport and Tourism Education,* **17**, 50-58. doi:10.1016/j.jhlste.2015.09.001

8

Parasuraman, A., Zeithaml, V. and Berry, L. (1985). A conceptual model of service quality and its implications for future research. *Journal of Marketing*, **49**, 41-50.

Penrose, E. (1959). *The Theory of the Growth of the Firm*. Oxford: Oxford University Press.

Price, A. (2007). *Human Resource Management in a Business Context*. London: Thomson Learning.

Richardson, S. and Butler, G. (2012). Attitudes of Malaysian tourism and hospitality students' towards a career in the industry. *Asia Pacific Journal of Tourism Research*, **17**(3), 262-276.

Roberts, K. (2012). The end of the long baby-boomer generation. *Journal of Youth Studies*, **15**(4), 479-497.

Roney, S.A. and Oztin, P. (2007). Career perceptions of undergraduate tourism students: A case study in Turkey. *Journal of Hospitality, Leisure, Sport and Tourism Education*, **6**(1), 4-18.

Rowson, B. and Lashley, C. (2005). *Student Employment Patterns in Nottingham's Tourism Sector: A Research Report for East Midlands Tourism*. Nottingham Trent University. Retrieved from: http://irep.ntu.ac.uk/id/eprint/4102

Ruzic, M. (2015). Direct and indirect contribution of HRM practice to hotel company performance. *International Journal of Contemporary Hospitality Management*, **49**, 56-65.

Rynes, S. L. (1991). Recruitment, job choice, and posthire consequences: A call for new research directions. In M. Dunnette and L. Hough (Eds.), *Handbook of Industrial/Organizational Psychology*, Vol. 2: 399-444. Palo Alto, CA: Consulting Psychology Press.

Sherrel, S. (1987). Give us a chance. *Caterer and Hotelkeeper*, 5th February.

Spender, J. C. and Grant, R. M. (1996). Knowledge and the firm: An overview. *Strategic Management Journal*, **17**(Special issue), 5-9.

Stanford Report. (2014). Stanford literary scholar traces cultural history of our obsession with youth. *Stanford Report*. Retrieved from http://news.stanford.edu/news/2014/november/youthful-book-harrison-111914.html

Thomas, R. (2000). Small firms in the tourism industry: Some conceptual issues. *International Journal of Tourism Research*, **2**(5), 345-353.

Ulrich, D. and Dulebohn, J. (2015). Are we there yet? What's next for HR? *Human Resource Management Review*, **25**, 188-204.

Walmsley, A. (2012). Pathways into Tourism Higher Education. *Journal of Hospitality, Leisure, Sport and Tourism Education*, **11**, 131-139.

Walmsley, A. (2015). *Youth Employment in Tourism. A Critical Review*. Oxford: Goodfellows.

Wan, P. , King, Y., Wong, A. and Kong, W. H. (2014). Student career prospect and industry commitment: The roles of industry attitude, perceived social status, and salary expectations. *Tourism Management*, **40**, 1-14.

Wanous, J. P. (1992). *Organizational Entry. Recruitment, Selection, Orientation and Socialization of Newcomers*. Reading, Massachusetts: Addison Wesley.

Warhurst, C. and Nickson, D. (2007). Employee experience of aesthetic labour in retail and hospitality. *Work, Employment and Society,* **21**(1), 103-120.

Warhurst, C., Nickson, D., Witz, A. and Cullen, A. M. (2000). Aesthetic labour in interactive service work: some case study evidence from the 'New Glasgow'. *Service Industries Journal,* **20**(3), 1-18.

Wernerfelt, B. (1984). A resource-based view of the firm. *Strategic Management Journal,* **5**(2), 171-180.

Witz, A., Warhust, C. and Nickson, D. (2003). The labour of aesthetics and the aesthetics of organization. *Organization* **10**(1), 33-54.

Wright, P. , McMahan, G. and Williams, A. (1994). Human resources and sustained competitive advantage: a resource-based perspective. *International Journal of Human Resource Management,* **5**(2), 301-326.

8

9 The Role of the Professional Body in the Development of Talent

Crispin Farbrother

Learning objectives

This chapter explores the value of professional bodies with a particular focus on talent management. After reading it and carrying out the suggested activities the reader will be able to:

■ Understand the history of professional bodies and view their role in today's society in a positive way.

■ Understand the value industry focused professional bodies have in developing talent management within the hospitality industry.

■ Understand the value academic professional bodies have in developing talent for the hospitality industry.

■ Consider the value membership of a professional body has in career development.

Introduction

Professional bodies offer their members many benefits and come in many shapes and sizes at both an international and a national level. Within the UK there are a significant number of institutions that represent members within the broad hospitality profession and they take on many forms. This chapter aims to explore the role and benefits of professional bodies and review a number of these institutions focusing on their value and purpose. A full listing is shown in Table 9.1, and whilst all of the institutions offer value to individuals, some will have more value than others to those with a role in hospitality management and particularly those hospitality organizations that are focused on talent management within the UK.

History

Professional bodies are the societies, institutions and associations that promote and further the careers of the people who practice in that particular field, discipline or industry. The Hospitality Guild, an overarching body for hospitality bodies defines a professional body as *'an organisation that helps individuals or businesses develop their skills in a particular industry or profession'*. 14 professional bodies are members of the recently formed Hospitality Guild, though there are also many bodies that have a significant role in supporting or promoting talent management within hospitality who are not members of the Hospitality Guild. Each body has a particular focus or purpose and they offer many reasons for their existence.

There appears to be a variety of definitions regarding bodies, institutions and associations. The original body though that represents people coming together under a profession is arguably the *guild*. The guilds held significant political influence and economic power across the world hundreds of years ago. Craftsmen, merchants and drapers, for example, held significant sway across their trades from the 13th century onwards, having come from original Saxon guilds whose name comes from 'gegildan' meaning 'to pay'. During the medieval period, guilds had taken on a central role in everyday life for people in Britain, with particular focus on its cities such as London. Guilds, as associations of artisans or merchants who control the practice of their craft, were mainly city- or town-centric. Sometimes referred to as *confraternities* the guilds were organized in a manner something between what we would recognize today as a professional association, trade union and a cartel. There were also traits of a secret society about many guilds. By the 12th century, groups of people in the same trade were drawn together for it was perceived to be convenient for those in the same trade to live and work closely together, and street names across many British cities and towns indicate which trades were based there. In London for example, the bakers would be near Bread Street, and the fishmongers in Friday Street, named after the Catholic demand for fish on Fridays. Whilst the cartel approach can be seen to have many negative commutations, these traditional guilds, operating as collectives, allowed individuals to work together in many aspects of business and trade, and in particular they worked towards the advancement of quality.

Benefits were evident to society via education through apprenticeships, and quality control implemented through stamps or marks of approval and a medieval approach to peer review. These collectives were able to show significant tangible benefits as well as more intrinsic values being developed by the members of the early guilds within Britain as well as across Europe. The main role of the guilds was to protect the quality and reputation of a trade and the members of a company. Over time, these loose groupings became official Livery Companies, named after the elaborate uniform, or livery, they wore for ceremonies and processions. The oldest charter of incorporation is for the Worshipful Company of Weavers in 1155.

The guilds developed rules of behavior about how their members should behave both within business and as a person. Rules of professional behaviour and an early view on ethical business and social behaviour became apparent with accounts from hundreds of years ago stating that individuals found guilty of spending too much time in the tavern, being lazy or enjoying spectator sports such as wrestling '*shal be put of for euermore of this companye*'. There were also similar warnings for anyone who should earn themselves 'an euel (evil) name' or to be accused of breach of the peace or theft.

The economic power and political influence wielded by the medieval guilds was significant, and by the early 14th century a closed shop approach to trade had developed, with no-one being allowed to practice a trade, set up shop, or take apprentices unless they were admitted to a livery company. Members of the guilds were appointed to the most important and influential positions in the community: the burghers, aldermen and even the Lord Mayor of London came from the ranks of, and were chosen by, the guilds. Richard Whittington, a member of the Mercer's Guild and the real-life Dick Whittington, was elected as Lord Mayor of London no less than four times by the guilds.

Although each guild had its own hall and coat of arms, this powerful and influential body needed a communal meeting place, so in the early 1400s London's magnificent Guildhall was constructed. This building is the only secular stone structure dating from before 1666 still standing in the City of London, having survived both the Great Fire of London and the Blitz. The Guildhall is a physical illustration of the power of the guilds, for as well as providing a venue for the guilds' commercial business, the Guildhall was also used for the civic and administrative duties of the guilds and their members.

The numerous guildhalls across the country continue to be physical legacies of the traditional guilds, and many are still used as meeting places today. Education was an important part of the traditional guilds and the emergence of universities at Bologna, Paris, and Oxford around the year 1200 is also in thanks to the guilds of that time. Along with the physical structures, the quality legacy is undeniably from the guilds and is still evident in both a historical and more modern context today. The Bakers' Marque is a standard of quality intended to help customers make informed choices about their bakery purchases. The Bakers' Marque is an independent organisation focusing on provenance, production and participation in the local community. Not unlike many of the traditional guilds. Customers buying their bread from a bakery awarded the Bakers' Marque can be certain of where their bread comes from and how it was made.

Whilst today there is evidence of the legacies, the well developed guilds, often referred to as fiefdoms, found their political influence and economic power diminish as capitalism and free markets grew across Europe, and in the UK in particular. They still exist today in many different forms, often with a different focus or purpose, though it is evident that they still have a role to play in the modern world of business, politics and the wider society. In the UK there are over

80 'chartered' professional institutions, covering areas of work including finance, engineering, construction, health, law, journalism, personnel and management. Within hospitality there are many professional bodies each with its own focus, and many of them either directly or indirectly have a role to play in enhancing quality standards, developing individuals and thereby influencing and supporting the development of talent specific to their area.

Professional bodies and their value to society

In an uncertain worldh where government, trade associations and trade unions often have to think short term, the professional bodies, with many years of stability do stand out as organizations that provide a constant and consistent drive for technical, productivity and welfare improvements over the long term. They have no political or economic gains as societies, as they are a collective representation of individuals and organizations within business sectors. Professional bodies have at their core the desire to make things better, and in the 21st century this is generally through the sharing and dissemination of information. Professional bodies will focus on issues that improve techniques and processes, maximize advances in technology or sometimes better worker welfare. This third issue is perhaps contentious amongst some professional bodies where the focus is on betterment for members rather than workers generally. Whilst members almost always exist in a competitive environment, the professional bodies are there to help members collaborate rather than compete and thereby maximize benefits to all appropriate stakeholders. With having superior talent being recognized as the prime source of sustainable competitive advantage in high performance organizations, the professional bodies have a clear role to play in supporting all members enhance their ability to develop superior talent to compete ever more effectively.

Whilst professional bodies can and will often promote best practices, these are only 'best' when they're applied in a given context; what works for one company may not work in another. Hospitality companies cannot just mimic the top performers, they need to adapt talent management practices to their own strategy and circumstances and align them closely with their leadership philosophy and value system, while at the same time finding ways to differentiate themselves from their competitors. So whilst the membership supports a collegiate collaboration and sharing, each business, in order to retain a competitive edge must share in this collaboration, but also use talent management for its own competitive advantage.

Professional bodies play a significant role in creating value and the focus on areas such as productivity and social mobility score high on the current political agenda. A recent report *Understanding the Value of Professionals and Professional Bodies*, shows some interesting findings. The report was based on a survey of more than 2,000 members of the public and over 150 MPs regarding their perception of professional bodies. The report indicated that value of professional bodies in UK society is poorly recognized by many people, with only 41% saying they know something about these organizations. So whilst they could perhaps be referred to as unsung heroes, the polling of the public found that 61% agree that professional bodies can help guide government on relevant policies and 48% of MPs scored highly for professional body effectiveness in supporting good policy making in their industry.

The report findings clearly indicate that professional bodies in the UK offer significant value to society in five areas that link to current social and political agendas. These are:

☐ **Productivity** – through increasing the capability of the workforce by promoting best practice and sharing the latest advancements;

☐ **Social mobility** – by providing routes to entry for all and in providing trusted qualifications that remain open to individuals at any point within their career;

☐ **Governance and ethics** – by setting standards for behaviour and competence and sanctioning those who contravene them;

☐ **International development** – by exporting qualifications and professional services via growing international networks;

☐ **Policy formation** – by undertaking research which advances understanding of important issues and by sharing specialist knowledge with decision makers.

An additional point that came from the findings was the indication that those who know about professional bodies would trust a professional more if they knew that they were a member of a professional body. This indicates the level of trust shown to professionals supported by membership of recognized bodies and this trust is from the belief that professional bodies are effective in promoting robust standards of compliance, governance and ethics in their relevant industry or sector.

It is evident that much of the value professional bodies provide both within their industry and to society as a whole goes unnoticed. A good example of this is within the area of talent management. Hospitality organizations, with the support of appropriate professional bodies such as the CIPD and the IoH, develop, coordinate and validate high level professional education and qualifications over many years with little, if any, pull on the Treasury and taxpayers' money. Professional bodies have tended to provide, through their qualifications, a consistent benchmark in education and training over the last 50 years or more. Whilst beyond education their value can be found in areas such as social mobility, productivity, governance and ethical standards, international development and policy formation, a number do play a clear and unambiguous role within education. Those listed in the table below are key players within the UK and international hospitality management field of education.

BHA: British Hospitality Association   www.bha.org.uk

BHA's mission is to champion the UK hospitality industry as the best in the world. They do this through the bringing together of hospitality businesses with government to deliver three clear aims: to secure valuable new jobs for our people; growth for our industry; and competitive advantage for our country. The causes which most matter to the hospitality community form the backbone of BHA's work.

BII: British Institute of Innkeeping   www.bii.org

BII is the professional body representing individuals working across the licensed hospitality industry. It supports its members with a wide range of benefits including: events, newsletters, business magazine, mentoring service, helplines offering advice on legal, licensing, financial and general business issues, as well as numerous other benefits designed to specifically meet the business needs of the individual members.

The BII has charitable status and works across the industry to promote professional standards, well-managed, profitable businesses and responsible drinking, as well as providing advice and support for those working in the industry. It also offers its own qualifications.

CHME: Council for Hospitality Management Education   www.chme.co.uk

The Council for Hospitality Management Education is a non-profit making organisation representing UK, European and international universities and colleges offering higher education programmes in hospitality studies, hospitality management, and related fields. It is CHME's stated purpose to contribute to the professional development and status of UK, European and International hospitality management education, through the sharing of best practice in scholarship and pedagogy.

Euro-CHRIE: European Council on Hotel, Restaurant & Institutional Education   www.eurochrie.org

The European Council on Hotel, Restaurant & Institutional Education is the official federation for Europe, the Mediterranean Basin and Africa of International CHRIE, the leading international organisation that supports education and training for the world's largest industry. The European Federation brings together educators from hospitality & tourism management schools and universities into a global network in close co-operation with industry representatives. Under the CHRIE umbrella, both education and industry combine their efforts to shape the future of hospitality & tourism.

ICHRIE: International Council of Hotel Restaurant & Institutional Education   www.chrie.org

ICHRIE is a not-for-profit professional association and provides programs and services to continually improve the quality of global education, research, service and business operations in the hospitality and tourism industry. ICHRIE is an inclusive, collegial association that values creative, ethical and progressive action and improvement of global hospitality and tourism education and research.

IoH: Institute of Hospitality   www.instituteofhospitality.org

IoH is the international hospitality professional membership body for managers and aspiring managers who work and study in the hospitality, leisure and tourism industries. The IoH helps more than 10,000 hospitality professionals in 100 countries grow their knowledge, professional profile and expertise by offering a wide range of high quality membership services. These include targeted and regular industry networking events, hospitality qualifications and extensive online quality resources, such as free management guides, *Hospitality* magazine, bi-weekly webinars, e-books and e-journals. Their vision is to provide international hospitality professionals with the highest professional standards of management and education in the hospitality, leisure and tourism sectors and help them become the best and most sought after managers within the industry.

PACE: Professional Association for Catering Education   www.paceuk.org

PACE is the representative body for the hospitality and catering education and training sector in England with links to colleagues in Wales, Scotland and Northern Ireland. Working with, and on behalf of the members they promote excellence and innovation within hospitality and catering education and positively champion the sector and its priorities within the hospitality and related industries.

Springboard: Springboard UK   www.springboard.uk.net

The Springboard Charity helps young people achieve their potential and nurtures unemployed people of any age into work. It helps alleviate poverty by supporting disadvantaged and underprivileged people into sustainable employment within hospitality, leisure and tourism. Springboard's work encourages, motivates, builds confidence, develops the skills required and mentors its beneficiaries to succeed in a career within hospitality, leisure and tourism.

Table 9.1: Key organisations impacting hospitality education

Each of the above bodies adds value to hospitality management education, albeit in different ways with a different focus. The IoH is an industry body that has always had a role in the development of talent within the industry and was prominent in the field of hospitality management education with its own higher education courses. The IoH works with CHME, PACE and Springboard in sharing good practice. With individual membership, it is closest in formation to a traditional professional body and thereby offers many career development benefits to individuals. It also works very closely with UK Universities and colleges in two distinct areas. Whilst the accreditation of many of the UK's degrees is of value to the sector as a whole, individual students can benefit through their universities and colleges being members of the very successful Education Membership Scheme. The IoH has also developed the Passion 4 Hospitality conference and student debate offering many young people the opportunity to network with prominent industry professionals. With support from organizations such as CHME the P4H event grows each year.

The BHA has a distinct role, as an organization membership body that brings businesses and government together, through its specific agenda and campaigning focus, in order to ensure that members' interests are effectively represented at a national level. It engages with government, the media and the general public to raise awareness of many important issues. In 2016 four core campaigns were running. The first two of these are specifically around the area of encouraging talent into the hospitality industry. The first is to inspire the next generation of hospitality talent through The Big Hospitality Conversation. The BHA is looking for the creation of 300,000 new jobs in the hospitality industry by 2020 with a focus of 60,000 job opportunities for young people aged 16-24. This campaign runs alongside the second of facilitating access of workers into the UK to fill the many vacant positions through asking the government to improve the process, the cost and the perception of visa access to the UK. The third and fourth campaigns fit comfortably into the role professional bodies have in improving quality and offering benefits to society overall. The campaigns focus on areas such as requesting the government to reduce VAT, as well as more educational campaigns promoting responsible hospitality practices to members on issues around salt intake, food safety, allergen awareness and food wastage.

The BII being industry sub-sector specific is like many other smaller professional bodies in supporting those working in the hospitality industry. As a membership organization is supports its members in a variety of areas and in particular it has its own, well developed, education training and awards through the BIIAB.

CHME and CHRIE share similarities though differ through geography and size. Whilst ICHRIE and EUROCHRIE are clearly on an international scale with members from across the world CHME is more UK-centric albeit with a growing European base. Whilst each are open to individuals, their membership profile tends to be predominately universities, colleges and other higher education institutions offering hospitality management education. All three bodies pride themselves on the sharing of world renowned research. Much of this is pedagogic in nature and thereby focused on the development of the next generation of managers presently in the universities. Most universities offering hospitality programmes will be members of one or both of CHME and CHRIE, giving the tutors access to world leading research in the fields of both hospitality and tourism through annual research conferences, as well as through peer-reviewed journal articles. With their focus on research and co-creation with the hospitality industry, they are often perceived to be at the forefront of developing talent for those early in their management careers.

PACE, whilst similar to CHME in that it is UK-based, is predominately made up of members more aligned to further education (16-19 year olds). PACE is very successful in bringing together industry and education, thereby helping the two parties most interested in the development of talent work together in knowledge and skill development. The annual conference is very successful in meeting this aim.

Springboard is not explicitly a membership organization, nor is it a professional body of any sort. It does however deserve to be mentioned due to the work it does in helping, supporting and encouraging young people to enter the hospitality industry and gain the skills needed to enhance their careers. Springboard, as a charity, does a lot of work in developing attracting young people into the industry assisting them in their early stages of careers development. A significant value that Springboard brings to higher education is the development of the INSPIRE standards for student placements. This is fully supported by CHME, BHA and IoH, giving just one example of how the different organizations can work in supporting one another.

Whilst the next section will highlight how individuals can take from and benefit from the relevant association, the bodies will not work as progressive collective organisations unless there are also individuals making an impact by positive involvement in issues and by giving back to their industry. Many associations work hard on behalf of their members to affect industry at government or societal level, allowing members to have a larger influence on their industries. It is much easier for a large association comprised of hundreds or thousands of companies, such as the British Hospitality Association's influence on the development of the Tourism Council, to affect change and leadership than it is for just one.

Professional bodies and their value to the talent pool and individuals

Whilst it could appear that outside of hospitality some professional bodies inhibit access to careers in specific fields to those who are unqualified, this is less evident within hospitality and tourism. The roles carried out by those listed above in promoting education and career choices can actually open up and propel the careers of many people at whatever stage they are in their career. Those educational organisations that are members of the bodies listed in the table are perceived to be offering trusted qualifications that remain open to individuals at any point within their career, thereby offering employers talented employees who can be selected on merit. Professional bodies have an important role to play to encourage their members to offer fairer access, whether social, gender or race, and thereby discourage discrimination. In hospitality they can, and do, reinforce the predominant culture that promotes aspiration for all. Members of the bodies work on commonly shared issues and thereby build a strong rapport between the key players.

The last decade has seen job availability stagnant, unemployment rates on the rise or remaining high and in particular the growth of zero hours contracts has reinforced insecurity in the job marketplace. At the same time manpower shortages in terms of both quality and quantity is one of the major HR challenges the hospitality industry faces. Research by Pricewaterhouse Coopers indicates that compared to other industries, hospitality and leisure rank second in terms of lack of skilled candidates. Among CEOs of hospitality/leisure organisations, 60% indicated that there was a deficit in skilled staff, 34% indicated that the hiring of staff had become more difficult. This has led to companies tightening their labour budgets and focusing on productivity levels through talent retention and development within the organization's labour force. Professional bodies play a role in ensuring quality standards are retained amongst member organizations and thereby retaining good employment practices. Within this environment of budget restraints, individual key relationships are become more and more important to individual professional success.

Associations are useful networks of people to approach, as an individual, and take advantage of when seeking changes in employment and/or new business opportunities. Membership of the relevant association will, through networking opportunities, allow individuals access to others of influence within the professional body that can, with proper investment yield returns in times of need. The relationship is reciprocal in that employers and those of influence will look within the association, or use the association's events for recruiting their new talent. Those individuals with active involvement within professional bodies will use the well known phrase *'it's all about who you know'* to their own advantage. Being actively involved in the relevant association can be valuable on a wide variety of fronts, both personally and professionally. It can be argued that annual membership fees may be one of the wisest investments to make, particularly in the present economy.

9

Hospitality professional bodies and their value to early careerists and students

Whilst in some professions, for example accountancy, surveying and many areas of engineering, a professional qualification can be essential to practice, the hospitality industry has no such demands. The lack of demand however does not negate the value offered of membership particularly early on in a professional career. The relevant professional body will set the formal route for qualification, covering examinations and assessment, competence and experience required, and standards for professional ethics. Within hospitality and its allied industries membership of a professional body is not essential. It is though certainly perceived to be of value. Membership can add value to a CV in a tangible way and the benefits from membership are evident to many.

Within hospitality, the IoH accredit many degree courses and offer the educational membership scheme to attract young talent into the association at an early stage in their career. The accreditation of qualifications is one of a range of important activities the IoH undertake to protect their profession's reputation, its practitioners and the general public. Membership as an individual allows one to have letters after their name and thereby have the moral expectation that the individual will need to maintain their professional standards to keep them. Professional institutions will then often provide guidance to encourage competences to be sustained and individuals continue to develop professionally through accredited CPD courses, e-learning and other methods for gaining experience, knowledge and skills.

Many bodies will attract those very early in their career through student membership, thereby allowing young people to benefit from the resources and knowledge base of a professional body. The IoH, like other bodies, argues that they can be great value in kick-starting a career. Making connections and building a network of peers and experts is one of the biggest benefits of being in a professional association and this can be done at a very early stage. The benefits of student membership are:

☐ **Kudos:** The membership will be an impressive addition to the CV, and also show a level of early commitment to a career area. This is particularly important if students get involved in the association's activities.

☐ **Advice:** the association will often give members access to career advice.

☐ **Information and resources:** regular news updates, the dissemination of key information and knowledge through publications and journals, online services and events are all accessible through membership.

☐ **Peer and professional networks:** meeting and networking with experienced professionals as well as like-minded students in regional branch activities and student-focused services is important particularly at early stages of a career.

☐ **Lobbying:** professional bodies work to represent all their members' interests and being part of a body that has a relationship with the media and the government regarding key issues.

Membership alone does not support career progression, not does it give the benefits above. Those bodies with the most to offer expect involvement at all levels of the organization by those in various stages of their career. The collegiate approach from hundreds of years ago is still important today. There are many ways for individuals to be involved within the many associations as well as within employing organizations. Working with other members, within the same sector, will not only establish relationships with industry colleagues but the sharing of skills and knowledge might one day pay-off as a referral and career advancement.

The human capital theory is a concept used by many hospitality organizations around the world and as such, has been implemented into many H.E. systems as Human Capital Theory links economic success to the education of the workforce. This is the notion that educated employees who obtain key interpersonal skills are the future success of any company trying to succeed. Associations such as the IoH offer professional development opportunities in many forms, and through participation in these sessions individuals are able to be up to date with industry trends and technologies, reinforcing the benefits of the association to society as a whole as well as to the individuals involved.

Although employees need key skills, they also need to be 'capable' in order to make important decisions with confidence. This means, capable people have confidence in their ability to:

1 Take effective and appropriate action,

2 Explain what they are seeking to achieve,

3 Live and work effectively with others, and

4 Continue to learn from their experiences, both as individuals and in association with others, in a diverse and changing society

Learning activities

1 Consider the role of Springboard as a charity. How much independence does this give the body in its campaigns and areas of influence?

2 Explore the campaigns being promoted by the BHA at present. Consider which of these are more important and why?

3 Watch the BHA video *Welcoming the World.* http://www.bha.org.uk/welcoming-the-world/ Consider the issues and solutions that are being highlighted by the different stakeholders.

9

References and further reading

Barron, P. , (2008). Education and talent management: Implications for the hospitality industry. *International Journal of Contemporary Hospitality Management*, **20** (7), 730-742.

BHA, (2016). http://www.bha.org.uk/bhconversation/why-does-it-matter/

Green, B. (2015). *Understanding the Value of Professionals and Professional Bodies*. Chartered Institute of Building (CIOB)

De Munck, B. (2011) Guilds, product quality and intrinsic value. Towards a history of conventions? *Historical Social Research*, **36**,103-124.

ILO. (2015). *World Employment and Social Outlook 2015: The changing nature of jobs*. International Labour Office. ILO. Geneva.

Knight and Yorke, (2002) *Learning & Employability: Embedding employability into the curriculum*. The Higher Education Academy. York.

Melling, J.K. (2003) *Discovering London's Guilds and Liveries*. Shire Publications. Oxford.

Pricewaterhouse Coopers (2012a). Delivering results through talent - the HR challenge in a volatile world. http://www.pwc.com/talentmanagement

Pricewaterhouse Cooper. (2012b) Key trends in human capital 2012 - a global perspective. http://www.pwc.com/talentmanagement

Raines, L. (n.d) The Value of Professional Organizations: Keeping a network of contacts current is an investment in yourself. The Atlanta Journal-Constitution. Available at: http://www.fernley.com/bestpractices/membership_recruitment/The_Value_of_Professional_Organizations.pdf

Stahl, G. K., Bjorkman, I., Farndale, E., Morris, S. S., Paauwe, J., Stiles, P. , Trevor, J. and Wright, P. , (2012). Six principles of effective global talent management. *MIT Sloan Management Review*, **53** (2), 25-42.

10 The Role of Situated Learning in Shaping Talent

Craig Wight

Learning objectives

Work based learning (WBL) is an increasingly popular mode of situated learning that is based on an emerging paradigm that considers learning through experience to be the foundation for tacit knowledge. This chapter reports on the findings of exploratory research undertaken during the academic year 2011-2012 on students studying hospitality management degrees at Plymouth University. Qualitative research was undertaken to make sense of student perceptions of situated learning in Food and Beverage Management at stage five of three hospitality management based programmes.

The paper introduces three organising themes and a set of recommendations to enhance teaching and learning strategies and to offer some insight into the role that this kind of capability-building can play in fostering talent amongst graduates on hospitality management programmes.

At the end of this chapter you should have achieved the following learning outcomes:

- Be able to analyse the underlying philiosophy of situated learning in the development of talent within an education setting.

- Have an awareness of the type of work based activities that can be built into a hospitality and tourism curriculum.

- Critically analyse the benefits that a situated learning approach brings to both students and employees.

- Consider a whole new approach to the hospitality and tourism curriculum in higher education settings.

Introduction

Early literature concerning pedagogical advancements in Higher Education (HE) has argued that the knowledge necessary to perform useful work cannot exist purely in the form of a body of information to be learned (Raelin, 1997). Work based learning (henceforth WBL) is an increasingly popular mode of situated learning that is based on an emerging pedagogical paradigm that considers learning through experience to be the foundation for tacit knowledge (Foster and Stephenson, 1998). The Higher Education Academy (2006) suggest that changing employment patterns in organisations have impacted on the demand for higher level skills such as flexibility and problem solving, and WBL is a response from HE institutions to equip graduates with the skills sought by industry.

This paper, based on interpretivist thematic research, explores student perceptions towards industry based situated learning experienced by a group of level 5 (stage 2) continuing students studying Undergraduate *Food and Beverage Management* as part of a wider, hospitality focussed programme of study at Plymouth University. Qualitative research was undertaken, based on a combination of two rounds of cross-sectional interviews (undertaken at the outset, and then again at the end of the academic year 2011–2012) with a focus group interview during a period of retrenchment, that saw a model of learning enrichment based on contributing to the operation of a training restaurant replaced with a new model of WBL to connect students with local enterprise. The research had the ultimate aim of producing a set of actionable recommendations designed to strengthen the approach to WBL as a central element of two food and beverage management modules in subsequent years. It is therefore a body of work that is produced with the specific intention to inform future practise in this area, certainly at a local level, and potentially at a broader level and it offers implications for the shaping of talent amongst undergraduates. These aims are achieved through the development of a thematic network that identifies three overarching or organising themes that are then used to form recommendations to enhance future academic practice towards the delivery of an efficient and comprehensive food and beverage management module developed around fostering talent. Specifically the study sets out to add to knowledge in the field of WBL as an enrichment strategy for learning about food and beverage management in hospitality. It therefore explores perceptions of work based pedagogical enrichment based on the first hand experiences of students enrolled on a work based learning module. As such, the study locates and analyses the perceived value of situated learning amongst a cohort of food and beverage management students who are required to develop skills and talent in hospitality management to enhance their chances of employability.

The motivation to undertake this research stems from a recent repositioning of learning strategies within the Tourism and Hospitality School at Plymouth University. Whereas the traditional model of learning saw students interact in an artificial trading environment, the university increasingly advocates the value of forming partnerships with local industry to produce students who are fit for 'practice, purpose, award and the world of work' (Plymouth University, 2012). This research provides some evaluative reflection over the success of this strategic repositioning as it applies in practice. Although WBL is accepted as 'the new frontier' in learning enrichment in the micro-environment of Plymouth Business School, there have been no attempts to date to carry out in-house research to support, and indeed to evaluate the idea that such a mode of learning adds value to the student experience and encourages talent. The paper begins with a discussion of contemporary concepts of situated learning before taking a closer look at this pedagogical approach in the context of vocational degree teaching, and in the terms of hospitality and tourism through the primary research undertaken.

Towards an understanding of work based learning

Boud and Garrick (1999) were amongst the first authors to note of educational institutions a trend towards engaging with the 'world of work' using ever more sophisticated approaches. Indeed the authors acknowledge the central proposition of learning as an aspect of any given career trajectory, since learning has historically been accepted as something that prepares people for work, yet it is increasingly acknowledged as the 'lifeblood' which now sustains it. The visible strands of the political and educational discourses that have emerged alongside these trends manifest as terminologies such as 'lifelong learning' and 'continuing adult education'. Bailey *et al.* (2003) suggest that WBL, if it is executed with care, can play an important role in strengthening the educational preparation of young people. To offer an overarching definition, based on an analysis of multiple suggestions (Boud and Garrick, 1999; Foster and Stephenson, 2006; Johnson, 2010; Rowley 2003 and Reeve and Gallagher, 2007), it is accepted by most that situated (or 'work based') learning is a transition-led strategy to support young people who have already chosen an occupational direction. It is an induction to a 'community of practice' (Bailey *et al.*, 2003) that is experienced to varying degrees through a pedagogical lens that orientates students within the workplace. In practical terms, WBL sees students undertake work experience over an agreed period of time with an employer external to the university with a view to completing some scheme of assessed output; usually a reflective analysis or evaluation against set criteria (Korthagen, 2010). Typically, the expectation of the academic is that WBL will form a major aspect of the student's studies and will offer them an opportunity to apply theory to practice (Rowley, 2003:131) by enhancing their skills and talent in the critical evaluation of theory based on the insights of its application to work, and by encouraging them to use theoretical concepts and models as a lens through which to make sense of the organisation. Such an approach also supports students in preparing an assessed output that demonstrates analytical ability in linking theory with practice. In terms of the assessment of WBL outputs, Costley and

10

Armsby (2006) note that the underlying purpose of this type of learning strategy should dictate the approach. Subsequently, assessment criteria are usually based either on a subject discipline or on generic work-based abilities. The context of the unit of analysis for this research is WBL rooted in a specific subject discipline which sees students immersed in commercialised food and beverage production and service operations.

In a food and beverage management context, WBL is about connecting students with experiences in commercial catering operations. The process of managing WBL is a challenging one, even when the student has been comprehensively prepared and briefed, and it is an initiative that depends on strong support in order to succeed. Indeed, some students have struggled with the application of theory to work, and others with the necessity to come up with a research strategy to collect and analyse data (Rowley, 2003). Self-reflection, particularly in writing and structuring an evaluation or assessment of a WBL experience also present difficulties for students. Indeed, Kirschner *et al.* (2006) note that instructional approaches delivered with minimal guidance have historically been considered to be less effective and efficient than approaches that place a strong emphasis on guidance. Crucially these authors identify that two assumptions underpin instructional autonomous learning approaches: they challenge students to solve 'authentic' problems or develop complex knowledge in applied settings in which they are challenged to construct solutions; and they presuppose that knowledge can be effectively acquired through experiences based on the observation of theory in practice. Regardless of these complexities, Rhodes and Shiel (2007) note that enquiry and evaluation skills are nonetheless explicit in all forms of WBL since participants are ultimately required to engage in a learning process that requires some engagement with practice, theory and context. Discovery learning is therefore keenly implied and, as such, must be supported and facilitated with an appropriate level of support and guidance.

In terms of the learning theories that support WBL, it has been suggested (Johnson, 2010) that any WBL approach needs to develop upon surface and deep learning (which encourage background reading and reflections over relationships with the topic and subject matter) towards a model of 'discovery learning'. The latter approach advocates that the principal content of what is to be learned is not provided by the teacher, but is instead 'discovered' by the learner. The centrality of the approach is therefore that the learner is active in the process. The related notion of Gestalt-insight theory (that insists the brain is holistic with self-organising tendencies) describes an active role for the student who develops new knowledge by appreciating the whole conceptual pattern of what is to be learnt (Johnson, 2010). Crucially, work experience must be related to some underlying problem which is puzzled over by the autonomous student, and the degree of this autonomy will depend on the level of the award that it is attached to (Savery, 2006). Such experiential learning should involve the definition of a problem and some analysis and understanding of the problem along with the generation of possible options to solve the problem (Cusins, 1995).

Central to these criteria is the notion that the student is part of their own research. Despite such assertions and despite the fact that traditional efforts to record, assess and accredit WBL formally have been developed over time, Foster and Stephenson (2006) reflect that the controversy around WBL has always been the extent to which control over the process is in the hands of education providers, rather than in the hands of the employers and students. Indeed, the authors acknowledge one of the central criticisms that is levelled at WBL, which is that despite the incorporation of work-based learning into degree programs, the courses and modules developed remain largely designed and controlled by universities and tutors, who reserve the right to regulate the validation process in the shape of teaching and assessment. These criticisms, to some degree, compromise the idea that WBL initiatives are produced based on the idea that preparing students for the expectations of the employer and of employment are central objectives (Zemblyas, 2006). Whilst a number of authors advocate placing emphasis on learner autonomy by allowing students to determine or negotiate the purpose, activities, programme, outcomes and assessment of their WBL development, research is required to evaluate the extent to which such autonomy is ultimately cultivated successfully. This paper produces tentative indicators in pursuit of a wider understanding of such perceived autonomy. Amongst the contemporary challenges raised in the discussion above is the identification of a suitable learning environment in which to carry out an employment experience to best foster the kinds of skills and talent sought by employers. It is with this aspect of WBL that this paper is concerned.

Of interest here are the views of Cornford and Gunn (2006) who challenge the effectiveness of off-site learning in suggesting many of the skills fail to adequately transfer from the training setting to the workplace. Knowledge, they argue, is situated and is therefore the product of the activity, context and culture in which it is developed and used. Indeed, the Higher Education Academy (2006) acknowledge that there are varied levels of emphasis on WBL provision and some are driven by institutional mission, whilst others occur as a by-product of some other initiative. Crucially, they further observe that learner outcomes are identified and developed increasingly by the learner, employer and academic institution, and these outcomes form the basis of a 'learner contract'. The challenge which motivated the research reported upon in this paper was to develop a module with a reflective experiential focus, from one that had previously been taught alongside exposure to an artificial training environment, to one that is based on a WBL evaluation. A further challenge was to simultaneously maintain recognition of a diverse group of students with varied skills sets, talents and aspirations. Lester and Costley (2010) develop upon the issue of maximising the value and effectiveness of WBL strategies and they suggest the most effective and valuable learning that can be undertaken in this context is responding to specific workplace issues as opposed to immersion in formal training or off-job programmes. Such an approach accommodates a strategy of placing students in environments of varying complexities that match their skills sets, yet challenge them to develop new talents in unfamiliar situations. However, Wood and Reeves (2007) caution that, whilst interaction is an essential ingredient in any such learning process, each interaction does not lead to increased learning, and only interactions that are subjectively meaningful to participants will yield real returns.

The centrality of WBL experience is summarised well by Gibson and Busby (2009:1,473) who note that industry contact of this nature:

> ...is intended to provide a vocational dimension to what can be a predominantly academic curriculum... (and to) provide familiarity with professional practice... raise graduate labour-market value and, arguably, enhance the individual's maturity

The nature of the WBL contact that students were asked to achieve was to be of a duration of some three 'shifts', lasting up to seven hours in any commercial food and beverage environment. The methodology section below locates the study on a particular philosophical and methodological horizon considered appropriate to identify and analyse student perceptions of WBL in two contrasting environments, each offering a unique set of challenges. Crucially, the research develops upon existing literature on WBL (which focusses most keenly on university and employer positions on the issues) by adding the voice of the student into the base of knowledge.

Methodology

This research is based on a small group of undergraduate students and is therefore naturally open to an interepretivist approach. Value is placed on exploring the perceptions and values of a sample of Food and Beverage Management students who were uniquely positioned to offer valuable feedback on two approaches to situated learning, having undertaken periods of work experience in an 'artificial' training restaurant during 2010/2012 and in a commercial environment during 2011/2012. As Boyce and Neale (2006) note, when in-depth interviews are conducted, generalizations about the results are untypical since small samples are chosen. Probability sampling is appropriate for research such as this (Bryman and Bell, 2007) since the participants are considered uniquely representative of the target population: level 5 students who have experienced work based learning. Although generalizability is not possible, the findings of research based on in-depth interviews are useful when informing the future direction of programmes of study in higher education. The class comprised of some 48 students and 8 students participated in two interviews. The size of sample was dictated by what can be considered a general rule for interview sample sizes; that when the '...same stories, themes, issues, and topics begin to emerge then a sufficient sample size has been reached' (Boyce and Neale, 2006).

Three qualitative research approaches were triangulated to identify permanencies and variations across contrasting sets of findings. Two set of cross-sectional semi-structured interviews were undertaken at the start and at the end of the academic year to contrast student expectations of situated learning with the realised experience. A focus group dovetailed with the second set of interviews in order to add rigour to the procedure and fortify the findings. Qualitative research interviews attempt to understand the world from the subjects' points of view and to unfold the meaning of peoples' experiences. Bryman and Cramer (1994) identify three kinds of interview technique as structured, unstructured and semi-structured. Semi-structured interviews were undertaken with cognisance of the need to access and speak to a small group of students in some depth. Such interviews are carried out based on an 'open' framework which facilitated a focused, conversational mode of two-way communication (Bryman, 2012). As Cohen *et al.* (2007) recommend, efforts were made to demarcate pragmatic, ethical and moral questions and to ensure questions remained impartial, non-invasive and relevant only to the research question. Students were given participant information sheets and were also offered the opportunity to withdraw from the research process at any time without the requirement to provide an explanation or notice. Recordings of interviews were destroyed following analysis.

In terms of the content of the first interview, students were asked to reflect on the experience of working in a training restaurant. The approach to contextualised learning in food and beverage management in the School of Tourism and Hospitality up to this point had been to place students in a training restaurant (*Pilgrims)* in order to carry out food and beverage service and preparation. The interview approach here was to gather a baseline of data in order to make comparisons between student perceptions of this simulated training environment with perceptions of work based leaning, in order to understand the challenges and the pedagogical support needs in each case. The second set of interviews therefore sought to explore student perceptions of situated (work based) learning in industry in order to make comparisons between the two experiences. On both occasions, students were asked to discuss the value of each learning experience and to identify the extent to which these experiences were successful learning experiences, in terms of the viewing the commercial environment through the lens of academic theory and market intelligence. Elaboration was provided around these issues where necessary.

Thematic (or textual) analysis was undertaken in order to make sense of the recorded interviews and focus groups. Such a form of data analysis is seen as a flexible method useful to identify and group key themes based on data that is collected qualitatively. Thematic analysis is a qualitative analytical tool that belongs to the broader methodological concept of discourse analysis (Boyatzis, 1998). Discourse as a concept arose out of the argument that social and cultural life is invested with meaning and value by regular symbolic representations. Foucault pioneered the argument that discourse acts as a predisposing mechanism and a social filter for possible meaning (Coupland and Gwyn, 2003:1) and his notions of power, discipline and knowledge have made profound imprints on thought in many fields of human concern. Textual analysis attends to more than analyses of coherent, structured and written sentences. Various analyses of texts can be carried out depending on the desired research outcome; for example, narrative analysis, rhetorical analysis, semantic and semiotic analysis. Each provides a different focus, and each is normally dependent upon the objective of analysis (Van Dijk, 1998). Examples of discourse can include conversation, news reports, lessons and teaching, and email. For this study, analysis was carried out on recordings of interviews and focus groups. Data familiarisation is as fundamental to thematic analysis as it is for other forms of qualitative analysis. It is therefore crucial, for this method to work, that researchers manage the data collection, transcription and analysis stages alone, to make sense of narrative (Bryman, 2012).

A key limitation of this research is its cross-sectional, ad hoc nature and the fact that it cannot be generalised in the absence of additional layers of quantitative analysis or further instances of qualitative enquiry undertaken in similar circumstances. In order to add value to this set of findings, it would pay to carry out further research based perhaps on other small groups of undergraduate students carrying out situated learning in other subject areas. Positivist research might develop new knowledge in this area based on statistical analyses of the variables that influence successful situated learning (such as age, gender and level of experience). Future research could also add value by extending qualitative enquiry to explore the views and experiences of academics on the delivery end of situated learning. This research is, however, self-consciously focussed, specifically on student perceptions of situated learning with a view to offering lessons for the pedagogical development of such approaches to learning.

Findings: Work based learning perceptions

Data analysis was undertaken based on a cross-referenced analysis of issues identified from the three research methods applied, and three core themes were identified in relation to the experiences of students undertaking WBL towards the completion of a level 5 (stage 2) module in Food and Beverage Management. These were organised into a thematic network (Attride-Stirling, 2001) which is based upon three 'organising' themes (see Figure 10.1). The themes are linked back to the research question; to understand the perceptions of students engaging with situated learning in food and beverage management. Each organising theme represents an aspect of WBL with potential for further pedagogical development.

The network is discussed below with reference to how teaching practice can respond to each of the 'organising themes' with implications for fostering talent. It is important to clarify that each of these themes is a summary of the more common aspects of feedback on WBL that students shared through interviews and the focus group. The purpose is to develop academic practice that responds to student perceptions of the situated learning experience in a food and beverage management context. The research was undertaken during a period of retrenchment that saw students who were used to participating in situated learning in a training environment asked to seek out employment in a local, commercial, food and beverage business. The findings therefore offer value particularly for new or evolving modules with a WBL focus in a hospitality management subject.

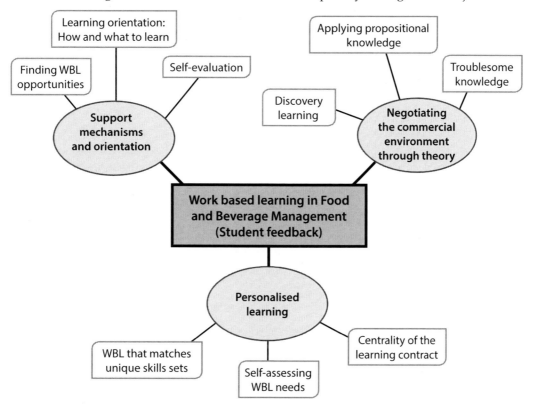

Figure 10.1: Thematic network of work based learning perceptions

Support mechanisms and orientation

Analysis suggests that the WBL experience is co-created between the academic, the student and the employer. Crucial to the efficiency of the arrangement is the need to establish and maintain links with local industry stakeholders and to broker the initial point of contact between student and employer. Beyond this, and from a learning point of view, it is important that students understand how to learn, what to learn, when they have learned and what learning is informed by (Brodie and Irving, 2007) in the situated learning context. Students that were interviewed spoke of the need to combine the process of seeking out employment opportunities with establishing the required 'return' on the employment opportunity from an assessment point of view early on in the process. One of the students suggested that:

> I think we need to be quite organised from the outset; so at the start of the year we can approach a number of participating F&B operations and know what to ask them.

10

The challenge for the teaching practitioner therefore, in communicating (early on) the principles of WBL, is to support students in being able to identify where learning has occurred and to equip them with the tools necessary to provide evidence of how learning has been achieved through assessment. As Brodie and Irving (2007) suggest, students need to establish the validity of the conclusions they come to through an analysis of their experiences and consequent learning, so assessment tasks will require them to reflect critically and effectively. Support is therefore required at a one-to-one level and in the form of seminar discussions throughout the academic year to ensure that WBL is not simply approached as a 'box ticking' exercise. Such support mechanisms must be in place even before the start of the academic year in order that students understand the requirements of the module and appreciate the need to seek out work experience locally. Finally, the experience of the WBL team behind the modules discussed in this paper has also been informed by involvement in a 'back to the floor' job shadowing experience day organised by Hilton Hotels UK. The author was invited to complete a shift within the hotel working with operations staff to appreciate the current issues and challenges associated with operational employment in hotels. Such an experience is valuable in negotiating and planning a situated learning module that is achievable and realistic from the point of view of the learner.

Negotiating the commercial environment through the lens of theory

Interviews would suggest that students who engaged well with WBL had adopted a personalised learning approach in the work place, based on the application of propositional knowledge. Cornford and Gunn (2006) identify the need for the student to negotiate the difference between work-*place* learning and work *based* learning. The former occurs when any kind of developmental up-skilling occurs within the place of employment, whilst the latter involves a combination of academia and workplace experiences with a specific outcome external to the workplace. As one of the students noted:

> *I think maybe you pay a bit more attention to the workplace since you know you need to do an assignment on it so you notice it (the environment) more.*

Understanding the requirements of WBL was clearly linked to the concept of 'discovery learning' and the requirement for the learner to be active in the process and to acquire and apply appropriate and relevant knowledge (Johnson, 2010). Yet aspects of the interviews also suggest that students were faced with the prospect of acquiring 'troublesome knowledge' and challenging threshold concepts (Perkins, 2006); that is to say that some experienced 'emotional turmoil' of the type that has been associated with the requirement to engage in critical thinking (Perkins, *op cit*). One student reflected on their attempt to locate propositional knowledge in the workplace and noted:

> *I could see what was happening to some extent but, like, I wasn't really seeing it (management practice) at face value and I had to ask (management) about some of the things (learning outcomes) to make sense of them.*

One of the issues mooted during interviews to support students in over-coming troublesome knowledge in WBL, was the idea of maintaining a reflective blog to record 'critical incidents' and other relevant observations in the workplace. The idea was met with some support, as one student noted:

> *Looking back now – it (a reflective blog) would help with the assignment; I know what I did but it would help with the assignment if you wrote it down.*

Such an approach has been tested with some success by Johnson (2010) and is recommended as a supportive tool for students engaging in hospitality based situated learning. The qualitative data for this research would suggest that students place value on directed study, and are more comfortable in modules where self-orientation is marginal. However, troublesome thresholds are accepted as the key to discovery learning and the type of critical thinking that is encouraged in the final year of an undergraduate degree; and where such learning is valued (as in situated learning) the experience can be supported with meta-learning approaches such as the maintenance of a reflective log or a learning diary to record the acquisition of new skills. WBL is therefore seen as a valuable threshold to cross towards the development of critical thinking during level 2 of a hospitality degree.

Personalised learning

According to Osbourne *et al.* (1998) matching the curriculum to the student is most effective when the curriculum adapts to student interests and needs, not vice versa. However, Reeve and Gallagher (2007) have observed that, increasingly, partnerships between the student, the faculty and the employer are agenda-led, and tend to overshadow the centrality of the learner in the situated learning setting. Crucial here is the need to develop teaching and learning strategies that involve students as active learners that can identify and develop upon their own interests (Osbourne *et al.*, 1998), with clear implications for the shaping of skills and talent. Interviews for this research would suggest that WBL as a strategy has been successful to some extent in promoting discovery learning that is independent and personalised.

Amongst the comments captured from students were the following:

> *Some found it (WBL) tough, but for me it was useful since I knew the material (learning outcomes) and the people I worked with – it was a good thing. The theory made sense and if I did not get (understand) it I would manage to get folk (ask colleagues) to make sense of it in context so it (WBL) was helpful.*

> *I would not have understood how the theory applied on the ground and how you would implement it if was not for WBL.*

The interviews holistically point to some success in WBL as a strategy to promote discovery learning and critical thinking. However, other feedback suggests that such learning was influenced to a significant degree by the level of engagement with the module and by individual student efforts to seek out and take advantage of WBL opportunities (even when such opportunities were guaranteed through arrangements made with external employers by the university). It was also influenced by the varied skills sets and knowledge of students at the time of embarking upon the module.

It is clear that those students already employed in a food and beverage management setting at the outset of the module had some advantage over those that were not, and those that commenced employment in a commercial food and beverage setting for the specific purposes of fulfilling the module. The following comments were captured in this regard:

> *For some with no job –they were thrown in at the deep end if they only took a few shifts. This is what was good about* Pilgrims *(the former training restaurant at Plymouth University) but WBL is a real industry and the challenges are also real.*

> *I had already done this (picked up work experience) before in the summer. I had an advantage since ... I have a good relationship with the managers anyway – the restaurant manager was not so helpful but the head chef was.*

> *Because I did it (WBL) over Christmas it worked well for me, but maybe if I'd had to stay on over here and work (over Christmas) it would have been too much. It was tough for some to source work.*

> *Yes – I was able to talk to one of the chefs so he helped with mine (understanding the WBL assignment) but if you did not have that relationship with staff it might be hard but it makes you think about how things work.*

The data would suggest that a systematic approach to supporting students in identifying and taking advantage of work experience opportunities is perhaps necessary. It also, however, suggests that learning arrangements (perhaps in the form of a learning contract) should be tailored to meet the needs of individual students; as opposed to creating a syllabus narrative that assumes all participants have equal levels of skills and similar talents in relation to the topic that is being covered. Crucial here is the inclusion of some of the criteria, identified by Osbourne *et al.* (1998), in the development of a learning contract that should task students with the identification of a suitable WBL operation, comprehensively defined critical incidents to identify and reflect over, appropriate levels of tutor support and the nature and criteria of assessment. In addition to these and in response to interviews, this paper recommends that students are exposed to a number of practical demonstrations and industry field trips to support and enhance learning at a generic level; to create a module that consists mostly of self-prescribed learning; and to ensure that existing skills and talents are capitalised upon, whilst latent skills and talents are unlocked. Such an approach recognises the diversity of students, from those with well-developed skills and knowledge in food and beverage management through to those with little understanding of the issues.

Discussions and development of practice based on findings

This paper has explored the perceptions of students undertaking WBL towards the completion of a level 5 (stage 2) module in Food and Beverage Management. The aim was to identify a set of recommendations to inform future pedagogical practice and to consider the implications for developing skills and talent. The research was undertaken during a period of retrenchment that saw, not only the introduction of commercial WBL as a teaching and learning strategy within hospitality subjects in the school of Tourism and Hospitality at Plymouth University, but also a shift in the emphasis placed on situated learning, away from the 'safety' of a training restaurant towards a model of student autonomy over the identification and pursuit of commercial employment opportunities with all the valuable risks and incremental learning that comes with this. The paper is confined to a discussion of food and beverage management, and in this sense is corseted by limitations to its scope. It is however useful to fulfil its intention; to produce a set of recommendations to inform future pedagogical practice in this specific module and field. The findings suggest that WBL in food and beverage management must be developed through focussed teaching and learning strategies, central to which are three organising themes of:

1 Negotiating the commercial environment through theory
2 Support mechanisms and orientation, and
3 Personalised learning to foster talent and skills development.

The importance of a reflective blog to record critical incidents in the workplace and the development of a focussed learning contract (unique to food and beverage management) have been identified as vehicles to enhance personal development and learning amongst students. The findings advocate placing emphasis on learner autonomy by allowing students to determine or negotiate the purpose, activities, programme, outcomes and assessment of their WBL development to see real returns in terms of skills development. One way of doing this that can be realistically supported through tutor contact is to identify three sub-cohorts of students that vary according to experience in food and beverage management, and tailor assessment outcomes to challenge each group according to these varied skills. Regardless of the approach, students should be encouraged to co-create realistic, challenging and personalised learning objectives to suit their varying personal and professional backgrounds. Such an approach is seen by the students interviewed for this research as key to developing new skills and talents. Finally, the importance of familiarisation visits and other industry contact undertaken by faculty involved in the delivery of WBL modules merits consideration in order to test the feasibility of WBL related module outcomes. Such familiarisation is also important to keep abreast of the skills and qualities that such employers seek from graduates.

10

Table 10.1 develops the organising themes that have been identified in this research into recommended enhancements to implement into pedagogical practice in the delivery of food and beverage management with a WBL focus.

Table 10.1: Developing pedagogical practice around organising themes

Organising theme	Recommended development/s in pedagogical practice
Support mechanisms and orientation	Relationship management with external WBL employers
	Learning orientation established early and reinforced through bespoke tutorial contact time to review personalised learning objectives
	Occasional immersion in the workplace (academic staff) or other industry familiarisation activities to evaluate the feasibility of learning outcomes and enrich the syllabus
Negotiating the commercial environment through theory	Agreeing an appropriate setting for WBL
	Supporting learning thresholds with meta-learning approaches
	Introducing the need to maintain a reflective blog to record and reflect over critical incidents and the development of news skills and talents
Personalising the learning	Assess capability and identify skills and talent deficits in discussion with the WBL tutor
	Agree standards of performance and match needs to the curriculum
	Agree the contents of a Learning Contract
	Enhance the WBL approach with other enrichment, such as skills focussed filed trips and professional demonstrations

Activities

You can now try the following activities:

1   Consider one of the modules or units that you are currently delivering or studying in the classroom. Design a new curriculum that will incorporate situated learning in the develvery of the module.

2   Critically analyse the advantage that situated learning brings to the development of talent for the sector.

3   Visit a local hospitality and tourism employer and observe how situated learning could be developed using their facilities and expertise. Write a short report of your findings.

4   Organise a focus group of students and/or emplyees to discuss the benefits that a situated learning approach will provide, in their opinion. Write a short report of your findings.

References

Attride-Stirling, J. (2001). Thematic networks: An analytic tool for qualitative research. *Qualitative Research*, **1**(3), 385-405.

Bailey, R.T., Hughes, K.L. and Moore, D.T. (2003). *Working Knowledge: Work Based Learning and Education Reform*, Routledge. New York.

Boud, D. and Garrick, J. (1999). *Understanding Learning at Work*, Routledge. New York.

Boyce, C. and Neale, P. (2006). *Conducting in-depth interviews: A guide for designing and conducting in-depth interviews for evaluation input*. Pathfinder International Tool Series. Monitoring and Evaluation 2. www.pathfind.org.

Boyatzis, R, E. (1998). *Transforming Qualitative Information*. Sage. Cleveland

Brodie, P. and Irving, K. (2007). Assessment in work-based learning: investigating a pedagogical approach to enhance student learning, assessment & evaluation. *Higher Education*, **32** (1), 11-19.

Bryman, A. (2012). *Social Research Methods*, 4th Edition, Oxford University Press.

Bryman, A and Bell, E (2007). *Business Research Methods*, Second Edition, Oxford University Press.

Bryman, A. and Cramer, D. (1994). *Quantitative Data Analysis for Social Sciences*. Routledge, London.

Cohen, L., Manion, L. and Morrison, K. (2007). *Research Methods in Education*, Routledge, London.

Cornford, I. and Gunn, D. (2006). Work based learning of commercial cookery apprentices in the New South Wales Hospitality Industries, *Journal of Vocational Education and Training*, **50**(4) 549-567.

Costley, C and Armsby, P. (2007). Work-based learning assessed as a field or a mode of study. *Assessment & Evaluation in Higher Education*. **32**(1) 21-33.

Coupland, J. and Gwyn, R. (2003). *Discourse, the Body and Identity*. Palgrave Macmillan, London.

Cusins, P. (1995). Action learning revisited, *Industrial and Commercial Training*, **27** (4), MCB University Press.

Foster, E. and Stephenson, J. (2006). Work based learning and universities in the UK: A review of current practice and trends, *Higher Education Research and Development*, **17**(2) 155-170.

Gibson, P. and Busby, G. (2009). Experiencing work: Supporting the undergraduate hospitality, tourism and cruise management student on an overseas work placement. *Journal of Vocational Education and Training*. **16**(4) 467-480.

Higher Education Academy (2006). *Work Based Learning: Illuminating the Higher Education Landscape*, The Higher Education Academy. York, UK.

Johnson, D. (2010). The use of learning theories in the design of a work based learning course at masters level, *Innovations in Education and Training International*, **37**(2) 129-133.

10

Kirschner, P, A., Sweller, J and Clark, R, E. (2006) Why minimal guidance during instruction does not work: An analysis of the failure of constructivist, discovery, problem-based, experiential, and inquiry-based teaching. *Educational Psychologist*, **41** (2), 75-86.

Korthagen, F, A, J. (2010). Situated learning theory and the pedagogy of teacher education: Towards an integrative view of teacher behaviour and teacher learning, *Teaching and Teacher Education*, **26** (1), 98-106.

Lester, S and Costley, C (2010). Work-based learning at higher education level: Value, practice and critique. *Studies in Higher Education*. **35** (5), 561-575.

Osborne, C, Davies, J and Garnett, J. (1998) Guiding the student to the centre of the stakeholder curriculum: Independent and work-based learning at Middlesex University, in Stephenson J.and Yorke M. (eds), *Capability and Quality in Higher Education*, Kogan Page, London: 85-94.

Perkins, D. (2006). Constructivism and troublesome knowledge. In J. H. F. Meyer and R. Land (Eds.) *Overcoming Barriers to Student Understanding: Threshold Concepts and Troublesome Knowledge*: 33-47. Routledge: London.

Plymouth University (2012). Work-based and placement learning. Available at: http://www.plymouth.ac.uk/pages/view.asp?page=28111. Accessed 16/04/2012.

Raelin, J, A. (1997). A model of work based learning, *Organization Science*, **8** (6), 563-578.

Reeve, F. and Gallagher, J. (2007) Employer–university 'partnerships': a key problem for work-based learning programmes? *Journal of Education and Work*, **18** (2), 219-233.

Rhodes, G and Shiel, G. (2007). Meeting the needs of the workplace and the learner through work-based learning. *Journal of Workplace Learning*, **19** (3), 173–187.

Rowley, J. (2003). Action research: An approach to student work based learning, *Education and Training*, **45** (3), 131-138.

Savery, J, R. (2006) Overview of problem-based learning: Definitions and distinctions. *Interdisciplinary Journal of Problem-based Learning*, **1** (1). Available at: http://dx.doi.org/10.7771/1541-5015.1002

Van Dijk, T.A. (1988). *News Analysis: Case Studies of International and National News in the Press*. Lawrence Erlbaum Associates, Hillsdale, New Jersey.

Wood, Y and Reeves, T, C. (2007). Meaningful interaction in web-based learning: a social constructivist interpretation. *The Internet and Higher Education*. **10** (1), 15-25.

Zemblyas, M. (2006). Work-based learning, power and subjectivity: Creating space for a Foucauldian research ethic. *Journal of Education and Work*. **19** (3), 291-303.

PART 3

TALENT MANAGEMENT MEANINGS FOR HOSPITALITY AND TOURISM COMPANIES

11 The Inclusive or Exclusive Concept in Practical Talent Management

Susan Horner

Learning objectives

This chapter considers the philosophical approach that an organisation can adopt to the implementation of talent management. The learning objectives of this chapter are as follows:

- To explore the meaning of the exclusive and inclusive approach to talent management and the underlying philosophies of each approach.

- To consider the links to other important concepts such as equality, trust, value and corporate social responsibility.

- To consider how organisations from the sector have implemented talent management and discuss the links to the academic theory and consider the influence of different types of organisation.

- To evaluate the likely outcomes from different approaches to talent management implementation.

- To evaluate some real life examples from the sector in relation to the above .

Introduction

We saw in Chapter 1 that an organisation can broadly use two different approaches to talent management. The first one is the exclusive approach where talent is bought in and exploited or certain in-house staff are selected for promotion/development. The second approach is the inclusive approach where the organisation tries to develop all staff within the organisation in an equal way or to an equal level. The adoption process depends on the type of organisation, the culture of the organisation and its position in the market place. Other factors such as the availability of labour, and social norms such as where women are denied the chance for certain opportunities or roles will also have an influence.

In the first chapter we saw that Gallardo-Gallardo *et al.*, (2013) suggest that there has been ongoing confusion about the meaning of 'talent' in the work place and that a suitable framework should be adopted to encapsulate the underlying concepts that are involved. This includes grouping theories into two broad areas. The first of these is the theoretical approach to talent as 'object'. This is where talent is considered as a natural ability: talent as master, talent as commitment and talent as some people. The second approach is to conceptualise talent as 'subject', i.e., people possessing special skills or abilities. They summarise these two approaches in a framework for the conceptualisation of talent. In this chapter we are considering the second – 'subject' – approach, and the two general principles that come under this heading of 'exclusivity' and 'inclusivity'.

We will start by thinking about the two approaches from a philosophical approach, then consider the underlying issues, and finally think about how organisations implement talent management in practice and the results that this brings them.

Talent management philosophy

One of the most common definitions of talent management was developed by Collings and Mellahi (2009) as follows:

> *Talent management are the activities and processes that involve systematic identification of key positions that differentially contribute to the organisation's competitive advantage, the development of a talent pool of high potential and high performing incumbents to fill these roles, and the development of a differentiated human resource architecture to facilitate filling these positions with competent incumbents, and to ensure their continued commitment to the organization. (Colling and Mellahi, 2009 p.304).*

This definition suggests that the organization has certain job roles that are mission critical to success of the organization, and other roles that are less strategic and therefore of less importance. If we accept this definition, then the process will be implemented by a combination of outside recruitment, and the development of existing staff to nurture them into senior management roles using a variety of techniques. The emphasis here is on analysis of critical job roles and the selection and development of the appropriate staff to carry out these roles. It is also about keeping the talent pool happy on an individual basis so that they stay in role and keep developing their skill set.

In the first chapter we considered the two types of approach to talent management that involve the consideration of people in the process. We can see that the exclusive approach involves the creation of a talent pool as detailed in the

11

definition above. Most of the elevated management development programmes are organised with this in mind. The inclusive approach involves the organization investing in all staff, and identifying and nurturing their skills and qualities in an appropriate cultural setting. We can see that on the face of it, this appears to be a much fairer system but is likely to cost more money to implement or will restrict spending on the mission critical staff, if they exist because the development budget will be more equally shared. It is less likely to happen in high turnover sectors and maybe a lack of it causes high turnover perhaps?

According to Sparrow and Makram (2015), the people philosophy incorporates two components: first the **individual talent** or **inter-personal approach** that stresses that the individual should do their best. This type of approach is best suited to a competitive culture where leadership is critical and employees are categorized into A, B and C players underpinned by a system where successful individuals are lavishly rewarded, and underperforming individuals are dispensed with. Second, the **collective** or **intra–personal approach** derives from the giftedness or excellence literature and involves individual coaching and mentoring. This approach is more egalitarian, although it is to be expected that high level performances cannot be expected from all staff (Sears, 2003). It is unlikely that an upscale service sector SME could afford this approach.

There has been discussion about the fact that the current talent management literature tends to focus on large multinational and private institutions and often does not apply in small or public sector organisations. Since the majority of organisations in the hospitality and tourism sector are small to medium sized enterprises (SMEs) then this could be a flaw in the work to date (Thunnissen *et al.*, 2013). Their analysis draws on work by other authors and suggests that there are three key limitations to the talent literature and also suggests different approaches to overcome these issues. These can be summarised as follows:

1 The focus is on a narrow set of HR practices. Possible solution – focus on people and their work and employment and work relationship (Boxall and Macky, 2009).

2 Unitarist approach: organization presented as a unified actor. Possible solution – consider the influence and well-being of actors at multiple levels. (Bourdieu, 1988).

3 The managerialist view predominates. Possible solution – consider the multi-faceted value creation of talent management (Kalleberg, 2009: Suchmann, 1995).

This seems to be predicated on the idea of people all wanting to do their best, progress, develop, and reach their full potential. This is probably not true of all staff, as some see work as of no value to them except cash and they change jobs regularly by choice. Also is there perhaps a difference between those wanting a career and those wanting a job? For a further discussion about these new approaches to talent management please see Thunnissen *et al.*, (2013). They suggest, towards the end of the paper, that talent management needs to be considered in a wider range of organisations. Research should focus on talent management at the level of individuals, with a focus on their well-being, and also whether they are treated in a fair and just manner, particularly when an exclusive approach is adopted because this could have an effect on individuals both inside and outside the talent pool. They suggest that the best approach is to introduce characteristics of the exclusive approach but to consider the health and well-being of all employees at the same time (Thunnissen *et al.*, 2013).What is clear is that talent management is not just about recruitment, training and development. The fact that hospitality and tourism organisations often employ transitory workers because of the seasonal nature of the business, also makes this process a particularly challenging one, it can be argued. For any approach to work, people must want and be prepared to be talent managed.

Alternative theoretical frameworks to the talent management process have been proposed by other authors. An example which was developed by Gallardo-Gallardo *et al.*, (2015) involves four alternative frameworks, placed in order of importance as follows:

☐ A **knowledge management approach** based on the creation and application of knowledge that comes from a collective learning process in the organisation. This involves the organisation in encouraging learning and communication across all individuals in this process. Hospitality and tourism organisations often need very specific knowledge in order that they can develop. The role of the celebrity chef, for example, often brings unique specialist knowledge and skills to the organisation and they are also often critical to the development of the organisation in terms of competitive success.

☐ A **career management approach** based on the way in which individual careers are shaped both by the person and within the organisation. This means that both the employee and the employer have to develop an individual understanding and relationship based on trust and openness if talent is to be effectively managed. The recruitment and promise of career development that certain organisations in the hospitality and tourism sector have developed, is an example of this type of approach.

☐ A **social exchange theory approach.** This approach relies on the reciprocal relationships interactions and obligations that exist between employees and their employers. It involves concepts of trust, fairness and fulfilment. The mentoring schemes that some organisations in the sector have introduced are examples of this approach. Many organisations, however, in hospitality and tourism need employees to work unsocial hours, or for long intense periods of time, and these issues can make this process difficult to achieve, it can be argued. You also have to see some positive outcome from mentoring in this situation to want to engage as an employee.

☐ A **strength based approach.** This approach advocates the development of a framework that allows employees to choose the type of work they

11

want to do based on their particular strengths and allow them to develop in this role using organisational and job design. This will bring employee engagement and motivation, it is argued. Organisations in the sector often have very specific career pathways for specific functions which make it difficult for them to change direction, however. Management development programmes are examples of this type of approach. (Gallardo-Gallardo *et al.*, 2015)

How do organisations see things?

The CIPD definition of talent management provides a good overview of how organisations in general understand the meaning of talent management.

Talent consists of those individuals who can make a difference to organisational performance, either through their immediate contribution or in the longer term by demonstrating highest levels of potential.

Talent management is the systematic attraction, identification, development, engagement, retention and deployment of those individuals with high potential who are of particular value to an organisation. (CIPD, 2006)

Interestingly it says nothing about how this super talent will gain super rewards! It also fails to see that many younger people now seem to be more concerned with what value an organisation is to them!

The alignment of talent to the organisation's business strategy to gain competitive advantage is seen as being critical as part of this. A one-day conference was organised by CIPD in 2015 to give delegates valuable insights into the development of flexible and agile talent management strategies to achieve business success. It is interesting to consider the headings of the various sections of the conference to gain an understanding of the current topical issues in the general business sector. These were as follows:

- ☐ Strategic talent planning to support future business priorities
- ☐ Widening your talent pool to overcome skills shortages
- ☐ Leveraging your brand to attract and engage talent
- ☐ Incorporating diversity into your talent strategy
- ☐ Understanding talent analytics and its application to business challenges
- ☐ Engaging your talent with innovative approaches to performance management
- ☐ Building talent development initiatives to retain competitive advantage
- ☐ Developing future leaders to maximise organisational success

CIPD (2015), http://www.cipd.co.uk/events/talent/conference/seminar-programme

This conference considered important issues such as the widening of the talent pool, new and innovative ways of talent management processes including the use of technology, and the incorporation of diversity into talent management, processes which are of critical importance for the hospitality and tourism sectors.

The situation in hospitality and tourism is considered to have many of the same characteristics but because of the skill shortages in many areas of the world, there are particular issues that considered even more critical for the sector. These issues are summarised below in Figure 11.1.

- Mainstream and prioritise talent management as a central corporate objective and have in place a talent strategy.

- Explore alternate talent sources outside of firms and the Travel & Tourism sector.

- Create partnerships to share part-time or seasonal workers between businesses in Travel & Tourism and/ or other sectors.

- Offer different work options to suit different workers (e.g. to females, older workers etc.).

- Provide clear career guidance information and communicate effectively with future talent pools.

- Offer clear career pathways to young workers to promote Travel & Tourism as a viable and rewarding career option.

- Offer more apprenticeships.

- Provide greater corporate input to Travel & Tourism education and training design and teaching.

Figure 11.1: Issues that need consideration by the tourism sector with regards to talent management. *Source:* Adapted from the World Travel and Tourism Council (2015) http://www.wttc.org/-/media/382bb1e90c374262bc951226a6618201.ashx

11

Research carried out with managers in Scotland about their views on the challenges and opportunities of talent management for their business in the tourism sector provided interesting observations. There were contextual, strategic and operational concerns around the implementation of talent management policies and processes. The managers had a clear commitment to the talent management process but felt that the policy areas were generally underdeveloped. The talent management practices were found to be driven by internal expertise and available resources and were a particular issue for the SME businesses that were part of the sample. The practical implications that were considered of particular interest by the respondents were **defining, attracting, retaining, developing** and **transitioning** talent in the organisations (D'Annunzio-Green, 2008). Another piece of work also showed the views of representatives from the Scottish hospitality and tourism sector in Scotland and this research is summarised in the illustration below.

Illustration: Scotland

This illustration is taken from a round table discussion in Scotland that investigated the practical application of talent management in practical hospitality and tourism businesses. The abstract is quoted to illustrate the issues that the participants thought were critical in 2008.

Abstract:

Purpose

The purpose of this paper is to explore the operational implications and strategic actions involved in talent management (TM) in Scotland.

Design/methodology/approach

The paper is based on a literature review and focus groups comprising members of the Board of the Scottish Tourism Forum.

Findings

This paper finds that, in an industry with generally high labour turnover and rather negative public image as an employer, TM – in attracting, developing and retaining people – has significant potential to contribute to changing approaches to managing people and to improving opinions on careers in this sector. The respondents also talked about the important issues related to the attraction, retaining, developing and transitioning employees from one role to another.

Practical implications

Practical implications are that:

- Individual businesses adopt TM approaches that best suit their business, employees and customers;

- Industry bodies and leaders present exemplary practice in TM;

- Business strategies including TM initiatives are actively supported by senior and operational managers in organisations;

- Educators develop, in liaison with the industry, toolkits for the implementation and evaluation of TM initiatives. Maybe educators need to be more directly involved in developing talent and finding the right positions for each student?

Source: Adapted from Maxwell and MacLean, (2008) p820.

Issues related to talent management approach

Elitism

An organisation that adopts an exclusive approach to talent management will be adopting an elitist approach to the process. It is important for us to consider the definition of elitism in the context of this approach:

> *The belief that a society or system should be led by an elite: 'local government in the nineteenth century was the very essence of elitism'*
>
> *The dominance of a society or system by an elite.*
>
> *The superior attitude or behaviour associated with an elite: 'he accused her of racism and white elitism'*

Source: Oxford English Dictionary online. http://www.oxforddictionaries.com/definition/english/elitism

This old fashioned view is based on the idea that elites are defined by socio-economic factors alone and the idea that experience and upbringing make you an elite. Yet today elites can also be defined in terms of knowledge of technology for example. Are our elites today young individuals such as the IT people, perhaps?

The creation of talent pools is a signal that the organisation recognises that certain individuals in the organisation have specialist skills that need to be nurtured and rewarded. It is interesting when we consider the definitions that this may signal dominance and may encourage a superior attitude which may alienate the individuals who are not in the talent pool, unless things are handled well in the organisation. It can also be suggested that it is hard to achieve elitism and equality especially when one type of person, such as males or specific races, dominates the talent pool, and they think that they know best regardless of the cultural setting.

11

Equality

One of the key issues facing the hospitality and tourism sector is the issue of diversity of the work force and whether organisations treat the diverse work force in a fair and equitable way, at the same time as capitalising on the skills and qualities that different individuals bring to the organisation. There are issues here such as gender, age, nationality, and sexual orientation. Organisations usually have equal opportunity policies, but may or may not operate fair and appropriate policies once the staff are recruited. They may also recruit individuals from specific backgrounds as part of their corporate social responsibility programmes and encourage their development because of an altruistic agenda. The case shown below of Jamie Oliver's 15 restaurant shows how influential individuals wanted to give young disadvantaged people the opportunity to develop their skills as chefs in Cornwall UK. The hospitality and tourism sector has many openings where this type of development can happen if managed well. This type of approach is admirable and an example of a company trying to be more inclusive.

Illustration: Jamie Oliver's 15 restaurant

Opened in 2006, Jamie Oliver's Fifteen Cornwall continues to transform lives using the magic of food.

— JAMIE OLIVER'S —

FIFTEEN

ESTᴰ 〉 CORNWALL 〈 2006

As a social enterprise our profits are used exclusively to help people in greatest need in Cornwall. Bringing together over 700,000 people since we opened nine years ago, every day, every year we help to create meaningful memories and experiences that inspire, connect and reward. We give young people the means to create a new direction for themselves and make some fantastic food whilst we're at it. But hang on, we know this I hear you say, so what about the beginning and how did it all come about? None of it would have been possible if it weren't for a few very determined individuals...

Back in 2004, Betty Hale was working in the community regeneration department at Restormel Borough Council. Betty had followed the success of Jamie Oliver's Fifteen London and could see the enormous benefit such a project would have in Cornwall, one of the most deprived areas in the country with the lowest average wage and high youth unemployment.

Armed with a vision to bring Jamie Oliver's concept to the county she enlisted help from local businessmen Will and Henry Ashworth, owners of the Watergate Bay Hotel. Will and Henry had the perfect venue overlooking the beach and the scene was set to approach the Jamie Oliver Foundation team in London and persuade them that Cornwall, in particular Watergate Bay, would be the ideal location for a second Fifteen restaurant in the UK.

By early 2005, the deal was done and Jamie was fully on board. Like all good stories this one had its fair share of tension and drama: a hectic building schedule to convert the top floor of the Beach Hut into a state of the art 120 cover restaurant and a relentless recruitment drive to appoint directors, managers, chefs and front of house staff for the restaurant, and trustees, and staff for the Cornwall Food Foundation. All within a narrow window ready for the May 2006 launch date.

With the teams in place came the biggest challenge of all, recruiting the first cohort of apprentice chefs. It was no easy task. There were over 300 applications for just 21 places. By January 06, after hundreds of phone calls, interviews, a boot camp and four months at Cornwall College studying NVQ1 in Catering we had our inaugural group of apprentice chefs. Job done.

Just nine months after we got the go-ahead from the Jamie Oliver Foundation, and after so much hard work from everyone involved, we opened our doors to the world on 18th May 2006 with Jamie Oliver leading the celebrations. The world's media turned up and the apprentices, thrust into the glare of the media spotlight, took it all in their stride.

Nine years on and we're still going strong. Graduating over 100 still cheffing today, we know we have the recipe for success. In 2014 we won a prestigious RegioStars award for Inclusive Growth, recognition by the European Commission for our ongoing work.

We are proud to continually invest in training not just our apprentices but in our staff, employing over 70 people year round. We work closely with Watergate Bay Hotel to push back the traditional seasonal limits of hospitality businesses in Cornwall.

Spending on average over £1M each year in Cornwall's food economy, buying as much as possible from local producers and suppliers, our artisanal sourcing means we've got twice as many suppliers as other kitchens and we enjoy cultivating these relationships and work in partnership with them to showcase Cornish produce, this is evident not just on our menus but also at our bi-annual seasonal food fayres.

We are committed to measuring and improving our social impact, whether it's the hundreds of school children we engage in healthy eating each year, the lives we've changed through our Apprentice Programme, the people we connect through Food Revolution or the communities we're starting to help through FoodWorks, community engagement programme.

Thank you for your continuing interest, support and love.

Source: https://www.fifteencornwall.co.uk/history/

Gender

Women make up a significant proportion of the hospitality industry's workforce. Despite this, women in the hospitality industry hold less than 40% of all managerial and supervisory positions in the international hospitality industry (Baum, 2013). The WTTC have highlighted the possible consequences of talent imbalances in the sector and as part of this identified the major issue of women being undervalued and their talent not being used effectively with a particular issue at senior management level (WTTC, 2015). The International Labour Organization (ILO) highlighted the challenges faced by women in the hospitality workplace when it noted that unskilled or semi-skilled women tended to work in the most vulnerable jobs, where they are more likely to experience poor working conditions, inequality of opportunity and treatment, and even violence, exploitation, stress and sexual harassment (Baum, 2013).

A piece of research carried out with women room attendants in five star hotels in The Gold Coast region of South East Queensland, Australia highlighted the fact that they were considered to be on the 'lowest rung' of the hierarchy and were never consulted, even to the extent of being treated as invisible in the hotels.

> *We don't seem to have any input. If you say something to someone higher up it doesn't seem to have any impact, they don't really listen. We are the lowest rung here they just don't seem to think we are important, even though the rooms are the hotel. (Kensbock et al., 2013, p 360)*

11

We can speculate, of course, as to whether the fact that they are women is relevant or not to their treatment. Maybe it is due to the fact that whatever their background, their role is considered menial and this is the real reason that they are excluded and ignored. It could be more about hierarchy rather than gender. It is interesting, because in places like the Gulf states and even Sri Lanka, menial jobs in hotels are always held by men, for example room attendants, as it is not thought appropriate for women to work in such positions. So the question is whether those women are being denied opportunities or saved from degrading work and exploitation?

Research carried out to underpin a white paper on female employment in the sector showed that there is not one single solution to the issue of the under-representation of women in senior positions in the industry. The paper identified a wide belief in the business benefits of diversity and motivation to improve the situation, and illustrates good practice with a number of key case studies. The paper also provides key recommendations for stakeholders to align with and implement across three core areas – policies and procedures, engagement and consultation, and education and training. This, it is argued, will improve the position of women in the sector (Baum, 2015). At the moment, however, evidence suggests that women are still excluded from the senior talent pool in hospitality and tourism organisations.

Diversity management

One of the key issues that hospitality and tourism organisations have to consider in their talent management processes is the way in which they handle the diversity of their work force in the context of their customer base. Research in the general business area has shown that employing individuals from diverse backgrounds will bring distinct advantages, particularly when the customer base is also diverse (Klein and Harrison, 2007). On a tactical level, we can think about the front office desk of large hotels, for example, and think of the advantage that multi-lingual team will bring to this area of the business. Multi-national teams also work well together at a strategic level if their knowledge and experience is harnessed well by the organization.

Research carried out, mainly in the US, has indicated that of the top hotel groups, 60% of them had diversity policies, which is a surprisingly low figure (Holcomb *et al.*, 2007). Research carried out in 2008 indicated that most of the hotel companies which had diversity management strategies had failed to communicate their policies in a clear and straightforward way on their websites. This, it was suggested is what had led to issues with recruitment and attraction of talent from different cultural backgrounds (Gröschl, 2011). Since this time the larger organisations have developed well thought out diversity strategies and focused on these on their web pages, so things have moved on and organisations are trying to be more inclusive.

Organisations may have diversity policies but discrimination in hospitality and tourism is even worse for people from ethnic minorities than it is for women perhaps. Many immigrants who have worked in London hotels for 20 years are barely able to speak English and are doing the same job they were on day one. How much talent is being wasted there! And on cruise ships, for convenience, whole areas of employment are reserved for particular nationalities and white western Europeans are the captains! Discrimination and wasted talent perhaps?

Research needs to be carried out in smaller organisations to investigate how they develop their own versions of diversity strategies.

Pay / reward and work-life balance

One of the key issues in relation to inclusive and exclusive approaches to talent management is how employees are rewarded and treated at work in terms of their work-life balance. The creation of a talent pool using an exclusive approach usually means that these individuals are more senior, or have more potential to be more senior in the future, and therefore earn more. This has to be compared with individuals who are lower down the hierarchy and not in the talent pool, who could be earning the minimum wage, if this a requirement. For organisations that are based in countries where there is no minimum wage legislation, then the pay for those that are not in the talent pool can be even lower.

It is interesting to note that in the UK where the national Living Wage for workers aged 25 and over was introduced by the government in October 2013, and the government has named and shamed employers who fail to pay at this level, hospitality companies have continued to feature prominently in the list of companies who owe staff money and have been named and shamed by the Department of Business, Energy and Industrial Strategy. It appears from the list that the companies that were identified had excuses such as moving a member of staff from an apprenticeship scheme to a full time job, and confusion about accommodation payments. This situation does illustrate how employees are often given poor rewards for tasks that are viewed as menial by the employers. The government has promised to keep naming and shaming companies that do not pay employees the fair wage.

> *The government is determined to build an economy that works for everyone, not just the privileged few. That means making sure everyone gets paid the wages they are owed- including our new, higher National Living Wage. It is not acceptable that some employers fail to pay at least the minimum wage their workers are entitled to. So we'll continue to crack down on those who ignore the law, including by naming and shaming them.*

Source: Margot James, Business Minister, quoted in *The Caterer*, August 12th, 2016.

There is also the issue of tipping – should staff in effect have to become pseudo beggars trying to elicit tips to earn a living wage? On the other end of the spectrum, we can consider the companies that are considered to offer excellent pay

11

and working conditions in the hospitality sector. The illustration below shows how organisations were highlighted in 2016 as offering the best working condition in the sector. It is interesting to note that these companies tend to pay higher wages, and also adopt more inclusive approached to talent management with employees saying they are included and valued in their day to day work.

Illustration: The top 10 best places to work in hospitality and what they do for their staff

How can employers support staff and guarantee a great working environment? Look no further than these innovative employers – and potential Catey award winners – for inspiration, says *Rosalind Mullen*

Key findings from this year's research show that a positive working environment continues to creep up the 'What makes a great employer?' priority list, moving up to fourth place from fifth in 2014. Such workplaces tend to encourage positive communication, team respect, inclusion and employee areas that are treated with the same attention as customer-facing ones. It is also positive to see that "trusting managers" has entered the listing for the first time this year; demonstrating that hospitality businesses are creating empowerment cultures where their people are encouraged and trusted to do what is right for the organisation.

Shortlisted for the best employer category: Cafe in the Park

In a nutshell: Set up in 2005 by Carly and Ian Trisk-Grove

Location: The Aquadrome, Rickmansworth

Employees: 14 full-time

Average labour turnover: People stay for a year on average. Four members of staff have been there for more than two years, one for over three and two for over four

Annual turnover: £740,000 (2015)

It's not just the staff who are close-knit at this family-owned café, it is also the customers. In fact, in February it was shortlisted for the People's Favourite category in the Sustainable Restaurant Association's Food Made Good Awards. You just have to watch the website video to see how much the friendliness of this cheerful venue means to the people who go there. When forced to pick out a few examples of what makes this café such a great place to work, there are two that stand out. First, the owners pay their staff a salary so they know what they will take home each month. They never give out zero-hour contracts and all staff get the same starting salary – £17,500 – because they all do the same job.

Second, they also work with a number of adults with learning difficulties, who volunteer from two to 10 hours a week. This has many benefits. The volunteers have an opportunity to gain work experience and to mix with adults without learning difficulties, and the full-timers gain an understanding of what life is like for people with a learning difficulty.

In recognition of its all-round best-practice, this café has been awarded three stars by the Sustainable Restaurant Association for its commitment to society, sourcing and the environment.

Shortlisted for the best employer category: Firmdale Hotels

In a nutshell: Tim and Kit Kemp's collection of uber-cool, unstuffy, luxurious boutique hotels

Locations: Five hotels and three townhouse hotels in London; one hotel in New York

Employees: 1,200

Average labour turnover: 28%

Annual turnover: £105m

Several recognition initiatives have been introduced at this cutting-edge company to promote communication, engagement and employee involvement. The aim is to build employee retention, reduce turnover and also to reward and celebrate success.

It's clearly doing plenty of things right. Last year, employee retention was 87%, while its loyalty awards, which recognise long service with additional holidays, reveal that just over 20% of employees have more than five years' service.

Breakfast clubs bring employees together every quarter to give feedback on what it is like to work at Firmdale. Over the past year, this has revealed that staff want more development and internal succession. This has triggered the implementation of a bespoke performance review and communications system (namely Purple Cubed's Talent Toolbox). The result is that some 23.5% of the team have been promoted or transferred within the company in the past year.

Staff Appreciation Weeks take place twice a year in every hotel where managers organise film clubs, bowling and lunch. This is in addition to afternoon teas every Friday so the team can kick-back and celebrate the week.

Training certificate presentations are held quarterly where those involved celebrate with Champagne and canapés. Some 20.5% of employees are trained every quarter, with more than 120 employees attending each event.

And last but not least, there is the annual company-wide incentive, where staff are invited to put forward a suggestion, spurred on by the fact they will receive a reward if it is implemented.

Shortlisted for the best employer catey: The Headland Hotel

In a nutshell: A 96-bedroom, four-star hotel with an award-winning spa, luxury cottages and surf school

Location: Newquay, Cornwall

Employees: 154

Average labour turnover: In 2014/15, average number of employees 149.75 with 97 leavers

Annual turnover: £7.1m

Last year, saw the pilot of the Headland Talent Development Plan (TDP), schooling employees and external candidates in the knowledge, skills and confidence they need to become a future manager. The programme gives an understanding of core hotel operations and provides credibility and a good foundation for candidates to build on. It's open to employees and external candidates, including students who want to put their academic knowledge into practice. For those with experience, the programme can be accelerated through external qualifications such as apprenticeships.

The TDP creates structured, hands-on learning using outcomes, assessment and feedback to help staff achieve their potential and deliver competent individuals equipped to become managers and leaders.

Some 10 months after implementation, the first candidate has completed the "accelerated" programme and joined the team as a junior duty manager. Having been with the company for 10 years, this was just the opportunity they needed to progress. This success has spurred the hotel on to begin a second rotation of the TDP, with enrolment taking place this spring.

Source: Adapted from Mullen, (2016) The top 30 best places to work in hospitality https://www.thecaterer.com/articles/366821/the-top-30-best-places-to-work-in-hospitality. Accessed 25/8/16

It can be seen in these case examples that the issue of work-life balance appears to be a critical factor for the employees when they rate organisations in terms of the preferred places to work. This mirrors the developing theme which has been an emerging issue in the literature. Research has shown that work life balance appears to be one of the key variables when addressing issues related to employee management, and it is suggested that it should become a major focus of the talent management practice (Deery and Jago, 2015).

Corporate social responsibility

In the more recent literature, talent management has been viewed at the societal level and part of corporate social responsibility (CSR). According to Carroll (1991), great emphasis was placed on the economic and legal responsibilities of the organization and it was only later that more consideration has been given to ethical and philanthropic functions. The inclusive approach to talent management, it can be argued, offers organisations to care for their employees as a whole, and may even involve them in helping the non-talented employees to find work without risking unemployment or loss of income if and when they leave the company. In this way, the company will be seen to be helping society as a whole, and not just satisfying their own economic targets (Thunnissen *et al.*, 2013).

Issues related to the type of organisation

Global or local?

The development of multi-national or global businesses in the hospitality and tourism sector has led to a more global dimension of talent management which has become known global talent management or GTM. This involves the selection, development and retention of employees in the most important roles in these newly developing work forces. A piece of research that was carried out on this in 2013, indicated that organisations should not mimic the actions of others but adopt six key principles in developing their GTM as follows:

1 Align the policy with the strategy
2 Develop internal consistency
3 Embed the policy in the organisational culture
4 Develop management involvement
5 Develop a balance of global and local needs
6 Use employer branding through differentiation (Arris, *et al.* 2014).

It is clear that when an organisation develops in a new market it will have issues with the development of a coherent talent management process. It will usually rely on senior managers from the home market in the initial stages to fill the senior roles but in the long term will have to develop local talent both at a strategic and operational level. This maybe the case in the longer term but many fifty year old hotels in Asia, Africa still have white managers from Europe or North America. This will be a particular challenge when the existing employees do not have a cultural understanding of the new market. In the hotel business, where properties are franchised, the company will be able to rely on staff from the local partner to advise on an appropriate strategy. But local views of talent management may be much less enlightened and progressive than they would be in Europe or North America, perhaps?

One of the most difficult issues in developing markets is the provision of well-qualified junior staff to fill the junior and middle management posts. One of the ways to develop in this area is to make strategic alliances with universities and colleges who are deemed to be excellent in their education provision with the aim of recruiting talented staff from their pool of graduates. The company can also develop these relationships by employing the students on internships during their studies so that the company can both assess their potential and encourage them to join the company workforce when their studies end. The illustration below of a strategic partnership between one of the best universities in India, and

11

Hilton Worldwide is an example of such an agreement which was forged during the rapid expansion period for the company in India.

Illustration: Hilton Worldwide strategic partnership with Christ University's Department of Hotel Management

Leading global hospitality company partners with one of India's premier educational institutions to offer aspiring talent the best of theoretical knowledge and practical training

BANGALORE, India and MCLEAN, Va. - Hilton Worldwide and Christ University's Department of Hotel Management, have signed an agreement to cultivate talent for the country's rapidly growing hospitality industry. Under the Hilton Class programme, Hilton Worldwide will offer students from Christ University rigorous on-the-job practical training and a theoretical curriculum designed to equip them for successful careers in hospitality.

"The introduction of the Hilton Class programme reiterates our commitment to developing our portfolio in India, one of the key strategic markets for Hilton Worldwide. We are delighted with this opportunity to nurture talent for the growing hospitality industry in this country. Besides providing Hilton Worldwide with access to best-in-class talent to support our expansion, we believe this initiative will also benefit the industry as more trained students enter the workplace," said Martin Rinck, President - Asia Pacific, Hilton Worldwide.

Under the partnership, every year, 15 first-year students will be selected for the Hilton Class programme by Hilton Worldwide and Christ University. Each student will be offered a 24-week internship at hotels and resorts operated by the leading global hospitality company through the four-year Bachelor in Hotel Management (BHM) course at Christ University. In addition, Hilton Worldwide will organise guest lectures, on-site visits and e-learning programmes specially designed to prepare students for the workplace. Upon graduation, outstanding students would also be able to secure job offers from properties operated by Hilton Worldwide.

"The Hilton Class offers our students an exciting opportunity to be trained by one of the biggest and highly-recognised names in the industry. The collaboration will also keep our faculty and students up-to-date with the latest trends in the industry. We are confident that the programme will better prepare our students for the workplace and enhance the employment opportunities available to them upon graduation," said Sushil Dwarkanath, Head of Department of Hotel Management, Christ University.

With the rising demand for talent in India's rapidly expanding hospitality industry, Hilton Worldwide is actively exploring initiatives to nurture a pool of talent for its expansion needs and to support the development of the industry. Apart from entering into strategic partnerships with hospitality and tourism institutions, the company also invests heavily in the training and development needs of its team members in India. Promising team members are offered career development opportunities across the company's more than 4,000 hotels globally with access to professional training and tailor made career development plans. A fast track management development programme is also in place to groom outstanding talent into senior roles within a reduced time frame.

About Christ University

Christ University is affiliated with Bangalore University. Established in July 1969, it became the preferred educational institution in Bangalore within the first three decades. In the past decade, it has been continually rated among the top 10 educational institutions in the country. In 2008, Ministry of Human Resources Development, Government of India, declared it a university.

The Department of Hotel Management was started in1991. The flagship programme of the department is the four-year Bachelor in Hotel Management (BHM), which is a combination of management and hotel operation courses. The department also offers a diploma and a few hands-on certificate courses. Visit www.christuniversity.in for more information.

About Hilton

Hilton (NYSE: HLT) is a leading global hospitality company, comprising more than 4,700 managed, franchised, owned and leased hotels and timeshare properties with over 775,000 rooms in 104 countries and territories. For 97 years, Hilton has been dedicated to continuing its tradition of providing exceptional guest experiences. The company's portfolio of 13 world-class global brands includes Hilton Hotels & Resorts, Waldorf Astoria Hotels & Resorts, Conrad Hotels & Resorts, Canopy by Hilton, Curio - A Collection by Hilton, DoubleTree by Hilton, Embassy Suites by Hilton, Hilton Garden Inn, Hampton by Hilton, Tru by Hilton, Homewood Suites by Hilton, Home2 Suites by Hilton and Hilton Grand Vacations. The company also manages an award-winning customer loyalty program, Hilton HHonors®. Hilton HHonors members who book directly through preferred Hilton channels have access to benefits including an exclusive member discount, free standard Wi-Fi, as well as digital amenities that are available exclusively through the industry-leading Hilton HHonors app, where Hilton HHonors members can check-in, choose their room, and access their room using a Digital Key. Visit news.hiltonworldwide.com for more information and connect with Hilton Worldwide on Facebook, Twitter, YouTube, Flickr, LinkedIn, and Instagram.

Source: http://news.hiltonworldwide.com/index.cfm/news/hilton-worldwide-signs-strategic-partnership-agreement-with-christ-universitys-department-of-hotel-management-to-groom-indias-hospitality-talent. Accessed 25/8/16.

11

The development of a GTM policy often involves a large company in the creation of an exclusive 'talent pool' which is seen as being the potential senior managers of the future. This pool is often encouraged to be mobile so that they can experience different country settings and cultures, although this process can be damaging to their personal lives in the long term, since their family is forced to move around different locations or stay at home and as a result the family is often split up.

Type of organisation and organisation culture

The type of approaches that are adopted to the talent management process will vary according to the size, type and organisational culture. A large hierarchical organisation will tend to adopt an exclusive approach and employ senior managers at the top who receive the most pay and reward. It can be argued that although small organisations can have problems understanding and adopting talent management processes, they are in the best position to do this, due to a much smaller and flatter organisation structure. They can also allow employees to have a much wider experience in a variety of functions due to the small number of staff on the payroll.

Conclusions

The hospitality and tourism sector has been characterised as being a 'low skill' environment, but what is becoming increasingly clear is that there is an increasing need for talent in the sector. The new skills include a wide range of business and personal skills depending on the type of organisation and the business function. Issues such as diversity, CSR and equality all have a place in the talent management debate (Baum, 2008).

It appears at the moment that the hospitality and tourism sector is predominately adopting an exclusive approach in an attempt to attract, develop and retain talented staff. Pricewaterhouse Coopers (PwC) (2007) have suggested that there are three scenarios for the management of talent – the first is the 'blue environment' where the management focus on hard business requirements; the second is the 'green context' where CSR is taken into account; and the third scenario is the 'orange world' where the talent is managed in an inclusive manner and engages staff at all levels in the organisation. It recognises and uses the diversity of talents that is available and assumes psychological empowerment in the work place (Lashley,1997). The 'orange world' seems the most appropriate to the hospitality and tourism sectors because it encompasses the range of business, communication and personal skills that are required. Finding the way to implement it in large and complex organisations is the challenge for the future in an increasingly uncertain world.

Learning activities

1 Design an interview that you could use to discover the approach used by a chosen organi-sation to their talent management process. Conduct the interview and then assess your findings in relation to the literature.

2 Critically assess how the size and complexity of an organisation has an effect on the type of talent management process that they adopt.

3 Choose an organisation from the hospitality or tourism sector that have developed a new international market and critically analyse what this development would have involved in terms of talent management.

4 Provide a short 2000 word summary of the key areas of literature that underpins the topic of inclusivity and exclusivity in talent management and highlight the key authors in each of the areas that you identify.

References

Arris, A.A., Cascio, W.F. and Paauwe, J. (2013), Talent management: Current theories and future research directions. *Journal of World Business.* **49**, 173-179.

Baum, T. (2008) Implications of hospitality and tourism labour markets for talent management strategies. *International Journal of Contemporary Hospitality Management.* **20**(7) 730-742.

Baum, T. (2013) *International Perspectives on Women and Work in Hotels, Catering & Tourism.* International Labour Organization.

Baum, T. (2015) *Hospitality Industry White Paper Women in Tourism & Hospitality: Unlocking the Potential in the Talent Pool.* Diageo.

Bourdieu, P. (1988), Vive la crise! For heterodoxy in social science. *Theory and Society.* **17**(5), 773-787.

Boxall, P. and Macky, K. (2009). Research and theory on high-performance work systems: Progressing the high-involvement stream. *Human Resource Management Journal.* **19**(1) 3-23.

Carroll, A.B. (1991). The pyramid of corporate social responsibility: Toward the moral management of organizational stakeholders. *Business Horizons.* **34** (4) 39-48.

CIPD (2006), *Reflections on Talent Management: Change Agenda,* CIPD, London.

Collings, D. and Mellahi, K. (2009). Strategic talent management: A review and research agenda. *Human Resource Management Review,* **19**(4), 304–313.

D'Annunzio-Green, N. (2008). Towards a greater understanding of senior managers' perspectives in the tourism and hospitality sector. *International Journal of Contemporary Hospitality Management,* **20**(7)807-819.

11

Deery, M. and Jago, L. (2015.) Revisiting talent management, work-life balance and retention strategies. *International Journal of Contemporary Hospitality Management* **27** (3) 453-472.

Gallardo-Gallardo, E., Dries, N. and Gonzalez-Cruz, T. (2013), What is the meaning of talent in the world of work? *Human Resource Management Review*, **23**, 290-300.

Gallardo-Gallardo, E., Nijs, S., Dries, N. and Gallo, P. , (2015), Towards an understanding of talent management as a phenomenon-driven field using bibliometric and content analysis. *Human Resource Management Review*. **25**, 264-279.

Gröschl, S., (2011), Diversity management strategies of global hotel groups. *International Journal of Contemporary Hospitality Management*. **23**(2), 224-240.

Holcomb, J., Upchurch, R. and Okumus, F. (2007), Corpoate social responsibility: what are the top hotel companies reporting? *International Journal of contemporary Hospitality Management*. **19**(6) 461-475.

Kalleberg, A. (2009), Precarious work, insecure workers: Employment relations in transition. *American Sociological Review*. **74**(1), 1-22.

Kensbock, S., Jennings, G., Bailey, J. and Patiar, A. (2013), 'The lowest rung': Women room attendants' perceptions of five star hotels' operational hierarchies . *International Journal of Hospitality Management*. **35**, 360-368.

Klein, E. and Harrison, D. (2007), On the diversity of diversity: tidy logic, messier realities. *Academy of Management Perspectives*, November, 26-33.

Lashley, C. (1997) *Empowering Service Excellence. Beyond the Quick Fix*. Cassell: London.

Maxwell, G.A., and Maclean, S. (2008), Talent management in hospitality and tourism in Scotland. *International Journal of Contemporary Hospitality Management*, **20**(7), 820-830.

Oxford English Dictionary (n.d.) http://www.oxforddictionaries.com, accessed 30/8/16.

Pricewaterhouse Coopers (2007) *Managing Tomorrow's People*, Pricewaterhouse Coopers, London.

Sears, D. (2003), *Successful Talent Strategies: Achieving superior business results through market-focused staffing*. New York: American Management Association.

Sparrow, P. R. and Makram, H. (2015), What is the value of talent management? Building value-driven processes within a talent management architecture. *Human Resource Management Review*. **25**, 249-263.

Suchman, M. (1995). Managing legitimacy: Strategic and institutional approaches. *The Academy of Management review*, **20**(3), 571-610.

The Caterer (2016), Rachel Pickford, August 12th. https://www.thecaterer.com/articles/368114/hospitality-firms-named-among-minimum-wage-offenders

Thunnissen, M., Boselie, P. and Fruytier, B. (2013), Talent management and the relevance of context: Towards a pluralistic approach. *Human Resource Management Review*. **23**, 326-336.

WTTC (World Travel and Tourism Council) (2015) *Report on Global talent trends and issues for the travel and tourism sector*. http://www.wttc.org/-/media/382bb1e90c374262bc9512 26a6618201.ashx

12 The Role of Diversity in Talent Management

Matthew Yap

Learning objectives

After reading this chapter you should be able to:

■ Understand diversity management and talent management in the tourism and hospitality contexts.

■ Comprehend and discuss the value of recruiting diverse workers in the global tourism and hospitality workplaces.

■ Critically appraise the role of diversity in talent management.

■ Evaluate the essential components of the diversity management in global tourism and hospitality talent management paradigm

Introduction

Sociological advancements and multi-culturalism in contemporary societies, and the demographic changes of the general population have led to greater visibility of diverse individuals (Ineson *et al*, 2013). For instance, the enlargement of European Union (EU) leading to the migrant mobility within EU member states (Yap *et al.*, 2015a) and migration of population from rural villages to modern cities to seek job opportunities in developing countries (Yap *et al.*, 2015b; Yap and Ineson, 2016). In general, individuals' diverse backgrounds can be visible and invisible. Visible characteristics include physical appearances, age, skin colour, gender, physical disability; whilst invisible characteristics comprise of sexual orientation, transgender, age, culture, education level, religion, immigration status, social class, political association, marital status, parental status, mental disability, personality, work style, departmental affiliations, ex-offenders statuses and asymptomatic illnesses (Cooke and Saini, 2010; Yap and Ineson, 2012; Yap *et al.*, 2015a). For instance, Yap and Ineson (2009; 2012) conducted a multi-year study in the Asian hospitality industry and found the HIV (human immuno-deficiency virus) infection to be an asymptomatic illness because patients display no symptom during early stages of infection. They concluded that HIV infection is an invisible diverse characteristic. However, some demographic profiles like age and gender can be ambiguous due to natural phenomena and/or surgical and cosmetic procedures.

The global tourism and hospitality industries are expanding quickly, especially in Asia, with China's (Yap *et al.*, 2015b) and Vietnam's (Yap and Ineson, 2016) continued industrial and economic transformation and social modernisation. For instance, the United Nations World Tourism Organisation forecasts China to be the world's leading tourism destination by 2020 (Lew *et al.*, 2008). These expansions have generated increasing numbers of domestic and international diverse customers (Yap and Ineson, 2016). The global tourism and hospitality industries are labour intensive and need to provide quality service to customers round the clock seven days a week or 365 days a year but they are experiencing qualified labour shortages due to excessive labour turnover and exhaustive occupational stressors (Lövhöiden *et al*, 2011; Yap, 2011). Hence, it is of no surprised that more diverse workers, through mobility and migration, have joined these industries to fuel their continuous expansions (Yap *et al.*, 2015a). However, discrimination, prejudices, stigmatisation, marginalisation, unf air treatment and stereotyping of diverse workers and customers have surfaced frequently (Andriessen *et al.*, 2012; Ineson *et al.*, 2013; Yap and Ineson, 2009; Yap and Ineson, 2016; Yap *et al.*, 2015a). As such, both potential and existing global tourism and hospitality managers are challenged to manage and treat diverse customers and workers fairly through diversity management (Yap *et al.*, 2015b; Yap *et al.*, 2016). In the following sections, first, the value of diversity in the tourism and hospitality workplaces will be appraised; next, concepts of diversity management and talent management will be elucidated; then, the role of diversity management in global tourism and hospitality talent management will be discussed.

The value of diversity in the tourism and hospitality workplaces

The nature of the global tourism and hospitality industries is dynamically involving cross-cultural interactions of stakeholders from different backgrounds. Hence, the presence of diverse workers in the tourism and hospitality workplaces can yield many advantages but some disadvantages as summarised in Table 12.1.

With reference to Table 12.1, tourism and hospitality companies can gain competitive advantages when their diverse workers attract diverse customers to patronise their establishments (Wrench, 2007); because diverse workers can understand the behaviour of those customers from similar cultures, religions and sexual orientations. For example, gay and lesbian tourists prefer to do businesses with specialist gay tour operators as they understand the discretion and safety that their clients seek (Pritchard *et al.*, 2000). Even so, diverse customers feel more comfortable and are more compelled to purchase when they are communicating with and informed by employees who speak similar languages (Holmqvist and Grönroos, 2012). Hence, Agrusa, Kim and Wang (2011) suggest that Hawaiian tourism and hospitality companies should have Chinese speaking employees, and menus and signs written in Chinese characters to attract Chinese tourists.

Table 12.1: Advantages and disadvantages of recruiting diverse workers

Advantages	Disadvantages
Attract diverse customers and workers (Wrench, 2007).	May invite backlash from non-diverse workers and community (Hanappi-Egger, 2012).
Facilitate global expansion (Wrench, 2007).	Cross-cultural and behavioural misunderstanding (Kirton and Greene, 2010).
Satisfy equality legislation (Kirton and Greene, 2010)	
Generate new ideas (Madera, 2013).	
Harness the uniqueness of diverse individuals (Kandola and Fullerton, 2001).	
Create a positive public image (Hon and Brunner, 2000).	

However, Li, Absher, Graefe and Hsu (2008) caution readers of the difficulty of profiling cultural and cross-cultural values in service delivery, as they are frequently indirect and complicated to determine during interactions; hence leading to tourism and hospitality service personnel misunderstanding their customers' cross-cultures and behaviours (Kirton and Greene, 2010). Further, tourism and hospitality organisations having a pool of diverse employees can attract other diverse employees from similar nationalities and ethnic groups to work in those organisations. These organisations with global outlook can fully utilise their diverse workers as part of an international business strategy to facilitate global expansion (Wrench, 2007). Employing diverse employees purely to satisfy national equality legislation, like the Affirmative Action in America, is not the best way to value the uniqueness of diverse workers, but it certainly can help companies to avoid expensive discrimination lawsuits (Kirton and Greene, 2010) and to project positive public images (Hon and Brunner, 2000). In truth, tourism and hospitality organisations with excessively diverse workers may invite backlash from non-diverse employees because they may feel isolated, threatened and left out (Hanappi-Egger, 2012). For instance, heterosexuals working in an homosexuals dominated environment may feel threatened due to their ego defensive behaviour (Lubensky, Holland, Wiethoff and Crosby, 2004).

Hence, the abilities of managers to harness the uniqueness of individual employees to work towards achieving the goals of their organisations are ultimately invaluable (Kandola and Fullerton, 2001). We should not forget that diverse employees with unique work styles can generate creative ideas to aid their companies' competitiveness (Madera, 2013). Previous discussions have justified the value of diversity in the tourism and hospitality workplaces. However, the

12

interactions amongst diverse workers, and diverse and non-diverse workers in the workplaces are very complex which can generate harmony, or disharmony if not managed carefully (Yap et al., 2015b).

Diversity management

The concept of diversity management originated in American corporations to address the Affirmative Action legislation using the 'melting-pot' metaphor (Yap and Ineson, 2016). This way American organisations could recruit workers from different ethnic minorities (Asian Americans, African Americans and Latin Americans) to blend with their existing white Americans in the workplaces in order to project to the Federal Government the image of an equal opportunity employer (Wrench, 2007). However, the melting-pot metaphor was criticised for under-utilising diversity management. Hence, the Europeans revolutionised the concept by keeping the equal opportunity employer rationale and adding the 'mosaic' metaphor, whereby the diverse uniqueness of individuals/workers were patched together to enhance the competitiveness of organisations (Kandola and Fullerton, 2001). However, the concept was further condemned for contradicting the reward system of meritocracy (Schwabenland, 2012).

Over the years, diversity management has been transformed into an overarching concept that aims to promote diversity tolerance, respect and harmony in organisations by fairly treating all stakeholders (Ineson *et al.*, 2013), and harnessing the uniqueness of individuals to strengthen the competitiveness of organisations (Mor Barak, 2014). Hence, it is a complex of systematic and planned tactics and commitment that involves all level of employees to comprehensively neutralise discrimination, prejudices, stigmatisation, marginalisation, unfair treatment, and stereotyping of all individuals in the contexts of legal, sociocultural, cognitive, organisational and business dimensions (Ineson *et al.*, 2013; Yap and Ineson, 2012). As such, diversity management is not a short-term quick fix solution but a long range human resources and organisational behaviour strategy that is resources consuming (Nishii and Özbilgin, 2007). Managers are recommended to include diversity management in

i   Their organisational policies and strategies formulation (Mensi-Klarbach, 2012);

ii All the human resources functions (recruitment, selection, employment, compensation, training and performance evaluation) (Kirton and Greene, 2010);

iii Promoting and understanding the psychological well-being of their workers (Blaine, 2013).

As the global tourism and hospitality industries are (diverse) labour intensive and international customers oriented, diversity management programme is of great significance to include both visible and invisible diverse characteristics.

One of the main reasons is because diversity management can act as a training and education mechanism to eliminate misunderstandings, misconceptions and fear of those diverse characteristics. For instance, Yap and Ineson (2009; 2012) interviewed many Asian hospitality managers and detected their misconception of HIV information and HIV mode of transmission leading to their fear of HIV infected workers and colleagues. Hence, Yap and Ineson (2009; 2012) suggested Asian hospitality managers to employ diversity management philosophy to guide their training and education programmes so as to eliminate workers' fear and misconception, and to enhance their level of tolerance. Successful implementation of diversity management programmes can yield many benefits. Increased revenue and profits, reduction of labour turnover and avoidance of discrimination lawsuits, and associated costs are the main quantifiable positive outcomes of diversity management (Yap and Ineson, 2016). In addition, improvement of an organisation's public image, work environment, workers' morale and performance, service to customers, and relationship with other stakeholders are achievable (Madera, 2013; Yap *et al.*, 2015b). Furthermore, diversity management can aid training and educating all stakeholders in an organisation to understand each other in terms of multi-culturalism and diverse behaviours (Harvey and Allard, 2012). However, implementing diversity management is not without obstacles. Executing diversity management is consistently challenged by all stakeholders' continuous commitment and support of financial resources throughout a long period of time (Ineson *et al.*, 2013). Moreover, there is no guarantee of success as this concept can be fragilely impacted by '*specific demographic profile and the legal, historical, political, and cultural contexts of equality*' of countries (Cooke and Saini, 2010: 481).

In summary, the success of global diversity management programmes in hospitality and tourism organisations highly dependent on their leaders involvement and commitment. Further, hospitality and tourism leaders must take into consideration of their organisations' socio-cultural norms, beliefs and communication issues when implementing global diversity management programmes. These programmes must involve global perspectives to clearly define diversity and its related policies and procedures to guide diversity practices in the context of human resource management to develop and achieve global competencies for the practicing organisation. As such, the involved organisation can create and share global knowledge, enhance performance and innovation, and deepen employee engagement. However, the organisation must be alert to the positive and negative reactions generated by the global diversity management programme. The mechanisms, elements and processes discussed above are necessary to avoid a failure of a diversity management programme.

12

Talent management

The topic of tourism and hospitality talent management has gained momentum in recent years due to an acute shortage of qualified labour, coupled with the continuous challenges of sourcing, attracting, retaining, engaging and nurturing capable workers in the global tourism and hospitality industries (Barron, 2008). In order to gain advantage in a competitive service industry, tourism and hospitality companies employ talent management programmes to develop and redevelop their employees through high quality human resources practices (Lewis and Heckman, 2006). However, talent management and its benefits in the tourism and hospitality industries lack empirical findings. Similar to diversity management, talent management has a broad meaning, and it takes into consideration both potential and existing capable employees in organisations. Although the concept of talent management has been criticised for being unfocused (Lewis and Heckman, 2006), it holistically encompasses human resources management strategies, execution and management of human resources functions, education and training, and workers' behaviour in organisations (Tarique and Schuler, 2010).

Both external and internal factors can have an impact upon the success of talent management practices in tourism and hospitality organisations (Hughes and Rog, 2008). In terms of external factors, Morton (2004) cautioned tourism and hospitality managers that the wider economy, mergers and acquisitions, and global expansion plans can influence the policy and practice of talent management. The global and regional economic outlook can affect the demand and supply of qualified tourism and hospitality talents; whilst mergers and acquisitions permit right-sizing and greater diversity of management positions. Then, global expansions require talented workers with cultural intelligence and diplomacy. On the one hand, unclear definition of talent management is one of the internal factors that can impact negatively upon policy and practices in tourism and hospitality organisations because of unclear direction and focus. On the other hand, upper management's commitment, alignment of strategic goals, and the company's existing approach to human resource management are the main internal factors that warrant attention (Hughes and Rog, 2008). The success or failure of talent management practices is highly dependent on upper management's commitment to allocate required/sufficient resources to support many activities that can achieve the organisations' strategic goals. Since talent management connects to human resource management, they must coexist. They are dependent on each other for success or failure. Nor must we forget, that (middle) managers must be given authority, financial resources and information to perform their duties and responsibilities to implement talent management programmes successfully.

In the context of research, the concept of talent management is multi-disciplinary and it connects strategic management, education, psychology, human resources management, applied human economics, and organisational behaviour. Future researchers are recommended to investigate tourism and hospitality talent management with the aforementioned disciplines. In essence, global tourism and hospitality organisations must consider the impacts of exogenous and endogenous drivers when employing global talent management to attract, develop and retain international talents (Tarique and Schuler, 2010). Exogenous drivers like globalisation, changing demographics of the constructive workforce, and the demand and supply of skillful labour can pose considerable challenges to organisations attempting to implement global talent management. In addition, managers must be aware that endogenous drivers like the formation of strategic alliances, sourcing talents through regio-centrism methods, and required competencies of talents can positively and negatively impact the operation of global talent management within their organisations. However, organisations that successfully implement global talent management programmes can yield competitive advantage, improve human resources' impact, and obtain stronger talent positioning.

Diversity management and talent management

Previous sections have explained the concepts of diversity management and talent management in the global context. These concepts and frameworks are applicable to the global tourism and hospitality industries. It is evident that both concepts can complement and supplement each other. In this section, these synergies will be discussed by exploring the role of global diversity management in global talent management suitable for the global tourism and hospitality industries as revealed in Figure 12.1.

With reference to Figure 12.1, external factors like changes of demographic profiles of the constructive workforce and the general population, demand and supply gap of qualified labour, socio-cultural norms of societies, globalisation of businesses and enactment of (equality) legislation can impact and drive the role of diversity management in talent management programmes of global tourism and hospitality companies. Global tourism and hospitality leaders must be committed to developing a diversity management culture in their organisations and incorporate such culture into their talent management programmes. With a view of their regions, tourism and hospitality leaders must understand their organisations' beliefs, strategic alliances and their employees' cultural intelligence, attitudes, competencies and openness to change and improvement before incorporating global diversity management within the talent management programme.

12

```
┌─────────────────────────────────┐
│       Exogenous Drivers         │
│         Demographics            │
│       Demand-supply gap         │
│      Socio-cultural norms       │
│         Globalisation           │
│          Legislation            │
└─────────────────────────────────┘

┌───────────────────────────────────────────┐
│         Leadership and Organisation        │
│            Beliefs and attitudes           │
│               Regiocentrism                │
│               Competencies                 │
│             Strategic alliances            │
│      Openness to change and improvement    │
│            Cultural intelligence           │
└───────────────────────────────────────────┘
                    ⇕
┌───────────────────────────────────────────┐
│         Global Diversity Management        │
│ Global diversity definitions, policies,    │
│        procedures and practices            │
│      Development of global competencies    │
└───────────────────────────────────────────┘
                    ⇕
┌───────────────────────────────────────────┐
│          Global Talent Management          │
│ International human resources management   │
│ activities – attracting, developing and    │
│ retaining global diverse and non-diverse   │
│ talents                                    │
└───────────────────────────────────────────┘
                    ⇕
┌───────────────────────────────────────────┐
│     Global Talent Management Effectiveness │
│          Competitive advantage             │
│      Knowledge creation and sharing        │
│          Diverse talent positioning        │
│       Improving human resources impact     │
│         Performance and innovation         │
│           Employee engagement              │
└───────────────────────────────────────────┘
```

Figure 12.2: Diversity management in global tourism and hospitality talent management paradigm.

Next, tourism and hospitality leaders will lead their employees in clearly defining diversity and establishing related policies, procedures and practices aiming to develop global competencies within their organisations. Then, the role of diversity management will be incorporated into global talent management programmes to influence international human resources management activities like fairly attracting, developing and retaining global diverse and non-diverse talents. During the development of talents, all employees' uniqueness will be pieced together towards achieving the goals of their organisations. As such, the global talent management programme, with the guidance of diversity management, can yield stronger competitive advantage and (diverse) talent positioning, enhance performance and innovation, increase knowledge creation and sharing, and improved human resources functions. However, global tourism and hospitality leaders must be aware that incorporating diversity management in talent management programmes is very time and resources consuming. Moreover, as the exogenous drivers are continuous changing, tourism and hospitality leaders must be flexible to adopt to changes quickly and swiftly. But it can yield tremendous benefits for global tourism and hospitality organisations when they are synergised.

Conclusions

The global tourism and hospitality workers' characteristics and background have modified due to sociological and demographical changes, and multiculturalism. Hence, the presence of diverse workers in the global tourism and hospitality workplaces is now more prominent. This chapter illustrates the value of diverse workers and their abilities to continuously support and expand the global tourism and hospitality industries. However, discrimination, prejudices, stigmatisation, marginalisation, unfair treatment, and stereotyping of diverse workers have continued to surface in the global tourism and hospitality industries. As elsewher in life, diverse workers require fair treatment in their workplaces. Hence, this chapter suggests the employment of global diversity management and its framework to buttress human resource functions, training and education, and workplace policies in order to build a harmonious and productive work environment for all workers in the global tourism and hospitality industries.

Due to the advancement of management theories, traditional human resources management alone is insufficient to address the acute shortage of qualified labour in the global tourism and hospitality industries. Moreover, contemporary skillful workers demand more to satisfy not only their physiological but also their psychological needs. As such, this chapter recommends the employment of global talent management and its framework to source, attract, retain, engage and nurture capable (diverse and non-diverse) talents in the global tourism and hospitality industries as a sustainable talents strategy.

As previously discussed, there are great synergies between the global diversity management framework and the global talent management framework. These frameworks can complement and supplement each other to maximise sustainable management efficiency and effectiveness in tourism and hospitality organisations. Hence, this chapter integrated both frameworks to form a diversity management

12

in global tourism and hospitality talent management paradigm. The essence of this paradigm is to employ the diversity management philosophy to guide the fair management of diverse and non-diverse talents and to sustain qualified labour in global tourism and hospitality organisations.

Learning activities

1   Explain diversity management and its metaphors.

2   Discuss the value of having a diverse workforce in tourism and hospitality organisations.

3   Discuss the functions of talent management.

4   Evaluate both exogenous and endogenous factors that can impact upon the success of talent management.

5   Discuss diversity management initiatives in various talent management functions of sourcing, attracting, retaining, engaging and nurturing capable workers in the global tourism and hospitality organisations.

References

Agrusa, J., Kim, S. S. and Wang, K-C. (2011). Mainland Chinese tourists to Hawaii: Their characteristics and preferences. *Journal of Travel & Tourism Marketing*, **28**(3), 261-278.

Andriessen, I., Nievers, E., Dagevos, J. and Faulk, L. (2012). Ethnic discrimination in the Dutch labour market: Its relationship with job characteristics and multiple group membership. *Work and Occupation*, **39**(3), 237-269.

Barron, P. (2008). Education and talent management: Implications for the hospitality industry. *International Journal of Contemporary Hospitality Management*, **20**(7), 730-742.

Blaine, B. E. (2013). *Understanding the Psychology of Diversity*. Thousand Oaks, CA: SAGE.

Cooke, F. L. and Saini, D. S. (2010). Diversity management in India: A study of organisations in different ownership forms and industrial sectors. *Human Resource Management*, **49**(3), 477-500.

Hanappi-Egger, E. (2012). Theoretical perspectives on diversity in organisations. In M. A. Danowitz, Hanappi-Egger and H. Mensi-Klarbach (Eds.). *Diversity in Organisations: Concepts and practices* (pp. 9-31). Hampshire, England: Palgrave Macmillan.

Harvey, C. P. and Allard, M. J. (2012). *Understanding and Managing Diversity: Readings, cases and exercises* (5th ed.). Upper Saddle River, NJ: Pearson Education Inc.

Holmqvist, J. and Grönroos, C. (2012). How does language matter for services? Challenges and propositions for service research. *Journal of Service Research*, **15**(4), 430-442.

Hon, C. L. and Brunner, B. (2000). Diversity issues and public relations. *Journal of Public Relations Research*, **12**(4), 309-340.

Hughes, J. C. and Rog, E. (2008). Talent management: A strategy for improving employee recruitment, retention and engagement within hospitality organisations. *International Journal of Contemporary Hospitality Management, 20*(7), 743-757.

Ineson, E. M., Yap, M. H. T., and Whiting, G. (2013). Sexual discrimination and harassment in the hospitality industry. *International Journal of Hospitality Management, 35,* 1-9.

Kandola, R. and Fullerton, J. (2001). *Diversity in Action: Managing the mosaic.* London, England: Chartered Institute of Personnel & Development.

Kirton, G. and Greene, A. (2010). *The Dynamics of Managing Diversity: A critical approach* (3rd ed.). Oxford, England: Butterworth Heinemann.

Lew, A. A., Yu, L., Ap, J. and Zhang, G. (2008). Foreword. In A. A. Lew, L. Yu, J. Ap and G. Zhang (Eds.). *Tourism in China* (pp. xvii). Binghamton, NY: The Haworth Hospitality Press.

Lewis, R. E. and Heckman, R. J. (2006). Talent management: A critical review. *Human Resource Management Review, 16*(2), 139-154.

Li, C-L., Absher, J. D., Graefe, A. R. and Hsu, Y-C. (2008). Services for culturally diverse customers in parks and recreation. *Leisure Sciences, 30*(1), 87-92.

Lövhöiden, C., Yap, M. H. T. and Ineson, E. M. (2011). Work-family conflicts and enrichment in the Norwegian hotel industry. *Scandinavian Journal of Hospitality and Tourism, 11*(4), 457-482.

Lubensky, M. E., Holland, S. L., Wiethoff, C. and Crosby, F. J. (2004). Diversity and sexual orientation: Including and valuing sexual minorities in the workplace. In M. S., Stockdale and F. J. Crosby (Eds.). *The Psychology and Management of Workplace Diversity* (pp.206-223). Oxford, England: Blackwell Publishing Ltd.

Madera (2013). Best practices in diversity management in customer service organisations: An investigation of top companies cited by Diversity Inc. *Cornell Hospitality Quarterly, 54*(2), 124-135.

Mensi-Klarbach, H. (2012). Diversity management: The business and moral cases. In M. A. Danowitz, E. Hanappi-Egger, and H. Mensi-Klarbach (Eds.). *Diversity in Organisations: Concepts and practices* (pp. 63-89). Hampshire, England: Palgrave Macmillan.

Morton, L. (2004). Integrated and integrative talent management: A strategic HR framework. *Research Report R-1345-04-RR.* New York, NY: The Conference Board.

Mor Barak, M. E. (2014). *Managing Diversity: Toward a globally inclusive workplace.* Thousand Oaks, CA: SAGE.

Nishii, L. H. and Özbilgin, M. F. (2007). Global diversity management: Towards a conceptual framework. *The International Journal of Human Resource Management, 18*(11), 1883-1894.

Pritchard, A., Morgan, N. J., Sedgley, D., Khan, E. and Jenkins, A. (2000). Sexuality and holiday choices: Conversations with gay and lesbian tourists. *Leisure Studies, 19*(4), 267-282.

Schwabenland, C. (2012). *Metaphor and Dialectic in Managing Diversity.* Hampshire, England: Palgrave Macmillan.

12

Tarique, I. and Schuler, R. S. (2010). Global talent management: Literature review, integrative framework, and suggestions for further research. *Journal of World Business,* **45**(2), 122-133.

Wrench, J. (2007). *Diversity Management and Discrimination: Immigrants and ethnic minorities in the EU.* Hampshire, England: Ashgate Publishing Company.

Yap, M. H. T. (2011). Hotel housekeeping occupational stressors in Norway. *Tourism and Hospitality Management,* **17**(2), 291-294.

Yap, M. H. T. and Ineson, E. M. (2009). HIV-infected employees in the Asian hospitality industry. *Journal of Service Management,* **20**(5), 503-520.

Yap, M. H. T. and Ineson, E. M. (2012). Diversity management: The treatment of HIV-positive employees. *AIDS Care,* **24**(11), 1349-1358.

Yap, M. H. T. and Ineson, E. M. (2016). Diversity management in Vietnam's hospitality industry. *Journal of Human Resources in Hospitality & Tourism.*

Yap, M. H. T., Ineson, E. M., Alexieva, I. and Tang, C. M. F. (2015a). Bulgarian hotel managers' recruitment perceptions. *Journal of Human Resources in Hospitality & Tourism,* **14**(2), 133-152.

Yap, M. H. T., Ineson, E. M., Tang, C. M. F. and Fong, L. H. N. (2015b). Chinese hospitality students' perceptions of diversity management. *Journal of Hospitality & Tourism Education,* **27**(2), 60-68.

13 Internships and Placements in the Talent Management Process

Mandy Aggett

Learning objectives

By the end of this chapter, readers should be able to:

- Understand the challenges relating to recruitment and retention in the tourism and hospitality industry;

- Identify the need for talent in the industry and the impacts on business performance;

- Identify the characteristics of Millennials and changing attitudes and expectations in the workplace;

- Understand the purpose of work placements and the benefits to both students and employers;

- Discuss the utilisation of placements in the talent management process;

- Recognise the impacts of the quality of placements on the attraction and retention of graduates in the industry.

Introduction

Organisations require a constant influx of talent that may be trained up for future management roles. Many businesses source this talent from the yearly output of university graduates, but attracting the best from this pool of potential candidates can be a very demanding process and, if done ineffectively, can impact on an organisation's performance and future (Venkataraman, 2014). Recent changes in higher education, and the mismatch between graduates' expectations and the *'realities of the working world'* (Venkataraman, 2014:11), have given rise to challenges in both talent acquisition and retention. As Robinson *et al.* (2015:1) explain, in an *'era characterised by uncertainty, constant change and increasing global mobility of employees, the tourism and hospitality [...] industries are frequently challenged with the problem of attracting and retaining quality employees who possess cross-domain abilities, as well as knowledge and competencies that match industrial trends and demands.'*

The competition for talent is further impacted by the characteristics of the so-called Generation Y, or Millennials, who *'possess a particular set of attitudes and characteristics that hospitality educators and the hospitality and tourism industry are struggling to cope with'* (Barron, 2008:74). The increased number of graduate opportunities, reported by High Fliers Research (2015) (up by 7.9% in Britain in 2014, and a further 8.1% in 2015), and the growth of the global tourism and hospitality industry (Fong *et al.*, 2014), is likely to intensify this problem.

Implementation, and effective management, of work placement opportunities for students can however, provide a solution (Yiu and Law, 2012; Fong *et al.*, 2014), and this chapter examines the role these may play in talent acquisition, development and retention in tourism and hospitality organisations. The chapter begins by focusing on the nature of the tourism and hospitality industry, and the challenges in recruitment and retention. This is followed by an outline of work placements, and how these may address attraction and retention problems, and includes an overview of the changing attitudes and behaviour of the current generation of students (referred to as Generation Y or Millennials). Recommendations and conclusions relating to best practice in the utilisation of placements in the talent management process are then provided.

The nature of the tourism and hospitality industry

Human resources are one of the most important assets of tourism and hospitality organisations. As noted by Kusluvan *et al.* (2010:171), *'the human element...is critical for service quality, customer satisfaction and loyalty, competitive advantage, and organisational performance.'* One of the greatest challenges faced by tourism and hospitality organisations however, lies in attracting and retaining employees. According to Chang *et al.* (2014:1), *'despite increasing demand, a substantial proportion of college-educated professionals are not attracted to careers in hospitality'*. In an industry that is characterised by low-pay, poor status, high staff turnover, and poor conditions (Nickson, 2013), tourism and hospitality jobs can be viewed as demeaning. Attitudes towards the nature of the work are often negative; thus challenges exist in recruitment, which in turn, threatens sustainability (Fong *et al.*, 2014).

Failure to address these issues can result in poor productivity and efficiency, and constraints in both innovation and the ability of organisations to meet customer demands (Christensen Hughes and Rog, 2008). The industry is already reportedly facing a productivity crisis, resulting from high employee turnover, which is currently around 30% (People 1st, 2015a), but can be as high as 300% (Barron, 2008), and a skills gap which has led to businesses being 58% less productive than those in other sectors (People 1st, 2015a). According to People 1st (2015b:2), '*21% of tourism and hospitality businesses report that their existing staff lack essential skills compared to only 15% across the UK economy as a whole*', and high employee turnover is costing the industry £274m a year. The loss of talented individuals, '*is a significant cost for every organisation*' (Lawler, 2008:21), and challenges in hiring for higher skilled and more professional roles is a particular issue in the sector (World Travel and Tourism Council, 2015).

The so called '*war for talent*', identified in the 1990s (Chambers *et al.*, 1998), was driven by the '*presumed scarcity of talent and the assumption that talented individuals have an extraordinary impact on the firm's performance*' (Eriksen, 2012:3). Talent is still viewed as a '*critical resource*' in shaping performance (Eriksen, 2012:3), and Amadeus (2010:8) stresses, '*the ability to attract, motivate, develop and retain sufficient talent will be a key success factor*'. It is therefore essential for the tourism and hospitality industry to consider their approaches to these processes. However, Rangan and Natarajarathinam (2014) note, in the current economic climate, finding and retaining a quality workforce, that's loyal to the organisation, is becoming increasingly difficult. People 1st (2015b) concur there two key challenges facing tourism and hospitality organisations: insufficient numbers of applicants and a shortage of applicants with the right skills. This has led to increased workloads for other staff, low morale, difficulties in meeting service objectives and standards, increased operating costs, and the loss of business to competitors (World Travel and Tourism Council, 2015).

As Raybould and Wilkins (2005:203) point out however, vocational degree programmes are '*intended to satisfy industry need for skilled future employees.*' Thus, many organisations source their talent from the pool of students graduating from universities, and promote opportunities through specialist recruitment websites such as Milkround and Prospects, or through university careers services. Higher education institutes (HEIs) have a '*pivotal role to play in the future of the industry*' (Barron, 2008:731). Robinson *et al.* (2015) agree, noting industry issues such as globalisation, rapid shifts in the market and environmental turbulence requires critical thinkers, such as those developed through university education. However, around a quarter of the UK's leading organisations increased their budgets for the 2014-2015 graduate recruitment period and there were more graduate positions available in 2015 than at any time in the previous decade (High Fliers Research, 2015). Coupled with record salaries on offer to graduates in other sectors (High Fliers Research, 2015), tourism and hospitality organisations face significant competition in graduate recruitment, but, as Chambers *et al.* (1998:1-2) argue, '*better talent is worth fighting for ...[as]... superior talent will be tomorrow's prime source of competitive advantage.*'

13

Scott and Revis (2008) identify a strong connection between 'graduateness' (the degree to which a student is prepared for the working environment), and the qualities an individual requires to be recognised as talent. Although the curriculum is often designed to meet industry needs, tourism and hospitality employers often complain that graduates lack the transferable skills required (Scott and Revis, 2008), thereby providing a rationale for work based learning. Work placement programmes, can provide organisations with an opportunity to identify suitable talent as they offer employers *'access to a pool of workers who are usually enthusiastic and dedicated to the industry'* (Yiu and Law, 2012:383).

High Fliers Research (2015:23) reports a *'noticeable change in the purpose and aims of placement programmes.'* Whereas previously, there were few direct links between placements and the graduate recruitment process, today, placements have become an *'integral part of recruiting new graduates.'* Indeed, up to a third of new graduates are now recruited directly through employers' work placement programmes (High Fliers Research, 2015). As noted by Scott and Revis (2008), the growing need for professional, career-driven employees in the industry, requires a strategy to identify, nurture and retain talent. David Cowsill (President and CEO of the World Travel & Tourism Council), notes, *'in the years to come, progress in developing and retaining talent will require a much stronger and more co-ordinated effort between the private sector, educational establishments and government'* (Cowsill, 2015:7). Talent management can however be initiated through a work placement programme, which *'provides undergraduates with a gateway into the industry'* (Kim and Park, 2013:70).

Work placements

A period of employment, as part of a university degree programme, is traditionally known in the UK as a sandwich placement, and sometimes as work experience, practicum, co-operative education or internship (Aggett and Busby, 2011). Placements range in duration, but students on a traditional sandwich placement are normally placed for 30-52 weeks (ASET, 2013). The purpose of a placement, from the students' perspective, is to enrich theoretical learning with some practical experience, with the expectation of enhancing their employability on graduation. Indeed, a number of students' expectations are met with the option to return to the placement provider on graduation (Aggett and Busby, 2011), as highlighted by Rate My Placement (2015), which reports that 60% of placement students will be offered a full-time role with the company. As well as practical experience and enhanced employment prospects, placement students also gain an insight into career opportunities, improve self-confidence and develop maturity (Robinson *et al.*, 2015).

From the employers' perspective, hiring placement students can lead to competitive advantage. They may benefit an organisation as a source of new ideas and perspectives from their studies (Maertz *et al.*, 2014a), improve company image and raise company awareness in the community, act as an inexpensive means of recruiting new employees, and increase employee productivity (Hurd and Hendy, 1997). Lawler (2008:17) adds, *'in many respects, it's a low-risk way to hire important human capital.'* Perhaps as a result, in 2015, the UK's leading employers were offering the highest level of placement vacancies ever recorded – an increase of 10% of that offered in 2014, and 40% more than in 2010 (High Fliers Research, 2015). Maertz *et al.* (2014a) stress that, as well as solving short-term labour needs, placements may also generate a talent pool for future openings. As identified by Bullock *et al.* (2009:481), *'the links between higher education and industry are considered fundamental in boosting the economy and enhancing the quality of the workforce.'* The link created by work placements, also allows for dialogue between education and industry, and therefore provides knowledge to education institutions on the skills and competencies required of graduates, thus providing industry with suitable candidates for employment (Garavan and Murphy, 2001).

Placements and the talent management process

Student interns are viewed by industry as a *'readily available, easily transformed and specifically trained workforce, that can be a valuable source of labour'* (Yiu and Law, 2012:384). Issues relating to finding and retaining quality employees may be resolved, as well-structured placements offer a route to creating high quality, loyal employees for future roles (Rangan and Natarajarathinam, 2014). Placements provide organisations with an opportunity to 'try before they buy'. They may be viewed as an opportunity to screen potential employees, and train and develop them for future graduate positions. Recruiting graduates, with previous experience in the organisation, saves on recruitment and selection costs (Maertz *et al.*, 2014b), will reduce training time, improve productivity and reduce churn rate (Rangan and Natarajarathinam, 2014). Maertz *et al.* (2014a) add that former placement students are more likely to fit an organisation's culture and values, and employers will benefit from more rapid contribution. Furthermore, they are also more likely to exhibit greater job satisfaction as their expectations will be more realistic (Fong *et al.*, 2014). In addition to recruitment opportunities, placements may also provide an opportunity for the development of existing staff, as supervisors/mentors will be needed to support interns. This can help to develop individuals' management capabilities, and will be particularly beneficial to those who don't have any line management responsibilities (CIPD, 2012).

Maertz *et al.* (2014a:3) recognise that offering placements to students can increase human resource fluidity through low cost labour, flexibility in labour capacity, flexibility in *type* of labour capacity, and flexibility in where labour capacity is sourced or deployed. Furthermore, they identify placements as the *'best single targeted talent acquisition method'*, as it costs far less than utilising head-hunting agencies, or other acquisition methods, and organisations may review performance before making a commitment. Placements allow for an extended test

13

of potential employees, which the authors note is *'among the most valid predictors of job performance.'* Yiu and Law (2012) agree, stating placements are frequently viewed as a recruitment and retention tool, and offer a very effective recruitment strategy. Competencies, they add, may be more easily assessed through a placement than through traditional recruitment methods, such as an interview. Accordingly, 37% of entry-level positions in 2015, were expected to be filled by graduates with previous experience in the organisation (Rate My Placement, 2015).

There are no guarantees however that offering placements will help an organisation to gain strategic advantage, or assist in talent acquisition and retention. While numerous benefits to hiring placement students have been identified, it should be noted that there are costs involved. In addition to compensation costs, employers will need to commit staff to plan, supervise and evaluate interns and the placement programme, equating to an opportunity cost for the organisation (Maertz et al., 2014b). Some students, particularly those with no prior experience at all, may require constant supervision, and evidence suggests *'interns sometimes lack the ability to manage their time, take initiative, and accept constructive criticism'* (Maertz et al., 2014b:131). Poor return on managers' time or dissatisfaction with the placement can also minimise potential benefits (Maertz et al., 2014a). As Yiu and Law (2012:381) note, placement experiences may have a *'significant effect on future career choices.'* While placements provide organisations with the option to 'try before they buy', they also offer students the same opportunity, and their experience could determine whether or not they stay in the industry when they graduate. Previous research suggests that 46% of tourism and hospitality students with work experience wouldn't work in the industry after they graduated, due to negative experiences (Richardson, 2008), and up to 70% are *'not willing or able to foresee a long-term career in the industry'* (Barron, 2008:736).

Surprisingly, many students enter onto tourism and hospitality degrees with very little, or no, knowledge of the industry or working conditions. Placement experiences offer a reality check and often do not meet the pre-conceived notions of glamour that students expect (Robinson *et al.*, 2015). Therefore, tourism and hospitality organisations and educators must understand the impacts that such unrealistic expectations can have on students' perceptions of the industry, and those wishing to acquire and retain talent through work placements, will need to understand and manage these expectations.

Lam and Ching (2007) acknowledge the rise in demand for labour, but note a significant decline in the number of tourism and hospitality graduates pursuing a career in the industry. Poorly structured and organised placements can be very discouraging for students, resulting in increasingly high fallout rates of graduates from the industry (Lam and Ching, 2007). Also, as Barron (2008:736) notes, *'poor quality employment early on leads to less opportunities for developing skills and learning which in turn engenders low levels of motivation, cynicism and lower work values.'* Positive placement experiences therefore, are beneficial to both students and the placement provider. With an estimated 993,000 additional staff required in the UK, by 2022 (People 1st, 2015b), and, at a global level, a shortfall of 14 million jobs in the travel and tourism sector (World Travel and Tourism Council, 2015), it is clear that if placements are to be utilised in the talent management system, these must be effectively structured and managed, in order to retain graduates. It is therefore important to select interns carefully, set goals and expectations from the start, and ensure adequate supervision is provided (Maertz *et al.*, 2014b). Knowledge of the current generation of students (part of the Millennial generation), and their needs and expectations will also prove crucial in attraction and retention.

Millennials

Graduates with more realistic expectations, are more likely to remain in the industry (Brown *et al.*, 2014). However, there is often a 'disconnect' between the expectations and perceptions of placement students and managers (Rangan and Natarajarathinam, 2014). This is partly explained by Barron (2008:732), who stresses that Generation Y (to which current students belong) *'think and behave differently'*. Brack (2012) refers to this generation as Millennials, but they may also be referred to as Generation Next, Echo Boomers, Facebookers and the MySpace Generation. Various sources differ in defining the age range of this generation, but it is generally accepted that it includes those born between 1980-2000 (Goldman Sachs, 2015), and will account for 75% of the global workforce by 2025 (Schawbel, 2013). However, Schawbel (2013:para. 1) notes this generation is going to make *'major shifts in corporations over the next decade'*, but most organisations, *'aren't ready for the amount of change that's coming.'*

Goldman Sachs (2015:para. 2) explains, *'Millennials have grown up in a time of rapid change, giving them a set of priorities and expectations sharply different from previous generations.'* Barron (2008) adds that Millennials are more demanding, demonstrate a lower tolerance for boredom, and are more inclined to voice their opinions. They are entering the workforce with different expectations and views on how work should be done (Schawbel, 2013), and meeting motivational, training and development needs is problematic (Barron, 2008). Their input needs to be recognised from the start, and they are used to being praised for their effort, rather than results. They also seek instant rewards and constant feedback and dislike menial and repetitive work (Barron, 2008). For this generation, Barron adds, long term means 12 months.

However, Millennials grew up with technology and are *'hyper-connected, tech-savvy entrepreneurial, and collaborative'* (Schawbel, 2012:para. 5). They are also *'the most diverse population to date ...[and]... the most-educated generation in history'* (Brack, 2012:4). Increasingly therefore, according to Brack (2012:2), *'business leaders are realising this generation's unique competencies and perspectives and employers are looking for ways to harness their strengths.'* Due to the sheer volume of Millennials, in comparison to their Generation X predecessors, and the increasing retirement

13

of Baby Boomers, organisations must look to Millennials to fill leadership gaps (Brack, 2012). Barron (2008) stresses that future employment strategies will need to adapt as this generation enters the workforce. As they have grown accustomed to instantaneous connection and immediate responses, through their use of technology, they expect the same in the workplace, and *'favour fast-paced work environments'*, and quick promotions (Schawbel, 2012:para.5-6). As their expectations and perceptions differ from those of previous generations, they also tend to exhibit lower levels of job satisfaction (Barron, 2008). Thus, Millennials may be even less attracted to staying in the industry following a negative work placement experience. In order to benefit from employing placement students, in terms of managing talent and meeting future staffing requirements, consideration must be given to the characteristics of Millennials and acquisition, development and retention practices.

Acquisition

To select the most suitable students for placement, employers will need to identify universities that offer degree programmes in tourism and hospitality. Relationships should then be developed with the relevant faculties, careers advisors, placement co-ordinators and students, and it is advisable to do this early in the academic year to avoid losing out to competitors (Rangan and Natarajarathinam, 2014). High Fliers Research (2015) reports the majority of top employers target between 10-25 universities each year, and some more than 30. Although the majority of students will undertake their placement after the second year of their degree, four-fifths of the leading employers are now holding events, such as taster sessions, open days and introductory presentations that are specifically targeted at first year students (High Fliers Research, 2015). This indicates that organisations recognise the benefits derived from placing students and recruiting graduates, and are seeking ways to get ahead of the competition, and, *'the sooner the business identifies interns, the longer they have to establish a mutually beneficial relationship'* (Rangan and Natarajarathinam, 2014:7).

Placement opportunities would normally be advertised to students via the careers service or placement officers within the universities, and often by attending careers fairs, but many organisations also promote these on the careers sections of their web-sites. As noted by Lawler (2008:11), the employer brand is a *'key part of what attracts talent to a company.'* The World Travel and Tourism Council (2015:16) agrees, a *'strong employer brand can both improve application rates for new employees and increase engagement and retention among the current workforce.'* The same principle may apply to placement students. The employer brand communicates what potential employees might expect from working for a particular organisation, and will therefore help them to assess how well they may fit into the working environment. It therefore needs to be devised carefully in order to manage expectations and to deter those that wouldn't fit well into the organisation (Lawler, 2008). Much the same as with regular recruitment practice, applicants should be short-listed and invited for interviews, and these should serve as an opportunity for both the employer and the student to determine suitability.

While Baby Boomers and Generation Xers valued job security and structure, Millennials are concerned with employability and flexibility and seek to *'add to their skills in meaningful ways'* (Brack, 2012:5). According to Barron (2008:733), they expect *'tangible and intangible rewards, empowerment, respect, workplace involvement, concern for employee welfare and supportive management.'* Career priorities for this generation include compensation, flexible work schedules, the opportunity to make a difference, trust in leadership, benefits and professional development opportunities (Brack, 2012). Information on organisational culture, an open communication policy, flexible work schedules and training and development opportunities should therefore be communicated to help attract Millennials (Brack, 2012).

Lam and Ching (2007) stress the need for effective collaboration between universities and industry in developing well-organised, quality placements, and emphasise this can only be achieved through an understanding of students' expectations, perceptions and overall satisfaction. Employers, they state, must be aware of placement objectives, and not view interns simply as a solution to labour shortages. At the same time however, the objectives should be aligned with organisational requirements (Rangan and Natarajarathinam, 2014).

Development

Scott and Revis (2008:783) assert talent management is *'ultimately about an organisation's ability to develop a pool of gifted individuals, who can individually help a company meet immediate and long-term objectives.'* A positive placement experience will increase students' confidence in their future career development (Chen and Shen, 2012), and may therefore encourage retention. Rangan and Natarajarathinam (2014:2) add, *'an effective internship experience is mutually beneficial to both the intern and the business.'* Thus, the design of the placement programme should involve both the student and the placement provider, and should consider pre-placement support, ongoing consultation and post-placement review (Chen and Shen, 2012). Robinson *et al.* (2015:2) remind organisations, that the design of a work placement is a *'key determinant as to whether students will commit to longer term careers in the industry.'*

A placement should expose students to *'best practices, effective management and an understanding of the skill sets and the application required to successfully transition into a productive contributor'* (Rangan and Natarajarathinam, 2014:2). Research suggests however that many placement experiences are less than beneficial to students, due to employers assigning unchallenging, routine tasks, which offer little in the way of learning or value (Maertz *et al.*, 2014b). Millennials are concerned

13

about developing the skills and training they will need '*to compete in the long run*' (Brack, 2012:9), and therefore, placement organisations that offer development opportunities and training will be more valued, and are more likely to retain students on graduation.

Brack (2012:11) asserts the differing attitude and expectations of Millennials' will require them to be trained in:

☐ Intergenerational dynamics;

☐ How to assimilate into a new workplace culture;

☐ How to work with team members assertively and diplomatically;

☐ How to process feedback;

☐ How to approach a supervisor for coaching and mentoring; and,

☐ How to set long-term career goals.

Lawler (2008:26) also notes the importance of motivation, stating '*even the best talent will perform at a high level only if motivated to do so.*' Millennials were '*raised under heavy supervision*' (Brack, 2012:4), and need coaching, as they are used to constant coaching and feedback. Though Brack (2012:7) highlights, this '*can be as simple as a quick email response, a text or a two-minute conversation.*' They are used to measurement systems and understand, and are accustomed to, being judged and assessed. A good mentoring programme will also help to retain staff. Brack (2012) highlights the results of a study that showed mentees had a 23 per cent higher retention rate, and mentors a 20 per cent higher retention rate, than those that didn't participate in a mentoring programme. Students need to be evaluated before their placement ends so that potential future employees may be identified and further mentored, thereby '*cultivating the recruitment benefits of internships*' (Maertz *et al.*, 2014b:136). Performance appraisals and other career management techniques can assist in this and help to plan for the succession of talent, as well as reduce staff turnover (Scott and Revis, 2008).

Retention

Research demonstrates that long-term career prospects and training are key in the decision graduates make when selecting an employer. Such opportunities can help an organisation to attract and retain the best employees (Scott and Revis, 2008), and '*Millennials are just as interested in how a business develops its people* […] *as they are in its products and profits*' (Salzberg, 2015:2). While small to medium (SMEs) enterprises may have traditionally lost out to larger competitors, who generally offer more attractive development opportunities, Branine (2008:499) suggests this gap is closing; '*Although large organisations still dominate the graduate recruitment market, an increasing number of small and medium-sized organisations employ graduates.*' This increase in competition for talent, and the rising salaries offered in other sectors, provides a challenge for the industry, and D'Annunzio-Green (2008) calls for a more proactive approach to attracting and retaining talent. She argues that, as the financial benefits of working in the industry are often limited, the identification of other factors that motivate employees to stay in the industry is crucial in informing attraction strategies. At the same time, there is a need to understand why employees leave, to help reduce staff turnover.

As mentioned, many students choose to pursue a career in other industries due to unsatisfactory placement experiences in tourism and hospitality organisations. Oliver's (1980) expectancy disconfirmation model, which posits that satisfaction is achieved when expectations are met or exceeded, is frequently cited by those researching student satisfaction with work placements (Siu *et al.*, 2012; Kim and Park, 2013; Fong *et al.*, 2014). If a student's perception of their experience matches their expectations, this results in confirmation, and if their expectations are exceeded, this results in positive disconfirmation. However, an experience that fails to meet expectations will result in negative disconfirmation, and it is this negative experience that may impact a student's motivation to stay in the industry.

While salary may partly influence students' perceptions, job satisfaction is also a crucial element. Placement students must feel they have a meaningful role to play in the organisation, and organisations must recognise this if they wish to recruit or retain more tourism and hospitality graduates. Maertz *et al.* (2014a) identify three factors that lead to successful placements: an engaged supervisor/ mentor, a quality on-boarding' experience, and meaningful work. Rangan and Natarajarathinam (Rangan and Natarajarathinam, 2014) identify eight factors, asserting placements should:

☐ Be planned;

☐ Be well-structured;

☐ Include tasks that challenge the student;

☐ Provide responsibility;

☐ Allow students to be mentored;

☐ Recognise and reward good work;

☐ Be meaningful; and,

☐ Pay well.

Chambers *et al.* (1998) suggest the best way to retain people is to create and deliver a great employee value proposition. The majority of employees that leave, do so simply because, '*they have found a more attractive alternative elsewhere*' (Lawler, 2008:22). Organisations must therefore obtain knowledge of the market, their competitors and what their competitors are offering, so they can assess how to gain competitive advantage in talent retention (Lawler, 2008). Compensation needs must also be reconsidered in the industry, due to the substantial increase in university fees and resulting debt. Perhaps most importantly, The World Travel and Tourism Council (2015:22) advises organisations must '*provide clear career guidance information and communicate effectively with future talent pools*', and '*clear*

13

career pathways' should be offered to help *'promote travel and tourism as a viable and rewarding career option.'*

A case study analysis of recruitment and retention practices (Lacey and Lavery, 2007:11) summarises the key factors contributing to effective retention:

- ☐ Probationary periods replaced with 'puppy walking' such as 'tailored support by line manager';
- ☐ The terms of employment (fairness, flexibility and clarity on the commitment the organisation is making to its employees);
- ☐ Management style ('devolved with emphasis on coaching and mentoring');
- ☐ Tailored individual career promotion; and,
- ☐ A 'welcome back' ('keeping in contact with ex-employees' and providing them with the opportunity to return when they 'take time out').

Brack (2012:13) also acknowledges the latter point, stressing, the doors should remain open to Millennials who leave the organisation, and former employees should be kept *'up-to-date on what is happening in the organisation'*. This may also be applicable to former placement students, and contact should be maintained with these students, when they return to university, particularly with those the organisation would like to retain.

Finally, it should be noted that placement students that don't return to their placement provider on graduation, may still act as an ambassador or PR agent for the organisation if they had a satisfactory experience (Maertz *et al.*, 2014a), and therefore may help to attract others. This further supports the need for effective management of students' placement experiences.

Conclusions

The purpose of this chapter was to examine the potential of utilising work placements in the management of talent acquisition, development and retention of employees in the tourism and hospitality industry. Talent management is critical to performance, but challenges still persist in recruitment and retention, due to negative perceptions of the industry, and the increasing number of tourism and hospitality students choosing to work in other sectors on graduation. In the context of skills shortages, changing expectations of the Millennial Generation, a lack of suitable applicants, and more attractive alternatives, the industry is suffering from severe productivity problems and higher than average employee turnover. The provision of work placement opportunities to university students however, is proven to be one of the best strategies for recruiting and developing talent, as it provides an efficient means of testing a pool of suitable candidates for future roles, and is more effective than traditional recruitment methods.

Numerous benefits to both employers and students have been identified, but in order to maximise the recruitment potential of placements, and retain graduates in the industry, the experiences of placement students must be effectively managed. Placements should offer students meaningful work, and develop the skills that the industry needs to address its skills shortages, and that Millennials value. Job satisfaction is crucial to students' perceptions of placement experiences and is critical in determining their future career intentions, as a negative experience can deter graduates from entering the industry. Expectations must therefore be managed, and this is the responsibility of both placement providers and universities. However, organisations must learn to adapt to the changing attitudes of the Millennial Generation as they form such a large and important component of the working population. As employability and skills are so significant to Millennials, organisations will need to provide, and clearly communicate, development opportunities and long-term career prospects to students, if they wish to attract placement students and retain them on graduation.

Growth in the industry, and the predicted increase in the number of employees needed in the future, will continue to prove challenging for tourism and hospitality organisations, and attraction and retention issues simply must be addressed. Those organisations that do manage to attract, nurture and retain quality employees, will prosper, as talent is shown to be critical to performance and success. In such a competitive industry, and in an environment of accelerating numbers of graduate opportunities, effective talent management is essential. While placements may provide an opportunity to identify potential talent, from a pool of students interested in careers in tourism and hospitality, the placement organisations are responsible for developing this talent and maintaining graduates' interest in the industry.

Learning activities

1   Reflect on the challenges relating to recruitment and retention in the tourism and hospitality industry. Why do these problems exist?

2   Why are talented individuals so important to the success of tourism and hospitality organisations?

3   Investigate the differences between Millennials and their Generation X predecessors. How might these differences impact on the work environment if organisations fail to adapt their employment strategies?

4   Analyse and evaluate the importance of a work placement to a tourism and/or hospitality student.

5   Investigate best practice in the design and management of work placements in the context of the talent management system.

6   Analyse and evaluate the impacts of the *quality* of placements on the attraction and retention of graduates in the industry.

13

References

Aggett, M. and Busby, G. (2011). Opting out of internship: Perceptions of hospitality, tourism and events management undergraduates at a British university. *Journal of Hospitality, Leisure, Sport & Tourism Education*, **10** (1), 106-113.

Amadeus (2010). *Hotels 2020: Beyond Segmentation. Strategies for Growth in an Era of Personalization and Global Change*. Amadeus. Available at: http://www.amadeus.com/web/binaries/1333077622343/blobheader=application/pdf&blobheadername1=Content-Disposition&blobheadervalue1=attachment%3B+filename%3DHotelsWhitepaper2020BeyondSegmentation.pdf. Accessed: 07/08/15.

ASET (2013). *ASET Good Practice Guide for Work Based and Placement Learning in Higher Education*. ASET. Available at: http://www.asetonline.org/wp-content/uploads/2014/11/ASET-Good-Practice-Guide-2014.pdf. Accessed 08/08/15)

Barron, P. (2008). Education and talent management: Implications for the hospitality industry. *International Journal of Contemporary Hospitality Management*, 20 (7), 730-742.

Brack, J. (2012). *Maximizing Millennials in the Workplace*. UNC Executive Development. Available at: http://www.avds.com/images/blog/UNC_Millenials_Workplace_Study.pdf. Accessed: 08/08/15.

Branine, M. (2008). Graduate recruitment and selection in the UK: A study of the recent changes in methods and expectations. *Career Development International*, **13** (6), 497-513.

Brown, E. A., Arendt, S. W. and Bosselman, R. H. (2014). Hospitality management graduates' perceptions of career factor importance and career factor experience. *International Journal of Hospitality Management*, **37** (Feb), 58-67.

Bullock, K., Gould, V., Hejmadi, M. and Lock, G. (2009). Work placement experience: should I stay or should I go? *Higher Education Research & Development*, **28** (5), 481-494.

Chambers, E. G., Foulon, M., Handfield-Jones, H., Hankin, S. M. and Michaels, E. G. (1998). The war for talent. *McKinsey Quarterly*, **1998** (3), 44-57.

Chang, S., Walsh, K. and Tse, E. C.-Y. (2014). Understanding students' intentions to join the hospitality industry: The role of emotional intelligence, service orientation, and industry satisfaction. *Cornell Hospitality Quarterly*, Nov, 1-14.

Chen, T.-L. and Shen, C.-C. (2012). Today's intern, tomorrow's practitioner?—The influence of internship programmes on students' career development in the Hospitality Industry. *Journal of Hospitality, Leisure, Sport & Tourism Education*, **11** (1), 29-40.

Christensen Hughes, J. and Rog, E. (2008). Talent management: A strategy for improving employee recruitment, retention and engagement within hospitality organizations. *International Journal of Contemporary Hospitality Management*, 20 (7), 743-757.

CIPD (2012). *Work Experience Placements That Work: A Guide for Employers*. CIPD.

Cowsill, D. S. (2015). Foreward. In: Oxford Economics. *Global Talent Trends and Issues for the Travel & Tourism Sector - January 2015*. World Travel and Tourism Council.

D'Annunzio-Green, N. (2008). Managing the talent management pipeline: Towards a greater understanding of senior managers' perspectives in the hospitality and tourism sector. *International Journal of Contemporary Hospitality Management*, 20 (7), 807-819.

Eriksen, B. H. (2012). *Dancing With the Stars: How Talent Shapes Firm Performance*. Academy of Management, 2012 Annual Meeting. Boston, MA. Available at: http://papers.ssrn.com/sol3/papers.cfm?abstract_id=2021899. Accessed: 05/08/15.

Fong, L. H. N., Luk, C. and Law, R. (2014). How do hotel and tourism students select internship employers? A segmentation approach. *Journal of Hospitality, Leisure, Sport & Tourism Education*, **15** (Jul), 68-79.

Garavan, T. N. and Murphy, C. (2001). The co-operative education process and organisational socialisation: A qualitative study of student perceptions of its effectiveness. *Education+ Training*, **43** (6), 281-302.

Goldman Sachs (2015). *Millennials Coming of Age*. Available at: http://www.goldmansachs.com/our-thinking/pages/millennials/. Accessed: 20/08/15.

High Fliers Research (2015). *The Graduate Market in 2015. Annual Review of Graduate Vacancies & Starting Salaries at Britain's Leading Employers*. High Fliers Research Limited.

Hurd, J. and Hendy, M. (1997). What we know about co-op employers' perceptions of cooperative education: A synthesis of research in the USA and in Canada. *Journal of Cooperative Education*, **32** (2), 55-62.

Kim, H.-B. and Park, E. J. (2013). The role of social experience in undergraduates' career perceptions through internships. *Journal of Hospitality, Leisure, Sport & Tourism Education*, **12** (1), 70-78.

Kusluvan, S., Kusluvan, Z., Ilhan, I. and Buyruk, L. (2010). The human dimension: A review of human resources management issues in the tourism and hospitality industry. *Cornell Hospitality Quarterly*, **51** (2), 171-214.

Lacey, M. and Lavery, T. (2007). *Recruitment and Retention Lessons from Beyond the Social Services Sector*. Rock Solid Social Research. Available at: http://lx.iriss.org.uk/sites/default/files/resources/Recruitment%20and%20Retention%20Lessons%20Research%20-%20Report%20.pdf. Accessed: 25/08/15.

Lam, T. and Ching, L. (2007). An exploratory study of an internship program: The case of Hong Kong students. *International Journal of Hospitality Management*, **26** (2), 336-351.

Lawler, E. (2008). *Strategic talent management: Lessons from the corporate world*. Madison, WI: Consortium for Policy Research in Education.

Maertz, C. P., Stoeberl, P. A. and Magnusson: (2014a). Finding strategic human resource advantage from building an effective internship capability. *Organizational Dynamics*, **4** (43), 303-311.

Maertz, P. C., Stoeberl, P. and Marks, J. (2014b). Building successful internships: lessons from the research for interns, schools, and employers. *Career Development International*, **19** (1), 123-142.

Nickson, D. (2013). *Human Resource Management for Hospitality, Tourism and Events* (2nd ed). Routledge, Oxon.

Oliver, R. L. (1980). A cognitive model of the antecedents and consequences of satisfaction decisions. *Journal of Marketing Research*, **17** (4), 460-469.

People 1st (2015a). *The Skills and Productivity Problem*. People 1st. Available at: http://www.people1st.co.uk/Research-policy/Research-reports/The-Skills-and-Productivity-Problem. Accessed: 07/08/15.

13

People 1st (2015b). *The Skills and Productivity Question: Hospitality and Tourism Sector*. People 1st. Available at: http://www.people1st.co.uk/getattachment/Research-policy/Research-reports/The-Skills-and-Productivity-Problem/Report-The-skills-and-productivity-problem-July-15.pdf.aspx. Accessed: 07/08/15.

Rangan, S. and Natarajarathinam, M. (2014). How to structure an internship that is great for the intern and the manager? *Proceedings of the 2014 American Society for Engineering Education Conference and Exposition*. American Society for Engineering Education.

Rate My Placement (2015). Rate My Placement University Presentation. Available online at: http://www.ratemyplacement.co.uk/universities. Accessed: 05/08/15.

Raybould, M. and Wilkins, H. (2005). Over qualified and under experienced: Turning graduates into hospitality managers. *International Journal of Contemporary Hospitality Management*, **17** (3), 203-216.

Richardson, S. (2008). Undergraduate tourism and hospitality students attitudes toward a career in the industry: A preliminary investigation. *Journal of Teaching in Travel & Tourism*, **8** (1), 23-46.

Robinson, R. N., Ruhanen, L. and Breakey, N. M. (2015). Tourism and hospitality internships: influences on student career aspirations. *Current Issues in Tourism*, (March), 1-15.

Salzberg, B. (2015). The purpose of business. In: Deloitte (Ed). *Mind the Gaps - The 2015 Deloitte Millennial Survey: Executive Summary*. Deloitte. pp 60.

Schawbel, D. (2013). 10 ways Millennials are creating the future of work. *Forbes Magazine*. Available online at: http://www.forbes.com/sites/danschawbel/2013/12/16/10-ways-millennials-are-creating-the-future-of-work/. Accessed: 18/08/15.

Schawbel, D. (2012). Millennials vs. Baby Boomers: Who would you rather hire? *Business Time*. Available online at: http://www.business.time.com/2012/03/29/millennials-vs-baby-boomers-who-would-you-rather-hire/. Accessed: 20/08/15.

Scott, B. and Revis, S. (2008). Talent management in hospitality: graduate career success and strategies. *International Journal of Contemporary Hospitality Management*, **20** (7), 781-791.

Siu, G., Cheung, C. and Law, R. (2012). Developing a conceptual framework for measuring future career intention of hotel interns. *Journal of Teaching in Travel & Tourism*, **12** (2), 188-215.

Venkataraman, R. (2014). *The Challenge of Attracting Graduates - A Strategic Process in People Resourcing*. MA in Arts in Human Resource Management, National College of Ireland, Dublin.

World Travel and Tourism Council (2015). *Global Trends and Issues for the Travel & Tourism Sector - January 2015*. World Travel and Tourism Council.

Yiu, M. and Law, R. (2012). A review of hospitality internship: Different perspectives of students, employers, and educators. *Journal of Teaching in Travel & Tourism*, **12** (4), 377-402.

14 Local, National or International Strategies for Talent Management

Deniz Kucukusta

Learning objectives

By the end of this chapter you'll be able to:

■ Understand the critical success factors for global and local companies

■ Identify existing challenges regarding talent management functions

■ Discuss possible solutions regarding the issues in global and local companies

■ Identify the cultural and demographic challenges in local companies in developing talent management strategies

■ Learn the current facts and issues about talent in emerging Asian markets such as China, Singapore, Hong Kong, Taiwan, Thailand, Korea and Japan.

Introduction

The chapter discusses critical success factors, challenges and possible solutions for talent management in global and local contexts. The first part focuses on international and global strategies and the second part concentrates more on the national or local talent management practices and strategies, and current issues being faced in emerging markets in Asia, namely China, Singapore, Hong Kong, Taiwan, Thailand, Korea and Japan. The third part includes cases in a Chinese context discussing the perceptions of talent management in China and a successful example from the industry.

Successful implementation of talent management in a global or local company depends on how it blends with the company's overall strategies and how successful it is in dealing with local or global challenges. Although talent management related problems seem to be similar, there are significant differences depending on the cultures or countries where the business is being developed. In Asia, for instance, the main concern for talent acquisition and development can be how to stay competitive in fast-growing Asian economies and rapidly growing businesses. The objective of this chapter is therefore to identify the issues that the industry is facing; provide possible solutions in terms of local and global companies; and present current situations in the Asian context. The emerging markets in Asia represent a huge portion in the hospitality and tourism industry on the global stage. Therefore, the chapter includes valuable cases of benchmarking and talent management practices from emerging Asian markets.

Global (multi-national) talent management

It is well known that the hospitality and tourism industry is highly people-oriented, which just brings the issues and challenges of managing the talent. Without mentioning more about the reasons and benefits of effective talent management in the industry, there are basically two fundamental approaches to viewing the optimum utilization of an organization's resources for enhancing its competitive advantages: resource based and talent based theory (Rabbi *et al.*, 2015). Another comprehensive theory of firms describes how those resources that are valuable, rare, inimitable, and non-substitutable, have the potential to sustain competitive advantage, and that these include the talent, also referred to the human capital (Barney, 1991).

Another definition of talent management in the global context is described as *'the strategic integration of resourcing and development at the global level which involves the proactive identification and development, thus strategic deployment of high-performing and high-potential strategic employees on an international scale'* (Collings *et al.*, 2009). This implies the significance of not just sourcing and acquiring the competence and intelligence, but also the mater of retaining and sustaining their contributions in the emerging markets globally (Farndale *et al.*, 2010). Thanks to, and because of globalization, the demand and supply of talent bring both opportunities and challenges to organizations; and hence the management of this matter remains significant (Lane and Pollner, 2008).

Critical factors for the successful implementation of talent management

Interactively, the successful implementation of talent management is just similar as the typical management of human resources, which requires a holistic and comprehensive collaboration with the strategies of managing other aspects in an organization, such as its marketing and financial objectives and goals. Talent management has to be integrated and aligned with the organization's overall strategies because of its vital importance to articulation (Rabbi *et al.*, 2015); therefore, human behaviour and culture are critical attributes identified in dealing with the implementation (Coleman, 2008). Considering that knowledge and skills are the factors that can be constant, because of free information flow and transparency, the organization's competitive advantage can be easily copied or learned by other firms, but not the competencies and intelligence of its talent. Therefore, overcoming the cultural challenges is not just a matter of simply sharing and transmitting knowledge and intelligence (Cole, 2004).

Another point of view for the management on acquiring that knowledge and intelligence can be expressed by how much the talent are offered; that is the compensation. Offer and acceptance can be simply interpreted as the demand and supply in the human capital market, in which the competitors 'fight' among each other by offering attractive and competitive 'motives' to acquire valuable and competent talent, and so the right incentive has to be given to those who are able to contribute success (Cole-Gomolski, 1997). It is also important that the talent themselves have to also understand the importance of the management's implementation, so that they are willing and able to contribute their efforts in knowledge sharing by accepting the reward of compensation.

Challenges and solutions for global companies

In the wider scope of the global context, a multinational corporation can confront a number of challenges in managing talent, particularly the following two key difficulties: global competition and new forms of international mobility (Farndale *et al.*, 2010). As the hospitality and tourism industry is definitely doing the business by crossing borders and territories, organizations are typically and commonly large and wide covering countries and regions, not just in competing for customers and markets, but also for the human resource and talent. Therefore, it can be predicted that the emergence of a common pool of global talent is being shared and fought over by the multinational organizations. Thus, this creates the issues of demanding increasingly high skill levels of staff and requiring more specifically those of their qualities which can differentiate and help the company stand out among its competitors (Dickmann *et al.*, 2008).

Further about the 'quality' requirement, there is the issue that the supply of sufficiently educated senior and managerial staff is not enough to satisfy the demand. As well as in the developed countries (Cappelli, 2008), it has been also a growing problem in transitional and developing countries, such as China and India (Doh *et al.*, 2008; Ma and Trigo, 2008); and therefore the multinational organizations have to broaden their search to a wider pool of talent (Boussebaa and Morgan, 2008). Strategically, the integration of holistic approaches on managing high quality human resources requires the extension of their talent pipelines into much more forward planning activities, such as sourcing and recruiting; and

14

it also means that the issue also involves market-mapping and employer-branding to assist in attracting and retaining high-performing employees with exceptional qualities (Farndale *et al.*, 2010). Such activities have to be highly and extensively executed on the corporate's agenda by considering many more aspects, including both internal and external opportunities and threats, particularly in the international and regional markets of human resources.

Substantially, the criterion of culture is again to be considered when managing talent from the perspectives of multinational organizations. Research suggests that there is a need for managers with distinctive competencies and a desire to operate the business in distant countries culturally and geographically (Bjorkman and Xiucheng, 2002; Li and Scullion, 2006). Specifically, the effective and successful management of cross-cultural and cross-regional talent requires several forms of capital competencies (Farndale *et al.*, 2010), namely cognitive, social, political and human capital. Cognitive capital refers to the effective mental competency of sharing and transmitting knowledge across the globalizing organization (Murtha, Lenway and Bagozzi, 1998); social capital is based upon social networking, which gives the necessary connections to perform boundary-spanning roles (Kostova and Roth, 2003); political capital means the legitimacy necessary to be recognized and confirmed as talent (Harvey and Novicevic, 2004); and human capital is the personal competencies necessary to operate in a cross-cultural context (Earley and Mosakowski, 2004). Previously, talent management in the global context has been focusing on the staffing senior positions in headquarters or at regional levels by considering the pattern of the expatriates' appointment in terms of ethnocentric, polycentric, regiocentric or geocentric aspects (Perlmutter, 1969); and now the trends are even more on the international transfer of expatriates or inpatriates with the inclusion of the above capitals (Collings *et al.*, 2009; Sorge, 2004).

Another key challenge arises from the new forms of international mobility, in particularly the emerging markets. Even though the supply of culturally-conscious and competent talent may satisfy the demand of the current market of human resources, the willingness and readiness of the talent to be relocated bring another big factor towards the success. As the emerging markets are usually in the stage of developing, the lack of support can set barriers for motivating or compensating the talent to the new locations, such as the living standard and environment of the host countries. The developments in emerging markets instantly create the issues of the preparedness of individuals' mobility in the international context; and the individuals' ethnocentric mentalities in coping with the global approaches to managing the cross-cultural business and operations (Farndale *et al.*, 2010). With the intense competition for scarce highly qualified senior staff, the talent is also able to be more selective in the offers of opportunities; hence the challenge of mobility is present. Such issues across international borders, particularly to the relatively higher risk locations such as the developing countries, is significantly difficult to overcome (Yeung *et al.*, 2008); for instance the failure of overseas appointments is reported to be the highest in China, India and Russia, with the typical reasons being immigration formalities, tax regulations, language and cultural difficulties, and the perception of salaries experienced by employees from higher cost locations (Farndale *et al.*, 2010).

To address the issues, the solution of self-initiated movers may help (Tharenou, 2003), by inviting and sourcing competent talent who are willing and ready to be relocated; while another condition can be also applied to make it more effective: the relocation of talent to a third country, which is neither the nationality of the talent nor the country of the corporation. Such practice has been proven successful in companies with foreign subsidiaries, in terms of standardizing and formalizing managerial policies, practices and incentive schemes (Harvey and Novicevic, 2004). Another strategy can be deploying the acculturated talent from developing countries to the desired location, with the experience of working in developed countries or the corporation's headquarters (Sebastian Reiche, 2006; Scullion *et al.*, 2007). It is because the deployed inpatriates can help socializing and integrating the cultural and geographical gaps with the corporate environment. The benefits are that a global core competency or a diversity of strategic perspectives can be created at the top management team; while the emergence of the developing markets can be provided with opportunities for the high-potential talent (Harvey, Speier and Novicevic, 1999). Nevertheless, the strategies are aiming to solve the challenges of scarcity and mobility but the cost pressure on offering compensation and benefits remains an ever-standing difficulty, as well as sustaining the appointments in a long run.

Local (national) talent management

Cultural and demographic challenges

Having been researched and discussed for years, the topic of talent management has broadened to address the challenges of managing talent at different levels and scales in terms of national, cultural and sectoral perspectives; but nevertheless the focus is primarily the pressing demands of talent shortages and surpluses, or the location and relocation of talent with effective compensation and utilization (Tarique and Schuler, 2010; Tatli *et al.*, 2013). Despite the cost of compensation and motivation, the challenge can be directed to the geographic and demographic levels in which the management of talent involves creative and competitive use of resources to achieve the individuals' full potential, and to meet the demand of industries by effectively deploying and employing the demand and supply of the labour market. One of the rationales is the changing and emerging demography, such as aging population, declining birth rate, feminization of higher education, increased economic migration and regional shortage of skilled labour (Tatli *et al.*, 2013).

It can be also predicted that the issue can remain ever-changing because of the macro environmental factors, which may not be a serious matter in one coun-

14

try but can be a big problem in other regions or nations. A study by Manpower illustrates that the global phenomenon is felt in different ways and extents across the continents, but the shortages of talent are an ongoing challenge for multinational employers and seem unlikely to be solved in the short term (Tatli *et al.*, 2013). To address the issue quickly, many innovative or traditional practices have been adopted, such as outsourcing, cross-border and on-demand employments, structural change on educational curriculum, and even migration policies. However the immediate tactics may probably be able to address the challenge in a decade without offering much to affect the true dynamics of talent management of retention and development, including the barriers of cultural and demographic contexts; for example, one of the most significant issues in Asia's talent resources is the gender discrimination. The phenomenon is not solely attributable to demographic reasons but is affected by the realities in different countries, which have their own stories and rationales; and hence the situations and challenges are definitely not the same because of cultural, political and historical backgrounds.

Talent management in Asian countries

China

In discussions about topics in a business context in recent years, China has inevitably been named, as the country has been influencing the entire world economically and politically. From the perspectives of managing people in organizations, the traditional ideology of Confucianism has long been been part of China's managerial and business systems (Ngo *et al.*, 2008). The ideology has been widely influencing not just Chinese society, but also the neighbouring countries such as Korea and Japan, by embedding a patriarchal notion and philosophy of gender roles and expectations, which shape the organizational practices and structure all the way from recruitment, promotion and even work-life balance in personal lives after work (Leung, 2002). One of its representing notions is that men's role has to have its emphasis on work while women's role is centered on managing the household's wellbeing. Another traditional Confucius notion also suggests that women have to be ethically virtuous, by not being professional academically. An analysis of evidence from recruitment advertisements reveals that gender discrimination has been present directly and indirectly through the use of gendered expectations and stereotypes on abilities and competencies, which reflect the traditional ideas of men and women's roles at work (Woodhams *et al.*, 2009). The disadvantages in employment because of gender are not limited to the stage of recruitment but also affect the subsequent career developments and compensation. A survey conducted in Beijing finds that women have lower levels of job commitment compared to their men colleagues because of strong perceptions of gender discrimination and bias in job assignments and compensation, such as less challenging tasks assigned to women but more promotional opportunities given to men (Peng *et al.*, 2009).

Another unique cultural factor in Chinese culture is relationship building, which is presented in literal Chinese phonetics '*guanxi*'. The existence of guanxi emphasizes the use of informal networks to get things done through the process of defining and formulating human relationships based on loyalty and trust. Such a way of handling interpersonal relationships has been being a vital element of career progression, as well as doing business, for determining one's future career in China (Fan, 2002; Faure and Fang, 2008). The culture and beliefs of guanxi play a prominent role, and need to better understood when formulating strategies or solutions in managing talent and human resources in China.

Taiwan

Similar to the situation in China, Confucian values and beliefs are strongly rooted in both private and public domains in Taiwan, which is also a territory of ethnical Chinese. The work and life styles of Taiwanese are constrained by the traditional thoughts of gender roles despite the efforts contributed towards talent development by education and training system (Tsai, 2006). Substantial restructuring has taken place in Taiwan in recent decades in terms of capital and knowledge, as a result of several major reforms in education systems such as vocational and professional developments (Lin and Yang, 2009; Rodgers *et al.*, 2006). The pool of talent has been adequate, yet shortages remain among both low and high end practitioners and professionals (Tatli *et al.*, 2013). The major challenge of managing talent in Taiwan was attributed by brain drain, which has been recorded at seriously high levels in recent years. Severe shortages of skilful and knowledgeable managers were reportedly due to emigration to China and other developed countries such as the U.S. and Europe (Wang and Hsiao, 2002), because the competent talent have the opportunities of jobs in international markets not just the limited choices within the territory.

Other than the problem of brain drain, there is a demographic imbalance in the work force because of the culture, which creates anadditional challenge in managing talent. The traditional values compose the society's structure by limiting the potential of women, who have less likelihood of progression and leadership in organizations because of their roles in families (Bowen, 2003; Lin and Yang, 2009; Rodgers *et al.*, 2006). Although the government has been promoting the elimination of inequality of gender by multi-dimensional efforts, such as the education systems (Lin and Yang, 2009), the labour markets are still largely gendered by salary ranges, promotion opportunities, job tasks, stereotyping, and even harassment (Bowen, 2003; Wu, 2006). The case in Taiwan illustrates that the retention of talent is another critical criteria in the holistic and successful approach of talent management despite the prior efforts of sourcing, recruiting and developing. Fair employment systems have to be used for tapping potential talent such as skilled and educated professionals and minor demographic groups (Chou *et al.*, 2005).

14

Thailand

Another Asian country, Thailand, also demonstrated the challenge of inequality in the workforce because of cultural and demographic factors. Without the influence of Confucianism, the culture of Thailand still has patriarchal values, which portray that gender and social status are critical factors for performing managerial roles, with certain degrees of prejudices and discriminations (Virakul, 2000). Although the authorities have dedicated resources to in training and developing talent and workforces, resulting in some narrowing of the gaps in salary and compensation, the higher and tertiary education systems are yet lacking the representation of demographic minorities, such as female and lower social classes with relatively less income (Nakavachara, 2010). Legislative and educational reforms have resulted in an improvement of equality in labour market status, but there are still barriers to women and under-privileged populations, for instance the labours from rural areas, for advancement and progression (Yukongdi, 2005). Other factors that are blamed include the discrimination and inequality that are brought in and deepened by some multinational firms operating in the country (Youngsamart, Fisher and Härtel, 2010). Evidence shows the presence of organizational barriers of inequality and discrimination for advancement and development across different practices, ranging from recruitment, selection and retention (Lawler, 1996) by maintaining the organizational cultures and status quo (Appold *et al.*, 1998). For instance, a study reveals that the social homophily of male preference causes sexual discrimination (Appold *et al.*, 1998). The case of Thailand gives the thoughts of closing the gaps of unfair treatments by interventions at multiple levels, including proactive state policies and changes in organizational policies and cultures (Virakul, 2000; Tatli *et al.*, 2013).

Japan

A special and unique example can be seen in the nation of islands in Asia, in which Japan seems to have the challenges in different ways than the cases above. The country has been long being limited in its talent in terms of diversity, which has been always criticized in the ever-changing world of globalization. Large companies in Japan still tend to recruit employees from the local talent pool, and even limit their selections of outstanding talent solely to a few local universities (Debroux, 2013). Subsequently organizations in Japan cannot remain competitive and advantageous without attracting qualified talent from rest of the globalized world; this problem cannot be easily solved by simply modifying policies and ordinances of talent immigration (Brannen, 2010). Yet, Japanese culture and society have certain degree of similarities as other Asian countries, such as masculinity, which denotes the dominance of male in most of the status including workplaces. Opportunities for females are far more limited than some other neighbouring counties, by having glass ceiling on career progression, role assignments, and roles of wives in terms of work-life balance; all the attributes result in the underutilization of potential resource of talent (Debroux, 2013).

One of the Japanese traditional values emphasizes social harmony and the hierarchy of seniority, which prohibits the promotion of talent with higher competencies over the heads of their supervisors; therefore organizations struggle to respond to the expectation of career progression and reward compensations. Because of this, the salary and career path of talent are no longer correlated with competencies and performance, which result in demotivation and lower productivity (Lazear, 1979). Another aspect of the values of social harmony and hierarchy is observed by legitimacy. Employees in Japan are likely to perceive their supervisors as people who have performed outstandingly and perfectly in a meritocratic system (Sugimoto, 2010); and that perception extends the acceptance of hierarchy to acknowledging its legitimacy. Employees are willing to act according to the prescribed roles and duties without questioning or even striving for alternative distributions of power, status and rewards (Debroux, 2013). The legitimacy can potentially bring issues; casually terminating relationships within the organization without understanding and following the traditional culture can result in conflicts and mistrust. Demographically, the country has been famous for its aging population which affects the management of not just talent but the human resource severely. According to studies and estimations, employees in Japan have to keep working until the age of 64 by the end of March 2025, if other factors remain constant as the current status, such as birth rate, life expectancy, economic stability and political environment (Lazear, 1979; Conrad, 2010). Such a huge burden on workforces does not only impose costs and challenges on organizations and society but also extend to other issues of morality and policies. Concurrently, the country has started to adopt a new trend of employing and integrating more and more 'non-permanent' workers, who are expected and required to perform and carry out duties the same as the other employees, but without any long-term commitment and protection of employments. This creates a big issue of social fairness and even causes moral hazard, thus deteriorating the organizations' efficiency and competitiveness (Debroux, 2013).

Overall, challenges exist as much as chances and solutions; and one of the cases to tackle the talent management in Japan can be benchmarked by referring to the practices of introducing explicit career fast tracks, which provide talent with long-term employment security but with greater certainty concerning remuneration and advancement. The trend towards professionalization gives opportunities to nurture higher specialized and professional talent with competencies and better treatment for upgrading and retaining in organizations (Froese and Goeritz, 2007; Meyer-Ohle, 2009).

Korea

Close to China and Japan, the peninsula country of Korea shares similarities and differences with its neighbouring countries in terms of cultural background and values in the context of managing talent. One of the similarities with Japan in the business sense is the presence of '*chaebols*', which like the famous '*keiritsu*' of Japan,

14

have dominated the country's economy (Kearney, 1991). The term '*chaebol*' means large conglomerates or corporations with extensive linkages with other firms and government,which heavily influence the country's economic development (Song, 1990); an example is the Shilla and Lotte group of hotels, shipping malls, and theme parks. Moreover, because of the deep and long history with China, Confucianism is rooted in Korea, with influential and determining impacts on many aspects of the country, including the management style. The conglomerates of chaebols are typically structured with a centralized authority, the chairman's office, which actually belongs to and is thoroughly controlled by the owners and their families.

The management of human resources is also directly affiliated and controlled by the chairman's office, which makes promotion decisions for executives and senior managers of all member companies based on the business direction of the conglomerate (Kim and Briscoe, 1997). The hierarchical and centralized style truly reflects on the management of talent from recruitment to development in Korea's entrepreneurial mechanism. Workforces are usually sourced twice a year from the few reputable universities across the territory by series of tests and interviews (Kim, 1997), followed by a month of in-house training with the requirements of strong emphasis on loyalty and obedience, resulting in the transformation of 'warrior workers' from 'naïve graduates' before being assigned to various work locations and roles (Kearney, 1991). By doing so, the newly recruited employees are intensively trained, and imbued with a sense of loyalty as well as of harmony and unity; thus the chaebols promise assignments and compensations for almost a life-time length.

The process of development is provided with extensive technical and managerial training, which is also emphasized by the conglomerates to be ongoing and continuous (Steers *et al.*, 1989). Although the situation does not predict any shortage of talent or brain drain, it seems that both the organizations and employees are relatively stable and satisfied; and therefore the lack of motivation and personal growth become barriers to competitiveness and efficiency. Traditionally, the employees' salary and compensation has been determined by seniority, because of similar reasons and rationales as the Japanese style and paradigm, but it has been changed with a common trend of an emerging reward system with performance based criteria for the purpose of increasing productivity and efficiency (Ahn, 1996; Byungnamlee and Rhee, 1996).

Another reason for the lack of motivation can be attributed to the impact of cultural believes and values on the evaluation of performance. Organizations do not seek objective performance appraisals since managers are unwilling to evaluate their subordinates' performances with unfavourable or extreme grades (Kim and Briscoe, 1997). The cultural impact from Confucianism highlights the collective or group harmony and teamwork, which is expressed as '*in-hwa*' in the Korean language. Performance appraisals are generally rated with central tendency without any significant difference among employees, who also perceive that the objectivity and legitimacy of job enhancement and career progression, as well as compensation, are fairly conducted according to seniority and hierarchy. To better cope with the globalized business environment, enterprises have already dedicated changes on managing their valuable and potential talent by breaking through some of the traditions, such as a new paradigm of adopting quality leadership instead of centralized authority, individualized incentives and reward based performance evaluation, and discriminant reward levels based on individual performance instead of the principle of seniority and hierarchy (Kim and Briscoe, 1997).

Hong Kong

Unlike other countries or territories in Asia, Hong Kong is an independent economic entity which has limited resources of land and human capital. With its unique historical and cultural background, the city has been well developed in terms of business and economic environment, while confronting its challenges of managing potential talent. The city's economy has been transformed to a knowledge-intensive and high value-added model after decades of investment and development in human capital; however the demographic and political attributes cause difficulties in its talent management, particularly in a long run (Varma and Budhwar, 2013).

With a relatively low unemployment rate, Hong Kong has also one of the lowest birth rates in the world, at 0.9% per female per annum and faces significant difficulties in tackling the problem of an aging population (Tatli *et al.*, 2013). Therefore, the city has been adopting less rigid immigration policies for attracting human capital, while reforming and reviewing frequently its education policies for coping with rapid changes in the business and economic environment (Olsen and Burges, 2007). Despite the quickly changing environment, companies report difficulties in retaining their human capital and required skilled workforce because of unfair discrimination and certain legislative constraints (Ng and Chakrabarty, 2005; Wong, 2005), though there have been new ordinances in recent years, including the anti-discrimination ordinance and the legal requirement on statutory minimum hourly wages.

Reported from findings of researching multinational organizations, one of the significant contributory factors is a family-unfriendly working environment and policies that cause difficulties in managing talent (Lo *et al.*, 2003; Ng and Chakrabarty, 2005), such as long and unstable working hours in the hospitality and tourism industry. Structurally and demographically, the workforce in the industry has also perceived the roles and career development with relatively low and unsatisfactory motives, resulting in high turnover rates because of plenty of alternatives from other industries, as well as the changing values of the newer generations (Lam *et al.*, 2001; Lam *et al.*, 2002). Rather than the difficulties caused by an aging population, the demographic shift brings low commitment and retention in the industry because of the absence of interest or opportunities for

14

advancement, and the lack of sense of belonging, as reported after investigations from current industrial practitioners (Wong *et al.*, 1999; Pang *et al.*, 2014).

In summary, the situation of Hong Kong presents an ever changing demand and supply of competent talent which has to be planned and organized appropriately and strategically in a long run (Varma and Budhwar, 2013), although prior requests of conditions have been fulfilled and managed including the adequacy of recruiting sources and comprehensive development plans.

Singapore

Similar to Hong Kong, the tropical country of Singapore shares a colonial background, but is independent both economically and politically without too many resources including workforces. Since its independence in 1965, the country's leaders have long realized that the need of competent and well-equipped manpower is one of the most critical surviving criteria and defining factors for the tiny country with its limited population of approximately four million, of which the multi-cultural and multi-racial nature makes the challenge even more unique and representing. To start developing the newly-established economy, the country has been progressively removing obstacles from all aspects by aiming at creating one of the most attractive and comfortable environments for foreign investors and multinational companies (Bhasin and Low Kim Cheng, 2002).

Although the challenges of managing talent in Singapore is innate in its background settings, the government has been visionary and pragmatic in tackling the problems politically by implementing means of policies on transforming the small country to one of the most well-developed economic entities in the region with an abundance of talent and human resources. Primarily, the favourable policies for attracting and retaining talent from overseas are aimed at bringing in expatriates to the country by offering citizenships, taxation and housing allowance, and visa waving scheme (Bhasin and Low Kim Cheng, 2002). In a long run, valuable talent are further attracted by referral schemes and scholarships to continue and prolong their stays in the country, such that the following generations can also enjoy the benefits and remain in the country to further contribute and make their living (Debrah, 1996; Budhwar and Debrah, 2008). The government also dedicates efforts to tackle talent shortages and enhance competitiveness by offering attractive employment deals to overseas students upon their graduation (Tatli *et al.*, 2013).

Consequently, and undoubtedly, the management of talent and development has been outstandingly conducted in the country; however certain degree of underutilization of potential manpower still remains as obstacles for the success of talent management (Lee and Pow, 1999; Windsor and Auyeung, 2006; Tatli *et al.*, 2013), such as the treatment of female and ethnic minorities in the hospitality and tourism industry. Such challenges are as typical as other countries in Asia because of cultural values and norms of masculinity and organizational hierarchy (Chi-Ching, 1992; Li and Wang Leung, 2001), although it is relatively not serious.

Cases in the Chinese context

Perceptions in China

Talent management has been recognised decades ago as being a key to organizational success and competitive edge, through the identification, development and redeployment of talented and competent employees (Michaels *et al.*, 2001; Iles *et al*, 2010). However, literature have also revealed that different definitions and interpretations exist with different aspects and points of views (Ashton and Morton, 2005; Lewis and Heckman, 2006); and as seen from the previous section, in different context and cultural settings.

After decades of economic development and growth since the 'Open Door' policy in 1978, the country has transformed into one of the biggest and most influential economic entities in the world by progressively participating in the global village (Newton and Subbaraman, 2002; Warner, 2008). Changes of enterprises' business operations include the decentralization of the planning and decision making process, the introduction of responsibility systems and so forth (Shen, 2007; Warner, 2008; Iles *et al.*, 2010); while the labour management marks one of the significant transformations.

Fundamentally, the management of talent is not much different in the Chinese context, with the attention paid to the shift to the knowledge economy, the importance of human capital and the retention of talented candidates (Wang and Wang, 2008; Zhao, 2008); as well as handling the issues of rising costs of employee turnover and shortage of managerial talent, because of fierce competition in the pool of talent. Research has specifically addresses the issue of growing talent shortages and the imbalance between the demand and supply of qualified managers; as well as the geographical discrepancy between cities and rural areas (Lane and Pollner, 2008). Big cities, such as Beijing, Shanghai and Guangzhou, have about 20% of the national population but possess more than 80% of the leadership talent (Lau, 2007). There is always reported a mismatch between university graduates and the competencies required by employers with differences in expectations (Iles *et al.*, 2010).

Nevertheless, the challenges and issues remain in China; the problems are perceived and interpreted differently and distinctively in Chinese society because of its historical and culture settings. A qualitative survey reveals how organizations perceive and implement talent management in China, in which the attribute of culture and situational factors apply (Iles *et al.*, 2010). It is observed that management of organizations do not essentially perceive talent management as different from typical human resource management, but is basically only the evolved and extended version of managing talent. Another thought is that talent management is an integration of human resource management with a selective focus, such as the selection and progression of 'top performers' and 'high potentials'. The findings are not surprisingly consistent with the country's cultural and historical settings, for instance elitism and rural-urban discrepancies.

14

Such perceptions and interpretation of 'no difference from human resource management' and 'inclusive people focus' may alter the focus and implementation of talent management.

A successful example

Opportunities come along with challenges and threats. While many hotels and tourism organizations are struggling with the problem of talent shortage, an example is observed in Shanghai, and is one of the best examples in China. An interview with the general manager, Mark DeCocinis, of the Portman Ritz-Carlton Hotel of Shanghai shares the leadership's practices and philosophy on talent management in China (Yeung, 2006). The hotel has been able to attract, develop, and retain high quality talent to deliver outstanding customer service with sustainable profits; but also has its previous experience of typical challenges on managing talent as other hotels and organizations in China. To tackle the relatively poor service attitudes and skills of employees in China, the general manager starts implementing his strategies from the selection process, which focuses on the talent's personal values, because those values are believed to be unchangeable. The general manager's choice is to recruit the talent who possess the same values and purposes as the company, instead of adjusting and fitting the company's culture and values to the local communities. They target the talent who 'genuinely enjoy meeting with people and helping others', which is the culture and philosophy of the company. Other than the criteria, the hiring process also brings the difference, because candidates are screened and interviewed by human resources, the line managers, and finally the general manager himself, enquiring into their skills, attitudes and motives; hence the selected talent are chosen and agreed by the group, and not just a manager.

The general manager also mentioned that genuine and natural smiles are important because it is something cannot be forced; and that makes the talent personally happy for bringing satisfactions. Further, the talent's satisfactions towards the job are described by the general managerwho notes that the low turnover rate has resulted in a long term relationship between the company and the talent. The management aims to develop and retain a long term relationship with every talent from their commencement of career with the company, including promotion and development plans. About 70 to 80 percent of the senior positions are filled from within the hotel or transferred from other properties of the group. Also, thorough and comprehensive training is offered so that talent are motived to commit, engage and become involved by knowledge and skills; and most importantly, empowerment and communication are emphasized by the general manager, who makes time for having breakfast with the talent every day for proactively listening to opinion and comments.

Nevertheless, the general manager answered and addressed the challenges on managing talent across cultural and national context by saying that relationship building and understanding set the fundamentals. Expatriates have to first adapt to the culture at the location assigned by gaining trust and relationships with the local people, before creating the success. The advantages and positive sides of the people have to be appreciated rather than making oneself look more important, advised Mark DeCocinis (Yeung, 2006).

Conclusion

Managing talent in the hospitality industry, which is highly employee-oriented, has its own issues and challenges compared to other industries. Moreover, as a result of globalization, supply and demand of talent bring many opportunities and additional challenges to multi-national or international companies. As discussed in the chapter, the criterion of culture has to be considered when managing talent from the perspectives of multinational organizations. As the most significant problem of the industry, talent shortage can emerge as the need for higher level of supervisors or managers with distinctive competencies and capability to operate the business in distant countries culturally and geographically.

The issues related to strategic talent management can remain ever-changing because of the macro environmental factors. While it may not be a serious matter in one country, it can be a big problem in other regions or nations. In this chapter different cases can be found from Asian countries how they utilized different solutions, such as outsourcing, on-demand employments, migration policies, and addressing the demographic issues.

Learning activities

Please form a discussion group to discuss on the following questions:

1 Identify the important factors for implementing talent management for global companies.

2 Discuss with your group on how to address the issues for the global companies.

3 How can cultural and demographic factors be a concern for talent managers in local companies.

4 Discuss and compare the talent management issues in Asian countries. Identify similarities and differences.

5 Read the successful example in China. Identify the problem and the strategies the General Manager utilized. How would you handle the situation if you were the talent manager of the company?

14

References

Ahn, H. (1996). *New Human Resource Policy of Korean Firms,* Korea Employer Association, Seoul.

Appold, S. J., Siengthai, S. and Kasarda, J. D. (1998). The employment of women managers and professionals in an emerging economy: Gender inequality as an organizational practice. *Administrative Science Quarterly,* **43** (3) 538-565.

Ashton, C. and Morton, L. (2005). Managing talent for competitive advantage: Taking a systemic approach to talent management. *Strategic HR Review,* **4** (5), 28-31.

Bhasin, B. B. and Low Kim Cheng, P. (2002). The fight for global talent: new directions, new competitors - a case study on Singapore. *Career Development International,* **7**(2), 109-114.

Barney, J. (1991). Firm resources and sustained competitive advantage. *Journal of management,* **17** (1), 99-120.

Bjorkman, I. and Xiucheng, F. (2002). Human resource management and the performance of Western firms in China, *International Journal of Human Resource Management,* **13**(6), 853-864.

Boussebaa, M. and Morgan, G. (2008). Managing talent across national borders: the challenges faced by an international retail group. *Critical Perspectives on International Business,* **4** (1), 25-41.

Bowen, C. C. (2003). Sex discrimination in selection and compensation in Taiwan. *International Journal of Human Resource Management,* **14** (2), 300-315.

Brannen, M. Y. (2010). Global talent management and learning for the future. In *Challenges of Human Resource Management in Japan,* Abingdon: Routledge, 124-130.

Budhwar, P. and Debrah, Y. A. (2009). Future research on human resource management systems in Asia. *Asia Pacific Journal of Management,* **26** (2), 197-218.

Byungnamlee, M. and Rhee, Y. (1996). Bonuses, unions, and labor productivity in South Korea. *Journal of Labor Research,* **17** (2), 219-238.

Cappelli, J. (2008). Talent management for the twenty-first century. *Harvard Business Review,* **86** (3), 74.

Chi-Ching, E. Y. (1992). Perceptions of external barriers and the career success of female managers in Singapore. *The Journal of Social Psychology,* **132** (5), 6 61-674.

Chou, W. C. G., Fosh, P. and Foster, D. (2005). Female managers in Taiwan: Opportunities and barriers in changing times. *Asia Pacific Business Review,* **11** (2), 251-266.

Cole, G. A. (2004) *Management Theory and Practice,* Cengage Learning EMEA.

Cole-Gomolski, B. (1997). Chase uses new apps to ID best customers. *Computerworld,* **31** (35), 49-50.

Coleman, D. (1998). Learning to manage knowledge. *Computer Reseller News,* **775,** 103-04.

Collings, D. G., Scullion, H. and Dowling, P. J. (2009). Global staffing: a review and thematic research agenda. *The International Journal of Human Resource Management,* **20** (6), 1253-1272.

Conrad, H. (2010). From seniority to performance principle: The evolution of pay practices in Japanese firms since the 1990s. *Social Science Japan Journal*, **13** (1), 115-135.

Debrah, Y. A. (1996). Tackling age discrimination in employment in Singapore. *International Journal of Human Resource Management*, **7** (4), 813-831.

Debroux, P. (2013). Human resource management in Japan. *Managing Human Resources in Asia-Pacific*, **20**, 64.

Dickmann, M., Sparrow, P. and Brewster, C. (2008). *International Human Resource Management: A European perspective*, Routledge.

Doh, J. P., Stumpf, S. A., Tymon, W. and Haid, M. (2008). How to retain talent in India. *MIT Sloan Management Review*, **50** (1), 6-7.

Earley, P. C. and Mosakowski, E. (2004). Toward culture intelligence: turning cultural differences into a workplace advantage. *The Academy of Management Executives*, **18** (3), 151-157.

Fan, Y. (2002). Questioning guanxi: Definition, classification and implications. *International Business Review*, **11** (5), 543-561.

Farndale, E., Scullion, H. and Sparrow, P. (2010). The role of the corporate HR function in global talent management. *Journal of World Business*, **45** (2), 161-168.

Faure, G. O. and Fang, T. (2008). Changing Chinese values: Keeping up with paradoxes. *International Business Review*, **17** (2), 194-207.

Froese, F. J. and Goeritz, L. E. (2007). Integration management of western acquisitions in Japan. *Asian Business and Management*, **6** (1), 95-114.

Harvey, M. and Novicevic, M. M. (2004). The development of political skill and political capital by global leaders through global assignments. *The International Journal of Human Resource Management*, **15** (7), 1173-1188.

Harvey, M., Speier, C. and Novicevic, M. M. (1999). The role of inpatriation in global staffing. *International Journal of Human Resource Management*, **10** (3), 459-476.

Iles, P. , Chuai, X. and Preece, D. (2010). Talent management and HRM in multinational companies in Beijing: Definitions, differences and drivers. *Journal of World Business*, **45** (2), 179-189.

Kearney, R. P. (1991). *The Warrior Worker: The history and challenge of South Korea's economic miracle*, IB Tauris.

Kim, S. (1997). *Traditions and Transformations: Human resource management in Korea. Human Resource Management in the Asia Pacific*, Nanyang University Press, Singapore.

Kim, S. and Briscoe, D. R. (1997). Globalization and a new human resource policy in Korea: Transformation to a performance-based HRM. *Employee relations*, **19** (4), 298-308.

Kostova, T. and Roth, K. (2003). Social capital in multinational corporations and a micro-macro model of its formation. *Academy of Management Review*, **28** (2), 297-317.

Lam, T., Lo, A. and Chan, J. (2002). New employees' turnover intentions and organizational commitment in the Hong Kong hotel industry. *Journal of Hospitality and Tourism Research*, **26** (3), 217-234.

14

Lam, T., Zhang, H. and Baum, T. (2001). An investigation of employees' job satisfaction: the case of hotels in Hong Kong. *Tourism management*, **22** (2), 157-165.

Lane, K. and Pollner, F. (2008). How to address China's growing talent shortage: The growing need for talented managers in China represents the biggest management challenge facing multinationals and locally owned businesses alike, surveys show. *McKinsey Quarterly*, **3**, 32.

Lawler, J. J. (1996). Diversity issues in South-East Asia: the case of Thailand. *International Journal of Manpower*, **17** (4/5), 152-167.

Lazear, E. P. (1979). Why is there mandatory retirement?. *The Journal of Political Economy*, **87** (6), 1261-1284.

Lee, J. S. and Pow, J. C. (1999). Human resource policies for women-a study in Singapore. *Journal of Management Development*, **18** (4), 326-341.

Leung, A. S. (2002). Sexuality at work: Female secretaries' experiences in the context of Chinese culture. *Journal of Managerial Psychology*, **17** (6), 506-522.

Lewis, R. E. and Heckman, R. J. (2006). Talent management: A critical review. *Human Resource Management Review*, **16** (2), 139-154.

Li, S. and Scullion, H. (2006). Bridging the distance: managing cross-border knowledge holders, *Asia Pacific Journal of Management*, **23** (1), 71-92

Li, L. and Wang Leung, R. (2001). Female managers in Asian hotels: profile and career challenges. *International Journal of Contemporary Hospitality Management*, **13** (4),189-196.

Lin, C. H. A. and Yang, C. H. (2009). An analysis of educational inequality in Taiwan after the higher education expansion. *Social Indicators Research*, **90** (2), 295-305.

Lo, S., Wright, P. and Wright, R. (2003). Job-family satisfaction and job-family satisfaction and female married professionals in Hong Kong: A dichotomy of attitude and outlook. *International Journal of Employment Studies*, **11** (2), 25.

Ma, S. and Trigo, V. (2008). Winning the war for managerial talent in China: An empirical study. *Chinese Economy*, **41** (3), 34-57.

Meyer-Ohle, H. (2009). *Japanese Workplaces in Transition: Employee perceptions*, Palgrave Macmillan.

Michaels, E., Handfield-Jones, H. and Axelrod, B. (2001). *The War for Talent*, Harvard Business Press.

Murtha, T. P., Lenway, S. A. and Bagozzi, R. P. (1998). Global mind-sets and cognitive shift in a complex multinational corporation. *Strategic Management Journal*, **19** (2), 97-114.

Nakavachara, V. (2010). Superior female education: Explaining the gender earnings gap trend in Thailand. *Journal of Asian Economics*, **21** (2), 198-218.

Newton, A. and Subbaraman, R. (2002). *China: Gigantic possibilities, present realities*. London: Lehman Brothers.

Ng, C. W. and Chakrabarty, A. S. (2005). Women managers in Hong Kong: Personal and political agendas. *Asia Pacific Business Review*, **11** (2), 163-178.

Ngo, H. Y., Lau, C. M. and Foley, S. (2008). Strategic human resource management, firm performance, and employee relations climate in China. *Human Resource Management*, **47**

(1), 73-90.

Olsen, A. and Burges, P. (2007). *Ten years on: Satisfying Hong Kong's demand for higher education*. Report by Strategy for Policy and Research in Education in Hong Kong.

Pang, L., Kucukusta, D. and Chan, X. (2014). Employee turnover intention in travel agencies: analysis of controllable and uncontrollable factors. *International Journal of Tourism Research*. **17** (6), 577–590

Peng, K. Z., Ngo, H. Y., Shi, J. and Wong, C. S. (2009). Gender differences in the work commitment of Chinese workers: An investigation of two alternative explanations. *Journal of World Business*, **44** (3), 323-335.

Perlmutter, H. V. (1969). The tortuous evolution of the multinational corporation. *Columbia journal of world business*, **4** (1), 9-18.

Rabbi, F., Ahad, N., Kousar, T. and Ali, T. (2015). Talent management as a source of competitive advantage. *Journal of Asian Business Strategy*, **5** (9), 208-214.

Rodgers, Y. V. D. M., Zveglich, J. E. and Wherry, L. (2006). Gender differences in vocational school training and earnings premiums in Taiwan. *Feminist Economics*, **12** (4), 527-560.

Scullion, H., Collings, D. G. and Gunnigle, P. (2007). International human resource management in the 21st century: emerging themes and contemporary debates. *Human Resource Management Journal*, **17** (4), 309-319.

Sebastian Reiche, B. (2006). The inpatriate experience in multinational corporations: An exploratory case study in Germany. *The International journal of human resource management*, **17** (9), 1572-1590.

Shen, J. (2007). Labour contracts in China: Do they protect workers' rights?. *Journal of Organisational Transformation and Social Change*, **4** (2), 111-129.

Song, B. (1990). *The Rise of the Korea Economy*, Oxford University Press, New York, NY.

Sorge, A. (2004). Cross-national differences in personnel and organization. In A.W. Harzing and J. Van Ruysseveldt (Eds.) *International Human Resource Management*, London: Sage Publications Inc. 117-140.

Steers, R. M., Sin, Y. G. and Ungson, G. R. (1989). *The Chaebol: Korea's new industrial might*, Harper and Row, Ballinger Division.

Sugimoto, Y. (2010) *An Introduction to Japanese Society*, Cambridge University Press.

Tarique, I., and Schuler, R. S. (2010). Global talent management: Literature review, integrative framework, and suggestions for further research. *Journal of world business*, **45** (2), 122-133.

Tatli, A., Vassilopoulou, J. and Özbilgin, M. (2013. An unrequited affinity between talent shortages and untapped female potential: The relevance of gender quotas for talent management in high growth potential economies of the Asia Pacific region. *International Business Review*, **22** (3), 539-553.

Tharenou, P. (2003). The initial development of receptivity to working abroad: self-initiated international work opportunities in young graduate employees. *Journal of Occupational and Organizational Psychology*, **76** (4), 489-515.

14

Tsai, C. T. L. (2006). The influence of Confucianism on women's leisure in Taiwan. *Leisure Studies*, **25** (4), 469-476.

Varma, A. and Budhwar, P. S. (2013). *Managing Human Tesources in Asia-Pacific*, Vol. 20, Routledge.

Virakul, B. (2000). Breaking the glass ceiling: a combined work of women's minds and HRD. *Human Resource Development International*, **3** (1), 8-17.

Wang, H. Z. and Hsiao, H. M. (2002). Social capital or human capital? Professionals in overseas Taiwanese firms. *Journal of Contemporary Asia*, **32** (3), 346-362.

Wang, Z. M. and Wang, S. (2008). Modelling regional HRM strategies in China: an entrepreneurship perspective. *The International Journal of Human Resource Management*, **19** (5), 945-963.

Warner, M. (2008). Reassessing human resource management 'with Chinese characteristics': An overview: Introduction. *The International Journal of Human Resource Management*, **19** (5), 771-801.

Windsor, C. and Auyeung, P. (2006). The effect of gender and dependent children on professional accountants' career progression. *Critical Perspectives on Accounting*, **17** (6) 828-844.

Wong, M. M. (2005). Subtextual gendering processes: A study of Japanese retail firms in Hong Kong. *Human Relations*, **58** (2), 249-276.

Wong, S., Siu, V. and Tsang, N. (1999). The impact of demographic factors on Hong Kong hotel employees' choice of job-related motivators. *International Journal of Contemporary Hospitality Management*, **11** (5), . 230-242.

Woodhams, C., Lupton, B. and Xian, H. (2009). The persistence of gender discrimination in China–evidence from recruitment advertisements. *The International Journal of Human Resource Management*, **20** (10), 2084-2109.

Wu, M. Y. (2006). Perceptions about male and female managers in the Taiwanese public relations field: Stereotypes and strategies for change. *Public Relations Quarterly*, **51** (3), 36.

Yeung, A. (2006). Setting people up for success: How the Portman Ritz-Carlton hotel gets the best from its people. *Human Resource Management*, **45** (2), 267-275.

Yeung, A., Warner, M. and Rowley, C. (2008). Guest editors' introduction growth and globalization: Evolution of human resource management practices in Asia. *Human Resource Management*, **47** (1), 1-13.

Youngsamart, D., Fisher, G. and Härtel, C. E. (2010). 19 Diversity management in Thailand. *Managing Cultural Diversity in Asia: A Research Companion*, 416.

Yukongdi, V. (2005). Women in management in Thailand: Advancement and prospects. *Asia Pacific Business Review*, **11** (2), 267-281.

Zhao, S. (2008). Application of human capital theory in China in the context of the knowledge economy. *The International Journal of Human Resource Management*, **19** (5) 892-817.

15 Technology and Talent Management

Fevzi Okumus, Wei Wei, Edwin Torres, Ahmet Ozturk and Trishna Gajjar

Learning objectives

This chapter discusses technology and talent management in hospitality and tourism. By the end of this chapter, you should be able to:

- Explain importance of technology in talent management;

- Identify existing talent management technologies in recruitment, selection, training, performance evaluation and motivating and retaining of employees;

- Explain how talent management technologies are used in recruitment, selection, training, performance evaluation and motivating and retaining; and

- Offer recommendations on how hospitality and tourism businesses can use talent management technologies.

Introduction

Talent management is one of the most critical factors that can assist hospitality and tourism organizations to achieve superior performance and gain competitive advantage (Cappelli and Keller, 2014; Deery and Jago, 2015; Huges and Rog, 2008; Okumus, 2008). As discussed in previous chapters, managing talent is a critical factor for hospitality and tourism organizations. Talent management refers to finding the right people with the right knowledge and expertise for the right positions and right organizations, and supporting them to grow and excel so that the business can grow and prosper (Deery, 2008). Talent management is one of the key sources of competitive advantage for hospitality businesses.

Increasingly, delivery, support and management of talent management practices greatly depend on the use of technology (Johnson and Gueutal, 2011a; Schweyer, 2010). It is evident that human resources technology offers web-based systems to deliver data and service including online recruiting, online application testing, online training, online benefit system and employee self-service (Johnson and Gueutal, 2011b; Schweyer, 2010; Stone *et al.*, 2015). Overall, talent management research has focused on recruitment, selection, training, development, retention and performance evaluation. This chapter will therefore particularly focus on the use of talent management technologies in these areas.

Technology use in recruitment

One of the main goals of talent management is to attract, recruit, develop, engage and retain the best talent in order to help the organization attain its goals. The goal has remained the same, but the procedures have changed over the past few years, as organizations have embraced the latest technological advances. The process of *recruitment* refers to the organization's efforts to attract a qualified pool of applicants, whereas *selection* entails choosing the best applicant for a given position. The field of recruitment has faced several technological changes in the past few decades. For example, in the past one of the primary means of advertising a job opening was through the local newspapers. As the Internet has evolved, newspaper circulation has decreased dramatically. Job advertisements still exist in print media, but their number has decreased, as more employers opt for electronic recruitment. Electronic recruitment can entail posting a job on a company's proprietary website or using a general job board such as Career Builder (http://www.careerbuilder.com) or one that specializes in a particular industry, as in the case of HCareers (http://www.hcareers.com).

Job boards may charge a fee for their services, but could potentially return a greater number of applications. On the one hand, online job postings have made it possible for applicants to easily access job information and apply for multiple positions. On the other hand, these electronic recruitment methods have resulted in an increase in applicants for companies, thus increasing their administrative costs (Stone *et al.*, 2015). Another challenge with electronic recruiting arises from the diversity of the applicant pool. Some individuals may be less technically savvy or have limited access to the Internet.

Another tool used in the recruitment of prospective employees is the virtual job fair. A virtual job fair may include webcasts, webinars, chat rooms, simulated environments, and a place to upload a resume (Stone *et al.*, 2015). There are several companies that offer the capability of hosting a virtual job fair. Some examples include the software providers Communique (http://www.virtualjobfairhosting.com) and Career eco (https://www.careereco.com). Using such software, companies can feature various simulated environments, hold various seminars, and create a branded image of their company online.

Social networking has also been used for recruitment purposes. Whereas some candidates use social media to network with prospective employers, others can go as far as submitting an application directly through the site. LinkedIn (https://www.linkedin.com) is an example of a company that has a platform that helps people create a professional network. While social media offers advantages as a recruitment tool, this technology may also allow employers to gain prior knowledge of the applicant's personal information. More specifically, information on gender, race, religion, weight and disability might become apparent from a personal profile. In light of this, several jurisdictions have created laws to regulate the usage of social media in the recruitment process and several court cases have emerged concerning its utilization for employment purposes (Morgan and Davis, 2013).

In recent years, blogs have also helped applicants gain information about the companies they apply for. For example, Glass door (https://www.glassdoor.com) allows individuals that work for a company to post their impression of what it's like to work for them. Similarly, it allows applicants to see what current employees think. Such technology can bring about the benefit of increased information and a realistic job preview, but it can also damage the company's reputation and hurt its chances of obtaining good applicants.

Recruitment efforts, whether electronic or traditional, should be measured for their effectiveness. According to Mathis *et al.* (2014), to determine the effectiveness of a recruitment method, an employer should consider the following:

- ☐ The number of applicants received
- ☐ The quality of its applicant pool
- ☐ The time it takes to fill gaps
- ☐ The diversity of its talent pool
- ☐ Costs versus benefits, and
- ☐ Retention.

A recruiting method may yield many applicants, but it may also generate a lot of unqualified applications, thus increasing the workload of the hiring manager. A method may attract great quality of applicants, but it may not be sufficient to meet the demands in terms of the quantity of applications the company needs to fill its employment vacancies. A third method may be good in terms of quality and quantity, but incur a prohibitive cost for the company. In deciding the combination of recruiting sources, companies should weight several factors and make a decision that helps them attain their recruitment goals in the most effective manner.

Technology use in selection

15

Once an organization has attained a reasonable applicant pool, the process of selection begins. There are multiple technologies that can aid employers in the selection process. For example, a software category used by many in talent management is that of applicant tracking systems. These systems allow employers to create job openings, set-up several levels of screening, review notes of various interviewers, track the status of each application, and produce reports on the effectiveness of your recruitment and selection efforts. There are several applicant tracking systems including Recruiter Box (http://recruiterbox.com) and Clear Company (http://info.clearcompany.com).

Organizations have also taken processes that were performed manually and transferred them to electronically. For example, cognitive abilities testing and personality inventories have been used by firms for decades. Today instead of administering paper and pencil tests, applicants can be given these tests electronically. Employers may even set up the system to prevent applicants from moving forward if they obtained unfavorable scores in these inventories.

You may ask why a company should engage in cognitive abilities and personality testing. Since the 1920s, research has examined the ability of various selection criteria to predict future job performance. Meta analyses by McDaniel *et al.* (1994) and Schmidt and Hunter (1998) demonstrated moderate correlations between structured interviews and work performance. When the interview is completely unstructured, that correlation is even less. In contrast, cognitive abilities testing and personality testing (particular on conscientiousness) have demonstrated better ability to predict long term retention and performance (Johnson and Gueutal, 2011b).

From a practical perspective, companies may also struggle with limited resources to review a large number of applications. In light of this, resume screening software exists. These platforms allow employers to quickly identify resumes with the desired qualification by considering key words. The applicant tracking systems often provide capabilities for resume screening. Some examples are: iCIMS, Recruiterbox, Workable, and Clear Talent (Capterra, n.d.)

Interviews have also undergone a transformation in the past few decades. The traditional modality of an employment interview was face-to-face. Later, employers began experimenting with phone interviews as a way to improve the efficiency of the process. With the advent of the Internet, employers have adopted web-based interviews. These interviews can be either synchronous or asynchronous. In a synchronous interview, the applicant uses his or her computer or mobile device to interview in real-time with the interviewer. Examples of technologies that enable these interactions include Skype (https://www.skype.com) and Go To Meeting (https://www.gotomeeting.com). As an example of research in this area, Chapman *et al.* (2003) explored the perceptions of justice, interview difficulty, intentions to accept an offer, and perceived interview outcome using three interview modalities: face-to-face, telephone, and videoconferencing. The research findings demonstrated that face-to-face interviews were perceived fairer by applicants as compared to videoconferencing and telephone modalities.

More recently, employers have adopted asynchronous video interviews (AVI) as a way to improve the efficiency of their processes (Milne-Tyte, 2011). Using a variety of proprietary software platforms, employers send a web link to applicants. Prospective employees will then record the interview at a time of their convenience using a personal computer, or laptop with webcam, tablet, or smartphone. The interview is recorded and the hiring manager reviews the contents at a later time. Companies that provide these services include Hire Vue (https://www.hirevue.com) and Interview Stream (https://interviewstream.com) among others.

Advantages of AVI include the reliability of a high-quality audio connection, availability of technical support, and opportunities for branding (Zielinski, 2012). Some drawbacks to AVIs include the lack of real-time feedback and the impersonal feeling experienced by some applicants. Within the hospitality and tourism fields, two research studies have emerged, with the first addressing the perceived fairness of AVI among applicants (Toldi, 2011), and the second reporting the effects on applicants regarding the selection process (Guchait *et al.*, 2014). More remains to be known about the effectiveness of these interviews. However, at the present time the AVI is a growing trend among large organizations.

Once the organization has decided to select an applicant, a conditional job offer will normally be made. This job offer is typically dependent on the applicant's ability to pass various screenings, which may include: criminal background check, employment reference check, identity check or verification of the ability to legally work in a given country, credit checks, drug screening, and others. Many of these tests traditionally included a stream of paperwork and took several days or weeks. Today, advances in electronic human resources enable employers to conduct some of these electronically and receive a quicker or even immediate response. For example, in the United States, employers are required to verify the ability of an applicant to work legally in the country. This process was done with a paper-based form and a visual inspection of document by the hiring manager. This process was less than accurate, as it allowed for the presentation of invalid identification and identity theft. Today, the Department of Homeland Security has launched an electronic system, whereby the information is verified electronically and a quick response is generated (US Department of Homeland Security, n.d.). Additionally, conducting a criminal background search can be performed by an outside company with a quick electronic response. All large and leading hospitality and tourism companies in the United States conduct background checks.

Technology use in training and development

Technology has transformed the way in which training and development are currently being developed and delivered. Hospitality organizations have adopted a variety of training technologies to effectively execute and manage training and development processes. These range from simply offering training materials online, to utilizing different technologies including web-based training, videoconferencing and virtual simulations in order to deliver training materials and enhance trainee communications (Stone *et al.*, 2015).

15

The effectiveness of technology use in training has been a hot topic in recent academic research. On the one hand, many benefits of technology-facilitated training have been identified by researchers. According to Stone *et al.* (2015), learning via technologies offers more flexibility, efficiency, and convenience for employees. It decreases costs for companies compared to traditional training techniques. In terms of assessing the effectiveness of technology use in training, knowledge gain and satisfaction remain the two most commonly measured outcomes (Johnson *et al.*, 2008). Lewis (2016) states that technology makes it possible to access company information and training programs from a distance, to train new and current employees in a virtual classroom and to assess their training performance.

According to Stone *et al.* (2015), satisfaction is one of the desired outcomes as it passively influences employees' post-training self-efficacy, motivation and knowledge. Alliger *et al.* (1997) proposed utility judgments as another important outcome of electronic learning, considering that trainees' perceptions of the training's utility may be more effective in predicting the training transfer in comparison to satisfaction or knowledge gain. On the other hand, the use of technology has been argued to be less effective due to the isolation of trainees from each other and the reduced communication accordingly (Piccoli *et al.*, 2001). This may further weaken trainee satisfaction (Richardson and Swan, 2003). To overcome these challenges, it is suggested that businesses use blended training methods, incorporating both online and face-to-face training components. These blended training methods could increase the social connection among trainees, result in higher levels of personal communication, and allow for managers' greater control of their subordinates' knowledge gaining process (Stone *et al.*, 2015).

Several factors, including training design, trainee characteristics, and financial feasibility, have been identified as influential factors in the effectiveness of technology use in training (Harris and Bonn, 2000). In relation to training design, the use of active learning techniques such as role-playing, games, case studies and simulations can enhance electronic learning outcomes (Derouin *et al.*, 2005). Communication and teamwork also play a significant role in the effectiveness of technology use in training; trainees who receive electronic training in a group environment seem to achieve better communication and results than their counterparts who are not in a group environment. Trainee characteristics, including computer experience, can also positively or negatively affect the effectiveness of electronic learning outcomes (Brown, 2001). In comparison to technology-mediated training, researchers have further found that trainees prefer face-to-face training due to the high level of interpersonal communication and the ample feedback opportunities it provides (Stone *et al.*, 2015).

Among the limited research tackling the use and effectiveness of technology use in training in the hospitality industry, researchers have found that in the present hospitality industry, training methods tend to follow a more traditional approach and are not technologically advanced to meet the diverse training and communication needs of today's organizations. Therefore, investment in service training may not be always effective enough to meet the demands of customers (Harris and Bonn, 2000). Business executives are thus advised to evaluate the thoroughness and quality of their service training programs, the methods of implementation, and the delivery techniques with the specific employee group in mind.

Technology use in motivation and retention

Today, one of the most critical issues that organizations face is how to motivate and retain talented employees. Many sectors experienced reduced turnover rates during the challenging economic conditions of 2008-2010, since employees were reluctant to leave their jobs due to limited employment opportunities. However, the turnover rate has increased in the last few years, which points out that employees have become more confident in the job market and are willing to look for another job (National Restaurant Association, 2015).

Research has provided evidence that overall costs associated with entry-level employees' turnover range from 30% to 50% of annual salary of the former employee; for mid-level and high-level employees it costs up to 150% to 400% of their annual salary to replace them (Borysneko, 2015). Hotel companies are no exception to this turnover and retention problem, despite their efforts to prevent loss of employees. For example, according to a recent study conducted by Deloitte (2015), an average hotel company devotes 33% of its revenue on costs associated with labor. Despite this, the employee turnover ratio is still as high as 31% in the hotel industry (Deloitte, 2015). These statistics clearly demonstrate that the hotel industry is still notorious for high employee turnover ratio. Excessive turnover is both costly and disruptive as talent management professionals are challenged with a continuous cycle of recruitment, selection, and training (Tews *et al.*, 2013).

Compensation is among the top motives that cause people leave their organization, and there is an extensive body of literature associated with employee retention, which demonstrated that well established compensation policies, and practices minimize turnover and maximize retention (Cho *et al.*, 2006; Davidson *et al.*, 2006). Therefore, hoteliers need robust retention strategies to retain their talented staff and to reduce turnover. One such strategy is the use of technology to facilitate the compensation and benefit process, which is commonly known as electronic compensation (e-compensation). E-compensation includes web-based software tools that allow administrators to effectively design, administer, and communicate compensation programs. More specifically, e-compensation provides a web-enabled platform that contains various types of compensation tools that organizations can utilize to gather, store, manipulate, analyze, utilize and distribute compensation data and information (Dulebohn and Marler, 2005).

E-compensation systems combine organization's internal data (e.g., salary history, job descriptions, and employee performance data) and external data (e.g., benchmarking information and salary survey data) to create pay structures and

15

job evaluations for specific positions within the organization (Fay and Nardoni, 2009). Some of the benefits of utilizing e-compensation tools include; (1) increased access to important compensation information without the need for complicated technology infrastructures or information technology staff, (2) the availability of meaningful compensation information to talent management professionals and executives, (3) simplified cumbersome bureaucratic tasks through real-time information processing (Dulebohn and Marler, 2005).

E-compensation systems' aforementioned features can be divided into two sections: compensation analysis and design tools, and compensation administration tools Compensation analysis and design tools facilitate the key mechanisms of building an organization's overall approach to compensation, such as compensation survey management, market pricing, salary structure development and merit distribution scenarios. Compensation administration tools, on the other hand, are mainly used for the communication of compensation programs to employees within the organization. Compensation administration tools allow managers to administer the salary review process, to create compensation documents, and to distribute incentives and merit budgets (IBM, 2014).

Technology use in performance evaluation

One of the most critical, invaluable functions for HR denotes the effective management of employees' performance, involving assessing current employees' performance and communicating the feedback to employees for improving future performance (Dennison and Weber, 2015). Performance evaluation enables managers to meet many needs in their organizations, from establishing employee objectives, to assessing training needs, to making compensation decisions (e.g., pay increases, promotions/demotions, terminations), to develop succession plans (Dennison and Weber, 2015; Spinks et al., 1999).

While conducting employee performance evaluations is the cornerstone of human resources management, it is a challenging task to judge the competence of another and to communicate performance feedback results to employees. Owning to the difficulties that arise from the process, performance evaluation is regarded as the major source of dissatisfaction for both management and employees (Pulakos, 2009). For managers, it can be an unpleasant task when insufficient investment is made in its preparation and implementation. For employees, it frequently causes undesirable concerns and anxiety. These difficulties are compounded when managers are poorly trained in interpersonal communication skills, when performance objectives are not clearly explained to employees, and when human judgments affect performance evaluations. It is thus of critical significance for organizations to integrate well-designed evaluation systems, which not only need to be effective and responsive, but more importantly, ethical, flexible, and fair (Woods et al., 2012).

A variety of software systems and tools have been developed to increase business productivity in various areas of employee performance evaluation, from assessing employees' performance to communicating evaluation feedback to employees (Cardy and Miller, 2005; Fletcher, 2001). According to a survey conducted by CedarCrestone (2014), 93% of U.S. organizations apply some sort of electronic performance management system, which was termed as 'e-PM' by Stone *et al.* (2015). Such electronic software systems and tools allow for faster communication, maximize time spent on strategic priorities, and increase project completion rates through the automation of processes (SAP SuccessFactors, n.d.).

In terms of assessing employees' performance, online business productivity software facilitates the process by enabling managers to more easily monitor employee progress throughout each phase of an evaluation period. Such electronic performance monitoring systems collect and store employee performance information in a central repository, allowing managers to better track employee performance (Ehrhart and Chung-Herrera, 2008). Technology also assists in analyzing employee performance. For example, computer systems can efficiently generate reports to tabulate the multi-rater evaluation results for gaining a better understanding of performance, and help executives and managers to easily access a wide variety of performance metrics and analytical reports for making modifications and improvements (Johnson and Gueutal, 2011a; SAP SuccessFactors, n.d.).

For conveying performance evaluation feedback to employees, performance management technologies provide assistance to document formal and informal evaluations on an ongoing basis. This enables managers to disseminate feedback more immediately, and frequently for employees to stay on track and to meet with managers for discussing needed improvement opportunities. Such online software also allows managers to have their feedback scanned to check for any potential legal concerns and errors in their use of language, protecting the organization in the long run (Cardy and Miller, 2005). Compared to traditional feedback provided by managers in person, employees seem to hold a favorable attitude toward computerized feedback, which can positively influence their performance, work motivation, and trust (Earley, 1988; Kluger and Adler, 1993).

The use of technologies in performance evaluation induces several pitfalls. For both managers and employees, people's attitude and proficiency of using technology potentially posts a significant challenge for companies to effectively and efficiently incorporate electronic performance evaluation systems. According to a survey conducted among organizations, insufficient training of technology-based human resources systems places the greatest barrier to the success of using technologies in performance evaluation (Levensaler, 2008). Without sufficient training, managers' and employees' reluctance and inability to use electronic systems could lead to companies wasting time and money on integrating technologies that may not run effectively.

From the perspective of managers, while electronic evaluation systems can automatically produce performance dimensions for evaluating employees' jobs

15

(Cardy and Miller, 2005), they could also lead managers to heavily rely on the oversimplified performance dimensions generated by computer systems, which may reduce rating accuracy (Gueutal and Folbe, 2005; Johnson and Gueutal, 2011a). Managers' reliance on computer systems to convey feedback to employees rather than spend quality time interacting with their employees face-to-face could enlarge the distance between managers and employees, weakening the interpersonal relationship (Cardy and Miller, 2005; Zuboff, 1988). In addition, some managers may not possess the required skills to interpret and communicate the analysis results and reports generated by computer systems, undermining their managerial competence, fairness, and authority as perceived by employees.

From the perspective of employees, in comparison to the traditional performance evaluation process where employees can apply impression management strategies to project a positive image, the use of performance evaluation technologies reduces or even replaces their opportunity to participate in face-to-face conversations with their supervisors, thus lowering their motivation, trust, and perceived justice (Stone *et al.*, 2015). In some studies, employees disclosed their concern about the rating quality and accuracy of electronic methods as compared to traditional face-to-face feedback processes, weakening their work satisfaction and confidence in their supervisors (Payne *et al.*, 2009). Further, the use of electronic system for delivering feedback increases the difficulty for employees to understand the computerized feedback independently and to identify areas for improvement (Stone *et al.*, 2015).

In order to minimize the above-discussed pitfalls of technology use in performance evaluation as well as to increase the accuracy and efficiency of using digital technologies, businesses are recommended to develop systems or to choose software features from an outside vendor wisely. For example, to avoid problems associated with the lack of interpersonal interactions using computer systems, managers are suggested to apply electronic evaluation systems to facilitate, rather than to replace, their conventional feedback process; face-to-face meetings with employees should still be conducted on a continuous basis, while information generated by electronic systems is referenced as a supplement to increase the objectivity of evaluation feedback (Johnson and Gueutal, 2011a).

In the event of facing geographic barriers, certain interactive technologies, such as virtual conferences, chat rooms, instant messaging, internal social media platforms, and microblogs, have been recognized as helping managers to collect information and communicate feedback in a more personal and timely manner (Stone *et al.*, 2015). Prior to their adoption of electronic performance evaluation systems, businesses should design and implement a series of training programs for both managers and employees, so that they not only understand why the company is adopting these technologies in performance evaluation, but also feel comfortable of using them. In recognition of the time and cost involved in the training process, some electronic human resources service vendors strive to promote the user friendliness of their services, advertising that their systems are easy to use with minimal computer skill. Furthermore, it is essential for organizations to tailor any technologically-mediated evaluation systems to their organizational needs, values, and culture (Gueutal and Falbe, 2005; Johnson and Gueutal, 2011b).

Concluding comments and recommendations

This chapter discussed the use of talent management technology throughout HR practices, including recruitment and selection, training and development, motivation, retention and performance evaluation in hospitality and tourism organizations. The presence of a highly motivated, capable, and committed workforce that can continually learn new skills and improve themselves, plays a vital role in enhancing the productivity and performance of hospitality and tourism organizations. By utilizing talent management technologies, hospitality and tourism businesses can be better equipped to manage the recruitment, selection, training, engagement and retention of their employees. These technologies can assist hospitality and tourism businesses make their employees engaged and feel appreciated, which are the key to employees' organizational commitment, work performance, job satisfaction, and retention. When used appropriately, the integration of talent management technologies in recruitment, selection, training, development, communication, engagement, motivation, retention, and performance management has the potential to bridge the gaps in communication, to lower costs, as well as to increase business productivity, efficiency, and competitiveness.

There are three strategies for adopting talent management technologies (Johnson and Gueutal, 2011b). The first one is having an integrated system such as PeopleSoft, Lawson, Unified Talent Management or Talent Management Cloud from a single vender that offers services in multiple areas including administration, recruitment, selection, training, performance management and workplace planning. The second one is the 'Best of Bread Approach' where the best applications in each area are selected from multiple vendors. The third one is outsourcing HR technology to a third-party vendor where the vendor manages the employee database and applications drawing data from it (Johnson and Gueutal, 2011b).

As shown in Table 15.1, SelectHub (2016) suggests specific features and requirements that talent management software should offer in recruitment and application tracking, learning management, performance management, competency management, compensation management, succession planning and management, IT requirements, user support and maintenance. In other words, hospitality and tourism businesses can select talent management software by evaluating and comparing these features and requirements listed in Table 15.1. SelectHub (2016) lists about 69 talent management software and the first 10 of them are Unified Talent Management by Cornerstone, Talent Management Cloud by Oracle, SilkRoad's Life Suite by Silk Road, Halogen TalentSpace™ suite by Halogen Software, SuccessFactors HR by SAP, Talent Expansion by SumTotal

15

Systems, Talent Expansion by SumTotal Systems, Total Talent Management by PeopleFluent, Lumesse ETweb by Lumesse and Dayforce HCM by Ceridian Education. There are certainly other platforms and businesses providing information and consultancy services about talent management technologies as well as many other talent management technology businesses. As noted by Bersin (2016), HR and talent management software is over a $14 billion market, including all industries globally. However, despite their importance, a large majority of HR management departments in all industries are not yet using talent management tools and technologies (Corbell, 2016).

Table 15.1: Select Hub talent management software features and requirements

Recruiting and applicant tracking

- Social media job postings
- Candidate prescreening
- Resume parsing
- Auto-response mechanism
- On-boarding formalities
- Career portal management
- User profile management
- Talent pool management
- Predictive analytics
- Reporting and auditing
- Interview scheduling
- Talent profile analysis
- Career ladder — skill and competency requirements

Learning management

- Course and resource management
- Skills and competency management
- Enrollment and registration
- Administration
- On-the-job training analysis
- Training, scheduling and tracking
- Enrollment prerequisite management
- Progress tracking
- Promotion interaction
- Email communication
- Vacancy requisition

Performance management

- Corporate/organizational objectives
- Performance review process tools
- Performance planning and review cycles
- Competency management
- Development planning
- Qualitative goals and objectives
- Performance management audit trail

Career management

- Employee education and experience profiles
- Talent profile review and analytics
- General interface workflow management and communications
- Profile development
- Talent profile comparisons
- Talent pool creation and development
- Interactive visual content
- Internal social network tools

Competency management

- Competency assessment
- Competency reporting
- Competency models
- Assessments and recommendations
- Organization health

Compensation management

- Compensation planning
- Salary administration
- Budgeting
- Pay for performance
- Multiple compensation plans
- Salary recommendations
- Salary benchmarking
- Merit increases
- Bonus versus commission
- Compensation payout history

Succession planning and management

- Succession assessment
- Candidate readiness evaluation
- Peer nominations for promotions
- Identifying successors
- Weighted criteria
- Candidate comparisons
- Talent pool visibility

IT requirements

- Software as a service model
- Integration
- Native mobile application
- Interface customization
- Third-party hardware or software handling
- Api integration
- Role-based system access
- Security applications and protocols
- Security audit and compliance
- Encryption standards
- Scalability
- Confidentiality

User support and maintenance

- Phone support
- E-mail support
- Hours of support
- Community support network availability
- Maintenance contracts,
- Uptime and downtime
- Availability of services

Source: SelectHub (2016). The Big List of Talent Management Software Features and Requirements. https://selecthub.com/hris/talent-management-software-features-requirements/

When selecting, designing and utilizing talent management technologies, it is important to remember that these technologies represent the HR department and the whole organization. Therefore, these talent management technologies and websites should be sophisticated and well-designed as well as easy to use by all employees from different socio-economic backgrounds, and whatever their age, race, gender, education, income and position (Johnson and Gueutal, 2011b; Schweyer, 2010). It is also necessary to point out that regardless of how advanced they are, such technologies should be used as a tool to offer better talent management strategies and practices rather than just focusing on greater efficiency and lowering cost (Schweyer, 2010). Bro (2013) further states that having such technologies does not always guarantee that all the intended outcomes will be achieved. It is all about how these technologies will be implemented and received by the employees and managers.

15

Talent management technologies can offer employees access to the information that provides transparency and assists employees to better understand the role of HR and HR practices. This in return leads to higher job satisfaction and engagement (Johnson and Gueutal, 2011b). However, such talent technologies should protect private information about employees and their performance. Given the rapid development of mobile phones and apps, another important issue is that talent management technologies should be available via mobile/smart devices. Utilizing such technologies requires that in addition to their traditional roles and responsibilities, HR staff and managers need to be better educated and have higher technical skills and also have skills to work closely with vendors and other functional areas in their organizations (Corbell, 2016; MacKenzie *et al.*, 2014; Schweyer, 2010).

Finally, it emerges from this chapter that while talent management has received much attention in the hospitality and tourism field (Deery, 2008; Deery and Jago, 2015; Huges and Rog, 2008), there is still limited research on the use of technology in talent management in hospitality and tourism businesses. Future research studies can collect data from employees, HR practitioners and senior managers on the use of such technologies in terms of advantages, limitations, challenges and their impact on employees' performance as well as on business performance.

Learning activities

1 Critically analyze the use of technology in a chosen hospitality, tourism or events business in the area of recruitment of talented staff.

2 Discuss the ways in which the use of technology in the talent management process can reduce the development of effective relationships between the employer and employee.

3 Choose one talent management software package and assess the benefits that the use of this would bring to a hospitality, tourism or events business.

References

Alliger, G. M., Tannenbaum, S. I., Bennett, W., Traver, H. and Shotland, A. (1997). A meta-analysis of the relations among training criteria. *Personnel Psychology*, **50**(2), 341-358.

Bersin, J. (2016). The HR Software Market Reinvents Itself, *Forbes*, http://www.forbes.com/sites/joshbersin/2016/07/18/the-hr-software-market-reinvents-itself/#661b47c64930

Borysenko, K. (2015). What was the management thinking? The high cost of employee turnover. Retrieved from: https://www.eremedia.com/tlnt/what-was-leadership-thinking-the-shockingly-high-cost-of-employee-turnover/. (11/01/2016).

Bro, M. M. (2013). 7 Hottest Trends in HR Technology. *Forbes*. http://onforb.es/1aZ7iYW

Brown, R. E. (2001). The process of community-building in distance learning classes. *Journal of Asynchronous Learning Networks*, **5**(2), 18-35.

Cappelli, P. and Keller, J. R. (2014). Talent management: Conceptual approaches and practical challenges. *Annual Review of Organizational Psychology and Organizational Behavior*, **1**(1), 305-331.

Capterra (n.d.). Top 10 Resume Management Software. Retrieved from: http://www.capterra.com/sem-compare/recruiting-software?headline=Top%2010%20Resume%20Management%20Software&gclid=CI3KsaKsktACFUg2gQod8hIFfA (11/05/2016).

Cardy, R. L. and Miller, J. S. (2005). eHR and performance management: A consideration of positive potential and the dark side. *The Brave New World of eHR: Human Resources Management in the Digital Age*, 138-165.

CedarCrestone. (2014). CedarCrestone 2014-2015 HR systems survey: HR technologies, service delivery approaches, and metrics (17th annual edition). Alpharetta, GA: CedarCrestone.

Chapman, D. S., Uggerslev, K. L. and Webster, J. (2003). Applicant reactions to face-to-face and technology-mediated interviews: A field investigation. *Journal of Applied Psychology*, **88**(5), 944.

Cho, S., Woods, R.H., Jang, S.C. and Erdem, M. (2006). Measuring the impact of human resource management practices on hospitality firms' performances. *International Journal of Hospitality Management*, **25**(2), 262–277.

Corbell, T. (2016). HR trends in talent management using technology. TheBizCoach. http://www.bizcoachinfo.com/archives/24479

Davidson, M., Guilding, C. and Timo, N. (2006). Employment, flexibility and labor market practices of domestic and MNC chain luxury hotels in Australia: where has accountability gone? *International Journal of Hospitality Management*, **25**(2), 193–210.

Deery, M. (2008). Talent management, work-life balance and retention strategies. *International Journal of Contemporary Hospitality Management*, **20**(7), 792-806.

Deery, M. and Jago, L. (2015). Revisiting talent management, work-life balance and retention strategies. *International Journal of Contemporary Hospitality Management*, **27**(3), 453-472.

Deloitte (2015). Hospitality 2015. Retrieved from: https://www2.deloitte.com/ie/en/pages/consumer-business/articles/hospitality-2015.html. (11/01/2016).

Dennison, D.F. and Weber, M.R. (2015). *Strategic Hospitality Human Resources Management*. Pearson-Prentice Hall. ISBN 978-0-135-08705-3.

Derouin, R. E., Fritzsche, B. A. and Salas, E. (2005). E-learning in organizations. *Journal of Management*, **31**(6), 920-940.

Dulebohn, J. H. and Marler, J. H. (2005). e-Compensation: The potential to transform practice? In H. G. Gueutal and D. L. Stone (Eds.), *The Brave New World of eHR: Human Resources Management in the Digital Age*, San Francisco: Jossey-Bass, pp. 166–189

Earley, P. C. (1988). Computer-generated performance feedback in the magazine-subscription industry. *Organizational Be havior and Human Decision Processes*, **41**(1), 50-64.

15

Ehrhart, K. H. and Chung-Herrera, B. G. (2008). HRM at your service: Developing effective HRM systems in the context of e-service. *Organizational Dynamics*, **37**(1), 75-85.

Fay, C. H. and Nardoni, R. E. (2009). Performance management, companesation, benefits, payroll, and the human resource information system. In M. J. Kavanagh and M. Thite, (Eds.), *Human Resource Information Systems: Basics, Applications, and Future Directions* (2nd ed.) (pp. 338–360) . Thousand Oaks: Sage Publishing.

Fletcher, C. (2001). Performance appraisal and management: The developing research agenda. *Journal of Occupational and organizational Psychology*, **74**(4), 473-487.

Guchait, P., Ruetzler, T., Taylor, J. and Toldi, N. (2014). Video interviewing: A potential selection tool for hospitality managers – A study to understand applicant perspective. *International Journal of Hospitality Management*, **36**, 90-100.

Gueutal, H. G. and Falbe C. M. (2005). eHR: Trends in delivery methods. In: H. G. Gueutal and D. L. Stone (Eds.) *The Brave New World of eHR: Human Resources Management in the Digital Age* (pp. 190-225). San Francisco: Jossey-Bass.

Harris, K. J. and Bonn, M. A. (2000). Training techniques and tools: Evidence from the foodservice industry. *Journal of Hospitality & Tourism Research*, **24**(3), 320-335.

Hughes, J. and Rog, E. (2008). Talent management: A strategy for improving employee recruitment, retention and engagement within hospitality organizations. *International Journal of Contemporary Hospitality Management*, **20**(7), 743-757.

IBM (2014).The Business Case for Compensation Technology. IBM White Paper. http://www.hr.com/en?s=5UhPSvb8Fhn6KUPq&t=/documentManager/sfdoc.file. supply&fileID=1398174714823

Johnson, R. D., Hornik, S. and Salas, E. (2008). An empirical examination of factors contributing to the creation of successful e-learning environments. *International Journal of Human-Computer Studies*, **66**(5), 356-369.

Johnson, R. D. and Gueutal, H. G. (2011a). *Transforming HR through technology: The use of E-HR and HRIS in organizations*. Society for Human Resource Management Effective Practice Guidelines Series. Alexandria, VA.

Johnson, R. D. and Gueutal, H. G. (2011b). Leveraging HR technology for competitive advantage. *SHRM Foundation Executive Briefing*. https://www.shrm.org/about/ foundation/products/documents/hris%20exec%20briefing%20final.pdf

Kluger, A. N. and Adler, S. (1993). Person-versus computer-mediated feedback. *Computers in Human Behavior*, **9**(1), 1-16.

Levensaler, L. (2008). *The Essential Guide to Employee Performance Management Practices*. Bersin.

Lewis, J. (2016). How does technology impact HR practices, http://smallbusiness.chron. com/technology-impact-hr-practices-37912.html

Mathis, R.L., Jackson, J.H. and Valentine, S. (2014). *Human Resource Management* (14th ed). Boston: Cengate Learning

McDaniel, M., Whetzel, D., Schmidt, F. and Mauer, S. (1994). The validity of employment interviews: A comprehensive review and meta-analysis. *Journal of Applied Psychology*, **79** (4), 599-616.

Milne-Tyte, A. (2011). Seeking Work? Ready your webcam. The Wall Street Journal, Sept 26. Retrieved from: http://www.wsj.com/articles/SB100014240531119045374045765549 43587087926 (11/05/2016).

MacKenzie, B., Sears, J. and Watson, T. (2014). What you need to know about talent management technology. *Workspan*, **3**, 27-30.

Morgan, H.A. and Davis, F.A. (2013). Social media and employment law: Summary of key cases and legal issues. Retrieved from: http://www.americanbar.org/content/dam/aba/events/labor_law/2013/04/aba_national_symposiumontechnology inlaboremploymentlaw/10_socialmedia.authcheckdam.pdf (11/05/2016).

National Restaurant Assoication. (2015). Hospitality employee turnover. Retrieved from: http://www.restaurant.org/News-Research/News/Hospitality-employee-turnover-rose-in-2014. (11/01/2016).

Okumus, F. (2008). Strategic human resources issues in hospitality and tourism organizations. In D. Tesone (Ed.). *Handbook of Human Resources Management in Hospitality*. Oxford: Elsevier.

Payne, S. C., Horner,M. T., Boswell,W. R., Schroeder, A. N. and Stine-Cheyne, K. J. (2009). Comparison of online and traditional performance appraisal systems. *Journal of Managerial Psychology*, **24**, 526–544.

Piccoli, G., Ahmad, R. and Ives, B. (2001). Web-based virtual learning environments: A research framework and a preliminary assessment of effectiveness in basic IT skills training. *MIS Quarterly*, 401-426.

Pulakos, E. D. (2009). *Performance Management: A New Approach for Driving Business Results*. John Wiley and Sons.

Richardson, J. and Swan, K. (2003). Examing social presence in online courses in relation to students' perceived learning and satisfaction. *Journal of Asynchronous Learning Networks*, **7**(1), 68-88.

SAP SuccessFactors. (n.d.) Using technology to increase your business productivity. Retrieved from https://www.successfactors.com/en_us/lp/articles/using-technology-to-increase-your-business-productivity.html

Schweyer, A. (2010). *Talent Management Systems: Best practices in technology solutions for recruitment, retention and workforce planning*. John Wiley & Sons.

Schmidt, F., and Hunter, J.E. (1998). The validity and utility of selection methods in personnel psychology: Practical and theoretical implications of 85 years of research findings. *Psychological Bulletin*, **124** (2), 262-274.

SelectHub (2016). The Big List of Talent Management Software Features and Requirements. https://selecthub.com/hris/talent-management-software-features-requirements/

Spinks, N., Wells, B. and Meche, M. (1999). Appraising the appraisals: computerized performance appraisal systems. *Career Development International*, **4**(2), 94-100.

15

Stone, D.L., Deadrick, D.L., Lukaszewski, K.M. and Johnson, R. (2015) The influence of technology on the future of human resource management, *Human Resource Management Review*, **25**(2), 216–231

Tews, M. J., Michel, J. W. and Ellingson, J. E. (2013). The impact of coworker support on employee turnover in the hospitality industry. *Group & Organization Management*, **38**(5), 630-653.

Toldi, N. L. (2011). Job applicants favor video interviewing in the candidate-selection process. *Employment Relations Today*, **38**(3), 19-27.

U.S. Department of Homeland Security (n.d.). E-Verify. Retrieved from: https://www.uscis.gov/e-verify (11/05/2016).

Woods, R., Johanson, M. and Sciarini, M. (2012). *Managing Hospitality Human Resources* (5th ed.). American Hotel & Lodging Association Educational Institute.

Zielinski, D. (2012). Find social media's value, The platform's return on investment often eludes measurement. A recent KPMG Report of 2011, *HR Magazine*, 53.

Zuboff, S. (1988). *In the Age of Smart Machines: The future of work and power*. New York: Basic Books.

PART 4

THE FUTURE OF TALENT MANAGEMENT

16 The Future of Talent Management: Meanings for organisations and educational delivery

Susan Horner

Learning objectives

The learning objectives of this chapter are as follows:

■ To provide an overview of the current academic thinking on the topic of talent management.

■ To predict what will happen with the topic from a number of perspectives over the next ten years.

■ To suggest a new model for the talent management process that can be used for the development of research topics or in practical application of the talent management process

Introduction

The previous chapters have given a full and well–developed picture of the issues that are current in the development of the talent management process in the hospitality and tourism sectors. The case studies at the end of the book also give examples of practical application of the process in real organisations. This chapter provides you with a final overview of the current thinking on talent management in relation to the research agenda, and organisational development in the hospitality and tourism sector. It also provides some predictions on the likely development of the topic in the next decade.

A summary of talent management

We have seen throughout the book that there are many concepts and issues that underpin the topic of talent management, and that the practical application of the concept in hospitality and tourism business is in its infancy. In order to try to summarise all the issues highlighted in the book and make predictions for the future, a simple model has been created in Figure 16.1. This chapter will consider each of these issues in turn and try to make predictions for the future, on the basis of what has come before in the book. It must be stressed, that like all predictions, they may or may not come true and we will be able to evaluate the outcomes in later editions of the book.

Figure 16.1: The interrelationships of talent management

It can be seen in Figure 16.1 that four main areas will be reviewed – **the research agenda** where there are still many questions, **educational programmes** that underpin the talent management process, **individual career progression**, and finally the **organisational perspective and action.** It is hoped that this division makes the analysis and predictions clearer and easier to comprehend. It appears from the book that there are four interrelated issues that are represented in the diagram. The first ideas on talent management came from the consultancy field and academics developed research programmes following this. As we have seen in the book, academic theory is still being developed and until more empirical research is conducted in real hospitality and tourism organisations, the link to industry will be present but weak. The research interest and the fact that organisations require talent in the area, has meant that universities have embedded talent management in the curriculum, and of course it is the universities and colleges that

16

provide the talent for the organisations, so there is a strong link there. Individual career progression is a critical part of the talent management process in terms of how organisations can attract and retain talent. Finally, the organisational perspectives and action on talent management are both critical to the process.

Talent management

We have seen earlier in the book that the hospitality and tourism sector has been characterised as being a 'low skill' environment, but what is becoming increasingly clear is that there is a growing need for talent in the sector. The newly recognised skills include a wide range of business and personal skills depending on the type of organisation and the business function. Issues such as diversity, CSR and equality all have a place in the talent management debate (Baum, 2008). We saw that at the moment the hospitality and tourism sector is predominately adopting an exclusive approach in an attempt to attract, develop and retain talented staff. Pricewaterhouse Coopers (PwC) (2007) have suggested that there are three scenarios for the management of talent: the first is the 'blue environment' where the management focus on hard business requirements; the second is the 'green context' where CSR is taken into account which includes issues of inclusion and diversity; and the third scenario is the 'orange world' where the talent is managed in an inclusive manner and engages staff at all levels in the organisation. It recognises and uses the diversity of talents that is available and assumes psychological empowerment in the work place (Lashley,1997). We can question whether workers want to be empowered, or is empowerment another word for getting extra responsibility for the same pay? This new approach needs novel management techniques and new organisational design features to reflect the changing business environment. Other commentators have predicted general trends which are not just specific to hospitality and tourism as follows:

☐ The global abundance but local scarcity of talent.

☐ Fewer younger people and more people heading for retirement in some areas of the world. In some parts of world young people make up an increasingly large proportion of the population.

☐ Differences in attitudes to work across generations but with some common themes such as issues of trust and respect. There are differences, however between cultures and countries.

☐ More diverse, remote and virtual work forces. This will even have an impact on service industries.

☐ New methods of working and new relationships between users and suppliers of talent.

Source: Adapted from Ariss *et al.*, 2013.

The importance and value of talent management as a process is something that all commentators agree on, and we have discussed the special nature of the sector in some depth earlier on in the book. It appears that these special characteristics mean that the talent management process is even more important in hospitality and tourism businesses compared to other types of organisations. The service nature of the sector and the seasonal nature of the business have a particular impact on the talent management processes that are required. It is predicted, therefore, that talent management in the sector will continue to be of primary importance for the next ten years, and even probably beyond. We shall now consider each of the components shown in Figure 16.1 to try to assess where we are now, and what the likely predictions are for this issue in the next decade.

Academic theory

We have seen that there is much debate about the academic theory that under-pins the talent management topic with diverging views as to which is the best approach, coupled with a recognition that the topic is in its infancy and there is a need for much more research in real organizations. There has been a boom in the publication of academic articles since the first publication by the McKinsey group in 1998-2001 (Michaels *et al.*, 2001).

A review of the literature to date on the topic shows that the theoretical base is being widened, and new avenues of research have begun to emerge (Gallardo-Gallardo *et al.*, 2015). A summary of these new angles includes:

☐ A new conceptual model has been proposed that emphasises the impor-tance of 'pivotal positions' (Collings and Mellahi, 2009).

☐ A new integrative framework has been developed for understanding global talent management (GTM) which now has a major importance in the rapidly developing global economy (Tarique and Schuler, 2010).

☐ A number of discrepancies, tension and taken for granted assumptions have been identified in the talent management literature (Dries, 2013).

☐ There has been growing commentary on both the economic and non-economic (social and moral) benefits of the talent management process (Thunnissen, *et al.*, 2013).

☐ The new labour market conditions which are a great challenge has been a focus of some commentators with regards to the talent management process (Capelli and Keller, 2014).

The literature to date has a marked bias to the USA, UK and western countries and there have been little published academic papers from outside these areas (Gallardo-Gallardo *et al.*, 2015). This could be explained by the fact that the recruit-ment and retention of staff is a particular issue in these regions or perhaps it could be just that commentary is in languages we cannot read. This means that there is a need for well-designed primary research to be conducted in Asia and other areas such as Africa, the Middle East and South America, where the hospitality and tourism sectors are growing rapidly at the present time. I suspect that in both job

16

seekers are keen to enter the industry and talent management is easy, in contrast to the UK where hospitality and travel is often a last resort rather than a career choice. Research has also tended to focus on large organisation, and neglected the small to medium enterprises (SMEs), so there is also a need to do research in small organisations to reflect the whole sector. There is also much to be learnt from the concept of 'trust' and how this relates to the talent management debate as we saw in Chapter 7.

My predictions for the next 10 years in the academic research arena are as follows:

1 There will continue to be a debate about whether it is better to allow diversity in perspectives on talent management or whether it is better to settle on a singular talent management paradigm The most commonly suggested framework is human capital theory (Collings and Mellahi, 2013).

2 There will continue to be issues in the research in relation to the economic and non-economic outcomes of the talent management process. It is my prediction that there will be an increasing emphasis put on the non-economic outcomes because of the growing importance of corporate social responsibility and ethical considerations of employment (Inkson, 2008). This will shape the type of research that is carried out.

3 There is a lack of empirical evidence that has been published in top tier journals, and it can be predicted that if researchers are to be considered seriously they must publish empirically based research in these types of journals. This will mean that the previous practitioner based research will be superseded by more serious, conceptually based empirical research in real organizations.

4 The growing interest in the topic of talent management as a module in academic programmes will mean that academics will continue to encourage research amongst the academic community, and we will begin to see more doctoral level studies being completed on different aspects of the topic. In the hospitality and tourism field it is highly likely that this research will be applied research that will take place in real organisations.

5 We need more cooperation with industry so the researcher has access to corporate data and industry figures can bring some real world sense to the rather esoteric, generalised academic research.

On the basis of the rest of the book there are areas that will lend themselves to academic research in the applied area. Thus, a number of questions need to be answered including:

☐ Could we carry out empirical research that would create new models of talent management that could be tested further in novel and new contexts?

☐ What are the outcomes of the inclusive and exclusive approaches to talent management in organisations and how are these approaches perceived by both the managers and the employees of the organization?

☐ What talents do hospitality and tourism organisations need in the rapidly developing business environment and how can these talents be found?

☐ What are the barriers to the development of an effective talent management process at an individual and organizational level and how can these be overcome?

☐ Is trust necessary between employee and employer for an effective talent management strategy to be developed? How is this trust developed and how can an organisation develop new management practices that foster this?

☐ How can employee engagement be developed in a local, national, and global setting?

☐ What are the ethical considerations that underpin the talent management process?

☐ What is the role of external stakeholders such as universities, governments, and professional bodies in the shaping of talent management practices? Also the role of trade unions/workers representatives?

☐ How can work-life balance be enhanced using the principles and practice of talent management?

☐ What role does technology play in the practical application of talent management?

These are ideas for possible research projects that can be investigated. It must be stressed that the list is only meant to give you some ideas. You will probably have to focus your ideas further or select one avenue of research, depending on the level of study and whether there is a need to do the research in a practical setting or not.

Educational programmes

Educational programmes in the hospitality and tourism sector have developed over the last thirty years as more institutions started to offer provision in the field. There has been a general long term move from the certificate and diploma level studies to the degrees and post graduate level courses which are now available in a wide range of educational establishments. The research agenda has also changed dramatically over the last few years with the growth in doctoral research in the hospitality and tourism areas, which has led to a growing desire to publish in top level journals, as well as in books and commercial journals.

We saw in Chapter 3 how the educational field has changed rapidly and there are also newly emerging initiatives such as a growing interest in apprentice level study, and the growing interest of business organisations offering educational programmes in the hospitality and tourism field rather than just training. There is also a growth in cross-national educational opportunities as the political and

16

economic agendas change. The era of the Swiss Hotel School offering elite programmes in hospitality management has evolved into a position where you can
study for a Swiss qualification without even being in Switzerland, and you may
even choose to study in cooperation with a commercial organisation. The role of
internships and placements is also changing, as students often work part-time
anyway in the sector, while they are studying and placement may not be as attractive as it was previously. We also saw in Chapter 9 the role of the professional
body in the educational development of talent as well as the use of work-based
experiences as part of the education development in Chapters 10 and 13.

In the light of all the discussion that came earlier in the book let me now try to
summarise the sort of developments that are most likely to happen over the next
decade:

1   From an individual perspective, students will continue to study hospitality
    and tourism because they see it as a way of getting a job, despite the nega-
    tive image that the sector often has among the young. Individual career
    progression will be a particular focus for individuals choosing institutions
    and courses. In the UK numbers will probably fall. Why go into debt to join
    a low wage industry you could join at 16 or 18 with few qualifications?

2   There will continue to be the 'elite' institutions that offer educational pro-
    grammes in the field and these will continue to be popular for the select
    few. One of the key advantages that these organisations offer apart from a
    strong brand, is the opportunity for students to network and develop their
    careers.

3   The use of work based learning opportunities will continue to grow. Some
    students will choose to study at an institution that actually runs practical
    hospitality and tourism businesses, others may choose to gain their work
    experience outside the educational establishment since this gives them the
    opportunity to 'butterfly' around a variety of institutions and build their
    CV. The key issue will be whether the student at the end can gain good
    career progression following their course.

4   Up to the 'Brexit' vote in the UK, the predictions were that students would
    begin to study further afield in Europe and vice versa. It is far too early to
    know what will happen following the decision of the UK to leave European
    Union. Will the decision make any difference at all to the educational pro-
    vision on offer and the movement of students across national boundaries
    either when they are studying or in work? Time will tell.

5   There will be an increasing emphasis placed in the curriculum both on the
    type of learning approach that is most effective, and the changing nature of
    the hospitality and tourism business. New topics will be introduced – rev-
    enue management and talent management being two recent examples, but
    more importantly new work-based learning approaches and experiential
    learning will continue to expand and be developed in the most advanced
    institutions. We saw a good example of this in the possible work diary of

a student in Chapter 3, where the majority of the week is spent on work-related educational experiences, rather than sitting in a classroom listening to lectures. This type of learning will suit the new type of student much more, and help them to achieve their career goals, it can be argued.

6   There will be an increasing number of commercial organisations in the field that will offer educational programmes to their employees only. Examples of these currently include the Accor Academy and the Taj Development programme in India. At the moment these tend to be focused at a slightly lower level but as these institutions start to cooperate more fully with the universities, then this trend could develop to a higher level and combine both work based training but also advanced educational development. Accor, for example, has MBA level apprenticeships with IMHI/ESSEC, part study, part work.

7   Educators will have to reflect more deeply on the needs of the new millennial generation and what they want from education. Students are not customers in the strictest sense of the word, but they will make increasing demands on educational institutions, particularly when the perceived or real cost of education is increasing. We analysed the issues surrounding youth employment in the sector in Chapter 8. The increased focus on student satisfaction will also mean that academics may well have to give up their research agendas, and return to teaching again, which will be valued more highly in the future. Or hospitality/tourism educators/universities will continue to change too slowly and will become less and less involved in talent management and more and more about research. League tables will be all that matters, and research is all that matters to them.

These predictions are based on the content of the book and my own personal views, but we will have to see in future editions how much of this comes to pass!

Individual career development

A key theme that has already emerged in the literature is the issue of individual career development. The special characteristics that an individual needs to produce hospitality and tourism services that make guests feel welcome is discussed in depth in Chapter 4. Hospitableness has to be based on an emotional bond between the staff and the guest and this requires a certain type of person who is empowered and properly developed. Individuals need to be special to match this type of requirement.

One of the key aspects of talent management is the individual and their views on personal career development. There is a distinction made between individual career management, which focuses on how the individual develops, and organizational career management which is concerned with the management practices that help individuals to develop. Alongside this it seems that long term careers in

16

organisations are becoming a thing of the past and individuals are either choosing or being forced to move jobs and companies if they are to progress. There is less loyalty on both sides of the equation. We discussed the boundaryless career earlier in the book and the concept of butterflying, where individuals flutter from job to job (Gallardo-Gallardo *et al.*, 2015).

We saw in Chapter 5 that individuals often take interesting career journeys in the sector, and there is no set progression pathway that they can take. This is one of the reasons that the organizations have issues related to the recruitment and retention of staff, because talented individuals have many opportunities open to them and can change employer regularly without getting a bad reputation. In fact, the appearance of a number of high profile employers on a CV can give the individual considerable advantages in terms of career progression. It seems that for organisations to attract and keep the most talented individuals they have to adopt a new stance, which is based on social exchange theory and involves them in developing reciprocal relationships, interaction and mutually felt obligations between the individual employees and the employers (Festing and Schäfer, 2014). We have also seen in the book some of the issues that influence personal career development in the sector. These include inclusivity and exclusivity, issues related to diversity, gender and ethnic group, and the innate and learned behaviour of the individuals in question.

So where does that leave us concerning predictions for the next ten years? I would like to provide my ideas here on the individual career development component of talent management as follows:

1 The hospitality and tourism sector will continue to require talented individuals to enable organisations to provide the required experiences. These talent requirements may change, but the underlying dependence on individual talent will mean that career opportunities will be available.

2 Individuals will have to think hard about their chosen talent or talents and make efforts to develop these themselves to build their CV. It is not enough any more just to do a degree, the individual must now gain extra experience wherever possible. They should look for colleges and universities that offer them opportunities for personal development, including experiential learning opportunities, work-based learning and curriculum enhancing experiences. We discussed these issues in Chapters 10 and 13.

3 The new approaches to talent management should focus more on the individual rather than a group, and techniques such as coaching and mentoring will help the individual to develop and build a relationship with the organisation. Individuals need to look for organizations that offer them strong and sustained psychological bonds and not just a job.

4 Individuals need to be convinced about the many opportunities that exist in the sector and need to be nurtured by appropriate job and career opportunities.

5   The prediction is that the way forward in talent management is to nurture individuals in their career development. This will be the way to attract the best talent, and keep it. This seems to be just as important in Asia, where the sector is experiencing skill shortages in the sector, like the rest of the world. We analysed this situation in Chapter 14.

Organisational perspectives and action

Much research in the past about talent management has focused on the organisation and what it does, but here we finish with this analysis as our final part of the model. The hospitality and tourism organisation has a hard job to consider all the issues we have already discussed when considering the implementation of their talent management process. But we must remember the sort of advantages that this process will bring in terms of competitive advantage. Some of the issues we covered earlier in the book can be summarised as follows:

☐ Organisations need to identify the type of talent they will require both now and in the future and decide where this type of talent is on offer.

☐ They must consider the type of underlying philosophy they want to adopt – inclusive or exclusive, targeted at the individual or groups, global or local etc. Once they have decided, then they must implement it in their development programmes.

☐ They must use new techniques to develop stronger relationships with prospective employees including employer branding, CSR, and advanced social media contacts so that they show they are a 'modern employer'.

☐ They should adopt the use of technology where it can offer advantages in terms of the talent management process. Governments need to also have policies on this so it is not left just to the private sector.

Finally in this section, let us consider the predictions for the future as follows:

1   Organisations in the hospitality and tourism sector will continue to struggle to employ the right talent for organizational success and will increasingly look to talent management practices in combination with marketing initiatives and the use of social media to come out top in the race for talent.

2   The most enlightened institutions will adopt a combination of exclusive and inclusive approaches to talent management, so that all employees can feel consulted and part of the organisation.

3   The larger organisations will develop their own training and educational offerings further and will even offer their own degrees in the longer term. This will put into question the value of the university experience for personal career development.

4   Small to medium enterprises (SMEs) have experienced difficulties with the more traditional approaches to talent management but they have

16

real advantages and these will be exploited further by the enlightened companies. They should offer individuals job variety and cross discipline experience, as well as opportunities to work side by side with the owner or senior management team.

5 Organisations will still target the elite educational institutions in terms of their recruitment activities and it is likely that we will see more strategic alliances formed between the commercial and educational sectors.

6 Competition will hot up further and consumers will look for increasingly new and different experiences, coupled with authenticity, and so the provision of talented staff who can deliver these types of experiences will be a key priority for all organisations in the sector.

Conclusions

I have tried to summarise the main themes that have emerged from the book and would like to thank all the contributors for their valuable inputs. I will now try to conclude and give my major predictions for the next decade.

So what will happen in the future?

My view is that the hospitality and tourism market will remain volatile for the foreseeable future thanks to both the political situation and the continuing economic crisis. This will mean that the quest for talent will continue to be an issue, but perhaps in the short-term it will be put to one side as organizations try to weather the storm. The recent Brexit vote has also put both employees and employers into a temporary turmoil which will only be resolved when decisions are made about what Brexit means for employment across Europe. In the rest of the world the challenge will be to attract and develop the talent and develop the educational provision in country to support this.

Ten major predictions

1 Talent management will continue to be of major strategic importance in the future, and have a major influence on youth employment and increasing employment of individuals approaching retirement.

2 There will be growing interest in the academic world where research programmes will be established and empirical research will be developed further.

3 Organizations will have to put an increasing emphasis on talent management and develop new and exciting ways of engaging employees in trusting relationships so that excellent service delivery is achieved.

4 New attitudes to work and working relationships will continue to develop and these will have to be reflected in the talent management programmes.

5   Employer and employee generated media will play an increasing role in how people choose who to work for and how organizations choose and develop their new and continuing recruits. There will also be ethical issues involved with social media, such as privacy, and the impact which personal contacts and reviews can have on both the employee but also the employer.

6   Employee branding will also have a major influence on the talent management process, with individuals wanting to work for large well established branded companies, or small companies that offer new and exciting products and services.

7   Employees will be made ever more aware of the ethical issues in hospitality and tourism thanks to the media, and issues like low wages, discrimination, diversity and work-life balance will become major issues. Potential and existing employees will seek to modify their behaviour for the benefit of the planet and the future of their families, and will look for the most appropriate companies to work for with this in mind. In particular, talented individuals will seek to work for employees who offer ethical and well thought out employment opportunities. They will also look for employees who seem to offer personalized development programmes and opportunities.

8   Asian markets will continue to grow, become more democratised and start to mature. It will be interesting to see what happens to the labour markets in countries with no real democracy and no tradition of labour rights. The hospitality and tourism industry will continue to grow and as a result will require talented individuals to help the further development of the business. There will be an abundance of labour in the world but scarcity at the local level. It is critical that the talent management processes integrate both local and global employees in a fair and systematic way in this process.

9   New types of educational opportunities will continue to develop and we will see the growth of high level educational qualifications being offered by commercial organisations. The elite universities and colleges will continue with their developments, but we will also see a return to the apprenticeship system and the increase in work-based learning and experiential learning in the hospitality and tourism curriculum.

10 There will be more effort put back on the quality of curriculum content and teaching methods, rather that research, so that new approaches to teaching can be adopted. This includes the experiential and work-based learning that was discussed earlier.

Talent management was 'named' for the first time in 1998, but it will come to maturity by 2026. This is the final 'big' prediction!

It will be interesting to see whether the predictions come true over the next few years or not.

16

A final thought

The talent of the future will be nothing like the talent of today. Individuals will develop their careers in a myriad of ways and ICT will help them with this process. Networking will be critical and the idea of *'it's not what you know but who you know'* will continue to be a big issue in the talent management debate. Educational programmes will continue to be developed and individuals will choose these on the basis of the perceived career advantages that they offer. Employees will continue to try to find the best solutions for developing and retaining their talent in whatever setting they find themselves. I hope this book has helped you to think deeply about all these issues and urge you to read and research further on this fascinating topic.

'The world is your oyster' is still the catch phrase for the talented and it is up to the various stakeholders to keep this dream alive. Employers and governments will perhaps prefer people not to want to move around if they are to get a return on their investment. Maybe it is only globalised corporations that will offer this opportunity, and they are a small part of the market! There are many unanswered questions.

Learning activities

You can try the following activities to help you to develop your knowledge at the end of this part of the book:

1   Develop a proposal for a small piece of empirical research which focuses on one of the issues mentioned in the research section of this chapter.

2   Identify two different types of hospitality and tourism degree courses and critically analyse their content and delivery style with regards to talent development. Which do you think is best and why?

3   Critically review the things that new graduates look for when choosing a future employer.

4   Identify a real example of an organisation that uses new techniques to attract and develop young staff. What can we learn from this example?

5   Create your own proposed model to summarise the talent management process.

References

Arris, A.A., Cascio, W.F. and Paauwe, J. (2013). Talent management: Current theories and future research directions. *Journal of World Business*. **49**(2014), 173-179.

Baum, T. (2008). Implications of hospitality and tourism labour markets for talent management strategies. *International Journal of Contemporary Hospitality Management*. **20**(7), 730-742.

Cappelli, P. and Keller, J.R. (2014). Talent Management: Coneptual approaches and practical challenges. *Annual Review of Orgnizational Psychology and Organizational Behaviour*, **1**(1) 305-331.

Collings, D.G. and Mellahi, K. (2009). Strategic talent management: A review and research agenda. *Human ResourceMmanagement*, **19**(4) 304-313.

Dries, N., (2013). The Psychology of talent management: A review and research agenda. *Human Resource Management Review*. **23**(4) 272-285.

Festing, M. and Schäfer, L., (2014). Generational challenges to talent management : A framework for talent retention based on the psychological-contract persepctive. *Journal of World Business*. **49**(2), 262-271.

Gallardo-Gallardo, E., Nijs, S., Dries, N. and Gallo, P. (2015). Towards an understanding of talent management as a phenomenon-driven field using bibliometric and content analysis. *Human Resource Management Review*. **25**, 264-279.

Inkson, K. (2008). Are humans resources? *Career Development International*, **13**(3) 270-279.

Lashley, C. (1997). *Empowering Service Excellence. Beyond the Quick Fix*. Cassell: London.

Michaels, E., Handfield-Jones, H. and Axelrod, B. (2001). *The War for Talent*. Boston:MA: Harvard Business School Press.

Pricewaterhouse Coopers, (2007). *Managing Tomorrow's People*, Pricewaterhouse Coopers, London.

Tarique, I. and Schuler, R.S. (2010). Global talent management: Literature review, integrative framework, amd suggestions for further research. *Journal of World Business*. **45**(2) 122-133.

Thunnissen, M., Boselie, P. and Fruytier, B. (2013). Talent management and the relevance of context: Towards a pluralistic approach. *Human Resource Management Review*. **23**, 326-336.

16

PART 5

CASE STUDIES

Talent Management in large organisations

Talent management in SMEs

Case study 1: Taj Hotels talent development in association with the Institute of Hotel Management, Aurangabad

Anand Iyengar and Satish Jayaram

The prelude

At the 46th International Film Festival of India (IFFI) held in Chennai, French filmmaker Nicolas Saada's version of the 26/11 attacks on the Taj Mahal hotel in Mumbai left the audience in tears (Kamat, 2015). This gripping film was screened as a tribute to those who lost lives in the terror strike on the 26th of November 2008. The film is about an 18 year old girl who endures this nerve wrecking ordeal but lives to tell the tale. Recounting the inspiration, Saada mentioned that a few days after the attack, he was talking to a friend whose niece was at the Taj Mahal hotel and had a first hand experience of this gruesome episode. Fortunately her survival instincts helped to return to the safety of her parents outside the hotel. She had good luck on her side, many did not. With the magnitude of global response evoked, this was termed as India's 9/11 (Svensson, 2012). Deshpande and Raina (2011) provide a detailed account of the strike and the associates' response to the guests. Within moments of this nefarious activity, the associates at the hotel quickly realized that something was wrong and swung into action to reduce casualties. The focus was clearly on guest safety rather than personal security. In this ordeal, associates sacrificed their lives to uphold the values of the Taj and looked after the interests of the guests in letter and spirit. These acts of valour were documented in both the academic and business press all over the world. This incident highlighted a unique aspect of the associates, which was their keen sense of customer-centricity that propelled them to go beyond the ordinary for the guests. This can also be traced to the values of the Taj and the Tata group that instil the values in every associate. Training and mentoring has always been a part of the Taj culture. Over a period of time training and mentoring may have become a process driven activity. But they remain a product of the Tata culture and ethos.

The Taj: Genesis and the Tata philosophy

According to a popular legend, Jamsetji Tata (the founder of the Tata group) was denied entry into a European hotel that flashed a signboard prohibiting dogs and

Indians. This led to the creation of the Taj Mahal, a hotel where Indians could entertain and be entertained without being affronted. Some chroniclers suggest that the lack of clean and safe hotels was a deterrent in attracting European and American visitors who were looking to invest in business opportunities in Mumbai, and that meeting this need was the *raison d'être* for the Taj, as conceived by Jamsetji Tata.

Whatever the motive, in an era when there were no luxury hotels in India and very few in Asia, the Taj was a bold statement that proclaimed that India was as good as anything in the world. After a successful stint in other businesses, Tata & Sons, a partnership enterprise, was formed as a vehicle for the Tata family to manage business ventures and interests (Witzel, 2010). However, the Taj Mahal hotel was not a Tata & Sons venture, but was funded by Jamsetji Tata. He had created this hotel as a gift to the city of Mumbai and not for any business gain. Since the group's inception, a diversified portfolio emerged through the creation of strategic talent in the business of steel, power, technology and financial services. However the group always restrained from any political interference, continuing to focus on philanthropy and nation-building activities. Some observers (e.g. Sen, 2009) believe that the group was hibernating and therefore in the 70s and 80s other younger companies raced ahead in markets and products that the Tata group had dominated for decades. Coupled with this, the Taj Group faced a different problem: the question of whether to be in the luxury hotel business. This could be attributed to the independence movement and perhaps key decision makers did not view a luxury aligned to Gandhi's nation building ideas. It remains an enigma as to why this jewel in the crown of the Tatas was almost liquidated and left unattended for a very long period of time. It is very fortunate that the successors of Jamsetji Tata held on the Taj and it is indeed a jewel that has been shining very brightly.

Around the same time, another hotel chain under the stewardship of M.S. Oberoi began emerging as a competitor to the Taj. With the acquisition of the Associated Hotels of India in 1934, M S Oberoi became the first Indian to own a high end hotel chain with properties all across British India (Leahy, 2010). Both these groups were uncommon in more than one way, but they shared the same penchant for hotels and people (associates).

Enter Ajit Kerkar

With customer-centricity at the core of the business model and with the aim of providing the best service for the customers, the Taj group under the stewardship of Ajit Kerkar, Chairman and Managing Director, started to develop firepower. Kerkar was very particular about the associates being recruited and would personally interview everyone, including cooks, bellhops and captains. This founded a sound tradition of mentoring, guiding and training to achieve the best operational and business results.

CS

In an interview with a popular financial daily, a former Chief Operating Officer of the Taj fondly remembers Kerkar's charismatic leadership and sway over people, and attributes their success to Kerkar. (Lokesh and Chatterjee, 2015).

Kerkar changed everything about the business of Taj, including the approach to sourcing fruits and vegetables, the food and beverage menus, the interiors of the rooms and the design of the restaurants (Thomas, 2016). A new wing was added to the existing palace structure in 1972, and this gained the immediate patronage of the wealthy business class in India's financial capital. From a turnover of INR 4 lacs in 1941, IHCL was grossing 2.5 Crores by the mid 1970s. The Taj could now charge a premium and even the Oberoi, with a brand new hotel and the emergence of ITC could not stop the Taj from growing. With the hotel now charging Rs 100 for a room night, without complimentary breakfast, the Taj had finally arrived! Through the 1970s Kerkar took the company to new heights. The Taj was responsible for popularizing destinations like Rajasthan, Kerala, Goa and Chennai amongst foreign tourists Thomas (2016). The Taj was the first company to convert two real time palaces to luxurious heritage hotels in Rajasthan. The sales strategy was aggressive and used every trick in the book to boost the occupancy percentage. For instance, 80 international writers were flown in to cover all the Taj properties in India. It is rumored that this event unnerved the rivals and attempts were successfully made to dissuade Air India from extending gratis travel to these high profile writers. But fortunately some other carriers agreed, and these efforts led to Indian destinations receiving a wide coverage across the globe. New concepts and cuisines were tried out for the first time in India. The Thai Pavilion and the Golden Dragon restaurant are examples of Kerkar's game plan for growth.

The human resources agenda

This rapid growth of the Taj needed able human resources that could contribute to the success story. To ensure that the current and future human resources requirements were fulfilled, the senior management decided to create a hotel school that would enable the percolation of the Taj philosophy at the school level. This may not have been radical, but it was revolutionary thinking on the part of the Taj to aim for the creation of such a school facility. There were a couple of established models in India that the Taj could emulate.

The Oberoi group established the Oberoi Centre for Learning & Development in 1966 as a complete in-house training hub, to develop the talent that could assume higher responsibilities in the future within the hotel chain. This was a post-graduate effort to acquire high quality and committed human resources for operations. This meant that a very small number could be absorbed in this programme to be groomed as future leaders.

On the opposite end of the spectrum, India had established the National Council for Hotel Management, and Catering Technology Institutes in all the metropolitan cities that were producing hotel graduates in large numbers. While graduate number was not an issue with this model, the quality of education needed a lot of improvement and changes. The bureaucratic edifice of the Indian education system was a huge deterrent to achieving the desired quality of the graduates. To this day, it is seen that ratio of Vocational Education and Training (VET) to wages is significant and positive. However, unemployment from VET is very high, particularly for those individuals who have undergone VET courses that are at lower levels of general education (Ahmed, 2016). The Taj was looking at a flexible and hybrid model that could provide substantial numbers without compromising on quality. It was also very clear that the establishment a new educational institute with a fairly broad vision would mean drifting from the Taj's core business of hospitality. The stakes were high as the risk and return dynamics appeared to be unclear. Therefore there had to be a catalyst or a factor that could mitigate the risk for the Taj and at the same time provide a credible solution to this problem.

Around the same time, Dr Rafiq Zakaria, a leading politician, was looking for a suitable industry partner to further his dream of providing quality education in the city of Aurangabad. Dr Rafiq Zakaria was twice elected by the city to the *Lok Sabha* (House of Commons) and also represented India at the United Nations in 1965, 1990 and 1996. He was elected to the newly constituted Maharashtra state assembly in 1962 from Aurangabad and appointed the Minister for Urban Development. Under his guidance, planning for new Aurangabad had commenced and been implemented with the involvement of the state development corporation. As an aspect of his personal commitment, Zakaria had formed an educational trust, called the Maulana Azad Educational Trust, to look after the propagation of educational institutes. The trust was involved in the development of many educational colleges and centers of excellence in Aurangabad and Mumbai. Zakaria had ambitious plans for furthering high quality education through great institutions. His image and political background could have attracted any business house that was keen on developing talent through formal education.

There was *consensus ad idem*[1], and after initial discussions it was decided that the Taj would offer certification with the Trust as the partner in this exercise. This worked perfectly for both parties as the Taj was absolved of the local administration. The Trust enjoyed the reputation and the credence that the Taj brought to this equation. The new venture was called the Indian Institute of Hotel Management. The Taj inducted all the graduates of the first cohort from the Institute that graduated in 1996 into employment. This was a great success to be celebrated.

This was a model of best practice, for India, where a large business conglomerate joined hands with educators to create an academic environment. From 1993 to 1996, the Taj evinced a lot of interest in the progress of the students. A five star hotel facility was created close to the campus to provide work experience for the students. This supervised learning atmosphere enabled students to quickly grasp and apply classroom learning under real life conditions. This was factored

CS

1 'Meeting of minds', used in contract law to describe the intentions of the parties forming the contract

into the course structure and since there was very little bureaucracy involved, the curriculum could be altered to suit the requirements of all the stakeholders. All that had been envisioned was being translated into reality. This optimistic progress continued for some time, then another party entered into this existing arrangement.

A polytechnic institute in the United Kingdom was granted university status in 1993. To augment the social responsibility vision, this new university was looking for an overseas collaboration. At the Institute level there was also some thought applied to the enhancing the diploma that was awarded by Taj to a formal graduate degree in Hotel Management. This was to prepare for future challenges as regards to thegovernment approval and the recognition of educational institutes and courses. This was a perfect time and setting for the agreement between the Trust and the Taj to now include the University of Huddersfield, UK. Though the partners had different backgrounds, and this was an odd combination in many ways, working towards the betterment of the students was the prime agenda and motive that kept them tied together.

Now Indian students could afford to study at an institute under the aegis of a largest hotel company in India, get an internationally accepted qualification at a very reasonable cost. The University provided every possible effort to upgrade the quality of staff and academic process to improve the quality of student experience at the Institute. All the quality standards implemented at the university campus in Huddersfield were now being applied to the institute in Aurangabad. This became one of the hallmark of quality education in India. With an international degree and adequate knowledge, graduates of the institute could work, start an enterprise or pursue overseas higher education with relative ease as compared to students graduating from other hospitality institutions in the country. However, just as everything appeared to be working in the favour of this new found academic success, there was trouble brewing somewhere.

The era after Ajit Kerkar

In 1938, J.R.D. Tata, popularly referred to as JRD, became the chairman of the board at Tata Sons. JRD, who was 34 and from the Tata family (his father was Jamsetji Tata's cousin) was all set to provide strategic direction to the company. The Tata group always revered the Chairman of the Board, however, JRD felt that it would be a disaster to throw his weight around beyond a certain point. He greatly appreciated the fact that many executives had a deeper understanding of the industrial complexities and were adept at handling routine matters. This consensual approach, probably evolved in the corporate environment, became JRD's management style and resulted in a managerial environment that featured decentralization, participatory decision making and astute professionalism. JRD also possessed an innate ability to continuously recruit, reward and support executives with high potential. While he set broad guidelines, JRD gave absolute freedom to top executives but never interfered with the day to day operations. Therefore the top management consisted of luminaries who took pride in working for the Tata group, an organization that they considered professional and ethical. Contrary to the policy of rewarding top performance, poor achievers were never penalized, and as a consequence, middle management level was choking with survivors and non-achievers. In 1981, JRD decided to now step down in favour of his grand nephew Ratan Tata.

With India ushering in a new liberalized era in 1991, and Ratan Tata heading the Tata group, the picture was completely different compared to the JRD era. There were many changes that Ratan Tata brought to the management structure, reporting pattern and rules on senior executive retirement. Though some of his initiatives were criticized bitterly, Ratan Tata surged ahead and towards the end of 1990s a new management structure was in place. Ratan Tata used authority with discretion and some executives who did not fall in line were forced to resign. In September 1997, Ajit Kerkar resigned as the Managing Director of the Taj, and R K Krishnakumar, was appointed the new managing director of the Taj Group. Ratan Tata stepped in as the chairman at the board at the Taj. While addressing the Annual General Meeting in 1997, Ratan Tata had said that 80 percent of the revenues came in from only 5 hotels, while all their other hotels had zero or very low revenue generation capacity. While initially there appeared to be a discontinuity in the approach of the top executives towards the institute, over a period of time it was business as usual.

This time R K Krishnakumar was in charge of the Taj leadership. He was very keen on the development of talent and appointed a senior human resources executive in charge of the developments at the Institute. The Taj also made significant progress in the hospitality business and new avenues were being opened for the graduates of the Institute. The Taj was taking great care to develop the infrastructure at the Institute. The kitchen, laboratories and classrooms were upgraded to help students keep abreast with the latest hospitality trends. The Taj did not think twice to make investments and provide expertise wherever required. Krishnakumar regularly attended the Institute's board meetings and student graduation ceremony with great interest. He also enthused the students with his addresses on a variety of occasions. Creating a think tank of academics, high quality internship and training opportunities were seen as basis of hospitality education to improve the competence level of fresh graduates entering the industry (Jauhari, 2006). IIHM, Aurangabad, was emerging as an example that demonstrated the presence of both an academic and industry think tank while building capability to become a world class institution of the future. While the focus remained on providing the best experience for the students, employability issues were resolved by partnering with the hospitality industry and sharing the institute's talent with competitors. The whole idea was to source and hone the best hospitality skills and give them to the world! During this period the Institute lost the extra 'I' in the name but did not lose its character, and was now called IHM instead of IIHM.

CS

This partnership was fêted when the Chairman of Tata Sons, Mr Ratan Tata, graced the graduation ceremony in July 2000. This was a high point in the Taj-Maulana Azad Educational Trust – University of Huddersfield relationship. In 2003, Krishnakumar retired as the managing director, paving way for Raymond Bickson to be at the helm of affairs.

Raymond Bickson, an alumni of *Ecole hôtelière de Lausanne*, Switzerland, was fine hotelier himself. He watched with great interest the development of the institute. He continued to provide support in upgrading the physical infrastructure and also provide structural support in terms of developing talent at the Taj relying on the Institute's experience. While things were beginning to settle down, critical regulatory changes surrounding educational institutions were announced by the government. The All India Council for Technical Education (AICTE) was the body that controlled technical education in India.

With hospitality education being categorized as 'technical' as per AICTE, it was mandated that the course duration be changed to four years as opposed to the earlier three years. From the earlier experience and feedback from the industry, students were provided with a complete year's work experience. The ancillary Taj hotel on the campus was reorganized to include luxury hotel standards to provide high quality training exposure. All the Taj hotels across India and some hotels in Maldives, Mauritius and Sri Lanka absorbed the institute's students on placement. There was a directive from the Managing Director's office to dedicate 5 percent of the hotel General Manager's Key Result Areas (KRA) to providing quality student experience. The institute hitherto provided three year courses in Hotel Management and in Culinary Arts. While the Hotel Management course was reasonably settled, the Culinary Arts required regulatory approval. This entailed that the quality of kitchen infrastructure be improved to enable additional students to enrol on the Culinary Arts course. The Taj again provided financial and other resources to plan for a technology based, ultramodern studio kitchen. All celebrity chefs and master chefs were invited to provide live demonstrations and conduct master classes for the students to practice and perfect culinary skills. With this concrete and cemented relationship, there was no difficulty in obtaining necessary regulatory approval to offer the Culinary Arts course.

The institute could now offer BA (Hons.) Hotel Management and BA (Hons.) Culinary Arts under the collaborative provisions of the University of Huddersfield, UK. The institute further made changes to the course structure to incorporate a full year of internship towards the end of the course. This ensured that the internship could be used for observing students on the shop floor and for a seamless transfer to employment. With a broader vision to include other Tata companies into the recruitment process and other group companies like Tata Croma (Infiniti Retail) were invited on campus. The final year students selected for employment with Tata Croma were given project based assignment prior to taking up employment. This can be viewed as a support to an academic argument that that students must be provided opportunities to work in varied settings and roles to have better grip of the operational environment Lashley (2015). This was a positive step to acculturate students for a smooth graduation to employment. Students were also provided with interesting topics and projects to work during the internship phase. Jauhari and Thomas (2013) thematically outline perspectives on improving university–industry partnership and state the Institute has a very strong industry link.

The imperative issue was to strike a balance between academics and skills, to ensure that students are not only trained in vocational skills but also get adequate exposure to social sciences content in order to become critical thinkers (Lashley, 2013). The fulfillment of this objective can be evidenced through the fact that a large number of students have been able to make a mark in areas such as revenue management, sales and marketing, global distribution, marketing communication and social media optimization in global hospitality and allied industry.

Concluding remarks

There are some interesting remarks in the academic world about the quality of hospitality education. There are varied viewpoints, but there is consensus on issues such as that the curriculum must be focused on the graduates attaining a higher goal in life and not merely on securing an immediate entry level position (Gross and Manoharan, 2016; Lashley, 2013). There must be emphasis on an inter-disciplinary approach to help students understand the purpose of what they are learning. The education provided must be well rounded. Students must be provided with a sound academic underpinning that will enable vocationally oriented incumbents to be able to also pursue higher goals in life.

Deshapande and Raina (2009) provide an insight into the success of the Taj human resources strategy in the aftermath of the 26/11 terrorist crisis. The paper recounts the action of one of IHM-A's graduates and provide appropriate links to the strategy of Taj. If this is an extraordinary deed, then the Taj is to applauded for having created a philosophy that encouraged associates to look beyond the ediocre. This has been enshrined in the Institute's existence that has now spread across the globe along with over 2000 graduates in the past 25 years. This has been the success of the Taj and Tatas.

References

Ahmed, T. (2016), Labour market outcome for formal vocational education and training in India: Safety net and beyond, IIMB, *Management Review*, **28** (2), 98-110.

Deshpande R., and Raina, A. (2011) The ordinary heroes of the Taj. *Harvard Business Review*, **89** (12) 119-123.

Gross, M.J. and Manoharan, A. (2016) The balance of liberal and vocational values in hospitality higher education: voices of graduates, *Journal of Hospitality and Tourism Education*, **28**(1), 45-57.

CS

Jauhari, V. and Thomas, R. (2013). Developing effective university-industry partnerships: An introduction. *Worldwide Hospitality and Tourism Themes,*5(3), 238-243.

Jauhari, V. (2006). Competencies for a career in the hospitality industry: an Indian perspective, *International Journal of Contemporary Hospitality Management,* **18**(2),123–134. http://www.emeraldinsight.com/doi/abs/10.1108/09596110610646673

Kamat, P. (2015). Taj Mahal: In memory of 26/11 attack victims. *The Hindu,* Nov 28. http://www.thehindu.com/news/national/taj-mahal-in-memory-of-2611-attack-victims/article7924236.ece.

Lashley, C. (2015). Hospitality studies: escaping the tyranny?, *Quality Assurance in Education,* **23**(4), 364 – 377.

Lashley, C. (2013). Managing the tyranny of relevance: Linking with industry - but not too much! *Worldwide Hospitality and Tourism Themes,* **5**(3), 283-295.

Leahy, J. (2010). An eventful life of luxury. *Financial Times,* p. 14, Jun 21.

Lokesh, R. and Chatterjee, R. (2015). JRD Tata, Kerkar, Bhowmick and Lobo taught me the art of hospitality. *Financial Express,* May 02.

Sen, S. (2009). Tata group: Transforming the sleeping elephant. *IUP Journal of Business Strategy,* **6**(1), 31-45.

Svensson, T. (2012). Stories of catastrophe, traces of trauma: Indian state formation and the borders of becoming, *Alternatives: Global, Local, Political,* **37**(3) 253-265. doi: 10.1177/0304375412450843

Thomas, P. M. (2016). The Taj Mahal of the hotel world. *Businessline,* Aug 12.

Witzel, M. (2010). *Tata: The Evolution of a Corporate Brand,* Penguin Books Ltd:India.

Mandy Aggett

Introduction

Founded by Stanley and Bea Tollman, Red Carnation Hotels is part of the family-owned travel and leisure group, The Travel Corporation (TTC). It owns and operates a collection of seventeen luxurious hotels, located in the UK, Ireland, South Africa, Geneva and the USA, and the company is well known for excellence in recruitment and retention (Pollitt, 2006; Best Companies, 2015). It has won numerous awards in recognition of the level of support and development provided to their employees, and has benefited from the high levels of care and attention paid to its staff, as highlighted in one of their key guiding core values:

> *We believe that care comes from caring and so we provide a level of care for our team members that inspires by example, generates trust, respect, open and honest communication and appreciation. Staff feel valued and are offered opportunities to develop and progress, and as a result our staff loyalty far exceeds the industry average. (Red Carnation Hotels, 2014a)*

Stanley Tollman's father bought his first hotel, the Paternoster, in South Africa in the 1920s. After moving to Johannesburg in 1938, the family purchased the Palace Hotel, where Stanley Tollman learned his craft and developed a passion for the industry after leaving university. He married Bea in 1954 and, in this year, the couple opened their first property, the Nugget Hotel in Johannesburg. Other hotels in South Africa followed, including the Tollman Towers in 1969, which was named one of the best hotels in the world. The couple and their four children moved to the UK in 1975 and, in 1984, purchased the Chesterfield Hotel in Mayfair, at which point, Red Carnation Hotels (RCH) was founded and named in honour of Stanley Tollman's love for wearing a red carnation in his lapel (Red Carnation Hotels, 2014b).

The hotels

Today, the collection is made up of seventeen hotels which includes six properties in London, two in Ireland, two in Guernsey, two in Dorset, one in Geneva, three in South Africa, and one in Florida, and is still led by its Founder and President, Bea Tollman. Each of the hotels is four or five star rated and is luxuriously, and individually, designed and furbished by Bea herself, along with her daughter,

CS

Toni. Original, antique or contemporary art and furniture may be found in each room, and this is sympathetically combined with up-to-date technology.

The company's motto, '*no request is too large, no detail too small*' (Red Carnation Hotels, 2014c), demonstrates their commitment to service and the comfort of guests. Exceptional service and memorable experiences is at the heart of the hotel group's business strategy and this is clearly communicated in their core values, and embedded in development programmes. This was acknowledged in May 2015, when twelve of the hotels were inducted into TripAdvisor's Inaugural Hall of Fame – a higher proportion than any other UK hotel group, and just one of the most recent of a long list of awards and accolades the company has received, which includes:

- ☐ Travel Media Awards – Best International Hotel Group (2015);
- ☐ Travel Weekly's Gold Magellan Award – winner in the Luxury hotel/resort category (2014);
- ☐ AA Hospitality Awards – Small Hotel Group of the Year (2013);
- ☐ TripAdvisor – Certificate in Excellence for every hotel in the company (2012 and 2013).

(Red Carnation Hotels, 2015a)

Each hotel in the collection has also won numerous individual awards, and a selection of these are outlined, along with details of the hotels, in Table C2.1.

RCH has also won recognition for its HR practices and the company's leadership and management:

- ☐ Springboard Awards for Excellence – Best Student Placement Provider (2013);
- ☐ HR in Hospitality Awards for Excellence – The Tom Crowley Award (2013);
- ☐ European Hospitality Awards – Hotelier of the Year - Bea Tollman (2012);
- ☐ Caterer & Hotelkeeper – Top 100 Most Powerful People in Hospitality - Jonathan Raggett (Managing Director), (2012);
- ☐ HR in Hospitality Awards – Excellence in Recruitment and Retention (2012);
- ☐ HR in Hospitality Awards – Excellence in Learning & Development (2011);
- ☐ People 1st – Top 100 Most Influential Women in the Hospitality, Leisure and Tourism Industry – Liz McGivern (Director of HR & Training), (2011);
- ☐ Investors in People – 1st company to achieve the Gold standard across its entire portfolio (2010).

(Red Carnation Hotels, 2015a)

Perhaps of most significance however, in 2015, the hotel group was named 2nd in the *Sunday Times'* 100 Best Companies to Work For (Best Companies, 2015). Therefore, this case study examines the policies and practices of RCH, as an example of best practice in the management of talent.

Table C2.1: The Red Carnation Hotels Collection

Hotel	Description	Rooms	Awards & Accolades
The Milestone Hotel www.milestonehotel.com ★★★★★ **London** - Royal Borough of Kensington and Chelsea	Grade II listed building overlooking Kensington Palace and Gardens, offering fine British dining, award winning afternoon teas and 24 hour butler service	44 deluxe guest rooms, twelve luxury suites, six long-stay apartments	TripAdvisor Travellers' Choice Awards 2015 *2nd Best Hotel in the UK;* Travel + Leisure 2014 *World's Best 500 Hotels*
41 Hotel www.41hotel.com ★★★★★ **London** – Belgravia	An 'intimate private hideaway in the heart of London', near Buckingham Palace, offering personal butlers, luxurious style, a striking black and white design, Executive Lounge with complimentary treats, and staff that outnumber guests two to one	30 luxurious rooms and suites	TripAdvisor Travellers' Choice Awards 2015 *Voted one of the Best Hotels for Service in the UK;* Travel + Leisure 2014 *World's Best 500 Hotels*
The Egerton House Hotel www.egertonhousehotel.com ★★★★★ **London** – Knightsbridge	Luxury hotel with the feel of a 'homely private residence' and staff that outnumber guests two to one, located near to the V&A Museum	28 individually designed rooms and suites	TripAdvisor Travellers' Choice Awards 2015 *12th in the Top 25 Luxury Hotels UK;* AA Hospitality Awards 2014/15 *Awarded 5 red stars*
The Chesterfield Mayfair www.chesterfieldmayfair.com ★★★★ **London** – Mayfair	Regency style hotel with the feel of a traditional private club, offering 'supreme comfort and luxury', excellent facilities and a relaxing environment, fine dining and 'ideal for weddings, meetings and events'	93 individually designed deluxe rooms and 13 luxurious suites	Condé Nast Traveller Gold List 2014 *Number 3 in the Best Hotels and Resorts in England;* Travel + Leisure 2014, 2013, 2012 *World's Best 500 Hotels*
The Montague on the Gardens www.montaguehotel.com ★★★★ **London** -Bloomsbury	Elegant Georgian townhouse hotel in a peaceful location, offering sophistication, with 'ample old-world charm', and 'rich furnishings throughout', bistro style restaurant, plus al fresco dining on the terrace, and in-room beauty treatments	88 individually designed and elegant deluxe rooms, 11 luxury suites and one apartment suite	TripAdvisor Travellers' Choice Awards 2015 *24th Best Hotel in the UK;* Trip Advisor 2013 *Certificate of Excellence*

CS

Hotel	Description	Rooms	Awards
The Rubens at the Palace www.rubenshotel.com ★★★★ London – Opposite Buckingham Palace	Offers 'aristocratic grandeur, serene comfort and traditional hospitality', combined with the latest technology, pet and family friendly, fine dining and award winning afternoon teas	143 deluxe guest rooms, eight royal rooms, ten luxurious suites and two self-contained apartments	Travel + Leisure 2015 *World's Best 500 Hotels*; TripAdvisor Travellers' Choice Awards 2014 *Number 23 Best Hotel in the UK*
Ashford Castle www.ashfordcastle.com ★★★★★ Ireland – Cong, County Mayo	Dating back to 1228 and set in 350 acres, fully restored and home to Ireland's first School of Falconry, fine Irish cuisine, and 'regular host to royalty, dignitaries and celebrities', and offering a range of estate activities	69 deluxe or Corrib rooms, six staterooms, three junior staterooms, one presidential suite and three suites	Virtuoso Awards 2015 *Hotel of the Year*; Travel + Leisure World's Best Awards 2015 *Number 3 Best Hotel in the World*
The Lodge at Ashford Castle www.thelodgeac.com ★★★★ Ireland – Cong, County Mayo	Situated in the grounds of Ashford Castle and overlooking Loch Corrib, originally built in 1865, offering country house hospitality, estate activities, and 'classic refinement with modern appeal'	24 luxurious guest rooms and 26 unique suites	TripAdvisor 2015 *Certificate of Excellence*
The Old Government House Hotel & Spa www.theoghhotel.com ★★★★★ Guernsey –St Peter Port	The only five star hotel in Guernsey, located a few minutes walk away from the quayside, offering a health club and Moroccan style spa, fine cuisine, afternoon teas and picturesque gardens	63 stylish, individually designed rooms and suites	TripAdvisor Travellers' Choice Awards 2014 *21st Best Luxury Hotel in the UK*; Visit Guernsey 2014 *Gold Award*
The Duke of Richmond Hotel www.dukeofrichmond.com ★★★★ Guernsey – St Peter Port	Luxurious hotel minutes away from the town centre, in a peaceful location overlooking a park, offering family services and informal dining	73 individually designed rooms and suites, including a penthouse suite	TripAdvisor 2014 *Certificate of Excellence*; Visit Guernsey 2014 *Gold Award*
Summer Lodge Country House www.summerlodgehotel.co.uk ★★★★ Dorset –Evershot	Grade II listed country house hotel, a Relais and Chateaux property located in a picturesque village, and set in four acres, offering fine dining, extensive wine cellar and spa treatments	20 guest rooms, cottages and four luxury suites, all individually designed	TripAdvisor Travellers' Choice Awards 2015 *Number 20 in the UK Top 25 Hotels for Service, and Number 14 in the UK Top 25 Small Hotels*

Hotel	Description	Rooms	Awards
The Acorn Inn www.acorn-inn.co.uk **Dorset** – Evershot	16th century property with original character, including old beams, oak panelling and flagstone floors, offering a 'home away from home', and award winning dining	Ten individually designed rooms including four poster rooms and a private loft suite	TripAdvisor 2015 *Certificate of Excellence*
Hotel d'Angleterre www.dangleterrehotel.com ★★★★ **Geneva** – On Lake Leman	Fantastic location overlooking the lake, offering fine dining, live music and cocktails, and is the 'epitome of refined Swiss style and traditional style'	39 luxury guest rooms and six suites	TripAdvisor Travellers' Choice Awards 2015 *Number 14 Best Hotel in Switzerland and Number 5 Top Hotels for Romance in Switzerland*
The Twelve Apostles www.12apostleshotel.com ★★★★★ **South Africa**- Cape Town	Boutique hotel and spa situated in Cape Town, near to the Table Mountain national Park and the Twelve Apostles mountain range, offering a private cinema and fantastic panoramic views of the ocean and mountains	55 deluxe rooms and 15 luxurious suites including a Presidential Suite	Travel + Leisure 2014 *World's Best 500 Hotels;* TripAdvisor Travellers' Choice Awards 2014 *Top 10 Best Hotels in South Africa*
Bushmans Kloof Wilderness Reserve & Wellness Retreat www.bushmandskloof.co.za ★★★★ **South Africa**– Western Cape	An 'ecological oasis' set in the northern Cederberg Mountains, offering a 'distinctive wilderness experience', spa facilities and outdoor dining experiences in the reserve	16 luxurious guest rooms and suites and a private, fully-catered villa	Condé Nast Traveller: Gold List 2014 *The World's Best Places to Stay in South Africa, and Number 2 Best African Safari Lodges*
The Oyster Box www.oysterboxhotel.com ★★★★★ **South Africa**– Durban	Located on the beachfront overlooking the Indian Ocean and a lighthouse, and the 'ultimate in colonial charm and style', offering a private cinema, dolphin watching from the terrace, spa facilities and fine dining	86 rooms, villas and suites, including a Presidential Suite	TripAdvisor Travellers' Choice Awards 2015 *Number 3 Best Hotels in South Africa;* World Luxury Spa Awards 2014 *Number 1 Luxury Hotel Spa in Africa*
The Chesterfield Palm Beach www.chesterfieldpb.com ★★★★ **Florida**– Palm Beach	Located near the designer boutiques and beaches and 'surrounded by palm-lined boulevards and elegant villas', offers a relaxed palm beach lifestyle, fantastic cuisine and live music	41 superior and deluxe rooms and 12 luxurious suites, all individually decorated	Condé Nast Traveller Readers' Choice Awards 2014 *Number 9 Best Hotels in Florida*

CS

Talent management

The link between talent management, and organisational success has been discussed in previous chapters. As highlighted by Scott and Revis (2008:783), talent management is *'ultimately about an organisation's ability to develop a pool of gifted individuals, who can individually help a company meet immediate and long-term objectives'*. In addition to the HR practices of recruitment, selection, development and succession management, talent management involves workforce planning, and a focus on skills, growth, retention and reward (Christensen Hughes and Rog, 2008). This section examines the evolution of talent management at RCH, from the introduction of its first management training programmes to its current status as the 2nd Best Company to Work For, according to the *Sunday Times'* list of 2015.

A brief history

Back in 2001, factors such as the 9/11 terrorist attacks, SARS, and foot and mouth disease, were severely impacting the hotel industry. Whilst other hotel groups were discounting their room rates to combat the problems, RCH focused on improving service, with the introduction of training programmes for its managers. At this time, staff turnover was just over 80 per cent, which the Vice President of HR, Liz McGivern, believed was due to a prior lack of training, and the inexperience of supervisors (Pollitt, 2006). The importance of staff retention was highlighted, a few years later, in an interview with RCH's Managing Director, Jonathan Raggett (*Hotel Industry Magazine*, 2013), who explained:

> Guest feedback shows that the most important thing is how our guests were greeted, remembered and treated upon arrival. So it makes good business sense if our returning guests can recognise faces at the hotel property. Equally, we want our key customer-facing employees to remember our guests and welcome them back.

Liz McGivern stressed that high staff turnover was a threat to the company's reputation, and supervisors also reported problems with staff motivation, and difficulties in delegation, communication and meeting management goals (Pollitt, 2006). The introduction of a two-tier training programme for supervisors, Ambassadors in Management (AIM 1 and AIM 2 – see Figure C2.1), helped to improve staff morale, job satisfaction and motivation, and enhanced the confidence of supervisors. This helped to boost room occupancy by 10 per cent, increased profitability and reduced staff turnover to below 30 per cent, which in turn reduced recruitment costs by £200,000 a year. The training also resulted in the promotion of 39 of its delegates within the first few years (Pollitt, 2006).

| AIM 1 | Training for new supervisors in skills required to achieve the Chartered Management Institute's Certificate in Team Leading. |
| AIM 2 | Training for supervisors with 6 months + experience to build on skills to enhance departmental and business goals, leading to the Institute of Leadership and Management's Introductory Certificate in First-Line Management. |

Figure C2.1: Ambassadors in Management Programmes

Current practice

According to Christensen Hughes and Rog (2008), it is important to align talent management with an organisation's strategic goals. Indeed, a strong focus on corporate strategy may significantly impact profit (Bethke-Langenegger *et al.*, 2011). Talent is viewed as a 'critical resource' in shaping performance (Eriksen, 2012), and it has been noted that long-term career prospects, motivation, mentoring and training can help organisations to attract and retain the best employees, and assist with the succession of talent (Chambers *et al.*, 1998; Lawler, 2008; Scott and Revis, 2008). In an industry that is plagued by high staff turnover and a skills shortage, attracting, developing and retaining staff is critical and drives the need for talent management. It is therefore perhaps no surprise that RCH now spends around £250,000 a year on staff development (Best Companies, 2014). The training and development programmes in place link directly to the company's business goals and strategy and has helped the group secure the Investors in People Gold Award across all of its hotels.

Today, RCH takes care to recruit those with the passion, personality, skills and enthusiasm required to deliver the exceptional service they are known for. This recruitment strategy ensures a fit between the organisation's goals and the service that is delivered. Additionally, *all* 872 employees at RCH are now given access to training and career development opportunities, from Induction Day onward, and are actively encouraged to grow in their roles and progress. This is very much an *inclusive* approach to talent management (Cappelli and Keller, 2014). Training includes:

- ☐ Foundation skills for team members
- ☐ Foundation skills for managers
- ☐ Technical skills
- ☐ Developmental skills
- ☐ College sponsorships

RCH also offers two management programmes; a 2.5 year programme for graduates, and a programme open to those without formal qualifications, but a demonstrable 'passion and desire to succeed' in the industry (Red Carnation Hotels, 2015b). Trainees receive mentoring support with a key member of the management or executive team, direct access to the Managing Director, support with accommodation, internationally recognised qualifications and permanent operational management opportunities.

Talent development is the key to successful talent management (Bethke-Langenegger *et al.*, 2011), and, if effective, will result in more engaged employees and lower staff turnover (Lockwood, 2006). Best Companies (2015) stresses, '*if there was one initiative alone that Red Carnation believe makes them stand apart from many other hotel companies, it is their excellently researched, planned and executed training programmes*'. Indeed, RCH recognises that the delivery of exceptional service, requires exceptional staff, so they recruit the best, then provide them with all the

CS

support and encouragement they need to develop. They understand that the level of service they provide to their guests *'cannot exceed the talent of [their] teams'* (Red Carnation Hotels, 2014c:13).

Progression opportunities are also evident and well communicated. Ninety per cent of managers have been promoted from within the hotel group, and, according to Jonathan Raggett (2011:4), one of the things that excites him most is, *'seeing so many talented people grow within our business and become tomorrow's assistant managers, deputy managers and general managers'*. Jonathan himself joined RCH as a General Manager of the Rubens Hotel in 1998, and was promoted to Managing Director of RCH within two years. The development and progression opportunities have contributed to RCH climbing from 71st in the *Sunday Times'* Best 100 Companies to Work For in 2012, to its current position of 2nd (2015).

Employee engagement and retention

Overall, the *Sunday Times* ranked RCH 1st for 'Personal Growth', but development opportunities alone, do not help to attract and retain talent. Previous studies also emphasise the importance of employee appreciation, reward and recognition in developing higher levels of employee engagement and job satisfaction (Lockwood, 2006; Bethke-Langenegger *et al.*, 2011). The development of talent may be viewed as a 'perishable commodity', as once trained, employees may leave for better opportunities elsewhere (Cappelli and Keller, 2014). Thus, the employee value proposition must offer more than just training and development programmes. The key is to balance the needs of the organisation with the interests of the employees (Cappelli and Keller, 2014), and to provide staff with the tools and support they need to do their jobs well. The benefits of internal service quality, and job satisfaction, are illustrated in Heskett and Schlesinger's (1994) Service-Profit Chain (see Figure C2.2), which clearly demonstrates the link to performance. As RCH plans to grow to 25 hotels (*Hotel Industry Magazine*, 2013), an attractive and well-communicated value proposition, and high levels of internal service quality, are essential in attracting and retaining the necessary talent for such growth.

As identified, RCH is still run by its Founder and President, Bea Tollman, who plays an active role in the operation and management of the hotels, and it is Bea's passion for excellent service, along with her 'naturally nurturing character' that drives her personal interest in staff care and development (Red Carnation Hotels, 2014c:13). Bea is supported by Managing Director, Jonathan Raggett, but it is her 'vision, passion and leadership' that is very much at the fore-front of the success of RCH, and an inspiration to all those that work for the group (Red Carnation Hotels, 2014c:2). She was named Hotelier of the Year in the European Hospitality Awards in 2012, in recognition of her commitment to high levels of service, but acknowledges her success would not be possible without the support of her staff, who she describes as 'all part of the same family' (Red Carnation Hotels, 2014c:13).

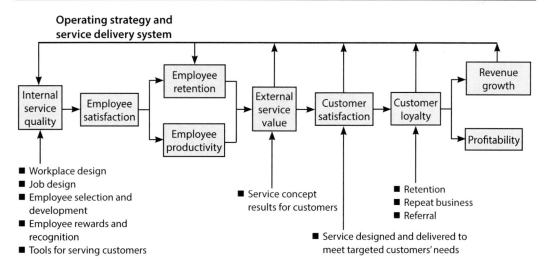

Operating strategy and service delivery system

- Workplace design
- Job design
- Employee selection and development
- Employee rewards and recognition
- Tools for serving customers

- Service concept results for customers

- Service designed and delivered to meet targeted customers' needs

- Retention
- Repeat business
- Referral

Figure C2.2: The service-profit chain (Heskett and Schlesinger, 1994)

Her gratitude is demonstrated in the annual black tie, Staff Appreciation Gala Dinner, and the personal Christmas gifts and messages she presents to every single employee each year. Staff are informed it is they who:

☐ 'Have turned her vision into an award winning reality;

☐ Kept alive her dream, for all these years, of offering the finest luxury hotel guest experiences at the best value;

☐ Are the embodiment of all that the RCH brand stands for as an enduring promise to its guests, staff and communities across the globe;

☐ Are responsible for making RCH so unique.'

(Red Carnation Hotels, 2014c:16)

Managing Director, Jonathan Raggett notes, *'we all need someone giving us a little nudge, encouraging us to be a better person. She makes things very personal. She genuinely cares that we be the best we can be'* (Red Carnation Hotels, 2014c:8).

Both monthly and annual reward and recognition systems are in place, including the Catch a Star programme, which *'celebrates achievement with public recognition and tangible rewards'*, and in 2014 internal promotions were awarded to 191 members of staff (Red Carnation Hotels, 2015c). According to the Careers Team, the group offers employees job security, competitive salaries, bonuses and incentive schemes. Employee benefits include:

☐ Free meals whilst on duty;

☐ Uniform provided and laundered free of charge;

☐ 28 days holiday per year, which increases with service;

☐ Loans to help buy a season ticket for travel to and from work in London;

☐ Pension scheme;

☐ Package of healthcare benefits;

CS

☐ Free use of the spa and gym facilities or a discounted corporate membership of local health clubs;

☐ Childcare Voucher Scheme and Cycle scheme at some properties;

☐ Volunteering for a charity supported by RCH for up to 2 days per year and paid as a normal working day;

☐ Discounted stays at the 4 star properties;

☐ Opportunities to travel worldwide with one of their sister companies at heavily discounted rates.

(Red Carnation Hotels, 2015c)

Best Companies (2015:7), notes, '*Bea strives hard to ensure that people are looked after, cared about, treated as individuals, feel supported and valued, have their welfare considered and are thanked.*' As a result, she received an 87% per cent positive score for being an inspiring leader in the *Sunday Times*' Best Companies listing, with only one other boss ranking higher than this. Additionally, staff turnover is now well below the industry average, at 26%, suggesting Bea's interest in her employees has positively influenced their loyalty. Her philosophy is that great service can only be delivered by staff that really care, and staff are more likely to care if they are looked after and treated well. As retention is one of the greatest challenges in the hotel industry, and talent is so crucial to success, this philosophy may well help inform the practice of other organisations.

Conclusions

The purpose of this case study was to examine the talent management practices of Red Carnation Hotels, as it was named 2nd in the *Sunday Times* Best 100 Companies to Work For. The family-owned and operated, luxurious hotel group has won numerous awards for the remarkable quality of its hotels, and memorable experiences and exceptional service are the focus of its strategy and deeply embedded into its culture. The Founder and President of RCH, Bea Tollman, understands the quality of staff is essential in delivering the promise that '*no request is too large, no detail too small*', and therefore recruits those whose ideals match the organisation, thereby aligning with the overall business strategy. Her hands-on leadership style appears influential in employee motivation, job satisfaction and retention, and her drive and passion for hospitality and service, and interest in the well-being and development of staff have won her both internal and external recognition.

As talent is such a critical resource in the success of an organisation, and is of particular importance in the service-oriented hotel industry, an effective approach to talent management is essential. The purpose of a talent management strategy is to attract, develop, and retain staff in order to achieve business goals. RCH clearly understands the relationship between job satisfaction and service quality, and the care shown to staff, along with development and progression opportunities has helped to retain those they've invested in. Effective practices, that may be gleaned from this case study, are to build an efficient recruitment plan, which aligns with the organisation's business strategy and attracts and recruits the right people; ensure all staff are given opportunities to develop in their roles; promote from within; understand that leadership style is critical to motivation and commitment; and recognise the importance of caring for staff and recognising and rewarding achievement.

Evidently, if hotel companies pay as much attention to their staff, as they do to their guests, performance may be improved. While the costs of training, development, and employee care can be high, RCH has seen a significant return on their investment in the form of employee satisfaction and low staff turnover, which in turn has lowered recruitment costs, improved service, and increased room occupancy and profit. This should be of interest to any hotel company looking for strategies to improve performance in this highly competitive environment.

References

Best Companies (2015). *Best Companies: Red Carnation Hotel Collection*. Available online at: http://www.b.co.uk/Company/Profile/343572. Accessed: 20/08/15.

Best Companies (2014). *Best Companies: Red Carnation Hotel Collection*. Available online at: http://www.b.co.uk/Lists/ListedCompanies/179/489. Accessed: 15/12/15.

Bethke-Langenegger, P. , Mahler, P. and Staffelbach, B. (2011). Effectiveness of talent management strategies. *European Journal of International Management*, **5** (5), 524-539.

Cappelli, P. and Keller, J. (2014). Talent management: Conceptual approaches and practical challenges. *The Annual Review of Organisational Psychology and Organisational Behaviour*, **1** (1), 305-331.

Chambers, E. G., Foulon, M., Handfield-Jones, H., Hankin, S. M. and Michaels, E. G. (1998). The war for talent. *McKinsey Quarterly*, **3**, 44-57.

Christensen Hughes, J. and Rog, E. (2008). Talent management: A strategy for improving employee recruitment, retention and engagement within hospitality organizations. *International Journal of Contemporary Hospitality Management*, **20** (7), 743-757.

Eriksen, B. H. (2012). *Dancing With the Stars: How Talent Shapes Firm Performance*. Academy of Management, 2012 Annual Meeting. Boston, MA. Available online at: http://papers.ssrn.com/sol3/papers.cfm?abstract_id=2021899. Accessed: 05/08/15.

Heskett, J. L. and Schlesinger, L. (1994). Putting the service-profit chain to work. *Harvard Business Review*, **72** (2), 164-174.

Hotel Industry Magazine (2013). Leading light: Jonathan Raggett of Red Carnation Hotels Collection. *Hotel Industry Magazine*. Available online at: www.hotel-industry.co.uk/2013/03/leading-light-jonathan-raggett. Accessed: 15/11/15.

Lawler, E. (2008). Strategic talent management: Lessons from the corporate world. *Madison, WI: Consortium for Policy Research in Education*, **7** (2010), 1-35.

Pollitt, D. (2006). Red Carnation blooms through management training. *Human Resource Management International Digest*, **14** (6), 11-14.

CS

Raggett, J. (2011). Welcome: A future that's bright. In: Springboard (Ed). *Careerscope Hotels: Your Definitive Guide to Careers in Hotels*. Springboard.

Red Carnation Hotels (2014a). *Core Values*. Available online at: http://www. redcarnationhotels.com/about/core-values. Accessed: 25/08/15.

Red Carnation Hotels (2014b). *The RCH Story*. Available online at: http://www. redcarnationhotels.com/about/the-rch-story. Accessed: 20/08/15.

Red Carnation Hotels (2014c). *Red Carnation Hotels: The Love Story Behind the Success Story (for Employees of the Red Carnation Hotel Collection)*. The Red Carnation Hotel Collection.

Red Carnation Hotels (2015a). *Awards and Accolades*. Available online at: http://www. redcarnationhotels/about/awards-and-accolades. Accessed: 20/08/15.

Red Carnation Hotels (2015b). *Management Programmes*. Available online at: http://www. redcarnationhotels.com/careers/management-programme. Accessed: 15/01/16.

Red Carnation Hotels (2015c). *What we offer our employees*. Available online at: http://www. redcarnationhotels.com/careers/whats-in-it-for-you/employee-benefits. Accessed: 14/01/16.

Scott, B. and Revis, S. (2008). Talent management in hospitality: graduate career success and strategies. *International Journal of Contemporary Hospitality Management*, **20** (7), 781-791.

Case study 3: The Rick Stein Group

Catherine Hine

Introduction

Rick Stein has been a household name since the 90s when he first started presenting television shows based on his life as a chef. Over the years he has written over 20 cookery books and created more than 30 different cookery programmes, where he has travelled the world and explored different culinary traditions and cultures. However *The Seafood Restaurant* in Padstow has been the bedrock of Stein's success and it was his work developing this business which ultimately lead to him being awarded on OBE in 2003 for his contribution to tourism within the West Country.

Rick and Jill Stein opened *The Seafood Restaurant*, Padstow in 1975. This remains their flagship restaurant, and has gained an international reputation for their use of the finest locally caught fish and shellfish. Following this they went on to open St Petroc's Hotel and Bistro, just up the road, to complement their thriving restaurant, this was later followed by a café, deli, patisserie, gift shop and cookery school, again, all based in Padstow. More recently they have opened properties outside of Padstow, meaning they have had to expand their team and recruit talent from new markets. While development of the group's portfolio has primarily been based within the South West of the country they now have properties in Winchester, Sandbanks and Marlborough, expanding the reach of their product offering.

The group currently has 11 restaurants, and offer both guest rooms and self-catering accommodation. Each venue is unique, thus unlike some restaurateurs the Stein's made a conscious decision that they did not want to create a chain of properties with a uniform style. Instead each operation is sympathetic to its local surroundings with its own design ethos, menu and network of local suppliers. The commonality amongst operations is their approach to managing talent and creating a family orientated organisational culture that fosters a commitment to service quality. Despite his ongoing dedication to television presenting and writing cookbooks Rick and Jill remain at the helm of operations. In addition to this their three sons all work within the business, maintaining the notion that, despite its growth, the Rick Stein Group remains a family operation.

CS

The business

The core of the Rick Stein Group business remains in Padstow, a popular tourist destination and working fishing port situated on the north coast of Cornwall. The abundance of freshly caught fish and shellfish here have helped carve out an international reputation for serving the finest seafood. Rick's affinity with fish and passion for local produce has played a large part in the development of the business and, in particular, the restaurants. As a result they were awarded Three Star Sustainability Champion Status by the Sustainable Restaurant Association in 2016. In order to achieve this all of their restaurants were graded against a rigorous list of criteria including sourcing, society and environment (Rick Stein, 2016a). In addition to this the business has won countless awards for their apprenticeship programmes, the quality of their guest accommodation and food (Rick Stein, 2016b). However this external recognition only goes some way to encapsulating the commitment that is placed on the provision of quality service and the HR related strategies that ensure this occurs.

Recent expansion within the Rick Stein Group has occurred relatively quickly. Table C1.1 (below) highlights growth of the company's restaurants. The catalyst for much of this has been the appointment of a new non-executive chairman to the business (Harmer, 2015). However Jill and Rick's three sons have also started to take a more active role in the business.

Within each of the new openings both Jill and eldest son Ed Stein have taken a creative lead, designing each of the properties so that they are sympathetic to their surroundings yet fresh and inviting. Similarly, youngest son Charlie – a wine merchant – has been instrumental in developing the wine lists at each of the properties. However it is the middle son of Jill and Rick, Jack, who has really helped to drive the business forward. Jack is Executive Chef overseeing all restaurants, the cookery school and the countless chefs that have found employment within the business. His commitment to the business has helped to drive the Rick Stein Group forwards so that each restaurant maintains a unique offering in keeping with the family's passion for food.

Talent management

As discussed in previous chapters there is a clear link between talent management and the strategic goals of a business (Akram *et al.*, 2014; Taylor, 2014). Clear talent strategies can positively impact service quality, customer satisfaction and profits (Christensen Hughes and Rog, 2008); thus they are beneficial to any business. The Rick Stein Group has developed a holistic approach to talent consistent with the work of Cappelli (2008: 74) who suggested that *'talent management is simply a matter of anticipating the need for human capital and then setting out a plan to meet it'*. While this definition appears to be somewhat simplistic in comparison to some of the others quoted elsewhere within this text, it encapsulates the need for individuals

Table C3.1: Rick Stein's restaurant businesses.

Business	Date Opened	Description
The Seafood Restaurant, Padstow, Cornwall	1975	The Seafood Restaurant is Rick and Jill's flagship restaurant. It was refurbished in 2008 when a seafood bar and an additional 2 bedrooms were added to the existing 14 rooms. Head chef, Stephane Delourme, and his team create simple seafood dishes with classic flavours using Rick's recipes.
St Petroc's Hotel and Bistro, Padstow, Cornwall	1988	Specialising in bistro food from Britain, France, Spain and Italy. St Petroc's offers a snug bar and lounge as well as guest accommodation.
Rick Stein's Café, Padstow, Cornwall	1994	Offering light lunches and relaxed dinners Rick Stein's Café serves food throughout the day in the heart of Padstow. Accommodation is also available here.
Stein's Fish & Chips, Padstow, Cornwall	2004	The menu here includes local fish as well as the more traditional cod and haddock, all cooked to order in beef dripping to make them nice and crispy. Dishes are served in the restaurant or to take-away.
The Cornish Arms, St Merryn, Cornwall	2009	Just up the road from Padstow is St Merryn where Rick and Jill run a local village pub. Serving British pub food and local St Austell Brewery's best ales.
Rick Stein's Fish, Falmouth, Cornwall	2010	Falmouth boasts a seafood restaurant and takeaway. Fish and Chips are at the heart of the menu however some of Rick's favourite fish dishes are also served here.
Rick Stein, Winchester, Hampshire	2014	Winchester was the first of Rick's restaurants to open outside of Cornwall. Situated in the city centre of Winchester the restaurant offers both an *a la carte* menu and a set menu option for lunch
Rick Stein, Porthleven, Cornwall	2014	The menu at Porthleven is inspired by Rick's travels to Venice and Istanbul. The menu boasts a number of sharing boards showcasing local and seasonal produce.
Rick Stein, Fistral, Cornwall	2015	Fistral offers a much more casual style of dining than many of the other restaurants. This restaurant specialises in serving fish and chips alongside curries, inspired by Rick's travels to India and the Far East.
Rick Stein, Sandbanks, Dorset	2015	Serving classic seafood dishes the restaurant is located with views overlooking the bay. The restaurant also offers casual lunches and evening dinners.
Rick Stein, Marlborough, Wiltshire	2016	Marlborough will be an 80 cover restaurant situated in the centre of the town. The menu will include meat, game and seafood dishes

CS

with certain habits and the social and personality attributes which the Rick Stein Group looks for in employees. The inclusive approach to talent is advocated by Baum (2008) who suggests that it is essential within the hospitality industry as a means of both recognising diversity within the business and helping to ensure that talented individuals are identified and remain within the business.

A focus on talent management is important as the world of work has changed in recent years (Pilbeam and Corbridge, 2010). The influence of Generation Y employees has fundamentally altered how businesses must think about their HR practices (Davidson *et al.*, 2011). For the Rick Stein Group this is particularly important as nearly half of their employees are under the age of 25. Prensky (2001:1) suggested the way in which these individuals '*think and process information is fundamentally differently from their predecessors*', therefore long established HR practices have had to be reconsidered by the Rick Stein Group. The following section will explore the talent management strategies adopted by the Rick Stein Group. Particular emphasis will be placed on the way in which the business is transforming as they grow and enter new markets.

Employer branding

Employer branding is an increasingly important component of talent management. According to Mandhanya and Shah (2010) the concept refers to creating a targeted and long term strategy aimed at managing the awareness and perceptions of employees, potential employees, and stakeholders with regards to a particular firm; it is a key method of differentiating a business from other, similar employers (Akram *et al.*, 2014). In terms of talent management it is therefore intrinsically liked to both the retention and attraction of individuals, something which is particularly important within the hospitality industry. In order to create an employer brand, Kristin and Surinder (2004: 502) suggest that a company must draw on information about their '*organisation's culture, management style, qualities of current employees, current employment image, and impressions of product or service quality*'; they must then market this value proposition both internally and externally. For Kucherov and Zavyalova (2012) the brand proposition is thus comprised of both brand attractions (feelings about the brand); brand image (including functional benefits such as pay along with symbolic benefits relating to the prestige of the company); and how attractive these are. Not all of these components are controlled by the employer, thus companies like the Rick Stein Group must be proactive in order to support the development of a positive brand proposition.

The Rick Stein Group draws on the family origins of the business as a core component of their organisational culture and employer brand image. While they acknowledge that the notion of a family business may not always have positive connotations they use the idea of family to inform the way in which they treat employees, which goes above and beyond most people's expectations. As a business the Rick Stein Group has very few formalised policies, however their commitment to this family ethos is upheld by a rigorous 'Dignity at Work' policy, designed specifically to ensure that all employees are treated fairly. The culture of harassment and bullying often associated with the hospitality industry (Ram, 2015) is therefore not present within the company. Instead, the Rick Stein Group offer a nurturing and supportive culture with a strong focus on learning and development within the organisation. This form of culture, leadership and commitment to training aids the development of a psychological contract between the employer and employee, supporting the employer brand image (Kucherov and Zavyalova, 2012).

In order to further support the development of an employer brand the Rick Stein Group has been successful in securing external recognition for their efforts. One way this has been achieved is through an award from the Sustainable Restaurant Association. The company received 100% for treating people fairly, in recognition of their employee training scheme and staff benefits (Rick Stein, 2016a) when audited for this award, showing how their talent management strategy and business development plans have taken into consideration the needs of their employees.

The company's commitment to learning and development is also a large part of their employer value proposition. This, coupled with extensive engagement strategies, and positive stories as to how individuals have progressed within the company helps the Rick Stein Group to provide further tangible evidence supporting their positive employer brand image. As the company grows and these brand attributes become more prevalent, it is anticipated that their brand image will increase (Kucherov and Zavyalova, 2012). However as a consequence of growth, and the increasing distance between restaurants, it can be difficult for this message to be disseminated. Thus while employer branding strategies have been successful in Cornwall, this is not yet evident in all of the new locations. As a result the company is beginning to formalise the way in which the employer brand is sold. Extensive work is being put into the development of what Berger and Berger (2010) refer to as a talent creed. This formally verbalises the company's principles and values, highlighting the family nature of the business, its history and what this means for employees, and potential employees. The proactive nature of this work demonstrates the importance of employer branding for the Rick Stein Group and emphasises its integral link to their talent strategy moving forwards.

Recruitment

Recruitment has historically presented occasional challenges for the Rick Stein Group; as a business they are arguably the largest recruiter within Padstow. As this is a small seaside town, with limited transportation infrastructure, the company have always had to be innovative in the way that they attract talent to the business. Lessons learnt through establishing themselves within this remote part of the country have informed both recruitment practises and strategic development within the Stein Group's growing portfolio of restaurants. Trying to break

CS

down the negative connotations of working within the industry, such as long and unsociable hours (Guerrier and Adib, 2000) and unclear progression opportunities (Richardson, 2010) have also been an ongoing challenge for the business.

Over the past year the Rick Stein Group have had to make around 500 new appointments to the business. Many of these have been due to the expansion of the business, however, as with all hospitality operations, staff turnover also contributes to demand. Hospitality operations are often characterised by high labour turnover (People 1st, 2015) resulting in significant financial costs for the business (Davidson *et al.*, 2010). For the Rick Stein Group, around one third of their turnover is due to the recruitment of seasonal staff and is therefore beneficial in managing headcounts during quieter times of the year. However when coupled with skills shortages within the industry (People 1st, 2013) any form of labour turnover places a burden on the recruitment team as they are constantly looking for individuals to join the business. As a result, the group have developed a 'best fit' approach to recruitment. This is consistent with the work of Baum (2008) who suggests that within the hospitality industry skills are not constrained to technical and practical definitions often found in other industries, but include the emotional, aesthetic and information processing attributes integral to the delivery of customer service, broadening the requirement from each potential employee. Thus for operational roles in particular the Rick Stein Group look for individuals who have a passion for food and hospitality and are looking to, potentially, progress within the company. This favours employees with the personality attributes and drive essential to the delivery of quality customer service. Individuals are then supported by the learning and development team in order to equip then with the practical skills and knowledge in order to effectively contribute to their team's performance. By approaching recruitment in this way, the organisational culture of the company naturally resonates with individuals; this results in strong, cohesive teams being developed within each operation. The Rick Stein Group also benefits from having an abundance of well trained and ambitious individuals within the company that can progress as the business grows, being deployed into more senior positions, or different locations. This approach to recruiting individuals, who want to develop within the company, also helps to address another skills gap within the labour market as, in addition to operational staff, it is often difficult to recruit individuals for more senior or managerial positions (People 1st, 2013).

Despite the seasonal nature of businesses, particularly in Cornwall, the majority of staff are employed on permanent contracts. This negates some of the disadvantages associated with employee commitment when casual or seasonal staff are employed (Davidson *et al.*, 2011). However for some employees of the Rick Stein Group the seasonal nature of work can be beneficial, allowing them to travel or study during the winter months and return to the business the following summer. In encouraging staff to return to the business after a break in employment, financial savings are made, as the core business values, organisational culture and knowledge of service standards have already been instilled within these individuals.

Learning and development

There has been a great deal of investment into learning and development. Key members of the centralised learning and development team have backgrounds in food and hospitality; their experience in the industry has helped to shape the company's training philosophy resulting in an approach that is both grounded and practical. The informal approaches to training synonymous with smaller businesses (Stewart and Rigg, 2011), which have traditionally been adopted by the Rick Stein Group have recently been replaced so that a more consistent experience is given to employees. Training is therefore embedded into all of the group's operations and forms a part of the organisational culture associated with the company. This supports commitment to the business from all employees (Baum, 2008) and is integral to the holistic approach to talent management and development that the group advocates.

A structured 12 week induction programme has been adopted across the company for all new employees. This means that there is consistency in the materials used, which have been specifically designed so that they contain relevant information, essential to help employees develop in their roles. This process is however not overly formal or detailed so as to disengage employees, as it has been noted that 'information overload' can occur within some induction programmes (Inman *et al.*, 2010). The initial induction period is also an opportunity to demonstrate the value of joining a business, therefore the core principles of learning, guidance and regular feedback are emphasised in order to foster engagement with the company's ethos.

Inductions for new members of staff have been identified as a core component of the learning and development function. Within this period operational staff are given essential information about service standards, and product knowledge associated with wine, coffee and fish are delivered alongside legislative training such as food handling. This can help to foster commitment to the business as, according to King (2010), disseminating information regarding the brand, service standards and expectations can have a significant impact of hospitality employees' role clarity and commitment to the organisation. A range of on-the-job training methods and an e-learning platform are used in order to help achieve this. Within the e-learning platform bespoke content can be developed and delivered to all sites. This not only ensures consistency in training but also means that completion can be monitored so that managers are able to easily identify employees that have engaged with particular training sessions (Nickson, 2013). As the company grows, and becomes more geographically dispersed these more formalised approaches are becoming increasingly common within the Rick Stein Group.

New employees entering the business at a managerial level undergo a slightly different induction process, particularly when they have been recruited to work within one of the company's new operations. When possible, these individuals are brought into the business ahead of premises openings. This means that they are able to spend up to 12 weeks working within an established team, learning about

CS

the company, the way in which support functions operate, and its organisational culture, before they start managing their new teams. For senior chefs (head chefs and sous chefs) this also gives them opportunities to learn some of Rick Stein's signature dishes in order to help inform menu development so that it remains true to the company's origins. This approach to inductions for managerial staff helps to ensure that the group's values and culture are shared with all employees, helping to support the development of a cohesive brand image in terms both the business and their status as an employer within communities. It also helps to foster engagement with the business and its underlying values by demonstrating a commitment to investing in employees even before they have started working in the position for which they have been recruited. This approach is important as managerial staff have greater involvement with the whole organisation and their understanding of the brand needs to be multifaceted in order for them to effectively implement brand management strategies within operations (King, 2010).

In addition to these internal learning and development initiatives, the Rick Stein Group also utilise externally accredited, and delivered, programmes in order to support staff. One area this is particularly prevalent is within their kitchens where a number of chefs complete apprenticeship courses. Working in partnership with local colleges the business utilises engagement with these programmes as a means of encouraging young people into the hospitality industry, inspiring, training and developing them into hospitality professionals (Rick Stein, 2015). While beneficial in some sections of the business, similar types of formal (and qualification-based) training have been less successful for management staff. Here it has been found that formal and classroom approaches to learning have disengaged some members of the team. An alternative model incorporating peer learning and shorter training sessions has therefore been adopted. This has the benefit of capturing and sharing organisational knowledge and can be effectively used as a method of helping to solve workplace problems by drawing on the experience and knowledge of existing employees (Hara, 2008). Shorter and more interactive sessions are also thought to help enhance learning (Nickson, 2013), maximising the effectiveness of training.

The learning and development function at the Rick Stein Group is integrally linked to their engagement strategy. By demonstrating that they want to invest in individuals, and that they value their employees the company aims to foster commitment. This in turn helps reduce staff turnover (Kucherov and Zavyalova, 2012) and produce high performing teams (Davidson *et al.*, 2011).

Employee engagement

Employee engagement is essential in order for the Rick Stein Group to deliver the level of service customers anticipate from the business. It is therefore a vital component of their talent management philosophy. As noted previously the employer brand image also depends on the success of initiatives such as the engagement strategy and the way in which this is internalised by employees (King, 2010). In line with the work of Gibbons (2006) the group's engagement strategy incorporates employee development; career growth opportunities; fostering good working relationships between co-workers and with managers; and offering employees autonomy within their job roles.

On a day-to-day basis the organisational culture and management style adopted by the business helps to foster engagement. Providing employees with continual, honest feedback and developing supportive relationships between co-workers and with managers is important to the business. Consistent with the work of Tews *et al.* (2014), the Rick Stein Group believe that these business philosophies can actively help to reduce employee turnover, and therefore contribute to the long term sustainability and profitability of the organisation. In addition, as individuals progress through their careers, and family circumstances change, the company will tailor working commitments to encourage individuals to remain within the industry. This flexibility again demonstrates the value that the business places on individuals and the lengths that they will go to in order to enhance employee retention as a component of their talent strategy.

The growth of the business has been particularly instrumental in supporting engagement. This has provided additional opportunities for career growth and development within the company. Opportunities to progress into more senior positions and transfer between operations are often seen as a core component of engagement as employees look to advance their careers (Gibbons, 2006). This is particularly important for the Generation Y employees within the Rick Stein Group as they are particularly concerned with progression opportunities as a component of their careers (Maxwell *et al.*, 2010) and often feel a sense of entitlement in relation to these (Davidson *et al.*, 2011). Within the business there have been a number of individuals that have benefited in this manner, taking on more senior roles within new premises; their stories within the business support the company's narrative surrounding promotion opportunities. Continued growth plans within the business also provide the potential for more opportunities to become available, again supporting engagement.

The Rick Stein Group does not offer a formalised graduate management development programme or internship programme, of the type which are often synonymous with a more exclusive approach to talent development strategies (Baum, 2008) as these involve focusing development on a finite, re-selected number of employees, as against all employees. Therefore the developmental stories noted above and the opportunity for employees to benefit from progression and deployment are accessible to all. In turn this ensures that engagement is achieved throughout the organisation and not just from those that have previously been identified with talent.

While pay is not often cited as one of the core motives for engagement, it is undoubtedly important to employees (Gibbons, 2006). As in most hospitality operations, within the Rick Stein Group the majority of employees receive pay in line with or above the national minimum wage. However this is supported by a

CS

number of additional rewards. These reflect the intrinsic benefits associated with work environments and help to support the underlying business culture:

- ☐ A share of tips from customers
- ☐ Staff discount
- ☐ Opportunities for paid overtime
- ☐ Annual staff party
- ☐ Summer events with Rick and Jill
- ☐ Progression opportunities
- ☐ Learning and development
- ☐ 28 holiday days each year

In order to help understand employee engagement within the Rick Stein Group the HR team have recently deployed the use of an employee engagement survey. This type of instrument is a means of helping to enhance employee engagement by measuring engagement levels across a number of environmental conditions within the company (Wiley, 2012). The survey offers a formalised, yet anonymous, voice for employees so that they can provide an honest opinion to the management team with regards to issues such as working practices and relationships at work. While a number of limitations associated with this form of measurement have been highlighted (Gruman and Saks, 2011) the Rick Stein Group have found the information gleaned within the survey results to be instrumental in shaping their business development. Thus by focusing on areas for improvement and identifying business practices that may have inhibited individuals in doing their jobs effectively the business have been able to make adjustments to management practices in order to enhance working conditions. It is anticipated this these changes will in turn help enhance engagement.

Conclusion

The aim of this case study was to consider the talent management strategies employed by the Rick Stein Group. The family owned restaurant and accommodation providers have undergone a period of expansion, which is set to continue into the foreseeable future. This has meant that their demand for labour has increased significantly and as a result some of their talent management strategies have had to be refined. Each of the company's operations is unique, however the level of customer service promised means that a heavy reliance is placed on employees to deliver this.

As the business continues to expand, it is anticipated that further developments will be made to the Rick Stein Group talent strategy in order help ensure that all employees have a similar experience when working for the company. The employer brand image will also be developed to help establish the business as an employer of choice within the hospitality industry, ensuring that they can recruit individuals capable of driving the company forward.

References

Akram, A. A., Cascio, W. F. and Paauwe, J. (2014) Talent management: Current theories and future research directions. *Journal of World Business*, **49** (2), 173-179.

Baum, T. (2008) Implications of hospitality and tourism labour markets for talent management strategies. *International Journal of Contemporary Hospitality Management*, **20**(7), 720-729.

Berger, L. and Berger, D. (2010) *The Talent Management Handbook: Creating a Sustainable Competitive Advantage by Selecting, Developing, and Promoting the Best People*. McGraw-Hill Education.

Cappelli, P. (2008) Talent management for the twenty-first century. *Harvard Business Review*, **86** (3), 74.

Christensen Hughes, J. and Rog, E. (2008) Talent management: A strategy for improving employee recruitment, retention and engagement within hospitality organizations. *International Journal of Contemporary Hospitality Management*, **20** (7), 743-757.

Davidson, M. C. G., Timo, N. and Wang, Y. (2010) How much does labour turnover cost?: A case study of Australian four and five star hotels. *International Journal of Contemporary Hospitality Management*, **22** (4), 451-466.

Davidson, M. C. G., McPhail, R. and Barry, S. (2011) 'Hospitality HRM: past, present and the future'. *International Journal of Contemporary Hospitality Management*, **23** (4), 498-516.

Gibbons, J. (2006) *Employee Engagement: A Review of Current Research and Its Implications*. New York: The Conference Board.

Gruman, J. A. and Saks, A. M. (2011) Performance management and employee engagement. *Human Resource Management Review*, **21** (2), 123-136.

Guerrier, Y. and Adib, A. (2000) Working in the hospitality industry. in Lashley, C. and Morrison, A. (eds.) *In Search of Hospitality: Theoretical perspectives and debates*. Oxford: Butterworth-Heinemann.

Hara, N. (2008) *Communities of Practice: Fostering Peer-to-Peer Learning and Informal Knowledge Sharing in the Work Place*. Bloomington: Springer.

Harmer, J. (2015) The Steins on 40 years of the Seafood Restaurant. *The Caterer*. Available at: https://www.thecaterer.com/articles/360320/the-steins-on-40-years-of-the-seafood - restaurant.

Inman, M., O'Sullivan, N. and Murton, A. (2010) *Unlocking Human Resource Management*. Oxon: Routledge.

King, C. (2010) 'One size doesn't fit all': Tourism and hospitality employees' response to internal brand management. *International Journal of Contemporary Hospitality Management*, **22** (4), 517-534.

Kristin, B. and Surinder, T. (2004) Conceptualizing and researching employer branding. *Career Development International*, **9** (5), 501-517.

CS

Kucherov, D. and Zavyalova, E. (2012) HRD practices and talent management in the companies with the employer brand. *European Journal of Training and Development*, **36** (1), 86-104.

Mandhanya, Y. and Shah, M. (2010) Employer branding- a tool for talent management. *Global Management Review*, **4** (2), 43-48.

Maxwell, G. A., Ogden, S. M. and Broadbridge, A. (2010) Generation Y's career expectations and aspirations: Engagement in the hospitality industry. *Journal of Hospitality and Tourism Management*, **17** (1), 53-61.

Nickson, D. (2013) *Human Resource Management for Hospitality, Tourism and Events*. Oxon: Routledge.

People 1st (2013) *State of the Nation Report 2013; An analysis of labour market trends, skills, education and training within the UK hospitality and tourism industries*. Available at: http://www.people1st.co.uk/getattachment/Research-policy/Research-reports/State-of-the-Nation-Hospitality-Tourism/SOTN_2013_final.pdf.aspx.

People 1st (2015) *The Skils and Productivity Problem*. Available at: http://www.people1st.co.uk/getattachment/Research-policy/Research-reports/The-Skills-and-Productivity-Problem/Report-The-Skills-and-productivity-problem-Oct-15.pdf.aspx.

Pilbeam, S. and Corbridge, M. (2010) *People Resourcing and Talent Planning: HRM in Practice*. Financial Times Prentice Hall.

Prensky, M. (2001) Digital natives, digital immigrants, part 1. *On the Horizon*, **9** (5), 1-6.

Ram, Y. (2015) Hostility or hospitality? A review on violence, bullying and sexual harassment in the tourism and hospitality industry. *Current Issues in Tourism*, 1-15.

Richardson, S. (2010) Generation Y's perceptions and attitudes towards a career in tourism and hospitality. *Journal of Human Resources in Hospitality and Tourism*, **9** (2), 179-199.

Rick Stein (2015) The Rick Stein Academy is launched. Available at: https://www.rickstein.com/the-rick-stein-academy-is-launched/.

Rick Stein (2016a) Latest News; Three Star Sustainability Champion Status received by the Sustainable Restaurant Association. Available at: https://www.rickstein.com/three-star-sustainability-status-received-by-rick-stein/.

Rick Stein (2016b) Rick Stein Awards. Available at: https://www.rickstein.com/about/rick-stein/rick-stein-awards/.

Stewart, J. and Rigg, C. (2011) *Learning and Talent Development*. London: Chartered Institute of Personnel and Development.

Taylor, S. (2014) *Resourcing and Talent Management*. ed. London: Chartered Institute of Personnel Development and McGraw-Hill Education.

Tews, M. J., Michel, J. W. and Allen, D. G. (2014) Fun and friends: The impact of workplace fun and constituent attachment on turnover in a hospitality context. *Human Relations*, **67** (8), 923-946.

Wiley, J. (2012) Achieving change through a best practice employee survey. *Strategic HR Review*, **11** (5), 265-271.

Case study 4: L'Aubier: Is talent management different for an ecological restaurant/hotel?

Saskia Faulk

Imagine you plan to visit the charming city of Neuchatel, at the tip of Switzerland's largest internal lake. You are looking for a place to stay there, perhaps because you are attending a conference at Neuchatel's picturesque university. Perhaps you wish to hike around the astounding rock formations in the neighboring Jura mountains or try adventurous aquatic activities on the lake and the river just over the border in France. Or maybe you are fascinated by economic history and dream of touring the many industrial museums and attractions in this region famous for watch-making and precision engineering. In your search for a hotel online, you come across L'Aubier, located in a small village adjacent to the city. Like most three-star hotels it is on Hotels.com and Tripadvisor, but you feel straight away that this one is unique. First of all, it's a bit more expensive than most which makes you want to find out what justifies the higher rate. Second, peering at the photos you see the hotel's design is very different from the rest (lots of untreated wood, indoor plants and a lush garden; a timeless and uncluttered décor). As you check the hotel's website you come across three rather unusual statements set in a large font on the home page of aubier.ch:

> "**Biodynamic:** *Stimulate living processes with natural preparations produced on the farm and dynamised at dawn on a beautiful day*
>
> **Applied ecology:** *where the fridges heat the water, rainwater does the laundry, recycled paper keeps you warm, and electricity is generated on-site*
>
> **Associative economics:** *we give thought to our sources and think of our suppliers, paying prices that enable them to live and raise their families in dignity*"

Scrolling down you read:

> "*L'Aubier is a pioneer site in ecology, biodynamic agriculture and associative economics. Organic restaurant and café, two ecological hotels, biodynamic farm and dairy, inter-generational eco-neighbourhood, and conference centre.*" [1]

Now you are intrigued that a hotel dares to state such values up front: are they sincere? Will they skimp on service and have bare-foot staff? Will you spend the evenings squinting in the shade of an ecological light bulb? Then, everything changes when you see guests' photos of the lake and mountains taken at the hotel.

---

1   Quotes from www.aubier.ch, consulted on 15 September 2016

CS

It is those views that clinch the deal. Several weeks later you arrive after a delayed flight, and your temper is frayed. Yet the receptionist makes you feel welcome the moment you step across the threshold. Your room is clean and fresh, smelling faintly of lavender soap and facing one of the most magical views you have ever set eyes on. Bookshelves well-stocked with philosophy, ecology, and politics line the walls of the corridors and the cosy corner you adopt in the restaurant. You unwind as you dine simply but well on organic fare and local wine, all the while savoring the serenity of the place and the kindness of attentive staff. As you doze off on your organic bedding you hear a cow mooing on the neighboring farm, and you wonder sleepily if working in a place like this has benefits that outweigh a simple salary.

Swiss innkeepers say 'La vie est difficile!'

The hotel business in Switzerland represents hard work and few rewards. Outside major ski resorts and world-renowned cities, life for hoteliers is even tougher. Over the past few years, the strong Swiss Franc made already high room rates inaccessible for some incoming tourists. For hoteliers wishing to renovate or expand, capital and loans are difficult to come by, in contrast to the situation for neighbouring competitors, such as Austria. In most regions tourism infrastructure improvements may take second place to other pressing economic priorities. Like utilities and taxes, labour costs are high in Switzerland. There is also a persistent labour shortage in the industry and to make matters worse, on the horizon there will be restrictions on hiring foreign workers. Similar to the situation in other affluent economies, the Swiss hospitality industry experiences relatively high turnover and managers find it difficult to motivate staff when a proportion of them are heading for the revolving door.

In addition, the world itself has changed, endangering the traditional appeal of Swiss mountains and lakes and its position, literally, at the crossroads of Europe. Low-cost airlines entice one to fly directly from Germany to Spain or England to Italy when formerly one took road or rail, stopping over in Switzerland. The aging Swiss hotel inventory is up against some very tough competitors with newer destinations that are better aligned with current trends.

Then, there are the tourists, a finicky lot who are not very loyal due to seeking new experiences and who are increasingly demanding in terms of service quality and quantity. The results of a national survey of 9000 tourists from 11 countries conducted in 2012 by SwissTourism, demonstrated that visitors here were mainly satisfied but 20% were not, citing the quality of service as the reason (Ruf, 2012). Service quality is therefore a top priority given higher room rates and menu prices—and the commensurately higher expectations of guests. With a well-established national network of hotel schools and training programmes which concentrate on developing technical expertise, it is up to companies to keep staff motivated, interested, and loyal. Which brings us back to the initial question:

Can a value-centred culture, incarnated by managers and shared on a daily basis, help attract and foster and keep the very best talent who can, in turn, provide the best service possible?

It is intuitively appealing to think that working for a company that puts ethical values above profits is intrinsically motivating. Specifically, it seems logical that people who are ecologically-motivated will work harder and be more loyal if working for an employer that promotes ecological practices. Beyond the apparent appeal of these assertions there are difficulties, such as how 'ecological' or 'ethical' is defined. 'Ethical' values include caring, citizenship, fairness, respect, responsibility, and trustworthiness according to the Josephson Institute of Ethics (2000); easy to list but difficult to implement. 'Ecological' values and principles are diverse, depending on the local priorities or underlying philosophy. In many cases 'ecological' refers simply to a number of practices such as re-using, re-cycling and re-using. Regarding 'ecological', we see claims for this in various and sundry places, and believe it less and less, partly because it is so difficult to pin down. For instance, does this mean simply that a business has taken several environmentally-friendly measures such as using power from renewable sources or that it simply conforms with the requirements of one of a myriad of eco-certifications? Further, concepts like fair-trade, corporate social responsibility and environmental management tend to be confused with ecological practices. Another problem is whence springs the company's interest in ecology: is it imposed from the outside (by clients or pressure groups), is it riding the wave of a current trend, or is it an enduring interest from inside the company? The differences in ecological outlook and behaviour described in the previous sentences would account for wide differences in the attitudes and motivation levels of staff. To compound any existing difficulty, there are the talent management variables that exist in all companies, whether ecological or not, and which affect staff in many ways.

Going back to the roots of L'Aubier

It is arguably a case apart from such considerations when companies are founded on ecological or ethical principles and continue to exist by and for these principles. One such hospitality company is L'Aubier, composed of a hotel and restaurant with a spa and conference centre, nestled next to a farm that feeds the guests in the rolling hills near Neuchatel, Switzerland, as well as a smaller city version. In order to understand this hotel firm it is essential to start by introducing the firm's history and philosophy, because both are constantly on the lips of anyone talking for and about L'Aubier.

Their story began as a working farm almost 40 years ago, founded by a group of friends seeking new and authentic methods to live and be kind to the earth. They settled upon *biodynamic* agriculture, which is similar to organic farming but more theoretical and far-reaching (see the Glossary: 299). The founders were driven spirituality based on self-development, termed *anthroposophy*, and an inter-

CS

connected economic perspective. Over time, the culture of care and sustainability developed further, and the hospitality business with its farm partnership became a way to demonstrate the relevance of the founders' values for a wider public. As a pioneer initiative, L'Aubier is well-known for its commitment as well as for its achievements, such as being Switzerland's first eco-hotel. Its constitution protects and ensures sustainability as well as participative management and finance, with community financial supporters today numbering 1600, happy to help a company with ideals and thereby reduce its reliance on banks. These stakeholders have been strengthened over the years thanks to transparent relationships and clear accounting procedures, and benefit from their input during annual meetings.

Basic facts about the hotel company and its properties

L'Aubier runs two hotels, the eponymous one in the quiet village of Montezillon, and a 'Café Hotel' in the centre of the city with nine rooms. The company has 50 employees, of which 30 work full time. The leadership team consists of five people, all of whom have been there for more than 15 years. Some key information about both hotels follows:

Facilities at L'Aubier, Montezillon

- 25 rooms
- The restaurant and café seats 80 guests and there is terrace seating as well
- Conference space: for maximum capacity of 200 people (256 square meters)
- Spa with sauna, hammam and treatment rooms overlooking a lake view
- There is an organic shop adjacent to the reception selling fresh and processed foods, accessories, and books
- Average occupation rate in 2015: 57% (higher than the Swiss and local averages)

Facilities at the Café-Hotel, located in the historic district of Neuchatel

- 9 rooms
- The café seats 45 guests inside and more than 16 seats on the balcony
- Average occupation rate in 2015: 61% (higher than the Swiss and local averages)

Such facts and figures do not appear to be exceptional in the 3-star hotel world. Yet, according to hotel manager Christophe Cordes, the biggest differentiator of L'Aubier from generic 3-star hotel competitors is its philosophy and values. To begin with, the facilities were ecologically-designed: the toilets and washing machines run on rain-water, solar panels provide electricity, the heating system uses wood pellets that are locally sourced. Heat is circulated from refrigerators to add several degrees to washing machine water. Cleaning products are biodegradable, and guest amenities are organic. In the restaurants only organic-certified ingredients are used, with the exception of beers and infusions (which are natural and local, but not certified). The L'Aubier farm provides biodynamic grains, meats (veal, beef, and pork), some vegetables, and dairy products. For the remainder, local farmers work within the framework of the hotel's supply-chain policies which demand a long-term partnership with suppliers rather than a bidding process that induces uncertainty. Such value-based decisions, already put into place in the early 1980s, were made long before ecology became mainstream.

Yet this case study is concerned with talent management, an area to which L'Aubier devotes a lot of energy due to the founders' conviction that human relations are at the centre of everything. The culture of the organisation is egalitarian, informal, and open, values that are embodied in the language used at L'Aubier. From day one managers and all staff use the familiar form of address ('tu') instead of the formal one ('vous'), which has the effect of knocking down social and status walls. Addressing one's manager as 'tu' is alone rather a shock for some new employees, given the typically strict and hierarchical culture prevalent in the Swiss hotel industry. The emphasis is clearly on trust, mutual respect, and friendly collaboration, rather than being 'buddies'.

One way to characterise the staff-management relationship is 'trust'. Managers at L'Aubier trust their staff to provide authentically welcoming service as part of their duties. They use a three-step process which puts trust at the forefront. First, managers provide the employees with a value-system and value-driven policies and practices expressed in terms of expectations of conduct. This begins on the first day during the employee induction procedure, which includes a tour of the site and explanations about the ecological foundations of the company's values and practices. Second, managers exude confidence in the capacity of their staff to make the appropriate customer-centred decisions, in other words they take ownership of their domains. Third , hand-in-hand with the egalitarian culture, managers are always easily accessible, and each day employees communicate with at least one of the founders which gives them an opportunity to have an exchange about what is really important.

Employees are encouraged to participate in decisions and take initiative and ownership rather than simply execute orders. They are not simply chess pieces to be moved at will or disposed of, and everything about the way we treat them makes that clear: they know their value. So even if staff members propose a new way of doing things that the management does not agree with, they will look at the good will that lies behind the initiative, and praise it independently of the acceptation or not of the proposal.

Problems can arise when new staff, accustomed to the almost military chain of command and unilateral communication prevalent in many Swiss hotels, can misinterpret this culture of mutual respect as a laissez-faire attitude. As a result, managers must consistently use positive reinforcement to communicate values and policies and their emphasis on how things are done at L'Aubier, for instance an *authentically* friendly welcome rather than the use of scripts or a required smile.

CS

And they know from customer feedback that customers, too, prefer this management philosophy which results in a welcoming, sincere, and serene atmosphere. Consistent with their philosophy, human relations are at the heart of talent management at L'Aubier, which means that employees are well-prepared to deal with the everyday human relations challenges that naturally occur with guests. Managers are realistic, however, they know that many of their employees come to work enthused by the ideals put into practice at L'Aubier. But not all do: because of the constraints in the small-city labour market it is impossible to uniquely hire people who share their values so management and staff know to be flexible in their collaboration with certain staff-members.

Menu planning and talent management values

Another practice inspired by egalitarian values is the restaurant's menu and pricing strategy. The prices are in line with competitors (generic countryside restaurants and urban cafés), quite a feat with organic ingredients and partnership-management of suppliers which prevents price-based negotiations and switching. Hospitality manager Christophe Cordes strongly feels that *'eating organic food should not be a luxury restricted to the elite'*, therefore management sat down with kitchen staff to design a strategy that would enable menu prices accessible to all. Formerly the kitchen emphasised creativity and presentation in a classical cuisine style, which raised food preparation and ingredient costs. Thus the menu prices were relatively high and fuelled the perception that L'Aubier may be elitist.

From the conviction that organic food should be accessible, a new concept was applied to the menu development process. This concept may be described as *simple country bistro food* based on four ingredient considerations: organic, fresh, local, and seasonal. Successfully installed over the past two years, the new menu reduces costs pertaining to complexity and creativity in the kitchen while raising the profile of the ingredients themselves. A certain latitude for creativity remains, of course. To be sure some older guests have been disappointed by the change—which included correlated changes in the dining room such as abandoning multi-layered white tablecloths—but most understand the values that are expressed in this change and appreciate them. In terms of talent management the new concept makes a great deal of sense for kitchen staff who are grateful to have stress levels reduced by a streamlined menu; as well as when kitchen staff change for seasonal or other reasons. What will now remain steady is a simpler menu, flawlessly executed.

When asked if the strongly-held values at L'Aubier support talent management, hospitality manager Christophe Cordes agrees strongly. One example is that bugbear of the hotel industry—turnover—is stabilising at L'Aubier. Thanks to a respectful work environment, doing work that has a meaning and a goal, employee loyalty is slowly but surely building, with a few clocking up more than a decade of service. As is the case with most hotels, a few temporary seasonal workers are necessary, and these are unlikely to adhere to the company's ideals. Such workers are exposed to the culture of L'Aubier, but the company does not believe in making 'converts' to its values. Yet a number of staff-members and all the managers have extraordinary longevity, many feeling a part of the history of L'Aubier's right from the beginning. Christophe Cordes puts it this way:

> Because we nourish ideals more than other employers, people who work with us generally want to give their best and stay with us. Some cite their love for this enterprise, this idea, our internal culture. I feel that we encourage and create a capacity for imbuing work with a meaning. Obviously we aren't an institution that teaches people the meaning of life, but if you're looking for a way to reduce the gap between your values and making a living, that we can give you.

Attracting talent: A 'help wanted' ad with a difference

One may wonder if L'Aubier is able to attract better talent given its values. They use specific channels to advertise when they need staff, starting with their corporate website. In some ways their 'help wanted' announcement resembles so many others: for the kitchen team they are looking for a person who is 'dynamic … experienced … conscientious … quick worker', but the resemblance stops there.

The text of the rest of the announcement asks potential candidates if they are 'interested in organic food and seeking to work in a restaurant unlike any other … with ethics and ideals'. It goes further, specifying that L'Aubier seeks colleagues who will be: 'committed and by our side to share a common goal and not just to have a job. It's good to know therefore what L'Aubier is, and what it stands for in terms of ideals, struggles, hopes and successes'.[2] The text goes on to invite interested people to get in touch, particularly if they want to contribute to the world as part of 'a company concerned by the growing problems of humanity and nature and which is committed to bio-dynamic agriculture, and associative economics in partnership with people who support us'.[3]

Clearly, such value-laden language could be enticing to like-minded people but could equally scare away some potential employees having the qualifications but lacking in introspection. In the case of generic hospitality industry employment platforms on the internet, fewer appropriate candidates are found possibly because it is more difficult on such platforms to go to the level of detail regarding the values and philosophy of L'Aubier, and also because people looking for a job on through this channel may be seeking a 'job', not a 'commitment'.

During the job interview, L'Aubier managers often converse with the candidate about values in order to discover affinities, yet it is not uncommon for job applicants to cite 'values' as a reason for applying at L'Aubier, in part because paying lip-service to ecological values is normal to a point where they have almost lost their meaning. During the recruitment process, even more emphasis is put on collaboration and his or her ability to work positively within a team, as

---

2   L'Aubier (2016). To Work and to Commit Oneself. Available at: http://www.aubier.ch/fr/des-collaborateurs-et-emplois.php [translation by Saskia Faulk]

3   Ibid.

CS

well as agreeableness. Otherwise staff is very diverse in age, sex, and origin (15 nations are represented currently), with a good number of students and others who are not originally hospitality professionals but have a strong interest in the L'Aubier project. If it were possible to define a personality profile of a strong candidate, it would include being authentic and open to new experiences and ideas, having integrity, being able to think beyond prejudices and out of the box. If they are interested in organic products and processes, that is positive, but not a precondition to being hired. *'It's easier to find people with ideals to work on the farm than in the hotels'*, smiles Christophe Cordes. Regarding values generally, Cordes has noticed over the years that young people increasingly look for meaningful work, or at least work that has a purpose transcending the task itself. And at L'Aubier, because of the strong underlying philosophy, all work has meaning and dignity.

Succession planning: Ensuring the perennation of company values

The current five-member leading team grew up and 'grew old' together because of their involvement as founders and protagonists in the history of L'Aubier. This is a strength due to the continuity of leadership and culture. Yet this longevity could stymie efforts to evolve, so the question of who will compose this core team in the future is an important one. There is a new generation of staff who are ideologically-motivated, and efforts are in place to ensure that these will continue to be attracted, retained, and developed into the future. One example of this is the investment made in apprentice programmes for certain positions. Another is a new strategic development: an innovative full-time internship at L'Aubier based on anthroposophy termed *'Become independent and committed to the world'*.[4]

The purpose of the internship is stated as: *'To discover the impulse of associative economics; to detect our own faculties; to engage our self in liberty and take the responsibility for it; to move near our own life project'*. This structured internship for eight young people over the age of 23 is composed of hands-on training in different hotel departments, courses, and artistic workshops. The anthroposophic course curriculum includes: humanity and civilisations, global ecology, self-knowledge, and the meaning of independence *'in one's head, heart and actions'*. Then there are management classes designed to encourage budding entrepreneurs on the subject of business plans, budgeting, accounting, financial control, and small-business creation. The workshops which combine spiritual development and awareness include: self-development work with horses, nature projects, theatre, languages, ceramics, eurythmics (a form of dance), and 'humour'. Participants finance their own tuition through work at the hotel's properties, and can live in shared accommodation on-site.

The programme begins for the first time in autumn 2016 so results of this initiative will not be known for a while. One demonstration of the company's

---

4 "Devenir indépendant et s'engager pour le monde!"

commitment to the internship programme is the direct participation by members of the board of directors in leading and teaching some of the courses and workshops. It is hoped that some talent will stay on at L'Aubier, and the programme will be continued in future years, depending on the results obtained in this area.

The philosophy that inspired L'Aubier: Spreading the word

People committed to a philosophy – particularly a less-known one – are often interested in sharing it with others. As we have seen, anyone who works at or with L'Aubier is aware of the unique philosophy that drives the organisation. Yet guests staying overnight, eating in the restaurant, or relaxing at the café are another big and diverse potential audience for the story and thinking behind L'Aubier. For this reason the company publishes a number of publications and hosts exhibitions and conferences on philosophical themes such as *'Towards a unique world economy: the works of Steiner, Keynes, and Dunlop'* or *'True price, true revenues: The proposals of Aristotle, Thomas Aquinas, and Rudolf Steiner'*.

The current exhibition, curated and designed by administrative staff, showcases the Swiss political philosopher Denis de Rougemont on a series of floor-to-ceiling wall panels in the lobby. These cite excerpts from his work with analyses by hotel manager Christophe Cordes to the side of the text. In 1947, de Rougemont made a speech about federalism in Europe and what principles would be needed for the future European Union to function effectively. Many of these principles have strong resonance today in countries with a federal system, such as Switzerland, and the European Union itself.

Although most of de Rougemont's work lies far outside the scope of this case study, some of it rings true for L'Aubier. First, that the tension between totalitarianism and federalism (the 'drama' of the 20th century) means there are no simple truths or easy answers: each citizen must be responsible for a perpetual quest of trying to find the right answer and with those right answers to build the society we would like to live in. Staff at L'Aubier are empowered and made responsible for situations they may encounter at work in a similar manner, as we have seen. Second, de Rougemont argued that a true federation could only exist if its members have equal status, and none can impose their will on others. This principle is applied in all human relations at L'Aubier: board of directors to managers, to employees, to investors, to suppliers, and even to customers. It is clear that, to use the phrase coined by hotel manager Christophe Cordes, in his brochure about the philosopher (Cordes, 2016), the principles described by de Rougemont comprise a *'basis for* any *group of people seeking to live or work together'* – not just big political entities like Switzerland or the European Union.

Into the sunset

Clearly, values are important whether for an international, national, or business entity. The importance of culture, values and ethics is made abundantly clear in

CS

the management literature. Hospitality and service-oriented companies strive to meet the daily challenge of exceeding customer expectations; they struggle to address the changing needs of younger talent who have a different view of the world. As we have seen in the case of L'Aubier, a strong value system—whether moral, ecological or otherwise—can assist companies in attracting and retaining the best. Among other factors, having strongly-held values and sharing and adhering to them through a coherent culture provides a sense of shared purpose and imbues work with meaning.

Glossary

Anthroposophy: '*A modern spiritual path that cherishes and respects the freedom of each individual… that real freedom is actually an inner capacity that can only be obtained by degrees according to the spiritual development of each individual*' (Anthroposophical Society in Great Britain, 2016). A neologism coined by Rudolf Steiner combining the Greek words for human, *anthropos*, and wisdom, *-sophy*, this 'spiritual science' postulated that the development of the spirit which is necessary for individual freedom requires scientific study of the spiritual knowledge available to humanity as well as an understanding of the cosmos.

Associative economics: The view that the study of economics as promulgated by Adam Smith is in need of a new focus and methodology, a perspective spearheaded by Rudolf Steiner after the first World War. His contributions to economic thinking included seeing economics in a closed system that is in need of regulation, and the need for inter-disciplinarity (notably history and sociology) in efforts to understand economic phenomena. Steiner's main tenet was to place humans at the centre of economic processes, and to advocate cooperation between humans and organisations as the next step in economics after 'market economics' (Allgemeine Anthroposophische Gesellschaft, 2016).

Biodynamic: A '*holistic, ecological and ethical approach to farming, gardening, food and nutrition*' first developed by Rudolf Steiner in the 1920s. Biodynamic farmers work to foster a farm ecosystem that is diversified and balanced, taking into account a triple bottom-line approach valuing ecological, social, and economic sustainability. Steiner envisaged a wider role for biodynamic farmers, ideally working in the context of community-supported agriculture in creative partnerships with other organisations such as hotels and restaurants (Biodynamic Association, 2016).

Ecology: Ecology views the natural environment holistically, as internally related components that interact in complex ways. It questions the role of humans with and in the natural environment and counsels a precautionary approach to any modifications that human activity might bring to such complex systems. Ecology is a worldview in addition to a scientific field of study that rejects an anthropocentric perspective of human activity, taking into consideration the ethical dimensions thereof. Prominent ecologist Aldo Leopold (1949) claimed that an ecological perspective *'changes the role of Homo sapiens from conqueror of the land-community to plain member and citizen of it'* (in Callicot, 2012).

Organic food: According to the Swiss organic certification organisation, BioSuisse, the 5,700 Swiss farmers who are certified organic work towards three higher goals of sustainable agriculture in harmony with nature and animals' needs, social equity, and transparency. Very strict rules apply to farmers who attain organic certification, which is a renewable process consisting of regular independently-run inspections and audits. On organic farms 90 percent of raw materials (animal feed and bedding among others) should be in a closed cycle – from the farm itself – or must be from Swiss suppliers. In addition the usual proscriptions exist: no synthetic pesticides, herbicides or fertilisers, no genetically-modified organisms, no growth stimulators or hormones. Animal welfare is top priority according to the needs of each species, and natural treatments are used for sick animals with no antibiotics unless required. In processed organic foods no additives (such as colours, flavours, or preservatives) are permitted. Two thirds of Swiss consumers consume organic foods *'regularly'* BioSuisse (2016), accounting for more than 2 billion euros of turnover in 2014 ((Leybold-Johnson, 2015).

Rudolf Steiner: (1861-1925) The Austrian developer of biodynamism and anthroposophy, Rudolf Steiner is more known today for the schools bearing his name than his views on a spiritual and human-centered philosophy, ecology and economics.

Value: (noun) As in 'moral' or 'cultural' value. *'Subjectively originating characteristics or properties — such as good and bad, right and wrong, beauty and ugliness — as are projected onto various things and actions in response to the objective characteristics or properties of those things and actions.'* (Callicot, 2012)

Questions and discussion points

1 Have you ever worked for an organisation that put its moral, cultural, or spiritual values at the forefront? What were your impressions at the time of mixing business and values, and were they favourable?

- If you were in agreement with those values did you feel more motivated to work there?

- If you were not in agreement with those values did it have a negative effect on your work? Whatever your answer to these two questions, do you believe that companies should be founded on values, or are they irrelevant to business practice?

CS

2 As a consumer are there examples of products or services that you prefer because of the values (moral, ecological, spiritual, or other) that the company puts forward? Do such values inspire you to want to work for that company? This question is best answered after having tackled Question 1.

If you need a reference point during your discussions on this topic, have a look at the company's website – for example the philosophy section – and identify how L'Aubier's values are showcased, and how you feel about them as (1) a potential guest and (2) a potential staff member. The website: www.aubier.ch/en

3 Debate the following statements in groups. Align your groups in agreement with one point of view, then debate its merits with another group holding an opposing viewpoint: *'What might be some of the dangers of a company wearing its values publicly on its sleeve and putting them to work in practice?'* The case study focused on the positive aspects from a talent management perspective. Consider the negative possibilities that could flow from a value-led culture (such as disillusionment; unreal expectations; the maintenance of trust; rigidity of values in a changing business environment; and avoidance of a self-righteous culture to name a few). Identify other possible outcomes, whether positive or negative.

What are potential outcomes of companies maintaining a value-neutral stance? Is the latter really possible?

4 The United Nations Educational, Scientific and Cultural Organisation (UNESCO) places values at the centre of planning and implementing sustainable development initiatives in the context of the *Earth Charter*[5]. The organisation recommends conducting an analysis of values for the following reasons:

"Understanding values is an essential part of understanding an individual's own worldview and that of other peoples. Understanding your own values, the values of the society you live in, and the values of others around the world is a central part of educating for a sustainable future. Each country, cultural group and individual must learn the skills of recognizing their own values and assessing these values in the context of sustainability." UNESCO, 2016.

Consider the values (sometimes referred to as 'principles') that are important in your organisation, whether ecological, ethical, social, business, or other. Where and when do they originate in the company's history? How are they communicated in the organisational culture? To what degree are they binding for management and staff?

References

Allgemeine Anthroposophische Gesellschaft (2016). *Associative Economics*. Economic Conference, Economics/Goetheanum. Consulted 15 September 2016 at http://www. economics.goetheanum.org/rudolf-steiner-associative-economics/

---

5   See the following UNESCO link for information about the Earth Charter: http://www.unesco.org/new/ en/education/themes/leading-the-international-agenda/education-for-sustainable-development/sustainable-development/values-sd/

Anthroposophical Society in Great Britain (2016). *About Rudolf Steiner: Anthroposophy*. Consulted 15 September 2016 at http://www.anthroposophy.org.uk

L'Aubier (2015). *Rapport d'activités* 2015. Montezillon: L'Aubier

Biodynamic Association (2016). *What is Biodynamics?* Available at http://www. biodynamics.com. Accessed 15 Sept, 2016.

BioSuisse (2016). *Le Bourgeon : Tout savoir sur le bourgeon en bref*. Available at http:// www.bio-suisse.ch/media/Konsumenten/Publikationen/bio_suisse_infobroschuere_ allgemein_a6_f_web.pdf. Accessed 15 Sept, 2016.

Callicott, J. B. (2012) Ecology: An ethical perspective. *Nature Education Knowledge* **3**(10),16 Available at http://www.nature.com/scitable/knowledge/library/ecology-an-ethical-perspective-80059530. Accessed 15 Sept, 2016.

Cordes, C. (2016). *Denis de Rougemont: L'attitude fédéraliste*. Montezillon: L'Aubier.

Josephson Institute of Ethics (2000). *Making Ethical Decisions: Core Ethical Values*. University of California at San Diego. Available at http://blink.ucsd.edu/finance/accountability/ ethics/core-values.html#. Accessed 15 Sept, 2016

Leybold-Johnson, I. (2015). Organic farming in Switzerland. *Swissinfo*, August 11. Available at http://www.swissinfo.ch/eng/fresh-from-the-farm_organic-farming-keeps-on-growing/41596974. Accessed 15 Sept, 2016

Ruf, M. (2012). Tourisme: Comment sortir de la crise. *Hebdo*, August 23. Available at http:// www.hebdo.ch/comment_sortir_de_la_crise_163365_.html. Accessed 15 Sept, 2016

UNESCO (2016). *Education: Values of Sustainable Development*. Available at http://www. unesco.org/new/en/education/themes/leading-the-international-agenda/education-for-sustainable-development/sustainable-development/values-sd/. Accessed 15 Sept, 2016.

CS

Index